Reconfiguring Slavery

West African Trajectories

T0355661

Reconfiguring Slavery

West African Trajectories

Edited by

BENEDETTA ROSSI

LIVERPOOL UNIVERSITY PRESS

First published 2009 by
Liverpool University Press
4 Cambridge Street
Liverpool L69 7ZU

This paperback version published 2016

British Library Cataloguing-in-Publication data
A British Library CIP record is available

ISBN 978-1-84631-199-4 cased
ISBN 978-1-78138-305-6 paperback

Typeset by Koinonia, Bury
Printed and bound by
CPI Group (UK) Ltd, Croydon CRO 4YY

Contents

Contents

List of Figures

Notes on Contributors

Alice Bellagamba
Department of Human Sciences for Education 'Riccardo Massa', University of Milan-Bicocca, Milan, Italy

Phil Burnham
Department of Anthropology, University College London (UCL), London, UK

Eric Komlavi Hahonou
Laboratoire d'Etudes et de Recherches sur les Dynamiques Sociales et le Développement Local (LASDEL), Parakou, Benin, and Department of Society and Globalisation, University of Roskilde, Roskilde, Denmark

Christine Hardung
Department of Social and Cultural Anthropology, University of Vienna, Austria

Martin Klein
Department of History, University of Toronto, Toronto, Canada

Olivier Leservoisier
Département d'Anthropologie, Université Lyon 2, Lyon, France

Tom McCaskie
Department of History, School of Oriental and African Studies (SOAS), London, UK

Benedetta Rossi
School of History, University of Liverpool, Liverpool, UK

Jean Schmitz
Centre d'Études Africaines (CEAf), Ecole des Hautes Etudes en Sciences Sociales (EHESS), and Institut de Recherche pour le Développement (IRD), Paris, France

Preface

The ideas presented in this book were first discussed at an international conference held at SOAS on 25–26 May 2007 and organised in collaboration with the Centre of African Studies of the University of London. When, in 2004, I applied for ESRC support to work on trajectories of slavery for the three following years, it had not occurred to me that the conference that was to be one of the outcomes of this research would fall on the bicentenary of England's abolition of the slave trade. When the conference took place, it was but one in a long list of slavery-focused events. Some of these events were targeted at a specialist audience; others were aimed at reaching the general public. Such a large set of initiatives focusing on slavery could not have simply been prompted by the bicentenary. Much of this work reflected a long-term engagement with slavery not just on the part of academics, but also of professionals working in the media, arts and policy. Retrospectively, the 2007 anniversary appears to have allowed the articulation of a generalised concern over historical slavery and its contemporary legacies. 'Slavery' translated concerns with related phenomena such as racism, discrimination and inequality, which chimed with public sensitivities. The reasons for such an intense professional and public interest in slavery at this particular time remain to be explored. Yet heightened public attention prompted new research and activism, and occasioned the opening of new study programmes, galleries and museums. Internationally, a series of large-scale initiatives set off new collaborative research agendas extending well into the future. The focus of these initiatives is on the interactions between identity and exclusion. They consider slavery in relation to citizenship, race, memory and European identity. Such mobilisation of resources, energy and creativity has great potential for achieving a firmer understanding of slavery in all its dimensions. However, as increasingly diverse projects converge within a loosely defined notion of 'slavery', the meaning of 'slavery' is broadened to the point that all it stands for is a generic condition of abuse. Contributions to this volume remind us that enslavement existed and, in some contexts, continues to exist, within specific historical and social dynamics. The book's emphasis on trajectories prioritises the detailed reconstruction of slavery's transformations in particular West African contexts. We need to be able to distinguish analytically between diverse forms of stigma and exploitation, while accounting theoretically for their being experienced and discussed as 'slavery' by the actors involved in them.

This volume benefited from widespread collaboration. My first thanks go to the contributors to *Reconfiguring Slavery* for their leap of trust in the book's inexperienced editor. Other participants to the conference from which this book originates also made important contributions to the ideas advanced here. I wish to express gratitude to the British Academy and Thriplow Trust for sponsoring the conference. My own research and work on slavery between January 2005 and December 2007 was made possible by an ESRC Research Fellowship (grant number RES-000-27-0147-A), located in the Department of Anthropology and Sociology of the School of Oriental and African Studies (SOAS). I benefited greatly from the support of my SOAS colleagues and students. I particularly wish to mention my then Head of Department Richard Fardon, who was always ready to discuss and support my ideas, and J.D.Y. Peel, for his invaluable help and encouragement. Olivier du Lac and William Simmons provided valued assistance with the organisation of the SOAS events (even on the day of their exams!), and Olivier helped in translating the book's French chapters. Karen Remnant of the SOAS Research Office dealt brilliantly with administrative and financial matters. I am grateful to the Centre of African Studies (CAS) of the University of London, where this project took its initial shape, and especially the CAS manager Angelica Baschiera. A particular thank you also goes to my father, Alessandro Rossi, for his expert advice on the artistic and graphic aspects of the conference and book projects. In September 2007 I started an RCUK Fellowship in International Slavery at the School of History of the University of Liverpool. I wish to acknowledge the UK Research Council's support and my Liverpool colleagues' understanding, as light teaching and administrative duties have allowed me to dedicate time to editing this book. In Liverpool I am particularly grateful to my Africanist colleague Dmitri Van den Bersselaar for his reliable and friendly collaboration. The book owes its title to John Thompson's suggestion at the Bloomsbury Centre. Henrietta Moore has always been there as a mentor and a friend; her support through the years made all the difference. Paul Lovejoy, Jan-Georg Deutsch, Martin Klein and Tom McCaskie have taken the time to read and comment upon drafts of some or all of the chapters. I am greatly indebted to them, even though I may not always have been able to do justice to their valuable advice. Finally, all of the work presented here originates in West Africa and has benefited, in one way or another, from the collaboration and support of West African colleagues and people willing to share their time and knowledge.

A Note on Language

Contributors to this volume follow the conventions in use in their respective fields for identifying various West African geographic, political and ethnic entities. However, for many vernacular words and expressions there is no single convention, and different forms are in use even within the specialist literature. This may account for differences in terminology and orthography across chapters in this volume.

Some groups are referred to by multiple ethnonyms. It is particularly the case of the Haalpulaar'en and Tuareg, which are internally diversified and broadly spread geographically. The Haalpulaar'en (sing. Haalpulaar), literally 'Pulaar speakers', include four main groups of free status, arranged in a hierarchy that has been changing in history. The most recent political elites in this hierarchy are the TooroBBe (imâms and quranic scholars, sing. Tooroodo), who replaced the FulBe (sing. Pullo) transhumant herders at the end of the eighteenth century; the ancient SeBBe warriors (sing. CeDDo); and the SubalBe fishermen (sing. Cuballo). FulBe groups situated west of the river Niger are called 'Peul' in French, and their language is called Pulaar. Those who live east of the Niger are designated as Fulani in the Anglophone literature, and their language is called Fulfulde. In the past the MaccuBe were slaves or slave descendants and the RimaayBe liberated slaves. Today these categories are being replaced by less stigmatising identities, such as GallunkooBe or HormankooBe, which identify themselves as liberated slaves and Muslim.[1] The term Tuareg has been contested as a generic name for all sections of this stratified society. Some authors prefer to use Kel Tamasheq (lit. 'those who speak Tamasheq'), to avoid possible references to the status of particular sub-groups. The term 'Imajeghen' (sing. Imuhag) usually designates elite or 'noble' sections only, but authors working in the Aïr region (Niger) may refer to all Tamasheq-speakers generically as 'Imajeghen'. This incongruence reflects differences in regional uses of the terminology. The first meaning (indicating elite status) is followed in this volume. 'Iklan' means 'slave' in Tamasheq, but today this meaning is contested and used also as an ethnonym. The ethnicisation of groups of slave origin results in orthographic inconsistencies. In general, authors who think of the terms used to designate slave groups as ethnic identities capitalise names such as *iklan* (Tamasheq), *buzu* (Hausa) and *bella* (Songhay), all three of which characterise slaves or ex-slaves in Tuareg society; or such as *maccuBe* and *rimaaybe* (Pulaar) in Fulbe contexts. On the other hand, authors who think of these terms as denoting social status use small capitals. Some names have anglicised, frenchised and/ or arabicised forms (e.g. *haratin, harratin, hrâtîn*).

With regard to the terminology of slavery, lacking further qualifications, the expressions 'freed slave', 'liberated slave' or 'ex-slave' are used interchange-ably in this volume to denote the slave origins of a person or group. The expres-sion 'of slave descent' indicates more specifically that someone is descended from slave parents or ancestors, but enjoys free status him/herself, however this is defined in a specific cultural and social context. This is particularly relevant where slave status is hereditary. The term 'master' does not imply a gender distinction, as both men and women owned slaves. 'Emancipation' is used to refer generally to the process through which individuals and/or groups categorised as 'slave' acquire free status. 'Slave' and 'free' refer to statuses the precise meaning of which may vary across contexts. Emancipation takes a variety of different forms. Ransom and redemption are different institutions for achieving emancipation, usually, but not always, through direct negotia-tions with the master(s). Legal measures, such as abolition and/or laws crimi-nalising enslavement, may not automatically imply the *actual* emancipation of slave populations.

A general Glossary of Foreign Terms at the end of the volume is directed principally at non-specialists, to facilitate the reading and understanding of vernacular terms that recur in the chapters.

Note

1   I owe these details on Haalpulaar'en nomenclature to the courtesy of Professor Jean Schmitz

Preface to the Second Edition

When *Reconfiguring Slavery: West African Trajectories* was first published, it made two main contributions to the field of African slavery studies. Firstly, it shifted the focus away from the 'end' or 'death' of historical slavery and highlighted slavery's reconfigurations throughout the twentieth century and into the present of West African societies. Secondly, by moving away from slavery's 'end' and directly addressing the slow and tortuous process of emancipation, it prioritised the lived experience of slaves and their descendants. Unlike earlier studies that produced bird's-eye views of slavery (and its supposed demise), this book's focus on 'trajectories' revealed strategies that were invariably 'from someone' and 'from somewhere' (Haraway, 1988) – strategies anchored in particular social landscapes and unfolded by individual men and women, youths and elders, ex-slaves still in contact with their former masters, or slave descendants generations removed from the enslavement of their forebears.

Seven years after the publication of the hardback edition, the themes of *Reconfiguring Slavery: West African Trajectories* continue to be relevant to the study of slavery and post-slavery in West Africa. Empirically, the case studies discussed in these pages are representative of circumstances that are still commonly found in many West African societies. And, analytically, it is still necessary, as suggested in this volume's introduction, to think of slavery today not as a unified reality, but as a fragmented phenomenon that requires qualification: *de facto* slavery, classificatory slavery, metaphorical slavery and extraverted slavery refer to distinct social and historical phenomena. These concepts were not introduced in an attempt to construct a rigid typology; they are qualifiers aimed at adding nuance and precision to the analysis of slavery in Africa. They continue to have heuristic potential for distinguishing across a plethora of practices characterised as 'slavery' in academic writings, heritage discourses, humanitarian appeals and policy reports.

This second edition comes out at a moment when the research field has on the whole embraced the emphasis on the experiential dimension of emancipation advocated in this volume, as attested by the multiplication of efforts to collect and analyse African testimonies on slavery and the slave trade, whenever possible by enslaved persons. This is an important historiographical turn, which has the potential to break a silence and integrate perspectives that had hitherto been marginalised (or altogether ignored) in the study of Africa's past and present. The very high slave/free ratios found in most West African societies up until the end of the nineteenth century imply that slaves were major contributors to the making of African societies. A renewed focus on their experiences, and on the collection of sources that foreground their experiences, will result in more accurate historical and anthropological analyses based on a polyphony of voices, with each voice considered critically to reveal the partial and circumstantial viewpoint of its author.

To be sure, there have been important precursors to this methodological reorientation (Curtin, 1967; Olivier de Sardan, 1975; Romero, 1988; Wright, 1993; to name just a few). But the last few years have witnessed an unprecedented effort to collect, analyse and make available to specialists and non-specialists alike African sources on slavery, including sources by slaves and their descendants. Examples include critical editions of African sources on slavery and the slave trade, such as the volumes edited by Alice Bellagamba, Sandra Greene and Martin Klein (2013; forthcoming); books and articles with an explicit focus on the biographic trajectories of enslaved persons (McDougall, 1998; Rasmussen, 1999; Lovejoy and Law, 2003; Greene, 2011; Getz and Clarke, 2011; Pelckmans, 2011; and many others); textbooks that emphasise the diversity of slave experiences in African history (Stilwell, 2014); and monographs detailing the options and choices of enslaved persons (e.g. McMahon, 2013; Rossi, 2015).

Part of this work is being carried out by African researchers, and this constitutes a major reorientation in an African historiography that has been treating interior African slavery as a taboo research topic until very recently (Thioub, 2005). This is beginning to change, as African researchers are turning to the study of slavery and emancipation in their societies. Research centres focusing on African slavery and its contemporary vestiges have been created in several West African countries – suffice it to mention as a key example the *Centre Africain de Recherches sur les Traites et les Esclavages* (CARTE), which brings together researchers working on slavery in the Université Cheikh Anta Diop de Dakar (Senegal), Université Abdou Moumouni de Niamey (Niger), Université de Ouagadougou (Burkina Faso), Université de Yaoundé 1 and Université de Ngaoundéré (Cameroun), and Université d'Etat d'Haïti.

Concurrently, slavery-focused NGOs have been collecting sources and making them available for research and public debate. The Nigerien NGO

Timidria supported the publication of a study on slavery in Niger that included case studies and quotes by persons of slave descent variously affected by the vestiges of traditional slavery (Galy, 2010). In 2014 the Malian NGO Temedt published a volume containing 101 Malian ex-slaves' testimonies with the support of the Rosa Luxembourg foundation (Temedt, 2014). This volume of testimonies followed the publication of Temedt's study *L'esclavage au Mali* in 2012 (Temedt, 2012). Both volumes were developed under the scientific direction of Naffet Keita. In Mauritania Mohamed Yahya Ould Ciré, founder of the Association des Haratine de Mauritanie en Europe (AHME), published a collection of his own articles on slavery and racism in Mauritania that discuss case studies on contemporary legacies of slavery (Ould Ciré, 2014). These volumes are but a few examples that testify to the rise of African anti-slavery activism and growing engagement by African intellectuals with slavery's survival in their countries.

In the last few years documentaries have been realised that illustrate how enslavement is remembered – or still experienced – by Africans of slave descent. *Les Esclaves d'Hier*, directed by Eric Hahonou and Camilla Strandbjerg, which combines an overview of the contemporary situation of Gando societies in Benin with a moving autobiographical testimony, is a case in point. This has been followed by *Endam Bilaali: Renégocier les identités en situation post-esclavagiste*, produced by CARTE under the direction of Ibrahima Thioub, Abderrahmane Ngaïdé and Ibrahima Seck (CARTE, 2014). Also in 2014 appeared *The Diambourou: Slavery and Emancipation in Kayes*, directed by Marie Rodet (Rodet and Challier, 2014). The Nigerien NGO Timidria, in collaboration with Alternative Productions, produced *Hadijatou Mani: La Courageuse*, directed by Abba Kiari Arimi (Arimi, n.d.). All of these films foreground the words of ex-slaves and slave descendants. They make the issue of internal African slavery accessible to a potentially wide public within Africa and in the world.

The field of African slavery studies has changed over the last seven years and new sources have become available. While the first edition of *Reconfiguring Slavery: West African Trajectories* probed researchers to fill a void, in today's transformed research field this new edition should encourage nuance, criticism, perhaps even a certain dose of scepticism. As a multiplicity of 'voices of slaves' become accessible, they force us to ask: whose voices, really, are they? Which agendas do they represent? Which voices attest to a life confronted with *de facto* enslavement, and which ones attest to the experiences and aspirations of people who this volume characterises as classificatory slaves? Which ones illustrate the metaphorical mobilisation of slavery as a powerful trope in African political fields reshaped by decentralisation policies? Which ones correspond to strategies of extraversion that flag 'slavery' as a word with high media-shock potential in global humanitarian discourses? This volume provides conceptual and methodological tools for coming to grips with these new questions, and its case studies serve as a laboratory to develop and test new answers.

Benedetta Rossi,
London, 6 January 2016

References

Arimi, Abba Kiari, n.d. *Hadijatou: La courageuse.* DVD. Niamey (Niger): Timidria and Alternative Productions.

Bellagamba, A., Greene, S. and Klein, M., eds, 2013. *African Voices on Slavery and the Slave Trade.* Cambridge: Cambridge University Press.

Bellagamba, A., Greene, S. and Klein, M., eds, forthcoming. *African Slaves, African Masters: Politics, Memories, Social Life.* Trenton, NJ: Africa World Press, Harriet Tubman series.

CARTE, under the direction of Thioub, I., Ngaïdé, A. and Seck I., 2014. *Endam Bilaali. Renégocier les identités en situation post-esclavagiste.* DVD. Dakar, Senegal: CARTE.

Curtin, P., 1967. *Africa Remembered.* Madison: University of Wisconsin Press.

Galy, K. A., 2010. *Esclavage au Niger: Aspects historiques et juridiques.* Paris: Karthala.

Getz, T. and Clarke, L., 2011. *Abina and the Important Men: A Graphic History.* New York: Oxford University Press.

Greene, S., 2011. *West African Narratives of Slavery: Texts from Late Nineteenth- and Early Twentieth-Century Ghana.* Bloomington: Indiana University Press.

Hahonou, E. and Strandsbjerg, C., 2011. *Les esclaves d'hier: démocratie et ethnicité au Bénin.* DVD. Copenhagen: Spor Media.

Haraway, D., 1988. 'Situated Knowledges: The Science Question in Feminism and the Privilege of Partial Perspective.' *Feminist Studies*, 14(3), pp. 575–99.

Lovejoy, P. and Law, R., eds, 2003. *The Biography of Mahommah Gardo Baquaqua: His Passage from Slavery to Freedom in Africa and America.* Princeton, NJ: Markus Wiener.

McDougall, A., 1998. 'A Sense of Self: The Life of Fatma Barka.' *Canadian Journal of African Studies*, 32(2), pp. 285–315.

McMahon, E., 2013. *Slavery and Emancipation in Islamic East Africa: From Honor to Respectability.* New York: Cambridge University Press.

Olivier de Sardan, J. P., 1975. *Quand nos pères étaient captifs. Récits paysans du Niger.* Paris: Nubia.

Ould Ciré, Mohamed Yahya, 2014. *La Mauritanie entre l'esclavage et le racisme.* Paris: L'Harmattan.

Pelckmans, L., 2011. *Travelling Hierarchies: Roads in and out of Slave Status in a Central Malian Fulbe Network.* Vol. 34, *African Studies Collection.* Leiden, NL: African Studies Centre.

Rasmussen, S., 1999. 'The Slave Narrative in Life History and Myth and Problems of Ethnographic Representation of the Tuareg Cultural Predicament.' *Ethnohistory*, 46(3), pp. 67–108.

Rodet, M. and Challier, F., 2014. *The Diambourou: Slavery and Emancipation in Kayer, Mali*. DVD. London: School of Oriental and African Studies, London.

Romero, P., 1988. *Life Histories of African Women*. London: Ashfield Press.

Rossi, B., 2015. *From Slavery to Aid at the Desert's Edge: Politics, Labor, and Ecology in the Nigerien Sahel 1800–2000*. New York: Cambridge University Press.

Stilwell, S., 2014. *Slavery and Slaving in African History*. New York: Cambridge University Press.

Temedt Association, under the scientific direction of Naffet Keita, 2012. *L'Esclavage au Mali*. Paris: L'Harmattan.

Temedt Association, under the scientific direction of Naffet Keita, 2014. *Esclavage au Mali: des victimes témoignent*. Paris: L'Harmattan.

Thioub, I., 2005. 'Regard critique sur les lectures africaines de l'esclavage et de la traite atlantique.' In I. Mandé and B. Stefanson, eds, *Les Historiens africains et la mondialisation*. Paris: Karthala, pp. 271–92.

Wright, M., 1993. *Strategies of Slaves and Women: Life Stories from East/Central Africa*. New York: James Currey.

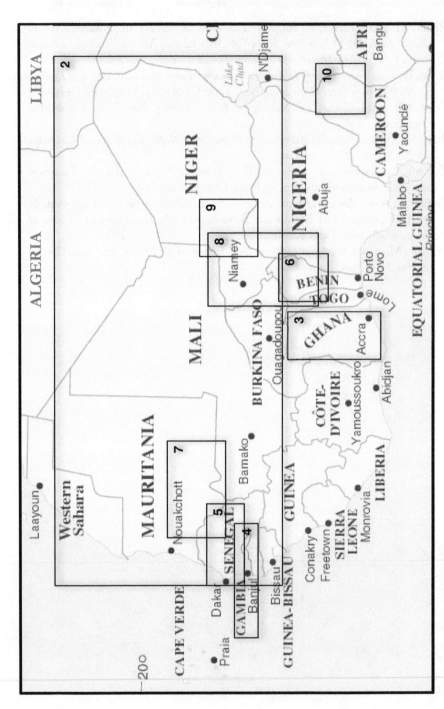

Study areas by chapter. Political boundaries c. 2008

1

Introduction: Rethinking Slavery in West Africa

Benedetta Rossi

Slavery has been pronounced dead many times in West Africa's modern history, yet it has not disappeared from research, the media, and reports of human rights organisations. This book does not retrace the aftermath of West African slavery, but rather it highlights the preliminary contours of its most recent reconfigurations. A number of publications have started documenting the new characteristics of African slavery.[1] Building on this new research, contributions to *Reconfiguring Slavery* show that, today in West African society, 'slavery' has acquired new practical and epistemological dimensions that cannot be explained by focusing solely on the end of historical forms of enslavement.[2]

Understanding the dynamics that define slavery's contemporary manifestations calls for new concepts and analytical frameworks. The notion of trajectory, which underlies this volume, attempts to trace transformations in how slavery has been perceived and experienced by different categories of actors in continuously changing circumstances. Most chapters focus on the trajectories followed by slave descendants. Yet, even within the same region or society, such trajectories vary. They lead not to a uniform end of slavery, but to its reconfiguration into new meanings and practices, often still identified as 'slavery', but embedded in new processes and institutions.

The notion of 'slavery' today covers a multiplicity of phenomena. New discourses of slavery, often originating outside Africa, developed around humanitarian activism and afrocentric ideas of heritage, legacy and race. Pre-colonial forms of slavery evolved differently in different societies, and within any one society, the category 'slavery' is used to characterise a variety of situations. In some contexts, the descendants of slaves are incorporated in the society of freemen, and the past is, for them, a buried memory. Elsewhere, slave status affects everyday opportunities and the sense of self of its bearers. New forms of dependence and exploitation coexist with the vestiges of 'traditional' slavery, while 'tradition' is itself manipulated by slave descendants trying to turn inherited stigma into a political asset. In order to comprehend how 'slavery' functions in contemporary West Africa it is necessary to delimit meaningful concepts that consider both the representations and practices, as both terminologies and practices have been changing.

Some West African societies include groups whose identity is marked, collectively, by slave status.[3] Yet these groups, whose name carries the stigma of slave origin, left behind most aspects of their life as slaves. Thus, against the contention that slaves are 'without history', people of slave status started articulating their own historical narratives (cf. Botte, 1994, 117ff; de Bruijn and van Dijk, 1994, 105; Vereecke, 1994, 43). In some cases, the memory of free origins is retained (Botte, 1994, 115; de Bruijn and Pelckmans, 2005, 90); elsewhere, new histories have been crafted. A key factor in definitions of slavery, the inability of slaves to own property, also requires revision in the light of extensively documented disputes between former slaves and masters over the property of land and productive resources (cf. Botte, 1994, 124; Leservoisier, 1994). In some West African contexts, ex-slaves are beginning to access religious knowledge and use it to develop a reformist ideology, in contrast with their traditional position outside their masters' faith (cf. Botte, 1994, 128–32; de Bruijn and van Dijk, 1994, 99; Vereecke, 1994, 36). The internalisation of the master's cultural and moral ethos, when it occurred, is being abandoned in favour of counter-ideologies that emphasise the capacity of slave groups to improve their status through hard work (cf. Hardung, 1997, 129; and in this volume). Against the view that slaves are 'without kinship', it has been noted that ex-slaves are increasingly able to forge and maintain durable kinship and affinal relations. In recent times, residual categories of West African slaves have been reproducing biologically.[4] As the ideology of slavery progressively loses its grip on the way people think and act, it becomes possible for slave descendants to talk about their ancestry and, in some cases, reconstruct their genealogies (cf. Schmitz, in this volume). Finally, the historical denial of slaves' political participation is being replaced by growing mobilisation (cf. Botte, 1999; Lecocq, 2005; Hahonou, in this volume; Leservoisier, in this volume).

Confusion, however, is generated by the fact that these domains (memory, religion, wealth, status, etc.) have evolved unevenly among different groups of slave descendants. The capability to change one's destiny depends on the existence of viable alternative livelihood options, as well as the relative resilience of past ideologies of hierarchy. Where the masters' class remained in power after colonial abolition, the rejection of such hierarchies would close avenues of social mobility that passed through the establishment of clientelistic relations with former masters (Kopytoff, 1988, 497; Schmitz, in this volume). Today, even within the same society, different categories of actors relate to traditional hierarchies in different ways. Elders, women and vulnerable groups are more likely to accept them than, for example, young male migrants. The ex-slaves' capacity and willingness to change status is partly determined by their assessment of available opportunities. These differ for men and women, elders and youths, more and less mobile people. Thus, the notion of 'voluntary slavery', which has become commonplace in African studies, should be considered in the light of the particular *context of choice* within which the residues of enslavement are tolerated.

This fragmentation of 'slavery' into a diversified range of circumstances and situations is poorly conveyed by existing terminologies. First, the English word 'slave' fails to express the subtle distinctions of status (gradations of dependence, age, gender, residence, etc.) articulated in certain African languages (cf. Hardung, in this volume; Rattray, 1956, 34ff.). This is not merely a problem of translation, but also of inadequate theorisation. Partly due to the denial of slave kinship (cf. note 4), we lack analytical tools to comprehend the process of creolisation, through which slaves became gradually integrated in the society of the free (cf. Klein, in this volume). As shown by Schmitz in this volume, arranged marriages between slaves and free, various forms of fictive kinship, and multiple strategies of status negotiation account for complex 'slave' (or 'part-slave') identities that have not been adequately explored. Moreover, as Burnham argues in his contribution to this volume, the meaning of words is not static but changes with other social and historical transformations. The meaning of the term 'slavery' changed in different ways in Euro-American and African contexts, retaining some of its original semantic dimensions and dropping others. 'Clashing globalised discourses on the interpretation of slavery' (Burnham, in this volume) generate ambiguities of meaning. While African Americans visit Ghanaian slavery heritage sites searching for an idealised history, their African hosts welcome them as potential avenues to an idealised wealth in Europe and the US (McCaskie, in this volume). Dreams of success in the West are crushed when young African migrants meet with xenophobia, and wonder whether they haven't left poverty behind only to become the 'willing slaves' of the West (cf. Bellagamba, in this volume). But interpretative clashes on slavery's past and present are not peculiar to transnational spaces. They occur also within the same country and community. Groups that distanced themselves from past hierarchies comment sceptically on neighbours and relatives who 'believe in slavery' (Bellagamba, in this volume), or 'cannot see with clear eyes' (Hardung, in this volume). Conversely, the ones who maintained relations with former masters reinterpret the nature of these relations, altering the meaning of 'slavery' accordingly.

Anthropologists employ vernacular terms when translations are misleading. In this case, turning to local terminologies does not necessarily provide a clearer picture. Within West African languages, status categories have been acquiring new meanings, and new identities and euphemistic expressions have been introduced. In Mali the Tamasheq term *iklan* has been replaced with euphemisms; instead, the term *bella*, Songhay word for Tuareg of low status, was used by the French for Tuareg slaves, then by Malian politicians in the 1950s to refer to Tuareg slaves whom they sought to liberate, then by 'intellectuals of unfree origins to refer to themselves as a separate ethnic group' (Lecocq, 2005, 49). In the Gambia the term *jonyaa*, a Mandinka word commonly translated as slavery, has transformed its late nineteenth-century meaning ('the one you sell or buy'), and has come to signify, today, the 'voluntary allegiance stemming from the reciprocal recollection of former master-slave relationships' (Bellagamba, 2005, 33). In ethnically plural contexts the situation is particularly complex, as status terms are multiplied by the number of societies trying to interpret their own and their neighbours' statuses and giving rise to competing theories of hierarchy. In Niger the term '*buzu*' was used by Hausa people to refer to the slaves of the Tuareg. As the distinction between slave (*iklan*) and various categories of liberated slaves (e.g. *ighawelan*, *iderfan*) became blurred even in Tuareg contexts, the name '*buzu*' was used interchangeably for Tuareg slaves or liberated slaves (cf. Norris, 1975, 6). In some contexts '*buzu*' is used by Hausa speakers in a derogatory way to refer to free Tuareg (Bernus, 1981, 62–63), and the term '*Buzanci*' is frequently used in Hausa in place of 'Tamasheq' for the Tuareg language without the derogatory connotation of '*buzu*'. But this term also has a separate history, more relevant in southern agricultural areas where groups of Buzu (also called Buzaye or Bugaje), detached from their old masters, settled amidst Hausa farming villages. Here, 'Buzu' is seen as an ethnic category, with mixed Tuareg and Hausa characteristics (cf. Nicolas, 1962, 153, '*l'ethnie des Bouzou*'). In other contexts it has been easier to change ethnicity than to change status. Former Tuareg slaves or liberated slaves have employed a 'Hausaisation' strategy in order to leave their inherited status behind (Oxby, 1986, 105; Rossi, 2009). In Mali some *iklan* groups have been adopting a Songhay identity (Gashoolt, 2007), and similar transformations have been documented in Fulbe society (cf. Hardung, 1997, 111; Burnham, in this volume).

Ex-slaves leading independent lifestyles have struggled with names that tie them to their past identity and carry stigma for them and their children. At the same time, terms used to designate slave status have changed meaning and slave descendants adopted new forms of self-identification.[5] What is the difference between a person of slave origin successfully passing as free, someone seeking security in old ties of dependence, someone with no choice but to inhabit traditional forms of slavery, and someone using slave status as a political agenda? Thinking of all of these cases as manifestations of 'slavery' may obfuscate the fact that groups engaged, alternatively, in avoiding hunger, escaping stigma and manoeuvring politics partake of different institutions, discourses and strategies. The chapters in this book shed light on at least four fields, each of which is regularly characterised as 'slavery' in the media, policy and academic writing:

- The persistence of pre-colonial forms of enslavement, ranging from the resilience of old hierarchies in hinterland areas to the voluntary retention of slave–master relations.
- Strategies of upward mobility of former slaves trying to conceal their own and their children's slave origins. This includes migration, the reinvention of history, the acquisition of new ethnic identities, and practices of silencing slavery.
- The political mobilisation of people self-identifying as of slave origin and seeking to state their claims on the basis of perceived shared interests.
- The introduction and manipulation of exogenous discourses on slavery. This includes the introduction of ideas of heritage and the legacy of slavery, which create new rationales and practices targeted at tourists, donors and humanitarian agencies.

This book focuses on the multiple trajectories of forms of dependence that existed in the past of the societies considered in its chapters. It does not include new forms of exploitation and coercion often characterised as 'new slavery' (e.g. child trafficking, prostitution, etc.), which nevertheless should be added to the list of phenomena currently labelled 'slavery'.

A Renewed Analytical Framework

Used to cover diverse manifestations, the term 'slavery' has lost interpretative value (cf. Miers, 2004). Today slavery appears fragmented and multiplied, as if seen through a kaleidoscope. New analytical tools are needed to make sense of the possibly diverse dynamics that underpin formally similar institutions. Here it is suggested that manifestations of 'slavery' in West Africa be analysed under four different rubrics: the circumscribed resilience of historical forms of enslavement (slavery); stigmatisation on the grounds of inherited or putative slave status (classificatory slavery); forms of exploitation akin to slavery (metaphorical slavery); and exogenous discourses opening new fields of thought and action around the notion of slavery (extraverted slavery). Unlike the first category, the other three should not be seen as types of slavery but as different phenomena variously related to it. It should be noted that these concepts are merely approximate categorisations and flexible tools for analysis. They are introduced to overcome the growing limitations of the single label 'slavery' for deciphering increasingly diverse dynamics, and are not necessarily used in the same way in this book's chapters. The following paragraph briefly discusses the practical implications of these four analytical concepts in contemporary West African society.

While vestiges of historical slavery can still be found today in some parts of West Africa, cases of people born into bondage and recognised as property of their masters are rare. On the other hand, being classified as 'slave' usually carries stigma and influences a person's opportunities and self-esteem. Yet the classificatory slave who freely disposes of his or her labour, property and progeny is not in the same situation as the slave. Other characteristics, such as caste, gender, 'race' or choice of sexual partner carry stigma for their bearers. Stigmatisation on the grounds of slave status and actual enslavement should be kept analytically distinct (cf. Morice, 2005). Metaphorical slavery ranges from the use of 'slavery' as a rhetorical trope to signal dependence (e.g. to characterise the continuing poverty of African countries) to new forms of exploitation of vulnerable groups (e.g. child trafficking), which can be so extreme as to constitute actual, not merely metaphorical, enslavement.[6] Yet exploitation, stigma and/or poverty are not always found in association with slavery.[7] Moreover, unlike slavery in the past, these forms of exploitation are illegal.

Now that slavery has been abolished everywhere, exploiting people as if they were slaves is illegal and sanctionable. One of the main questions raised by contemporary uses of the term 'slavery' is thus whether, once slavery is banned by law, the violation of fundamental rights of *de jure* free people should still be discussed as 'slavery', or if it should rather fall under different legal rubrics. In the majority of cases, different positions in this debate are actually closer than it seems. They converge in finding intolerable practices that some authors call 'slavery' (in order to achieve greater political impact and media-shock potential) while others qualify them as similar to slavery, in certain, but possibly not all, respects (in order to highlight change in historical forms of dependence and exploitation).

This introduction opts for a narrow definition of slavery. Clearly, slavery is 'not one social status, but many' (Searing, 1993, 48). It should be studied as a dynamic phenomenon, which implies different cultural associations in different contexts and evolves along with changing historical and social conditions (Deutsch, 2006, 5; Villasante de Beauvais, 2000, 17). Yet, for the sake of clarity, it is necessary to identify elements of a 'lowest common denominator' of slavery that would include certain phenomena and exclude others. Slavery refers to the individual or communal ownership of another person or group, whereby 'ownership' is understood to reflect culturally specific meanings and forms of rights in things and persons, as well as their modes of transmission and exchange. In the case of slavery, this commonly includes rights over the productive and reproductive capacities of slaves, rights over any assets they may own or use, and rights over their offspring.[8] The ideological assimilation of slaves to chattels and their actual saleability are not necessary conditions (cf. Curtin, 1976, 303).[9] It has been a historical leitmotif that what makes it possible for a human being to be enslaved is his or her outsiderness, a trait that may refer to real external origins or to ideological characterisations of slaves as intrinsically (physically, intellectually, morally) *other* than the free (cf. Cottias et al., 2006, 12ff).[10] The slave as the institutionalised outsider stands outside the laws that protect free members of society from extreme exploitation. Slave status, thus, designates a condition of abuse from which all humans are supposedly shielded, *except for the slave*.[11] This institutionalised exception justifies the slave's otherwise unjustifiable exploitation, and is a defining characteristic of slavery across time and space.

If slavery must be institutionally legitimised, the legal abolition of slavery in all countries may seem to imply its worldwide disappearance. In normative contexts where slavery has been abolished, the illegal enslavement of people does not imply the existence of slavery as an official institution. However, legal pluralism recognises that state law can coexist with parallel normative universes. Alternative legal frameworks operate in semi-autonomous social fields (Moore, 1978), where customary law, or alternative norms of governance, are invoked to legitimise enslavement. Hence, the existence of anti-slavery legislation does not automatically imply the disappearance of slavery. This accounts for vestiges of slavery in contexts falling outside the reach of state sovereignty (for example, remote regions where traditional hierarchies are particularly resilient).

Opting for a narrow interpretation of slavery sets this work in contrast with activist positions. Activist organisations tend to adopt the legal definitions of slavery provided by national and international institutions. These definitions are phrased so as to maximise the coverage of exploited and abused people (cf. Miers, 2003, 415). If the question one asks is of an interventionist order ('what should be done about slavery?'), reference to 'slavery' is likely to raise public attention and provoke faster official reactions, at the possibly trivial cost of definitional nuances. Yet these nuances matter more if the question one sets out to answer is 'how should slavery be understood?' An example will clarify this point. Forced marriage, as a practice that transfers fundamental rights over a woman's person against her will, is sometimes assimilated to slavery. But how can we compare the forced marriage of a free woman to a master's rights over the sexuality of his slave (that he can exercise or transfer to others, against compensation) if we collapse the two under the same category?

In hinterland Niger there have been cases of traditional masters turning persistent ties to their ex-slaves into a lucrative business by selling girls of slave descent to wealthy Nigerian businessmen.[12] As today these practices are illegal, the masters pretend to receive bridewealth and pass it on to the girl's father. Instead, they keep this sum, which signifies the transfer of rights over their slave who becomes the payer's concubine. Surely, this camouflaged 'bridewealth' and the bridewealth paid for the forced marriage of a free woman are understood and experienced differently by the actors involved. A similar case is described by Bellagamba in the context of colonial Gambia (2005, 27–30). Some of the 'wives' of Mussa Moloh sought to gain freedom by explaining to British authorities that they were not (free) 'real wives', but slaves. They provided evidence, which, in their eyes and in those of colonial officers, clarified the difference between slave concubines and real wives, who may or may not have consented to their marriage. Clearly, it is possible to assimilate to slavery various cases of un-freedom, exploitation, coercion and social stigma. But we should be able to distinguish analytically between these practices. We ought to ask *whose eyes* behold the proverbial similarities. Phenomena that appear similar to activists may look different to the actors directly involved. Any account of change must make the most of definitional and practical nuances, lest centuries of transformations be collapsed under the single referent 'slavery'.

The Times of Slavery's Transformations [13]

A study of slavery's transformations must consider changes occurring at different rhythms in various places (cf. Klein, in this volume). It is useful to borrow Braudel's idea of different historical temporalities: the slow time of society's relation to its surroundings; the intermediate one of societal change; and the fast-moving time of events, 'a surface disturbance, the waves stirred up by the powerful movements of tides' (Braudel, 1972). These three levels are matched, respectively, by distinct reconfiguration patterns in the history of slavery. The laws and decrees that marked the legal history of abolition and emancipation can be seen as legislative events, punctuating the 'deep-running currents' of social change. The intermediate time of societal change interests a plurality of interrelated domains, each of which bears upon the reconfiguration of slavery. These domains include, *inter alia*, economic processes (trade and production), labour regimes and forms of governance and rule. Finally, Braudel's first temporal scale, defining society's relation to its surroundings, is so slow that it can be seen as opposing resistance to changes occurring at the other two levels, rather than as a level that is itself slowly evolving. Thus, the slow pace attested for hierarchical transformations in Saharan regions is due, partly, to the implications of enduring environmental insecurity, as subsistence vulnerability puts a premium on the maintenance of patronage and clientelistic relations.

In the decades following the abolition of the slave trade, some of those slaves who would have been exported were redirected within West Africa as slave labour. Moreover, dynamics internal to the Western and Central Sudan, such as the consolidation of recently created *jihad* states through extensive warfare, and the expansion of the economic activities of the ruling classes of these states led to the expansion of internal slavery (cf. Lovejoy, 1983, 158ff.; Lovejoy and Hogendorn, 1979, 220–21). While a minority of slaves were able to negotiate with their masters limited freedom to conduct business and trade on their own account, they usually owed the masters a fee or part of their earnings. Later, with colonial control firmly established, the masters' power to enforce their domination was progressively eroded. 'Pacification' (what British administrators referred to as *pax Britannica* and their French counterparts as *paix Française*) restrained the military power of previous rulers and/or warrior elites. Progressively, the old masters class had to renegotiate the terms of its relations with ex-slaves who could, and in many cases did, choose flight over continued dependence. Klein in this volume considers the factors that played a role in the choice to stay or to go, and suggests that access to land and wage labour were key to the emancipation of slave populations. This was recognised early by colonial administrators, who used land and labour legislation to exercise an indirect leverage on the slavery question (see, for example, Lovejoy and Hogendorn, 1993, 127–58, 201–13). Yet avenues to emancipation had existed within African societies before colonial occupation. They often followed different logics from the ones that characterised colonial abolition. Thus, in some large Tuareg confederations in the second half of the 1800s, ecological and political factors at the regional level determined the onset of diminishing returns to slavery, leading to the transformation of slaves into tributaries, clients and sharecroppers (cf. Rossi, 2009). In this book, Schmitz shows that in the Futa Toro's Islamic society, pre-colonial emancipation took the form of a transition from bondage (slavery) to clientage. Becoming the clients of their masters, ex-slaves obtained access to land and, through marriages arranged by former masters, to a legitimate line of descent. In pre-colonial Islamic West Africa, religious piety offered avenues out of slavery. These avenues did not simply vanish with the introduction of colonial paths to emancipation, but persisted as alternative routes, their underlying rationales interacting in complex ways with colonial anti-slavery ideology.

At the beginning of the 1900s colonial powers in West Africa abolished the legal status of slavery. However, slavery was embedded in social processes that took a long time to adapt to decrees, particularly as colonial administrators hesitated to enforce anti-slavery laws (cf. Olivier de Sardan, 1976, 16). In both French and English West Africa, European powers initially refrained from actions that would spoil their relations with ruling African elites, and feared the political instability that could result from the sudden achievement of freedom on the part of ex-slaves (cf. Klein, 1998, 134; Klein, in this volume; Lovejoy, 1983, 271). Emancipated slaves were sometimes expected to work in colonial projects and were known as 'the slaves of the *Commandant*' (Cooper, 1996, 88; cf. Klein and Roberts, 1980, 383; Lovejoy, 1983, 258). Forced labour recruitment and forced military conscription particularly hit servile and low-status groups. Local administrative chiefs were often charged with recruitment and labour supervision, and they selected those people whose support they did not need and whose resentment they did not fear (Coquery-Vidrovitch, 1988, 223; Manchuelle, 1989, 101). But travel conditions had become safer and new opportunities of free employment available, not only in plantations and centres of rural production but also in cities, where slave status was not easily recognisable. Destitute free workers and slaves trying to turn the insecurity of emancipation into concrete livelihood strategies readily seized these opportunities (cf. Duffill and Lovejoy, 1985, 163). Recruitment in institutions structured by different codes of honour, like the military or some sectors of the public administration, provided avenues of social mobility to people of servile origins (cf. Mann, 2006).

By the 1940s dependence on cash had become more pressing even in rural areas; some West African cities had developed into urban poles of labour attraction; and a series of ILO reports had set the framework for the abolition of forced labour. Two related phenomena characterised the labour question (cf. Cooper, 2002): the 1935–48 strikes that joined the discontent of urban workers with the ideals proffered by nationalist intellectuals; and the less politically destabilising question of rural farmers practising seasonal labour migration. Both constituencies included ex-slaves. Both constituencies also included people of free descent who could be metaphorically likened to slaves in new social struggles against forced labour and, later, colonial domination. As slave and free people mixed, 'slavery' seemed to split into two: inherited slave status was silenced and metaphorical uses of 'slavery' multiplied. Focusing on the Gambia, Bellagamba in this volume suggests that in the 1940s and 1950s the slave origins of a multitude of recently emancipated West Africans became a 'public secret', that is,

> knowledge widely shared within society, but hardly articulated except for comments, gossip, and fragments of recollections and oral traditions that might spontaneously surface in daily conversations. For a while, when the mask cracks, this knowledge becomes visible and discussed. Then manners, courtesy, and self-control bury it again in the underground of social life, together with the painful emotions associated with this kind of remembrances.

While the slavery inherited by individuals was silenced (see Schmitz, in this volume), the idea of slavery turned into a powerful political metaphor with different evocative potential in the imaginary of West Africans, still renegotiating slave identities, and Europeans, who represented themselves as a civilising force. This potential was fully realised, for example, by the group of Africans led by Félix Houphouët-Boigny advocating the abolition of forced labour: 'Millions of men have sent us here giving us a precise mandate, to struggle with all our might to abolish the slavery which is still practiced in Black Africa [...]'.[14]

In 1946, just two years after the Brazzaville Conference, where the Free French led by General de Gaulle revised their relation with France's West African colonies, all forms of forced labour were abolished in French Africa. After the Second World War, the new 'development' ideology was introduced to deal with the factors underpinning urban labour unrest and seasonal rural–urban migration. Yet these two domains were compartmentalised into separate 'problems', calling for different remedies. In the last two decades of the twentieth century a growing 'informal sector' has been absorbing both seasonal migrant labour and the dropouts from urban wage and contract labour. The rhetorical separation between these phenomena conceals their related causes and deflates their political significance. The increasing size of these two constituencies is partly related to the impacts of externally induced liberalisation policies. West Africans of slave and free descent have become citizens of independent African states, but ascribed status remained a determinant factor for accessing political rights (cf. Hahonou, in this volume). In many West African contexts the stigma of slavery continues to make ex-slaves 'second-class' citizens, a situation that is worse for female descendants of slaves, doubly marginalised in terms of both status and gender (Mahdi, 2008; Robertson and Klein, 1983, 5–12; Wright, 1975).

The Contributions

The chapters in this book examine recent trajectories of slavery rooted in the processes outlined above and in more specific regional and local dynamics. The volume includes both historical and anthropological contributions, which rely on different sources and argumentative styles to support their interpretations. Even within the same discipline, personal approaches and agendas differ. This makes for an eclectic mix of essays that requires some flexibility on the part of the reader asked to shift across methodologies and intellectual frameworks. Yet such diversity joins the broader scale of historical reconstruction to the close-up look of the anthropologist. Thus, for example, Martin Klein reviews a vast cross-section of primary and secondary historical sources to show that, in a set of West African societies, codes of honour matter as much, if not more, than material wealth in the maintenance of hierarchy. In turn, Hardung's in-depth study of the Gannunkeebe provides a detailed illustration of how these very honour-codes matter, why they matter, when they cease being meaningful, and how the idea of honour works in the society she discusses. Thus, while chapters have different analytical styles, they converge in aim and purpose.

In chapter 2 Martin Klein traces the historical evolution of West African patterns of emancipation into the present. Some of his observations introduce themes that are developed in the following contributions. He notes that change occurred in two separate ideological systems, the colonial and the Islamic (cf. Schmitz, in this volume). The availability of money incomes through cash cropping or wage labour constituted an enabling factor in the slaves' capacity to negotiate a new position. However, status distinctions persisted unless the dominant codes of honour were also changed to allow slave descendants to occupy roles from which they had hitherto been excluded (cf. Klein, 2005).

Klein's wide-ranging paper is followed by Tom McCaskie's 'history of the present'. This is a detailed mosaic of different views, statements and positions on Ghana's 'heritage of slavery'. McCaskie focuses on the work of the Association of Black Psychologists (ABPsi) and reflects critically on the implications of certain Afrocentric professional discourses and activities. He shows how these discourses (of 'legacy' and 'heritage') project the ideological positions of their authors onto the past, and then invoke this reconfigured 'past' to interpret present circumstances. These discourses have become increasingly influential in international representations of slavery. But they conceal very different views and agendas, such as those of ABPsi members, Asante elites, aspiring international migrants, beneficiaries of ABPsi aid projects and national politicians. McCaskie's analysis is a long-overdue examination of the implications of Afrocentric discourses of slavery in contemporary Ghana.

Both chapter 3's focus on slavery in Ghanaian transnational spaces and Bellagamba's subsequent chapter on the Gambia highlight the polysemic potential of 'slavery'. As in Ghana, internal historical slavery is almost entirely silenced in the Gambia. Yet this 'silencing' of internal slavery occurs in parallel with slavery's metaphorical extension to the experience of poverty and continuing exploitation in contemporary Gambian society. The very absence of verbal registers to characterise internal slavery attests to its hold on people's imagination and its power as a political metaphor. Hence, in the 1950s and 1990s, Gambian struggles, respectively, for national independence and against poverty were expressed in the idiom of slavery. In Ghana Afrocentric discourses of slavery are introduced from the US and manipulated locally according to particular interests, without reference to the historical experience of internal slavery. In both Ghana and the Gambia, the slavery that *is voiced* glosses over *silenced* past domestic slavery, and present social inequalities between people of free and slave descent.[15]

In chapter 5 Jean Schmitz addresses the question of the silencing of internal slavery from a different angle. Rather than discussing slavery that is visible, he begins to unveil the concealed trajectories of internal slavery in the Senegal River Valley (Futa Toro). Schmitz reconstructs endogenous trajectories of upward mobility among the slaves of a number of Almaami. He also considers what happens to internal emancipation trajectories when new trajectories, inspired by colonial abolitionist ideology, become available (e.g. the military and school-teaching). This chapter highlights differences and continuities between Islamic and colonial strategies of emancipation. According to an influential strand of scholarship, the ideology of emancipation introduced by colonial conquest hinges upon the slavery–freedom opposition, whereby freedom implies severing ties of dependence and acquiring individual autonomy. However, this opposition does not, in itself, provide a satisfactory interpretation of avenues out of slavery in Islamic contexts. Schmitz suggests that the model of emancipation that prevailed historically in Islamic West Africa privileged the transformation of slaves into clients, through access to productive and reproductive resources, that is, land and wives granted mostly by former masters. Colonialism made available alternative 'careers', where slave identity could be transformed and reconstructed by reference to new indices of status. Schmitz shows that integration into new ideologies of hierarchy has been a crucial element in Senegambian paths to emancipation, pre- and post-colonial. Moreover, the ex-slaves' social mobility through colonial careers was often facilitated by former masters and did not signal the outright rejection of dependence.

Christine Hardung's chapter examines the strategies of Gannunkeebe communities of Northern Benin. It explores the hold of ideologies of hierarchy on the ideas and behaviours of ex-dependent groups and addresses one of the main questions in the field of slavery studies: the persistent low status of slave descendants in spite of their economic success. At the ideological level, the authority of a Fulbe master is exemplified by ongoing belief in his power to curse and bless. Hardung enquires into the conditions for hierarchy's resilience or demise by studying changing dispositions towards the masters' perceived supernatural power across groups and generations. She suggests that, in any particular context, 'dependence' should be understood in relation to the cultural significance of 'freedom'. Some Gannunkeebe choose to maintain their tie to former masters, but try to reinterpret the meaning of this relation. Paradoxically, epistemological negotiations to alter the negative connotations of slave status presuppose the acceptance of hierarchy.

This paradox is explored further in Olivier Leservoisier's chapter on MaccuBe[16] groups in Mauritania. Having described the MaccuBe's position in the spheres of ideology, marriage, religion, ritual, land tenure and politics, Leservoisier discusses various forms of MaccuBe resistance. He focuses on strategies aimed primarily at *crossing* social boundaries, rather than at challenging these boundaries and the hierarchical structures they belong to. Also here, change presupposes continuity, as moving up the social ladder implies preserving this ladder in the first place. Thus, in spite of the political mobilisation of groups of servile status striving to influence politics in their own interest, the social mobility of ex-slaves fits in a conservative view of society. This argument is also supported by Hahonou's comparative study of the contemporary political mobilisation of people of slave status in three contexts in Niger and Benin.

Hahonou describes the acquisition of a political voice on the part of slave descendants in the context of decentralisation. While the Songhay aristocracy has been able to maintain political control over its dependents, in Tuareg and Fulani societies slave descendants have now assumed the direction of municipal power. Hahonou's paper explores 'slave' politics at the micro-level and in a comparative framework. It highlights the diverse elements (social, economic, political) that play a role in the acquisition of a political voice on the part of slave descendants. The chapter suggests that associative forms of organisation are central to reshaping the collective consciousness of individuals. Yet he rejoins' Leservoisier's conclusion that the strategies of upward mobility of ex-slaves do not fit a broader project of social reformism.

My own chapter also focuses on Tuareg society, but turns from the voice option to the exit option (cf. Hirschman, 1970). It looks at the rearrangement of axes of physical mobility as privileged strategies for social mobility. I suggest that in the Ader region of Niger particular patterns of mobility are indicative of social status. The transformations of interrelated patterns of movement of former master and slaves since the second half of the 1800s reveal the changing nature of the master–slave relationship. Today, poorer people of slave status (Buzu) choose between 'dependent movement' tied to local forms of patronage (sometimes of former masters), and independent movement to places where they often endure exploitative and stigmatising labour conditions.

Finally, in the book's last chapter Phil Burnham reflects on the evolving discourses of slavery that he encountered in different contexts in the course of his forty years of research. His continuity of research and familiarity with certain fieldsites in Cameroon allowed him to witness changes on slavery discourses across generations. Hence, in the space of two generations, the slave origin of a Gbaya chiefly lineage was progressively forgotten. The slave status of the chief's father went from being an issue of collective concern to a hidden memory only reactivated during disputes. This steadfast assimilation would have been difficult in Mbororo contexts, also discussed in the chapter, where an exclusivist ethnic discourse grafts the stigma of slavery onto ethnicity. Here ex-slaves are less likely to be integrated in the society of the free than to become the object of racialised discrimination. As changes in the slaves' status become possible, the meaning of the word 'slavery' is transformed, giving rise to clashing discourses of slavery across contexts. Burnham's last example illustrates a debate between festival organisers and West African guests on the role of the Oni of Ife at the 150th festival for the abolition of apprenticeship in Trinidad. While festival organisers invited the Oni, whom they saw as the contemporary analogue of a West African traditional chief, a Nigerian guest saw him as representing African middlemen who collaborated with European slave traders. This chapter aptly concludes the book by showing that African 'slavery' has become increasingly fragmented, as groups variously associated with it have followed different trajectories and developed different perspectives.

Contributions to this book emphasise how particular groups and actors negotiate the experience of slavery, past and present, in their everyday lives. In spite of the diversity and complexity of these processes, the following section advances some generalisations.

Reconfiguring Slave Identities

M. I. Finley suggested that societies change, historically, from structures in which status runs along a continuum of rights in persons towards structures in which statuses are polarised around the slave and free poles. The direction of change is not teleological. Under new circumstances, a system polarised into the slave–free opposites can revert to a continuum of statuses (cf. Finley, 1964, 249). Some authors have seen this distinction as characteristic of the difference between African and Western societies. Thus Kopytoff has argued that

> [...] what was deeply engrained [in African societies] was not the narrow 'slavery' of Western conceptions but the wide institutional complex of inter-related and interchangeable dependencies, containing within it numerous functional alternatives. The abolition of one of these dependencies – slavery as the West defines it – could not undermine the larger complex on which so much of the structural continuity of African societies rested. (1988, 502)

Others, however, highlighted that also in Africa some slaves 'wanted freedom in the Western sense of maximum personal autonomy' (Miers and Roberts, 1988, 30), and suggested that Kopytoff's view may come close to implying that those African slaves who 'sought to break rather than bend bonds of dependence, did not understand African society as well as the Western anthropologist' (Cooper et al., 2000, 6).

This book's chapters emphasise the prevalence of paradox and ambiguity. In Mauritania ex-slaves trying to change status reproduce ideologies of hierarchy *vis à vis* other slave descendants (Leservoisier). In Benin many Gannunkeebe reassert past hierarchies in the process of reinterpreting their subordination (Hardung). A Nigérien chief of slave descent regrets the loss of power of former masters, as his village now lacks protection against outside attempts to take advantage of its people, exposing them to new exploitative conditions (Hahonou). In the Gambia, at independence, the struggle against a metaphorical 'colonial slavery' passed under silence the tensions within parties composed of ex-free and ex-slave members (Bellagamba). And while ordinary Ghanaians see African American tourists as 'white men' (*oburoni*), one Asante chief wondered what the slaves sold by his ancestors were doing back in Ghana (McCaskie). The contradictions internal to the same country, group or even family are difficult to grasp in terms of theories that attribute fixity and unity to 'cultural' or 'local' dispositions. Surely, human choice becomes meaningful contextually. But 'the West' and 'Africa' can hardly be seen as contexts. Culturalist interpretations of 'context' are too broad and too rigid to account for the variety of situations illustrated within confines much narrower than 'culture'. Now that slavery cannot be enforced legally, this variety of situations leaves two questions open: what explains the well-documented, if increasingly rare, resilience of ideologies of hierarchy and subordination to former masters? And, when things *do* change, how is hierarchy transformed?

Contemporary vestiges of enslavement are found in correspondence with semi-autonomous fields that escape the enforcement of anti-slavery legislation. In physical environments characterised by climatic instability, production scarcity and subsistence insecurity, webs of hierarchical obligation offer protection from the risk of livelihood failure (Campbell, 2004, xxv; Klein, in this volume; Roberts, 1987, 127). Bonds to old masters might break when these become impoverished and are unable to meet the expectations attached to their status (cf. Giuffrida, 2005). But unless vulnerability decreases, new forms of patronage, sometimes akin to slavery, take shape (cf. Amselle, 1981, 14–15). *In loco* this tends to continue for as long as the system of production and labour regime change (e.g., due to climatic or political transformations, or technological innovation). Instead, for those who can move, migration represents the main alternative. This is why the history of physical mobility is so important for understanding social mobility in West Africa.

Seeing labour migrants as relics of old systems of production intermittently plunging into modernity ignores the integration of urban and rural contexts in today's West African economies, where both sites partake of equally contemporary dynamics (cf. Cooper, 1980, 9). Yet this movement may well reveal a Braudelian insight in the migrants' choice to travel from settings where certain changes (e.g. industrialisation, wage labour) have been taking place more slowly to settings where these transformations are already accomplished. Upon return, migrants of slave descent may be reintegrated in their village of origin, without a substantial renegotiation of their low status (cf. Boyer, 2005). However, at destination migrants leave their status behind and become anonymous workers, joining what scholars in the 1960s called 'ethno-professional' networks, governed by new status criteria (e.g. Cohen, 1969, 191–92; Wallerstein, 1965, 155). Here labour relations assumed new forms through rapid societal changes that are not, as it were, 'hindered' by factors that slow down social transformations. In these contexts courage and entrepreneurship may be rewarded with economic success and fast status mobility. However, less fortunate migrants of slave descent in Africa's large cities or international destinations merely swap inherited dependence for new forms of stigma. Paradoxically, for them slave origin works as a source of 'belonging'[17] to familiar patron–client relations at home, while, at destination, their 'outsiderness' exposes them to xenophobia, corruption and exploitation.

But 'marginality' (spatial, economic, political) is not the only reason for the resilience of traditional hierarchies. And migration is not the only pathway to emancipation. Religion plays an ambivalent role. Vestiges of slavery are found in association with communities headed by maraboutic and religious groups (cf. Boyer, 2005, 782; Hahonou, in this volume; Rossi, 2009). Hahonou reports some slave descendants' assumption that slavery originates from the Qu'ran and cannot therefore be challenged. Hardung (in this volume) suggests that the belief in the supernatural power to curse of the Fulbe masters underscores fear of disobeying them or denying their superiority, even where ex-slaves have attained economic and political emancipation. On the other hand, Islam generated important pre-colonial reformist movements. Schmitz mentions 'emancipation through religious piety' as one of the main axes of emancipation in the Futa Toro. Burnham reminds us that Islam predicates the emancipation of converted slaves and that in some contexts it facilitated the adoption of an 'inclusivist' attitude towards slaves, blurring status differences within the Muslim community.[18] However, in contexts where identity was not primarily defined along the believer/non-believer axis, exclusivist ethnic attitudes act as obstacles to the assimilation of former slaves (Burnham, in this volume). Ongoing prejudice against ex-slaves accounts for the ethnicisation of identities that originally implied slave status (Burnham, Hardung and Hahonou, all in this volume). In such situations, legacies of slavery have a tendency to mutate into racism and discrimination rooted in the body and physical characteristics of the stigmatised group.[19] Accordingly, changing ethnic affiliation becomes a precondition for social mobility.

As paradoxical and ambiguous as the trajectories discussed above may be, they are not inconsistent. Everywhere, even when they appear to hang on to past hierarchies, slaves or ex-slaves strive to change their status. They do so either by moving up local hierarchies, or by entering new ones in which they were never categorised as 'slave' and where they can assume new positions. Hierarchies have properties of indexicality. They use signs (e.g. physical traits, demeanour, clothing style, speech variety) to 'point to' social status.[20] Mobility 'from within' implies the alteration of indices of status: when ex-slaves remain in the same hierarchy, they strive to reinterpret the 'signs' of their subordination as positive signs of value, or to lessen their negative implications (cf. Hardung, in this volume); or they try to pass as non-slave by acquiring the characteristics of higher status groups (cf. Leservoisier, in this volume). Alternatively, they can enrol in new hierarchies, to which they move through migration or which become available from the outside (e.g. through colonial conquest or the introduction of exogenous ideologies). Here ex-slaves use their skills to attain new identities in new ideologies of hierarchy (e.g. in the military, in education, in political associations – see Schmitz and Hahonou, both in this volume).

The cases discussed in this book illustrate the multiple trajectories through which such repositionings have occurred, and continue to occur, in some West African contexts. Such patterns often reveal strategic detours that defy conventional understandings of emancipation. Several chapters illustrate how status mobility within the same (spatial and social) system of reference can be achieved through the patronage of ex-masters (cf. Schmitz). This pattern requires willingness to negotiate change on both sides, master and slave, patron and client. It is noteworthy that this path requires belief in hierarchy on the part of slave descendants as well. Insofar as status promotion is obtained through the support of social superiors, the latter's superiority must be taken seriously, as well as the inferiority ascribed to others (cf. Leservoisier). When status ideologies are changed from within, transforming the meaning of slave status requires epistemological negotiations. Burnham's changing 'keywords' belong to this pattern. So do Hardung's examples of Gannunkeebe who reinterpret the implications of slave labour, turning it into a 'gift' to masters who 'need their (ex-) slaves' to perform demanding tasks. Finally, as illustrated by McCaskie, change may occur through confrontation and interaction across different rationales. In this sense, the sociological implications of clashing international discourses of slavery remain to be seen.

The chapters of this book do not provide a representative sample of West African states or societies. The main omission is Nigeria, and particularly the case of Osu groups in Eastern Nigeria. This introduction and Klein's historical overview do not focus on any single group or state. Following the order in which they are presented in the book, reference is made to the history of the regions falling in the following contemporary West African states: Ghana, the Gambia, Senegal, Benin, Mauritania, Niger and Cameroon. It would be reductive to classify contributions according to the Anglophone–Francophone divide derived from colonial domination, even though this aspect underlies the analysis of all chapters. Arabic language and Islamic influence also play a major role, as well as internal divisions within African societies. Some societies are better represented than others. This is the case of the Fulbe or Haalpulaar'en and their various ranked sub-groups, which are discussed in four contributions (Burnham, Leservoisier, Hardung, Schmitz). Tuareg groups are discussed in two chapters (Hahonou and Rossi). Other societies examined in the book are Asante, Gbaya, Songhay and Hausa. Burnham's wide-ranging comparative chapter contrasts two West African contexts with events witnessed in Trinidad; and Bellagamba's paper is more geared to Gambian political dynamics than to 'ethnic' or cultural divisions.

Reconfiguring Slavery derives unity from its intellectual purpose. The chapters' findings and conclusions suggest that after the 'end of slavery' there still is 'slavery'. This reconfigured 'slavery' acquired new meanings in distinct historical trajectories and today partakes of contemporary social processes. Some of its general features and broader implications have been preliminarily advanced in this introduction, and are explored in greater depth in the chapters. It is hoped that further research and debate will elaborate, and possibly correct, this book's hypotheses.

References

Abdelkader, G. K., ed., 2004. *L'Esclavage au Niger.* Report conducted by Anti-Slavery International and Timidria. London: ASI.

Amselle, J. L., 1981. 'Famine, prolétarisation et creation de nouveaux liens de dependence au Sahel: les réfugiés de Mopti et de Léré au Mali.' *Politique Africaine*, I/1, pp. 5–22.

Austin, G., 2005. *Labour, Land and Capital in Ghana. From Slavery to Free Labour in Asante, 1807–1956.* Rochester, NY: University of Rochester Press.

Baier, S. and Lovejoy, P., 1975. 'The desert side economy of the Central Sudan.' *The International Journal of African Historical Studies*, VIII(4), pp. 551–81.

Bellagamba, A., 2005. 'Slavery and Emancipation in the Colonial Archives: British Officials, Slave-Owners, and Slaves in the Protectorate of the Gambia (1890–1936).' *Canadian Journal of African Studies*, 39(1), pp. 5–41.

Bernus, P., 1981. *Touaregs nigériens: unité culturelle et diversité régionale d'un peuple pasteur.* Paris: Editions de l'Office de la Recherche Scientifique et Technique d'Outre-mer.

Botte, R., 1994. 'Stigmates sociaux et discriminations religieuses: l'ancienne classe servile au Fuuta Jaloo.' *Cahiers d'Études Africaines*, 34(133–35), pp. 109–36.

Botte, R., 1999. 'Riimaybe, Haratin, Iklan: les damnés de la terre, le développement, et la démocratie.' In A. Bourgeot, ed., *Horizons nomades en Afrique Sahelienne.* Paris: Karthala.

Bourdieu, P., 1991. *Language and Symbolic Power.* Cambridge, MA: Harvard University Press.

Bourdieu, P., 1998. *Practical Reason: On the Theory of Social Action.* Stanford, CA: Stanford University Press.

Boyer, F., 2005. 'L'esclavage chez les Touaregs de Bankilare au miroir des migrations circulaires.' *Cahiers d'Études Africaines*, 45(179/180), pp. 771–804.

Braudel, F., 1972 (1949). *The Mediterranean and the Mediterranean World in the Age of Philip II.* New York: Harper and Row.

Campbell, G. 2004., 'Slavery and Other Forms of Unfree Labour in the Indian Ocean World.' In G. Cambell, ed., *The Structure of Slavery in Indian Africa and Asia.* London: Frank Cass.

Cohen, A. 1969., *Custom and Politics in Urban Africa: A Study of Hausa Migrants in Yoruba Towns.* Berkeley, CA: University of California Press.

Cooper, F., 1980. *From Slaves to Squatters: Plantation Labor and Agriculture in Zanzibar and Coastal Kenya 1890–1925.* New Haven, CT: Yale University Press.

Cooper, F., 1996. *Decolonisation and African Society. The Labour Question in French and British Africa.* Cambridge: Cambridge University Press.

Cooper, F., 2000. 'Conditions Analogous to Slavery.' In Cooper, Holt and Scott, eds, 2000.

Cooper, F., 2002. *Africa Since 1940: The Past of the Present.* Cambridge: Cambridge University

Press.

Cooper, F., Holt, R. and Scott, W., eds, 2000. *Beyond Slavery. Explorations of Race, Labor, and Citizenship in Postemancipation Societies*. Chapel Hill, NC, and London: University of North Carolina Press.

Coquery-Vidrovitch, C., 1988. *Africa: Endurance and Change South of the Sahara*. Berkeley, CA: University of California Press.

Cottias, M., Stella, A. and Vincent, B., eds, 2006. *Esclavages et dépendances serviles*. Paris: L'Harmattan.

Curtin, P., 1976. 'The Atlantic Slave Trade 1600–1800.' In J.F.A. Ajayi and M. Crowder, eds, *History of West Africa*, vol. I. New York: Columbia University Press, 2nd edn.

de Bruijn, M. and van Dijk, H., 1994. 'Drought and Coping Strategies in Fulbe Society in the Hayre (Central Mali): A Historical Perspective.' *Cahiers d'Études Africaines*, 34(133–35), pp. 85–108.

de Bruijn, M. and Pelckmans, L., 2005. 'Facing Dilemmas: Former Fulbe Slaves in Modern Mali.' *Canadian Journal of African Studies*, 39(1), pp. 69–95.

Deutsch, J. G., 2006. *Emancipation Without Abolition in German East Africa c. 1884–1914*. Oxford: James Currey.

Doyle, S., 2007. 'Bunyoro and the Demography of Slavery Debate: Fertility, Kinship and Assimilation.' In H. Medard and S. Doyle, eds, *Slavery in the Great Lakes Region of East Africa*. Oxford: James Currey and Athens, OH: Ohio University Press.

Duffill, M. and Lovejoy, P., 1985. 'Merchants, Porters, and Teamsters in the Nineteenth-century Central Sudan'. In C. Coquery-Vidrovitch and P. Lovejoy, eds, *The Workers of African Trade*. London: Sage.

Farias, P. Moraes de, 1985. 'Models of the World and Categorical Models: The "Enslavable Barbarian" as a Mobile Classificatory Label.' In J. Willis, ed., *Slaves and Slavery in Muslim Africa*. London: Frank Cass.

Finley, M. I., 1964. 'Between Slavery and Freedom.' *Comparative Studies of Society and History*, 6/3, pp. 233–49.

Fisher, H., 2001. *Slavery in the History of Muslim Black Africa*. New York: New York University Press.

Gaasholt, O. M., 2007. 'Renegotiating Slave Identity or Hanging On To It? Strategies of Social Mobility (or Immobility) in Gossi, Mali.' Paper presented at the conference *African Trajectories of Slavery: Perceptions, Experiences, Practices*, held at the Centre of African Studies of the University of London, 25–25 May 2007.

Giddens, A., 1984. *The Constitution of Society: Outline of the Theory of Structuration*. Berkeley, CA: University of California Press.

Giuffrida, A., 2005. 'Metamorphoses des relationes de dependance chez les Kel Antessar du Cercle de Goundam.' *Cahiers d'Études Africaines*, 45(179/180), pp. 805–30.

Grace, J., 1975. *Domestic Slavery in West Africa, with Particular Reference to the Sierra Leone Protectorate, 1896–1927*. London: Frederick Muller.

Hardung, C., 1997. 'Ni vraiment Peul, ni vraiment Baatombu: le conflit identitaire des Gando.' In T. Bierschenk and P.Y. le Meur, eds, *Trajectoires peules au Benin*. Paris: Karthala.

Hirschman, A., 1970. *Exit, Voice, and Loyalty*. Cambridge: Cambridge University Press.

Klein, M., 1998. *Slavery and Colonial Rule in French West Africa*. Cambridge: Cambridge University Press.

Klein, M., 2005. 'The Concept of Honour and the Persistence of Servility in the Western Soudan.' *Cahiers d'Études Africaines*, 45(179–180), pp. 831–51.

Klein, M. and Lovejoy, P., 1979. 'Slavery in West Africa.' In H. Gemery and J. Hogendorn, eds, *The Uncommon Market: Essays in the Economic History of the Atlantic Slave Trade*. New York: Academic Press.

Klein, M. and Miers, S., 1999. *Slavery and Colonial Rule in Africa*. London: Frank Cass.

Klein, M. and Roberts, R., 1980. 'The Banamba Slave Exodus of 1905 and the Decline of Slavery in the Western Sudan'. *The Journal of African History*, 21(3), pp. 375–94.

Kopytoff, I., 1988. 'The Cultural Context of African Abolition.' In Miers and Roberts, eds, 1988.

Kopytoff, I. and Miers, S., eds, 1977. *Slavery in Africa: Historical and Anthropological Perspectives*. Madison, WI: University of Wisconsin Press.

Lecocq, B., 2005. 'The Bellah Question: Slave Emancipation, Race, and Social Categories in Late Twentieth-Century Northern Mali.' *Canadian Journal of African Studies*, 39(1), pp. 42–67.

Leservoisier, O., 1994. *La question foncière en Mauritanie. Terres et pouvoirs dans la région du Gorgol*. Paris: L'Harmattan.

Levtzion, N. 1985. 'Slavery and Islamization in Africa: A Comparative Study.' In J.R. Willis, ed., *Slaves and Slavery in Muslim Africa*. London: Frank Cass.

Lovejoy, P., 1981. *The Ideology of Slavery in Africa*. London: Sage.

Lovejoy, P., 1983. *Transformations of Slavery: A History of Slavery in Africa*. Cambridge: Cambridge University Press.

Lovejoy, P., 1989. 'The Impact of the Atlantic Slave Trade on Africa: A Review of the Literature.' *The Journal of African History*, 30(3), pp. 365–94.

Lovejoy, P. and Hogendorn, J., 1979. 'Slave Marketing in West Africa.' In H. Gemery and J. Hogendorn, eds, *The Uncommon Market: Essays in the Economic History of the Atlantic Slave Trade*. New York: Academic Press.

Lovejoy, P. and Hogendorn, J., 1993. *Slow Death for Slavery. The Course of Abolition in Northern Nigeria, 1897–1936*. Cambridge: Cambridge University Press.

Mahdi, H., 2008. 'Gendered Ideology of Slavery and Hausa Identity in the Sokoto Caliphate.' Unpublished paper presented at the conference *Hausa Identity: History and Religion*, University of East Anglia, 11–12 July 2008.

Manchuelle, F., 1989. 'Slavery, Emancipation and Labour Migration in West Africa: The Case of the Soninke.' *The Journal of African History*, 30(1), pp. 89–106.

Mann, G., 2006. *Native Sons: West African Veterans and France in the Twentieth Century*. Durham, NC: Duke University Press.

Manning, P., 1990. *Slavery and African Life: Occidental, Oriental, and African Slave Trades*. Cambridge: Cambridge University Press.

Meillassoux, C., ed., 1975. *L'Esclavage in Afrique precoloniale*. Paris: Maspero.

Meillassoux, C., 1991 [1983]. *Anthropology of Slavery: the Womb of Iron and Gold*. London: Athlone Press.

Miers, S., 2003. *Slavery in the Twentieth Century. The Evolution of a Global Problem*. Walnut Creek, CA: Altamira Press.

Miers, S., 2004. 'Slavery: A Question of Definition.' In G. Campbell, ed., *The Structure of Slavery in Indian Africa and Asia*. London: Frank Cass.

Miers, S. and Roberts, R., eds, 1988. *The End of Slavery in Africa*. Madison, WI: University of Wisconsin Press.

Moore, S. F., 1978. 'Law and Social Change: The Semi-Autonomous Social Field as an Appropriate Field of Study.' *Law and Society Review*, 7(4), pp. 719–46.

Morice, A., 2005. '"Comme des esclaves", ou les avatars de l'esclavage metaphorique.' *Cahiers d'Études Africaines*, 45(179–180), pp. 1015–35.

Nicolas, G., 1962. 'Un village bouzou du Niger. Etude d'un terroir.' *Les Cahiers d'Outre-Mer*, 15(58), pp. 138–65.

Nicolaisen, J. and Nicolaisen, I., 1997. *The Pastoral Tuareg: Ecology, Culture, and Society*, 2 vols. London: Thames and Hudson.

Norris, H., 1975. *The Tuaregs: Their Islamic Legacy and Its Diffusion in the Sahel*. Warminster: Aris and Phillips.

Olivier de Sardan, J. P., 1976. *Quand nos pères etaient captifs… récits paysans du Niger*. Paris:

Nubia.

Oxby, C., 1986. 'Women and the Allocation of Herding Labour in a Pastoral Society (Southern Kel Ferwan Twareg, Niger).' In S. Bernus et al., eds, *Le Fils et le neveu.* Cambridge: Cambridge University Press.

Peirce, C., 1992. *The Essential Peirce: Selected Philosophical Writings*, ed. N. Houser and C. Kloesel, Vol. 1. Bloomington: Indiana University Press.

Quirk, J., 2006. 'The Anti-Slavery Project: Linking the Historical and the Contemporary.' *Human Rights Quarterly*, 28, pp. 565–98.

Rattray, R. S., 1956 [1929]. *Ashanti Law and Constitution.* Oxford: Oxford University Press.

Roberts, R., 1987. *Warriors, Merchants, and Slaves. The State and the Economy in the Middle Niger Valley, 1700–1914.* Stanford, CA: Stanford University Press.

Robertson, C. and Klein, M., 1983. *Women and Slavery in Africa.* Madison, WI: University of Wisconsin Press.

Rossi, B., 2009. 'Tuareg Trajectories of Slavery: Preliminary Reflections on a Changing Field.' In I. Kohl and A. Fisher, eds, *Tuareg Moving Global.* New York: I.B. Tauris.

Searing, J., 1993. *West African Slavery and Atlantic Commerce. The Senegal River Valley, 1700–1860.* Cambridge: Cambridge University Press.

Smith, M. G., 1954. 'Slavery and Emancipation in Two Societies'. *Social and Economic Studies*, 3(3–4), pp. 239–90.

Stilwell, S., 2004. *Paradoxes of Power: The 'Mamluks' and Male Royal Slavery in the Sokoto Caliphate, 1804–1903.* Portsmouth, NH: Heinemann.

Thioub, I., 2001. 'Regard critique sur les lectures africaines de l'esclavage et de la Traite Atlantique.' Unpublished paper presented at the 3rd Congress of the Association of African Historians *Historiens Africaines et Mondialisation*, Bamako, 10–14 September 2001.

Vaughan, J., 1977. 'The Slave as an Institutionalized Outsider.' In Kopytoff and Miers, eds, 1977.

Veerecke, C., 1994. 'The Slave Experience in Adamawa: Past and Present Perspectives from Yola (Nigeria).' *Cahiers d'Études Africaines*, 34(133–35), pp. 23–53.

Villasante-de Beauvais, M., 2000. *Groupes serviles au Sahara.* Paris: CNRS.

Viti, F., 2007. *Schiavi, Servi e Dipendenti: Antropologia delle Forme di Dipendenza Personale in Africa.* Milan: Raffaello Cortina Editore.

Wallerstein, I., 1965. 'Migration in West Africa: The Political Perspective'. In H. Kuper, ed., *Urbanization and Migration in West Africa.* Berkeley, CA: University of California Press.

Willis, J. R., 1985. 'The Ideology of Enslavement in Islam.' In J. R. Willis, ed., *Slaves and Slavery in Muslim Africa.* London: Frank Cass.

Wright, M., 1975. 'Women in peril: a commentary in the life stories of captives in nineteenth century east Central Africa.' *African Social Research*, 20, pp. 800–19.

Notes

1   Primarily in special issues of journals. See, for example, *Journal des Africanistes*, 2000; *Cahiers d'Études Africaines*, 2005; *Canadian Journal of African Studies*, 2005; *Social Anthropology*, 2006.

2   The 'end of slavery' in West Africa has formed the object of numerous important contributions. Of direct relevance to the present work are, *inter alia*: Klein, 1998; Klein and Miers, 1999; Lovejoy, 1981; Lovejoy, 1983; Lovejoy and Hogendorn, 1993; Meillassoux, 1975; Meillassoux, 1991; Miers, 2003; Miers and Roberts, 1988; Robertson and Klein, 1983; Villasante-de-Beauvais, 2000; Viti, 2007. Works that do not look at West Africa, but contribute to understanding the structure of African trajectories

'out of slavery', are Campbell, 2004; Cooper, 1980; Cooper et al., 2000; and Deutsch, 2006.

3   They include the *iklan* (Tamasheq), *bella* (Songhay) or *buzu* (Hausa) in Tuareg society; the *maccuBe*, *rimaaibe*, Gando, or Gannunkeebe in the Fulfulde-speaking world; groups referred to as *abd* by the Arab-speaking Bidan nobility of Mauritania; the Songhay *horso*; the Mande *woloso*; and so forth.

4   Contra Meillassoux (1991, 78; 1975, 18), biological reproduction seems to have played an important role in the maintenance of slave constituencies also in the past (cf. Botte, 1994, 111; Botte, 1999, 59; Doyle, 2007; Nicolaisen and Nicolaisen, 1997, 611). Slave families were surely more ephemeral than the families of free people and had no legal autonomy, as slave adults were considered legal minors. This does not mean that 'slave kinship' did not exist, but only that it had to function in hegemonic conditions (cf. Oxby, 1986).

5   This is not a specifically modern phenomenon. Under particular historical and social circumstances, categories once 'hooked' to certain social referents can become 'unhooked' from reality and acquire new meanings, as a result of human projects or unplanned processes, as happened in the case of the name 'Zanj' (Farias, 1985).

6   Metaphorical and classificatory slavery are conceptually related. Categories have metaphorical qualities, they extrapolate one characteristic shared by the units of a group and make it stand for the whole group. This characteristic is often derogatory, generating stigma and abuse. Thus, misogyny turns certain aspects of female sexuality into a social handicap, and racism constructs physical traits as a 'sign' of inferiority. In the case of slavery, it is particularly hard to essentialise common characteristics for the highly diverse category of 'slaves' and thereby root the exploitation of slaves into a supposed shared 'nature'. Hence, slavery has always been more contested and unstable than other forms of inequality. Critiques of slavery and various forms of anti-slavery activism developed in relation to all historical forms of slavery. Despite the obvious relations between metaphorical and classificatory slavery, here I choose to keep them separate to highlight that while classificatory slavery is defined by the consequences of the *category* used to identify a group of slave origin (e.g. *iklan*, *maccuBe*, etc.), people whose identity is not associated to slavery (e.g. migrants, prostitutes, etc.) can be compared to slaves due to the exploitative conditions in which they work or live (metaphorical slavery).

7   For instance, the *servi caesaris* of ancient Rome and the royal slaves (e.g. Hausa *bawan sarki* or Wolof *fekk bayyeetil*) attached to the rulers of West African kingdoms and polities proudly enjoyed privileges well above those of many free commoners (cf. Finley, 1964, 247; Searing, 1993, 41ff; Smith, 1954, 274; Stilwell, 2004), and slave warriors were usually more powerful than other slaves (cf. Klein and Lovejoy, 1979, 192; Roberts, 1987, 35; Searing, 1993, 33).

8   Article 1 of the 1926 Slavery Convention defines slavery as 'the status or condition of a person over whom any or all of the powers attaching to the right of ownership are exercised' (text available at http://www.unhchr.ch/html/menu3/b/f2sc.htm). John Grace noted that concepts of property in West Africa have not always or not everywhere been the same as in Europe (1975, 6), a point substantially developed in Kopytoff and Miers (1977). More recently, Joel Quirk insightfully criticised the Convention's definition on the grounds that 'it is […] by no means clear how far a "right of ownership" extends, since this could theoretically include married relationships, or even professional athletes whose contracts are bought and sold' (2006, 568). This point is reminiscent of Kopytoff and Miers' argument (1977) that African societies were characterised by a continuum of rights in persons, and that slaves were not substantially different from other people, as specific sets of rights were held by any particular category of actors on other social categories. Yet, both quantitatively

and qualitatively, the range of rights that can be held upon the slave and the limited obligations of the master towards him/her constitute an extreme case, singling out slaves as disposable beyond what is considered acceptable for free people. While it can be argued that free people are also partially 'owned' – in the sense that claims can be made to their persons and capabilities – the type and amount of rights exercised upon the most marginalised slaves is so encompassing and unidirectional as to make (pervasive, unreciprocated) ownership a defining characteristic of slavery. This 'proto-typical' slavery did not, in practice, apply to all actual slave–master relations, as trusted or second-generation slaves acquired more rights and were treated with less rigour (e.g. see Roberts, 1987, 123, on the (skewed) reciprocity of slave–master relations in Maraka society).

9   However, in particular social and historical contexts, it is exactly these accessory condi-tions (assimilation to chattels and saleability) that became defining characteristics of slavery. Arguably, this is the case for slavery in the American South, which provided a template for modern definitions of slavery in Euro-America.

10   The rhetorical 'othering' of slaves, or of groups considered potentially enslavable, provided an ideological justification for their economic exploitation. However, in some cases the enslavement of *actual* outsiders (raided or imported foreign popula-tions) was a more efficient strategy in purely economic and/or political terms (see Austin, 2005, 160–61). Cf. Searing's discussion of the enslavement of local and foreign peoples in the Senegal river valley (1993, 30).

11   In classical legislation this sometimes takes the form of a distinction between the law of nature (*ius naturale*), by which all humans are born free, and the *ius gentium*, which introduces slavery (cf. 1, Justinian Institutes; *Digesta*, 1.1.4).

12   I recorded this practice in my 2005 fieldwork in the region of Tahoua. Similar practices are mentioned in the responses to Timidria's survey discussed in Abdelkader (2004). Another example is the case of Hadijatou Mani, forced to be the slave concubine of the man who bought her from her mother's master and unable to remarry even after she had been liberated. In April 2008 Hadijatou Mani brought her case before the ECOWAS Community Court of Justice, claiming that Niger had failed to enforce existing anti-slavery legislation (http://www.antislavery.org/archive/briefingpapers/ Niger_case_at_ECOWAS.pdf). It should be noted that these cases illustrate persisting gender inequalities as much as they shed light on the vestiges of slavery (cf. Mahdi, 2008).

13   In chapter 2, Martin Klein provides a detailed reconstruction of the historical recon-figurations of slavery in West Africa. Here, I shall merely situate the book's contribu-tions within some broader regional processes.

14   Letter to the French colonial minister quoted in Cooper, 2000, 138.

15   Ibrahima Thioub (2001) identifies two main intellectual strands within African histo-riography that contribute to this 'silencing' of domestic slavery, while emphasising Atlantic slavery. The first strand is that of nationalist and panAfricanist historiography, which espoused an idealised view of 'black' African internal hierarchies as humane and paternalist until they are brutally disrupted by 'white' colonisers. The second strand fits in the dependency paradigm and sees African domestic slavery as playing a minor role in the production of Africa's structural underdevelopment. Both schools of thought, as Thioub cogently shows, build their arguments upon simplistic 'chromatic' assumptions (black/white opposition) and reduce the historical role of African societies to one of victims, dismissing internal differences of status and strategies. See also Manning, 1990, 2.

16   On the term MaccuBe, see Note on Language, p. xi.

17   Kopytoff and Miers (1977) argued that the opposition between slavery and freedom is not a characteristic of African slavery. With Vaughan (1977), they suggested that what

distinguished slave status in African societies was the 'institutionalisation of marginality', i.e. the slave's alienation in contexts where sociality is defined by belonging, more than by individual autonomy (freedom). This perspective seems to imply that, unless they are part of solid migrant networks, some slave-status migrants are more marginalised and, hence, 'slave-like' abroad (where they are 'free' from the memory of their past identity) than back home where their slave past now constitutes a form of belonging. This is less paradoxical if the emphasis on belonging is not contrasted to a supposedly 'Western' emphasis on freedom, but considered in relation to high levels of insecurity in Africa, affecting the decisions of people of both free and slave status (cf. Klein and Lovejoy, 1979, 184).

18   Whether the conversion of slaves was encouraged or discouraged by Muslim masters remains a contested, and to a large extent contextual, issue. Discussing the Hausa-Fulani context, M. G. Smith argues for the relatively smooth conversion of slaves and assimilation into the free (Smith, 1954, 249). For a broader comparative discussion of this debate, see Fisher, 2001: 64; Levtzion, 1985.

19   Looking at different ideologies of enslavement within Islam, Willis comments on the greater rigidity of ideologies that racialise slavery, as opposed to ideologies that assimilate the slave primarily to the infidel, without strong racial connotations: 'while the bane of infidelity might dissolve in the healing waters of Islam, no rational refutation could hope to dissolve a simile shaped on the premise of racial superiority' (Willis, 1985, 10).

20   Charles Peirce provided many definitions of the index. Yet his focus on 'pointing' underestimates the political implications of indices ('The index asserts nothing – it only says: "there"!' Peirce, 1992, 226). Clearly the index does not just lie in a sea of grammar. If, indeed, indexicality of contexts produces a meaningful social world that does not imply context dependence (Giddens, 1984, 100), meaning is generated through interactions between actors who have different capacities to influence official visions of the social world (cf. Bourdieu, 1998, 75). Hence, 'pointing to' the blackness or coarseness or cowardice believed to be characteristic of the slave may be, with Peirce, a 'mere' assertion. But such an assertion becomes a dominant stereotype and a stigma as a consequence of social inequalities and political struggles.

2

Slave Descent and Social Status in Sahara and Sudan

Martin A. Klein

Over a century after European powers took what seemed to be decisive action against slavery and the slave trade, there are probably a couple of million people in West Africa who are referred to in their native languages as slaves. These people all descend from people who were slaves, who were captured or perhaps enslaved as a penalty for crime or a parent's debts. They experienced the shame and humiliation of enslavement and, thus, many of their descendants are stigmatised as being different. The terms vary from place to place. The *bidan* nobility of Mauritania often refer to all people of African descent as *abd*, which means slave in Arabic. Some use a local term such as *jaam*, which means the same thing in Wolof. Others use terms such as the Mande *woloso*, the Songhay *horso* and the Poular *rimaayBe*, which refer to second-generation slaves 'born in the house'.[1] The actual obligations of such persons vary nowadays, but generally are limited to symbolic payments or token acts. Still, one can go into most villages in West Africa, and all villages among the more hierarchical societies, ask where the 'slaves' are and be directed to certain hamlets or special quarters of the village. At the same time it is considered bad manners in many of those villages to confront persons of slave origin with their status. In spite of this formal discreetness, status regulates social relationships, particularly marriage, and hierarchy is often indicated by kinship terminology, the descendant of the master being addressed as father and the descendant of former slaves being spoken to as if they were children. This chapter seeks to assess the transformation of slave status in West Africa since the late nineteenth century. It does not deal with all societies.

Many people in West Africa lived in decentralised societies, which got involved in slaving but never became large-scale slave-users. In such societies integration tended to be rapid and slave origins relatively unimportant, though sometimes memories of the slave trade remain vivid.[2] Most of the people of West Africa, however, lived in highly structured societies, in many of which slaves were a majority of the population and the source of most labour in pre-colonial times. These societies also made strong distinctions between different statuses. When such societies were threatened by emancipation of their slaves, slave-owners struggled to maintain control of slave labour, and when that collapsed, to maintain a social hegemony, often with a significant decree of success. They managed this in spite of the hostility of many slaves to their pretensions and in the absence of open support from the state. Emancipation by colonial regimes was not the end of a process of struggle, but the beginning. The stigma of slave origins does not limit the possibility of peoples of slave origin earning a living – some are wealthier than their former masters – but it does affect marriage, social position, career options and identities.

The Struggle for Freedom

There was always resistance to slavery in Africa. The system depended on coercion, but when there was opportunity, slaves took advantage of it. Actual rebellions were rare, but slaves often ran away and sometimes formed maroon communities like the Nikhifores of coastal Guinea. They also rallied to the cause of egalitarian Muslim reformers such as the Hubbu of upper Guinea (I. Barry, 1971; B. Barry 1998). Elsewhere slave flight was a constant threat. The abolition of slavery by the British in 1833 and by the French in 1848 aroused among states bordering the colonies fears of slave flight (Walvin, 2005). When the French abolition of the slave trade was proclaimed in 1848, Trarza suspended the gum trade, villages on Cape Verde stopped selling fish to Goree, and other states threatened suspension of trade if the French freed their slaves.[3] The Gambia also returned slaves to their masters. On the Gold Coast, the British provoked a war with Asante when they refused to return Asante runaway slaves. In 1863 the failure to do so led to an Asante war with the British (Getz, 2004, 56–59). In spite of the efforts of European governors to avoid provoking slave-using neighbours, there was a constant flow of runaway slaves to both colonial towns and to Christian mission settlements. In the 1870s and 1880s the pressure of European public opinion forced a change in these policies. In 1874 the British abolished the slave trade in the Gold Coast and prohibited the import of slaves into the colony (Dumett and Johnson, 1988; Getz, 2004, 96–102). The French abolished slavery in the new towns of Dakar and Rufisque, and began enforcing the prohibition of transactions in slaves within the colony. An 1883 decree provided that any slave making it to areas under French direct administration was free (Klein, 1998, 61–64).

In both cases, colonial administrators were cautious about enforcing the new laws. In French Africa they actually disannexed areas that had been occupied and turned them into protectorates, which, for about one generation, acted as a device to permit toleration of slavery and slave-trading (Klein, 1998,

66–67). In spite of this, as colonial armies pushed into the African interior in the 1880s and 1890s, slave flights increased. Newly established military regimes wanted to protect the authority of their allies over their slaves, but they needed workers and soldiers. The liberty villages set up by the French from 1886 automatically freed the slaves of enemies of the French, but others were subject to reclamation by their masters for up to three months, reduced to one month if the runaway enlisted in the French army. Runaway slaves often used these villages as way stations where they could get a few meals before moving further away from their masters' pursuit. The heavy labour obligations imposed by the French meant that there was always a steady stream of departures (Klein, 1998, 84–88, 165–66). They were always particularly numerous during or after a military conflict.

By 1898 the French had defeated their most important enemies. At the beginning of 1899 the first civilian governor was appointed in the French Soudan (then named Haut-Sénégal-Niger). The conquest of northern Nigeria began in 1897.[4] In Sierra Leone the Hut Tax War cemented British control of the interior, as did the defeat of Asante in 1901.[5] Whatever policies the colonial government pursued, these events led to increased slave flight to colonial towns, to mission stations or, when they were safe, to earlier homes. Colonial regimes often moved to ban the slave trade, but most continued at first to return slaves to their masters except where there was evidence of substantial physical abuse. Where action was taken against slavery, it was usually the 'Indian formula', which simply withdrew the colonial state from support for slave systems. Given that slavery depended on force, this often led to substantial flight. In northern Nigeria about 10 per cent of the slaves fled their masters. Lugard prohibited slave-raiding and tribute in slaves, but not transactions in slaves within an emirate. He also declared free children born after 31 March, 1901, though that had little immediate effect because those children continued to live with their parents. Lugard instructed officials not to return slaves to their masters, but in other ways discouraged slave flight. Lugard feared disorder and the decline in agricultural productivity, which depended heavily on slave labour. Fugitive slaves, for example, were denied the right to move and access to land (Lovejoy and Hogendorn, 1993, 31–32, 67–88). Slaves instead were encouraged to purchase their freedom. Some slave raiding continued until after 1920 and slavery itself was abolished only in 1936.

In Asante slave-trading was abolished after the conquest in 1896, but most officials in Asante opposed the abolition of slavery. Slavery was abolished in 1908 in response to missionary pressure, but enforcement was very reluctant (Austin, 2005, ch. 11). In the southern area called the Colony slaves were free to leave their masters but not encouraged to do so. In the Northern Territories, hitherto the major source of slaves, the British conquerors moved to close slave markets, to end slave-raiding and to stop the slave trade. A small illicit trade, largely in children, persisted. The colonial administration prided itself on the creation of security in what had been a lawless area. They carefully avoided any attack on slavery and restrained the so-called Hausa constabulary, many of them of northern slave origin, from interfering with local institutions. Only in 1930 was slavery clearly abolished (Dumett and Johnson, 1988, 100–05). In Sierra Leone slavery was abolished only in 1929.

The French, however, moved more radically. In 1903 Ernest Roume, the Governor-General of French West Africa, proclaimed a new law code. Along with the new code, local administrators received instructions that they were no longer to receive the complaints of slave masters:

> Do not hesitate then in rejecting definitively any claim by would-be masters who own rights over the person of other natives based on slavery, whoever they may be. You will warn any who try to seize those they claim as slaves that such an act will expose them to legal action. To those who come to complain against their masters or simply to claim their liberty, you will explain if they are adults or at least in a condition to understand their situation, that they are free under the law and that French authority will insist on respect for their freedom.[6]

Two years later Roume proclaimed a comprehensive anti-slavery law, which prohibited any transactions in persons. It did not actually abolish slavery, though it is often believed to have done so.

The system was breaking down before the law was proclaimed. In the spring of 1905 slaves in settlements around Banamba, the most important market town in the Soudan, began to leave. As serious conflict threatened, the French tried to mediate and then supported the efforts of the masters to use force to keep the slaves in place. Then, a year later, the movement began again. This time Lieutenant Governor William Ponty told the local administrator to let the slaves go if they had paid their taxes and indicated where they were going. In a two-month period about 3,000 left. Often without food or goods that could be traded for sustenance, they walked, often a journey of over a month. Some of them went to Bamako to look for work, but most went home. In the years that followed the exodus spread from one area to another. In almost every part of the Soudan there was a period of several years when slaves left their masters in large numbers. Establishing exactly how many is difficult because many left without registering their departures. From 1906 to 1911 and 1912, government reports indicate a constant flow of slaves to earlier homes. I think that the number could have been over a million. Similar movements took place in other areas, but nowhere was there as massive a movement as in French West Africa. These slave liberations often saw people leave areas of slave-based plantations that produced both export crops and foods needed for the sustenance of large populations, but they also created a body of workers willing to travel to seek any kind of work.

In spite of surface differences, there were surprising similarities in the policies pursued by colonial regimes in Africa. Throughout the nineteenth century European officials in Africa were cautious about alienating the powerful slave-owning states with which they did business. In the latter part of the century pressures from missionaries within the colonies and from anti-slavery groups in Britain and France forced changes in policy, but colonial administrators were hesitant about applying anti-slavery laws. Both of these countries and the late-arriving Germans recruited their African armies largely from slaves. The French army actually distributed slaves to their officers, their African soldiers and their agents. It is probable that the British and Germans sometimes did the same thing. Then, once in firm control, policy changed, most dramatically in the case of the French. All colonial regimes moved quickly to end slave-raiding and slave-trading. With colonial forces stretched thin, they were not always completely successful, but such raiding as took place was largely on the margins of the colonial state and the trade largely a clandestine trade in children and occasionally in women. They were hesitant about undercutting slavery because slave-owning elites were their allies and agents in the government of colonial Africa. At this point, however, slaves themselves forced the situation by leaving their masters in huge numbers. They were able to do so because colonial regimes would no longer use their police power to reinforce slavery.

Those Who Stayed Behind: Domestic Slavery in Colonial West Africa

Enormous as the exodus was, most slaves stayed behind. It is fairly clear that those who left were largely those who remembered earlier homes. Many had spent a generation or two in slavery. Some did not remember their clan names or exactly where their homes were, but they knew who they were and what area they came from. Some did not leave because they were old or not strong enough to make the trip, though in later years, family members often returned to sites of servitude to find older relatives. Those born in slavery sometimes left with parents, but most of those born in servitude no longer spoke their original languages. They spoke their master's language, had kinship ties in the slave communities and were at home in the master's culture. The same was probably true of many of those enslaved young. Many had married. Many women were concubines of their master or of a male member of his family. Others were married to fellow slaves.

Certainly, the condition of those who remained behind changed radically. They were generally conceded the right to farm for themselves, but then, throughout the savanna and southern Sahara, those born in slavery were essentially Creole slaves, born within the household, raised as slaves and part of the master's culture. Many, probably most, Creole slaves had the right to farm for themselves. Meillassoux has described a series of statuses (1991, 116–21). The first, the *esclaves de peine* or drudge slaves, were the newly enslaved who worked only under supervision, usually in gang labour. The second, the *esclaves mansés* or allotment slaves, usually worked five days a week up to early afternoon prayer on the master's land, and then spent the rest of their time on their own plots. The third, *esclaves casés* or settlement slaves, were essentially share-croppers who paid their master a fixed part of their harvest every year. Finally, there were slaves who were manumitted, but still dependent on the families of their former masters. During the first decades of the twentieth century, the first two categories disappeared except in the desert and a few conservative areas. They were largely the ones who went home. Essentially, all slaves became Creole slaves. These former slaves also won the right to control their own family life and their work life. Whereas masters had in pre-colonial Africa the right to control the marriages of their slaves, and in fact, to use women as they wished and to appropriate slave children, the former slaves now negotiated their own marriages and raised their own children.

The process of change did not stop. It has, in fact, been a continuing process, sometimes slow, but with periods of revolt. There were, for example, new liberations. The African soldiers who served the French in the First World War were largely of slave origin. When they returned home there was in many areas, particularly in upper Guinea and eastern Senegal, a process of contestation (Clark, 1994, 51–71; Klein, 1998, 216–19). Many of the veterans led family members to new settlements. Few were willing to return to submissive behaviours. In general the years between the two World Wars was a period of change, particularly in areas where market production was expanding. In Senegal there were two processes. Former slaves who came from densely populated areas and did not have access to land flocked to the Mouride religious fraternity, which offered land and equality to those who joined the agricultural settlements that colonised hitherto under-used lands. In areas where land was available former slaves formed their own households, though they often continued to maintain social links with former masters (Klein, 1998, 200–03).

In the Gold Coast, the labour of slaves was often crucial in enabling chiefs to establish their cocoa farms but, increasingly, the inability to acquire more slaves meant that cocoa farmers had to hire labour. Former slaves proved quite enterprising, earning money as labourers or porters, and eventually becoming cocoa farmers themselves. Austin argues that 'emancipation owed much to the initiative of slaves themselves and their kin' (Austin, 2005, 215).[7] In south-western Nigeria slaves took advantage of the British conquest to flee their masters in massive numbers. Slave-owners and colonial authorities did their best to slow the process but, at the same time, the British abolished slavery in Lagos in 1901 and in the rest of Yorubaland in 1916. More important, however, than colonial legislation was the availability of wage labour in Lagos and in railway construction, and then the opportunity to earn money and acquire land by growing cocoa. By 1930 slavery was largely moribund (Falola, 1999). In southeast Nigeria the British were less tied to slave-owners and, in fact, saw them as their most vigorous opponents. Two ordinances in 1903 tried to free the slaves, but tied them down as apprentices or as subaltern members of costal canoe houses.[8] The slaves, however, did not accept this. Ohadike argues that

> slaves took advantage of colonial laws and of conflicts that raged between indigenous entrepreneurs and incoming Europeans to assert their freedom. Not all slaves left. Many remained but worked for themselves. Some converted their slave villages into autonomous settlements... Although officials tried to discourage mass desertion and social unrest, thousands of slaves ignored these precautions and simply walked off. Some migrated into newly created urban centres, seaports, mining districts and cocoa and rubber plantations. Some joined nearby farming communities as labourers, and others, presumably returned to their native homes. (1999, 201–02; see also Brown, 2003)

In northern Nigeria the conservative approach to abolition favoured by Lugard meant that change was very slow. Kidnapping, pawning and isolated raiding continued to provide slaves for a furtive slave trade into the 1930s, mostly in children. The attentions of various League of Nations committees put pressure on the colonial regime from 1927. Land policy was used to limit the access of slaves to land, but tax policy was used to encourage slave-owners to free their slaves.[9] While many slaves certainly used increased mobility to acquire dry season occupations and cash crops to increase their income, they still worked mostly as tenants and share-croppers. Lovejoy and Hogendorn argue that 'slaves on the official estates of the aristocracy continued to work under conditions that were more akin to the plantation agriculture of the late nineteenth century than to the peasant farms of the colonial period' (Lovejoy and Hogendorn, 1993, 286). Lugard's vision was that 'slaves would have to earn their freedom by selling their labor on the open market, using the cash so acquired to compensate their masters' (Lovejoy and Hogendorn, 1993, 201). It left a peasantry, largely of slave origin, that was indebted and impoverished.

Change was slower in the desert, in parts of the Sahel, in Masina and in Guinea's Futa Jallon. Certainly, there was always slave flight, and in some desert-side areas there was a southward movement into better-watered lands (Roberts, 1988). Migration was less of an option in the Sahara where slavery persisted. Saharan nomads raided the Sahel into the 1940s. French control was tenuous and dependent on alliances. Climate and distance made it difficult for slaves to flee. To be sure, many of the Bellah, dependents of the Tuareg, were freed after revolts that took place during the First World War I. Bellah fractions sometimes used the French, but they also depended on the Tuareg nobility for livestock, land and protection. Lecocq argues that real emancipation only began after the Second World War (Lecocq, 2005). In the southern Sahara a series of departures took place in the period immediately after the Second World War.

Some change took place after independence, but in Mauritania slaves found themselves in a state ruled by Arabic-speaking *bidan*, who identified as white and were determined to maintain control over slave and *harâtîn* dependents. In what is now Mali the Tuareg nomads were a minority in a state dominated by black agriculturalists. They were subject to the rule of politicians they scorned. They first revolted unsuccessfully in 1962. Then, in the 1970s, famines were disastrous for slave-owning elites throughout Saharan and Sahelian regions. When a Tuareg revolt broke out in 1990, Bellah intellectuals organised a *Mouvement pour l'Eveil du Monde Bellah*, but the most effective opposition to the Tamasheq was the organisation of the Ganda Koy militia among the Songhay. Many Bellah joined. The emergence of a counter-force led to the negotiation of a peace settlement in 1996, which left the Bellah in a stronger and more independent position (Lecocq, 2005). At the same time a revolt against military rule established a democracy that gave real influence to servile groups. In Mauritania slavery was abolished by presidential decree in 1981, but many slave masters refused to obey it because promised compensation never arrived. The state did little to enforce the decree, but increased activity by militants of servile origin and the pressure of international opinion made it possible for servile persons to organise and free themselves. Then, in 2005, a military coup created a democratic regime. In August 2007 a law was passed making slavery a criminal offence punishable by up to ten years in prison. A subsequent law made it a crime to defend or glorify slavery.

Elsewhere, some former slaves drifted away to seek work and never returned. Others formed separate villages, sometimes near former masters, sometimes far enough away to give them autonomy. De Bruijn and Pelckmans argue that formal slavery broke down in Hayre in the bend of the Niger only after the Second World War, and then rarely completely. Often former slaves were wealthier than former masters because they were willing to do different kinds of work and to work hard (de Bruijn and Pelckmans, 2005). Generally the obligations of former slaves were reduced over the years and many left, but many former slaves among Fulbe and Soninke populations in desert-side areas remained in dependent positions.

In general, there are two key variables that shape the speed of the process. The first is the availability of money incomes either through cash cropping or wage labour. This was clearly crucial in Senegal, Ghana and Nigeria. The second is the availability of land. In most of West Africa land was available to people willing to clear it. Where slaves could form their own settlements or simply clear land at the edge of their villages, they could free themselves from the control of their masters and achieve a measure of autonomy. Land was not, however, available in much of northern Nigeria because the British restricted access to it. In Masina in central Mali or the Futa Jallon in central Guinea high population densities limited availability of land. In Masina servile dues were replaced by land rent before the First World War, but that left the *rimaayBe* under the control of their former masters. With time a land-owning *rimaayBe* population emerged, but the opposition between Fulbe and *rimaayBe* remained tense throughout the twentieth century. Masina was, however, very fertile because of the annual Niger flood. The Futa Jallon was and is poor. A significant number of slaves left. Others moved into new occupations such as taxi driver or auto mechanic, but the existing elite maintained a tight hegemony with the support of many colonial administrators. In Guinea slavery was ended by Sekou Toure, but the Fulbe sarcastically referred to the former *rimaayBe* as 'Fulbe of the 28 September', and did not easily bend to government fiat (Botte, 1994). Botte argues that the process was slow because the slave's status was regulated by two different legal systems – on the one side, a French colonial system, on the other, a traditional and Islamic one that operated independently of the colonial system (cf. Botte, 2003).

What we have here again are similar processes of change, but the chronology is radically different. What took place quickly in southern Nigeria is taking place a century later in Saharan and desert-side regions today. This change is never a complete one. In many places, some financial obligations persist. Thus, in many savanna areas, slaves continued to pay the *assaka*. This was nominally the Qu'ranic tithe, which was supposed to be paid to the poor. Former slaves paid it to their wealthy masters, though it has been reduced to much less than a tithe.[10] In some areas the personal dues of the slave were converted to rent, but this was often accompanied by the right to purchase land, which permitted many hard-working former slaves to accumulate property. People of slave origin were also expected to pay for their emancipation before making the pilgrimage to Mecca. Those of slave origin often do the cooking for the noble's festive occasions. They generally cannot become imams and in some areas, if allowed in the mosque, can only sit at the back.

In general the reduction of financial obligations took place over a long period of time. For those of slave origin, the effort to achieve some autonomy has been a long and sometimes bitter struggle. It has also involved a complex process of give and take, not a formal negotiation process, but one in which slaves sought greater autonomy and, in particular, control of their work and family lives. Lacking coercive power, masters were forced to reduce what they extracted from their slaves. We are still forced to ask why servile status has persisted, and why former slaves, who sometimes earn more than their former masters, continue to accept elements of a servility they clearly dislike.

Slavery generally depends on the state to coerce and punish those seeking to abandon their masters. We then have to ask why in most areas, long after the economic logic of slavery disappeared and long after the state has withdrawn all support for the system, it has remained important as a status system. In some cases only vestiges remain. In others there is still substantial control. For a long time I looked for the answer to this question in the material roots of continued submission. There are, to be sure, good economic reasons for many former slaves to operate within the system. They get gifts, they get land and they profit from economic ties. The economic explanation was not, however, adequate. Sons of slave-owners clung to the status distinctions long after slavery ceased to give them any economic benefit. The basis of these status distinctions is codes of honour that exist throughout the western Sudan. The Fulbe speak of *pulaaku*, the Bambara of *horonya*, the Gambian Mandinka of *horomaa*. These codes demand that the noble be brave and generous.[11] He is also restrained in behaviour. He does not eat in front of others and is discreet about bodily functions. He is not crude and does not speak in a loud voice. The noble woman is chaste. The slave is loud, often coarse and shameless. The slave has licence to do many things a free man will not do. Ames writes that 'it is said that the slaves are fearless and without shame, even able to accuse a person of adultery in public, which a freeborn could never bring himself to do' (1953, 17).[12] Bellagamba writes: 'Slaves lacked "honour"... and all those positive social and personal qualities, which the master's ideology attached to the freeborn identity, i.e. self-control, shame and initiative' (2005, 13).

Behaviour that affirms the former slave's inferiority is licensed. Thus, it is acceptable for those of slave origin to beg. In begging they get the money and resources they need, but in the process they affirm their lower status. Many former slave-owners claim, probably correctly, that they give their 'slaves' more than they receive. It is difficult for a noble to deny assistance to a former slave in need. Major rites of passage such as marriage and naming ceremonies demand gifts that affirm the noble's generosity. Sexual licence also serves the same function. Riesman, Ames and Vincent describe the attraction of the slave village for freeborn (Riesman, 1977, 121; Vincent, 1963). Ames tells of lessened restraint when freeborn men were with slave women: 'They may caress them in public, and tell risqué stories in their presence as they never would with women of their own class' (Ames, 1953, 17). This, of course, means that social relations between the two groups often depend on role-playing, which underlines the nobility of the freeborn and the moral inferiority of the slave.[13] For the former slaves, playing a role was a way to deal with and entertain the nobles, but the effect was to confirm the difference between the two cultures. Music has also been an important boundary. As Islamic practice has become stricter across the western Soudan, many villages have prohibited dancing. In some cases everyone is forbidden to dance, but in others only members of caste and servile groups dance. Others gather and watch, but do not dance themselves. Interestingly, in Hayre slaves have moved into the making of music, hitherto the exclusive domain of griots (de Bruijn and Pelckmans, 2005).

Slave behaviour can be and is explained in different ways. It is very easy to argue that they are simply 'putting on ole Massa', that they do what they do because they profit from it or because that is how they survive in communities in which they and their families live. Certainly, in the few slave narratives I have been able to collect in coastal Senegal there is an undertone of bitterness and resentment. There is also, particularly in areas that have been resistant to change, evidence of a hegemonic ideology in which slaves to some degree internalise their status. Certainly, many nobles believe that slaves accepted their status. For example, in 1958, when Robin Maugham was exploring slavery in the Timbuktu region, one of his informants told him:

> Of course, a slave can go to the Commandant and the Commandant will tell him that by law he is not a slave, and by law, his master is not his master. But the slave probably knows that already. In his head, he knows that he is a free man. But in his heart he does not believe it. He knows that he is a Bela [*sic*] – and that a Bela is a slave. If he buys his freedom from his master, that is different. But otherwise, he believes that he belongs to his master, and so do his children. (Maugham, 1961, 164)

De Bruijn and Pelckmans argue that the continuing inequality between former slaves and their masters is rooted in 'the way slaves perceive themselves and how they define their own position by reflecting on the past'. It is the lack of history that is central: 'having a history is central to the construction of one's social identity. Without […] a *tarikh* (a written history), one is considered a non-person' (de Bruijn and Pelckmans, 2005, 72). That was the essence of the slave's social position. Slaves lost their names and were given new names. Marriage and inheritance was regulated by the master, who owned everything: the land, their possessions and their children. They could not create their own descent system and effectively had no family but the master's family. It is fairly clear that, to some degree, many of those raised in slavery accepted some notion of their place in society, but perhaps more important, they grew up within a group with its notions of kinship, mutual assistance and protection. Igor Kopytoff rightly points out that in most of Africa it is difficult to live as an isolate.[14]

One dimension of the slave's struggle has been the struggle against a hegemonic ideology. Some struggled by leaving home, but others remained within their natal communities and struggled by establishing their autonomy. I collected numerous tales of pride in Senegal. For example, there was an old man in a village near the Trans-Gambian Highway who pointed to the big trucks and claimed that many were owned by *jaam* (slaves); he then added that he had only one master, President Leopold Senghor. Another was the wealthy peasant who paid 18,000 francs (about $70 US) to free himself under traditional law so that he could make the pilgrimage to Mecca, but angered his master because he did not ask the master to set a price. He was not properly deferential. And even in the world that Maugham wrote about in the 1950s, there was a large community of former slaves in Timbuctou. In Hayre or in rural Mauritania self-assertion was more difficult, but even there slaves often had a breaking point and masters had to recognise it.

Once the forces of the state no longer protected the authority of the master, masters had to find ways to tie the nominally freed slaves into their society as dependent members. In some areas, particularly where slavery was not an intrinsic part of the social structure, slavery ceased to exist in any meaningful way. Elsewhere masters were forced to develop ways to integrate slaves more tightly into the hegemonic society. In doing so, they accepted change, albeit reluctantly, in order to keep the former slaves in a dependent position. The following case studies give some idea of how they did it and of the inevitable ambiguities of the servile situation.

Yaya Sy tells a tale of two lovers in Paris who violated the ultimate taboo, that of a sexual union between a male slave and a female noble (Sy, 2000). The male did menial tasks for the family of his master, but soon got involved with a daughter of the master's family and was seen leaving a hotel with her. Called to appear before an assembly of nobles, he refused to present himself and refused to pay a 5,000 franc fine. When the young woman became pregnant, she wisely moved out of her father's residence and even sought the protection of the police. The young man was denied all access to mutual aid as were his uncles. Like many immigrant groups, Soninke immigrants put a regular sum into a fund that can be used to deal with problems. Being cut off deprived the lovers of any possible assistance if struck by ill health or unemployment. In the village the young man's family was excluded from community prayer at the mosque, denied access to a cemetery, denied the right to get married in the village, and some in the village were deprived of land allocated to them. His supporters in Paris were cut off from the village association there. The young woman was totally excluded from her family and her sisters were sent back to Mauritania. In rural Mauritania or Senegal a dissident could leave, but that could involve cutting himself off from his family or from networks that provided work and security. While fears of physical coercion were present, the most important threats were of exclusion from the material and psychological benefits of being part of the community. Group sanctions were also used.

Another instructive study is a series of interviews done by Meskereme Brhane in Nouakchott. These involved people who were mostly *harâtîn*. The *harâtîn*, like the Bellah among the Tuareg, resembled the *woloso* and *horso* in agricultural societies. They were all essentially Creole slaves born in the society and raised within its social institutions. Though often seen as freed slaves, they remained highly dependent.[15] There were two significant differences. First, the slaves of nomads served either in the camps or in villages that provided grain and were the focal point of nomadic migrations. This meant that they were rarely under the direct supervision of their masters. Secondly, slavery persisted longer in the desert because the French did not feel they had the power to end it (McDougall, 1988). Mauritania abolished slavery in 1980. This meant that, though in general slaves became *harâtîn* during the colonial period, emancipation was for many a later process. Events in Mauritania in the 1990s mirrored events that took place almost a century earlier in Senegal and Mali.[16]

One of Brhane's interviews involved Brahim, a butcher in his sixties, whose consciousness was raised when his 90-year-old mother died and his masters arrived to take her possessions – two goats and two huts. As she had been their slave, they had a right to her possessions. Brahim and his wife were offended and contacted a neighbour, who put them in touch with an organisation called SOS Esclaves. As a result, when a group from the master's family arrived to take possession of the old woman's belongings, a group of *harâtîn* militants was stationed around the residence. In spite of efforts at negotiation by the head of *qabila* (tribal group), Brahim ended up a militant because his masters pushed their 'rights' too far. By contrast, Hadama, a young woman, who lived with her master's family, left the household from time to time when they did something that offended her, but always returned. Anti-slavery activists in her neighborhood regularly tried to raise her political consciousness, but to little avail. She eventually moved in with her master's brother. M'barek was the 60-year-old slave of one of the most venerated *shaykhs* on Mauritania. He remained in the *shaykh*'s service even though members of his family did not think he should continue to do so, because of his respect for his master's religious position. Lemine was a young man with a job and a higher income than his masters. Though he had the possibility of greater autonomy, he took pride from the religious prestige of his *qabila* and continued to take part in the life of the *qabila* with its gifts, ritual obligations and services. Mahmoud also had a job, though not as well-paid as Lemine. His family in Nouakchott lived separately from their former masters, but continued to make contributions to the *qabila*, which he saw more as an investment than as payment of tribute.

How do we see all of this? I see a conflicting set of goals, a desire to free themselves from onerous obligations, a concern to establish dignity and status, a continuing participation in the *qabila*, which probably offered some security, but all coupled to self-doubt. Furthermore, these conflicting obligations were filtered by the differing talents and relationships of both masters and slaves and the particularities of each situation. Brahim's political consciousness was raised by what seemed to him an offensive request. M'barek clearly was influenced by the status of his master. Hadama felt surer of her physical attractiveness than of her rights. Other studies also picture a range of different behaviours. De

Bruijn and Pelckmans talk of continuing to fulfil 'the roles expected of them in order not to lose the rights linked to their position as slaves'. Others moved away or created villages nearby. Some detached themselves, but continued to maintain relationships that could be useful to masters or slaves.

In all of this Islam was often a battleground. Denied a Muslim education in slavery, many freed slaves turned to Islam. In areas like the Futa Jallon, where they were denied full participation in the masters' mosque, *rimaayBe* communities built their own mosques. Muslim communities in many areas imposed restrictions on former slaves. In the Futa Jallon they could not sit at the front of the mosque or wear a starched white boubou (cf. Botte, 1994). Elsewhere they could not be imams. At the same time, it seems probable that the quest of former slaves for a Muslim education was a source of revenue for hard-pressed former slave-users, whose capital had been destroyed by the emancipation of their slaves.[7] But Islam could be at the same time the master's religion and the slave's religion. Islamic religious orders such as the Mourides and probably the Hamallists and Yakubists gave land and protection for former slaves, proving in many cases to be better patrons than former masters.

Any Gramscian theory of slaves internalising their exploitation has to be counter-balanced both by a clear picture of the steady erosion of the privileges of the master class and by the regular eruption of movements of liberation: the original exodus, the veteran-led departures after the First World War, the southern Sahara conflicts after the Second World War. In the 1950s radical parties in Guinea and Mali exploited slave–master tensions in the quest for votes and, once in power, sought to deliver on their promises (Cissé, 1978; Schmidt, 2005). In those areas where slavery has remained significant, movements of liberation have emerged from within the former slave communities. In Mauritania two groups, El Hor and SOS Esclaves, mostly with a *harâtîn* base, put pressure on the state from 1978. Though relations with the government have sometimes been ambiguous – SOS Esclaves was banned – they were a factor in the 1981 abolition of slavery and the 2007 act. Timidria was founded in 1991 in Niger. Its membership has been estimated at 200,000 to 300,000 former slaves. Like groups in Mali and Mauritania, it assists both servile communities and individuals seeking to escape abusive relationships. These groups have used democratic openings and exploited other tensions in their societies that make them helpful and valuable allies for slave descendants trying to set themselves free from the last vestiges of dependence.

Conclusion

Much of the discussion of 'trajectories' results from the different uses of the term slavery. It is often used metaphorically. It is also used in many societies to refer to social status. I am arguing that, if the term slavery has any precise meaning, it no longer exists for most of West Africa. The heritage of slavery is very important, but people referred to as slaves in local discourse are neither owned not controlled by others. Scholars date slavery's death to different periods: the 1920s, the end of the Second World War, the coming of independence and, sometimes, the present. In fact the process goes back to the nineteenth century, though early emancipations affected very few people and colonial administrators did their best to limit their effect. During the latter part of the nineteenth century colonial regimes were under a great deal of pressure from Christian missions, from European public opinion and from a democratically elected political leadership that could not ignore that public opinion. Thus, in the early years of the twentieth century, all colonial regimes acted to end the slave trade and slave raiding. They were not totally effective because in areas where slavery was still the major source of labour there was a market. Thus, raiding persisted on a small scale in the distant corners of empire. In northern Nigeria Hamman Yaji, a colonial chief, actively raided for slaves until he was removed in 1927. There was also a clandestine trade, mostly in children. Most colonial regimes depended on slave-owning chiefs and some administrators had little sympathy for slaves. These regimes were reluctant to abolish slavery, but they distanced themselves from its protection and eventually, under pressure, abolished slavery.

Colonial administrators were often reluctant to enforce anti-slavery legis- lation, but slaves generally took matters into their own hands. There is a mythology, common not only in Africa but in other societies threatened by abolition, that slaves are lazy and will not work without coercion. There is fear that emancipation will lead to vagrancy, crime and prostitution. In fact the one thing that slaves knew how to do was to work. In the first decade of the twentieth century there was a huge exodus from slavery of slaves who either wanted to go home or to go somewhere they could benefit from the fruits of their labour. This exodus put pressure on masters to ease the demands on slaves and, in particular, to recognise their control over their own labour and their family life. From that time forth, the process was a constant one. Most of the time it was gradual, but there were periods of rapid change, for example, after the First World War in French West Africa, after the coming of constitutional government in the 1940s, during the droughts of the 1970s and in the Tuareg revolts of the 1990s in Mali and Niger.

I am also arguing that people referred to in various African languages as slaves are not really slaves. I think that there are two essential characteristics of slavery. First, slaves are property and can be used in any way the master wishes. That means sexual exploitation and the control of the slave's labour. Secondly, the slave is kinless. He or she is stripped of any independent identity. There is an argument about whether Creole slaves are really slaves, but I think that their rights were limited and that they could be sold or pawned. Today there are very few people who come anywhere near this definition. They are largely in the desert, but those regimes that claim sovereignty over the desert have in recent years acted to end formal slavery there.

What exists is the heritage of slavery. There are significant differences in the way it operates. Among the Akan of southern Ghana, slaves were assimilated as junior branches of the master's lineage. One is not supposed to ask about another's origins, but slave origins often become an issue in questions of political succession. In many areas slaves tend to be wealthier than their former masters because of their willingness to work hard and to take jobs that the freeborn are reluctant to take. In many places they are eligible for local office. Thus a study of rural Senegal showed that people of slave origin were less likely to hold office in the local cooperatives, but many did hold office. The stigma is there, however, and it shapes the way people relate to each other. By contrast, the situation is worse in areas where neither land nor wage labour are easily available. People of slave descent had a harder struggle in areas such as northern Nigeria, where the colonial state restricted access to land and tried to force slaves to purchase their freedom, or in Masina, where recognition of the nobles as land-owners forced those who worked the land to pay rent. Even in those areas, control has broken down and the major concern is status.

In all this we have to recognise the ambiguities. There are differences between societies, which sometimes reflect geography but, in other cases, values and customs. Thus most of the larger communities in the western Soudan have castes and a tradition of hierarchy. Though caste and slavery are different – casted artisans were always free and usually quite mobile – the sense of hierarchy shapes social structure. By contrast, the Igbo have an egalitarian social structure, which means that there were few inhibitions on economic behaviour, but a strong taboo against marriage with a person of slave descent remains. As Brhane's interviews show, there are also always differences between people. Finally, most West African states are today multi-party democracies. That makes it possible for groups such as El Hor, SOS Esclaves and Timidria to put pressure on the system, and as de Bruijn and Pelckmans illustrate, it also shapes the way people treat each other. Ambitious politicians learn to address different constituencies.

References

Ames, D., 1953. 'Plural Marriage among the Wolof in the Gambia.' Unpublished doctoral dissertation, Northwestern University.

Austin, G., 2005. *Labour, Land and Capital in Ghana: From Slavery to Free Labour in Asante, 1807–1936*. London: University of Rochester Press.

Barry, B., 1998. *Senegambia and the Atlantic Slave Trade*, trans. Ayi Kwa Armah. Cambridge: Cambridge University Press.

Barry, I., 1971. 'Contribution à l'étude de l'histoire de la Guinée: Les Hubbu du Fitabe et les Almami du Fuuta.' Master's dissertation, Institut Polytechnique Julius Nyerere, Kankan, Guinea.

Baum, R., 1999. *Shrines of the Slave Trade: Diola Religion and Society in Precolonial Senegambia.* Oxford: Oxford University Press.

Bazin, J., 1975. 'Guerre et servitude à Ségou.' In C. Meillassoux, ed., *L'Esclavage en Afrique précoloniale.* Paris: Maspero, pp. 135–82.

Bellagamba, A., 2005. 'Slavery and Emancipation in the Colonial Archives: British Officials, Slave-Owners and Slaves in the Protectorate of the Gambia (ca. 1890–1936).' *Canadian Journal of African Studies,* 39, pp. 5–41.

Brhane, M., 2000. 'Histoires de Nouakchott: discours des hrâtîn sur le pouvoir et l'identité.' In M. Villesante-de Beauvais, ed., *Groupes serviles au Sahara: Approche comparative à partir du cas des arabophones de Mauritanie.* Paris: CNRS Editions, pp. 195–234.

Botte, R., 1994. 'Stigmates sociaux et disciminations religieuses: l'ancienne classe servile au Fuuta Jaloo.' *Cahiers d'Études Africaines,* 34(133–35), pp. 109–36.

Botte, R. 2003. 'Le droit contre l'esclavage au Niger.' *Politique Africaine,* 90, pp. 127–43.

Brown, C., 2003. *'We Were All Slaves': African Miners, Culture and Resistance at the Enugu Government Colliery.* Portsmouth, NH: Heinemann.

Cissé, S., 1978. 'L'esclavage "domestique" dans la partie Gourma du Moyen Niger: Structure sociale et comportement de classe.' Thesis, Université de Paris-VII.

Clark, A., 1994. 'Slavery and its Demise in the Upper Senegal Valley, 1890–1920.' *Slavery and Abolition,* 15, pp. 51–71.

de Bruijn, M. and Pelckmans, L., 2005. 'Facing Dilemmas: Former Fulbe Slaves in Modern Mali.' *Canadian Journal of African Studies,* 39, pp. 69–95.

Dumett, R. and Johnson, M., 1988. 'Britain and the Suppression of Slavery in the Gold Coast Colony, Ashanti, and the Northern Territories.' In S. Miers and R. Roberts, eds, *The End of Slavery in Africa.* Madison, WI: University of Wisconsin Press.

Falola, T., 1999. 'The End of Slavery among the Yoruba.' In S. Miers and M. Klein, eds, *Slavery in Colonial Africa.* London: Frank Cass, pp. 232–49.

Getz, T., 2004. *Slavery and Reform in West Africa: Toward Emancipation in Nineteenth Century Senegal and the Gold Coast.* London: James Currey.

Grace, J., 1975. *Domestic Slavery in West Africa.* London: Frederick Muller.

Hawthorne, W., 2003. *Planting Rice and Harvesting Slaves: Transformations along the Guinea Coast, 1400–1900.* Portsmouth, NH: Heinemann.

Klein, M., 1998. *Slavery and Colonial Rule in French West Africa.* Cambridge: Cambridge University Press.

Kopytoff, I., 1988. 'The Cultural Context of African Abolition.' In S. Miers and R. Roberts, eds, *The End of Slavery in Africa.* Madison, WI: University of Wisconsin Press.

Lecocq, B., 2005. 'The Bellah Question: Slave Emancipation, Race and Social Categories in late 19th Century Northern Mali.' *Canadian Journal of African Studies,* 39, pp. 42–68.

Lovejoy, P. and Hogendorn, J., 1993. *Slow Death for Slavery: The Course of Abolition in Northern Nigeria, 1897–1936.* Cambridge: Cambridge University Press.

Maugham, R., 1961. *The Slaves of Timbuktu.* London: Longman.

McDougall, A., 1988. 'A Topsy-Turvy World: Slaves and Freed Slaves in the Mauritanian Adrar, 1910–1950.' In S. Miers and R. Roberts, eds, *The End of Slavery in Africa.* Madison, WI: University of Wisconsin Press, pp. 379–90.

Meillassoux, C., 1991. *The Anthropology of Slavery: The Womb of Iron and Gold,* trans. Alide Dasnois. Chicago: University of Chicago Press.

Ohadike, D., 1999. '"When Slaves Left, Masters Wept": Entrepreneurs and Emancipation among the Igbo People.' In S. Miers and M. Klein, eds, *Slavery and Colonial Rule in Africa.* London: Frank Cass, pp. 189–207.

Olivier du Sardan, J.P., 1984. *Les Sociétés Songhay-Zarma (Niger-Mali).* Paris: Karthala.

Pollet, E. and Winter, G., 1971. *La Société Soninke (Dyahunu, Mali)*. Brussels: Université Libre.

Renault, F., 1972. *L'Abolition de l'esclavage: l'attitude de l'administration française, 1848–1905*. Paris: Paul Geuthner.

Riesman, P., 1977. *Freedom in Fulani Social Life*. Chicago: Chicago University Press.

Riesman, P., 1992. *First Find Your Child a Good Mother: The Construction of Self in Two African Communities*. New Brunswick, NJ: Rutgers University Press.

Roberts, R., 1988. 'The End of Slavery in the French Soudan, 1905–1914.' In S. Miers and R. Roberts, eds, *The End of Slavery in Africa*. Madison, WI: University of Wisconsin Press, pp. 282–307.

Schmidt, E., 2005. *Mobilizing the Masses: Gender, Ethnicity and Class in Nationalist Movement in Guinea, 1939–1958*. Portsmouth, NH: Heinemann.

Sy, Y., 2000. 'L'Esclavage chez les Soninkés: du village à Paris.' *Journal des Africanistes*, 70, pp. 43–70.

Vincent, Y., 1963. 'Pasteurs, paysans et pecheurs du Guimballa (Parties Centrale de l'Erg du Bara).' In P. Galloy, Y. Vincent and M. Forget, eds, *Nomades et paysans d'Afrique occidentale*. Nancy: Faculté de Lettres et de Sciences Humaines.

Walvin, J., 2005. 'British Abolitionism 1787–1838.' In T. Tibbles, ed., *Transatlantic Slavery: Against Human Dignity*. Liverpool: Liverpool University Press.

Wright, R., 1947. *Black Boy: A Record of Childhood and Youth by Richard Wright*. London: Readers Union.

Notes

1   Terms such as *abd* and the Poular *maccuBe* refer to slaves, but the more common terms, at least in languages that make the distinction, are to slaves 'born in the house'. There was a similar distinction made in the Americas between *bozales*, slaves born in Africa, and Creoles, slaves born in the Americas. The major difference is that the Creole slaves were not supposed to be sold.

2   Thus, the Balanta of coastal Guinea became very effective slave-raiders, but Hawthorne argues that the egalitarian nature of their age-grades made it difficult for them to absorb male slaves as inferiors. Women were absorbed as wives, but male children became full members of age grades (see Hawthorne, 2003, 139–42). Baum has discussed the shrine system that evolved to facilitate the trade among the Diola (Baum, 1999). It is deeply embedded in memory, but there are few persons left of slave origins.

3   Klein, 1998, 26–27. In an unpublished manuscript, Mohammed Mbodj has described similar policies in the Gambia.

4   On slave flight in northern Nigeria, see Lovejoy and Hogendorn, 1993, 11–12 and 31–63.

5   On Sierra Leone see Grace, 1975, 25–27.

6   Circular of 10 December 1903, Archives Nationales, Section Outre-Mer, Sénégal XIV 28. Also in Archives de la République du Sénégal, K 16. Part of it is reprinted in Renault, 1972, 100.

7   See in general Austin, 2005, ch. 12.

8   In the delta region of Nigeria, canoe houses were cooperative economic and political institutions comprising up to thousands of free and slave members who used canoes for their trade business.

9   See Lovejoy and Hogendorn, 1993, ch. 5 and 6.

10 I read some of the reports filed by research teams from the *Ecole Nationale du Développment Agricole* in Senegal, which included family budgets. I only saw one that referred to the *assaka*, but that suggested that it was a minute fraction of the family's

income. The absence of *assaka* in other budgets is also important. If it were an important part of family budgets, others would have mentioned it.

11 On *pulaaku*, see Riesman, 1992; on the Bambara, see Bazin, 1975; on the Songhay, see Olivier de Sardan, 1984; on *temushaga*, the Tamasheq term for code of honour, see Lecocq, 2005; see also de Bruijn and Pelckmans, 2005.

12 Eric Pollet and Grace Winter (1971, 432) make the same point.

13 Role-playing has probably been important to slaves in many cultures, for example ancient Rome, where a Sambo-type stereotype existed, and perhaps even more so in post-slavery societies. In *Black Boy*, his autobiographical account of growing up in Mississippi, Richard Wright describes how his seriousness and the absence of 'happy talk' threatened whites. He had to use subterfuges to get books and never mentioned his reading in front of a white (Wright, 1947).

14 Kopytoff (1988) sees emancipation as re-marginalisation, and therefore unattractive for the slave. He is right up to a point, but slaves often had the option of immersing themselves in new groups. Many also at some time risked re-marginalisation.

15 Meillassoux would not consider the *woloso/woroso* as slaves largely because he believed that slaves were produced only by violence and not by birth.

16 Brhane's interviews were the heart of a thesis defended at the University of Chicago in 1997. Five of them were discussed in a recent article (Brhane, 2000).

17 One of the intriguing aspects of emancipation is that in many areas the merchant families who were the most systematic users of slave labour and the biggest losers in emancipation were able to recoup their losses and re-surface as wealthy traders a generation or two later. Students were a source of labour and of gifts. On a 2006 visit to Guinea, I was able to interview two old merchants who were also teachers. Data from Banamba also suggests this.

3

African American Psychologists, the Atlantic Slave Trade and Ghana: A History of the Present

Tom McCaskie

'The pain of what has happened to my ancestors is very deep'[1]

Let me begin by identifying a network of African Americans who play a key role in the essay that follows. The links between them are set out below, as is their activist-intellectual project and the nature of their involvement with Ghana.

Molefi Kete Asante's *The History of Africa: The Quest for Eternal Harmony* (2007) is a comprehensive restatement of the author's well-known Afrocentric ideas. The book, produced by a respected academic publisher, is clearly aimed at a scholarly as well as a partisan historical readership. Its Afrocentric agenda proclaims the cultural unity of all African peoples in a historical line of descent from the original black civilisation of ancient Kemet/Egypt. Asante's conceptualisation of the transmission of African ideas and values across time and space is rooted in the core Kemetic/Egyptian principle of Maat. This was the archetypal belief that 'it was necessary to possess order, balance, harmony, justice, truth, righteousness, and reciprocity' to hold back 'chaos in every aspect of life'.[2] To possess Maat conferred strength and unity. By corollary, to lose it fostered weakness and alienation.

Asante's book argues that the centuries-long impact of white European and latterly American interventions in Africa – the Atlantic slave trade, territorial imperialism, neo-colonialism, the neo-liberal world order, a fragmented and alienated diaspora – constitute a calculated subversion of African unity and a sustained assault on Maat. The final section of Asante's book is headed 'Nothing remains except to do Maat', and it ends with the Draft of a Preamble to the Constitution of the African Federative State or United States of Africa drawn up under the auspices of the African Union in South Africa in 2002. This declares that Africans are 'a collective people with long traditions in intensifying a common bond', and restates the principles of Maat in 'a commitment to freedom, harmony, order, balance, justice, and reciprocity in all our relations with each other' (Asante, 2007, 350).

In his book's Acknowledgments, Asante thanks W. E. B. Du Bois and other forefathers of Afrocentrism as well as colleagues in and alumni of the African Studies department he heads at Temple University in Philadelphia. Also included in this list is Wade Nobles, 'an experimental and social psychologist', who is Executive Director of the Institute for the Advanced Study of Black Family Life and Culture and Professor of Africana Studies at San Francisco State University. Nobles was a founding figure in the 'New Black Psychology' movement of the 1960s. This posited a distinctive 'black personality' and aimed to treat its problems in the American diaspora by fostering a variety of therapies and educational initiatives to promote positive black images and to raise individual, family and communal self-esteem.

In 1968 Nobles and other like-minded psychologists founded the Association of Black Psychologists (ABPsi). This is now a flourishing organisation with a large nationwide membership, an annual convention and its own journal and research publications. In 1994–95 Nobles served as President of ABPsi. By then he had added Afrocentrism and African history to his project of psychological research and community activism. In his *African Psychology: Towards its Reclamation, Reascension and Revitalization* of 1986, Nobles argues that a specifically African psychology is dedicated to recovering and rejuvenating ancient Kemetic/Egyptian thought, and particularly Maat, as the key for restoring the 'psyche' of all people of African descent. Similar themes run through his more recent publications.[3]

Na'im Akbar, at one time Director of the Office of Human Development for the Nation of Islam in Chicago and since 1979 Professor of Psychology at Florida State University, is also a founding member and a past-President of ABPsi (1987–88). Like Nobles, Akbar is a 'Black Psychologist' and an 'Afrocentric scholar' who thinks the Atlantic slave trade and everything that followed it ruptured and traumatised the black psyche and its expression in the historic unity of peoples of African descent. Also like Nobles, Akbar is a prolific writer. In his *Light from Ancient Africa* of 1994, he argues for the Kemetic/Egyptian origins of the very concept of psychology.[4] This book has a Foreword by Nobles.

Another of Akbar's many books is *Know Thy Self* (1998). This has a Foreword by Asa Hilliard, a Professor of Urban Education at Georgia State University with a joint appointment in educational policy and educational psychology. Hilliard is a founding member and first Vice-President of the Association for the Study of Classical African Civilizations (ASCAC). This avowedly Afrocentric body is very widely known and is dedicated to the advancement and dissemination of knowledge about black African ancient Kemet/Egypt. In 2007 ASCAC's twenty-fourth Kemetic Studies Conference, 'Return to the

Black Land', took place in Aswan, Kemet/Egypt, in 'the sacred land of our ancestors'. Those making the trip at an average of US$2–3,000 per person listened to papers and discussions and undertook conducted tours to Philae, Abu Simbel, Kom Ombos and other sites. Hilliard was involved in this, and among the list of 'invited participants' are Wade and Vera Nobles. Also included on that list are James Small and Rosalind Jeffries.[5]

James Small taught for thirteen years in the Black Studies department at City College of New York (CCNY). He is a prominent member of ASCAC and worked together in that body with Nobles and Hilliard. He is 'a priest in the Yoruba religion', but is also a sometime associate of Malcolm X who performed the Hajj and served as Imam of the Muslim Mosque Inc. He is a 'Transformational Speaker and Consultant', and his lectures on topics such as 'Kemetamorphosis' and 'Post-Slavery Trauma Syndrome' are available on DVD.[6] Rosalind Jeffries is a faculty member in the School of Visual Arts in New York who specialises in the interpretation of African arts produced on the continent and in the diaspora. She works 'to uplift the oppressed, give new insights to the intellectual, and spark community zealots'.[7] She is married to Leonard Jeffries, one of the best-known and most controversial black intellectuals in the United States. We will return to Leonard Jeffries in due course, but for now let us note that he is a leading proponent of the ASCAC view that 'Egypt–Nubia–Ethiopia' was 'the basis for the cultural unity of Africa through its traditions and institutions'.[8]

Many things link Asante, Nobles, Akbar, Hilliard, Small and the Jeffries. All share in the idea of the deep historical and cultural unity of peoples of African descent worldwide. All trace this unity to the black civilisation of ancient Kemet/Egypt, and give prominence to the abiding influence of Maat. All hold that the unity and strength of the black African community has been under unrelenting assault from racist white Europeans and Americans since the era of the Atlantic slave trade. All, and especially the psychologists among them, think that the collective and individual personalities of Africans have been alienated and fractured by oppression. All are social activists who want to 'heal' and 'uplift' diasporic and African psyches and self-esteem. All believe in the regenerative power of a properly understood Afrocentric history. All think that there is a white conspiracy to deny and suppress the facts of that history.

All these individuals have at least one other thing in common. They are all long-time and frequent visitors to Ghana. Nothing encapsulates this better than the fact that most of them have been granted Ghanaian chieftaincy titles and stool names. Thus Asante is Nana Okru Asante Peasah, the Kyidomhene of Tafo in Akyem Abuakwa; Nobles is Nana Kwaku Berko I, the Nkosuohene of Akwasiho in Kwawu; Akbar is Nana Osei Nkwantabisa III, the Nkosuohene of Abono on lake Bosomtwe in Asante; Hilliard is Nana Baffour Amankwatia II, the Nkosuohene of Mankranso in Ahafo Ano South to the west of the Asante capital of Kumase; Rosalind Jeffries has chieftaincy titles and names from Agogo in Asante and the Edina Traditional Authority at Elmina; Leonard Jeffries is Nana Kwaku Dua Agyeman III, the Nkosuohene of Agogo in Asante; Small appears to have no chiefship or title thus far, or at least none that I can trace.

'They tried to destroy us with the Slave Trade. But we will RETURN'[9]

In April 1995 the government of President Rawlings held a conference in Accra on the Slave Route in Ghana. This took place under the sponsorship of the Slave Route Project initiated by UNESCO, the World Tourism Organization and several African states. Ghana was an obvious venue for this gathering, for European forts at Elmina, Cape Coast and other coastal towns are the most tangible reminders of the Atlantic slave trade in West Africa. The outcome of the conference was the 'Accra Declaration on the Cultural Tourism Slave Route Project'. This promised 'to rehabilitate, restore and promote the tangible and intangible heritage handed down by the slave trade', and to reveal the 'common nature' of the Atlantic slave trade 'in terms of Africa, Europe, the Americas and the Caribbean'.[10]

Other initiatives included PANAFEST (the Pan-African Historical Festival), first held in 1992 and more or less triennially thereafter, a gathering to recall the Atlantic slave trade and celebrate the vitality of African culture. The Rawlings regime also endorsed the celebration of Emancipation Day, the anniversary of the 1834 liberation of British slaves in the Caribbean and elsewhere in the diaspora. There is now a small but good and insightful literature on these matters. It deals in general terms with the matter of memorialising the Atlantic slave trade from the points of view of Ghanaians and the mainly African American diaspora.[11] Here I want to focus precisely on those African American individuals already mentioned.

As a part of PANAFEST in 2003 Small addressed a gathering of African Americans, Ghanaians and others at the former slave market at Asen Manso. He said, 'we are here on a pilgrimage to know the history of our ancestors, both those who went and those who stayed'. He declared that African Americans 'understand the need to understand our histories'. In the diaspora, he continued, 'we are beginning to be Africans again'. However, 'paying homage symbolically' was not enough. African Americans should take 'knowledge' from Ghana and invest in its economy so that 'we all work together to build the future'.

Four days later Jeffries gave a speech at the PANAFEST Opening Ceremony at Cape Coast Castle. He reiterated some of Small's themes, declaring that African Americans and Ghanaians 'need to do business together' and have 'to plan to be successful'. He then turned to the Atlantic slave trade and its legacy, starting with the statement that 'whoever controls the history controls the images'. The slave trade was 'an enormous process of genocide', but it was still being written as 'their' (European) and not 'our' (African) history.

Jeffries said he did not want to hear about Africans selling other Africans, for Asante 'slave traders' were 'victims themselves', and 'the real villains' were in Amsterdam, London, Nantes, etc. He then demanded 'reparations' for the Atlantic slave trade and linked this to the present condition of Africa. Whites today, he stated, still controlled 'minds and mines', and all of Africa's oil, gold, diamonds and other wealth were the objects of 'recolonisation'. He ended by declaring Ghana, with its tangible reminders of the Atlantic slave trade, 'sacred ground to all Africans worldwide'.[12]

Small expanded on his views in a speech at Cape Coast. He declared that he was an Imam, but had studied and learned at a Tigare shrine in northern Ghana. 'Western miseducation', he said, was a decline from the sacred and cosmic to the profane and material. What was required was to get rid of the dominant 'Greco-Roman or Anglo-Saxon' system, and to take 'the best of our ancestral wisdom' to replace history textbooks 'designed on the models of our enemies'. Africans 'cannot be instructed by any tradition other than our own'. He totally rejected 'failed socialist politics' in favour of a liberation based on culture, a culture derived from 'Ancient Egypt when it was still African'. Maat, with its emphasis on internal and communal harmony, was the key to reinserting culture into politics and economics. He emphasised that 'African spiritual integrity' was essential, and he quoted with approval Hilliard's dictum that the goal was 'to be African, or not be at all'.[13]

Jeffries too expanded on his views in a speech given at Cape Coast on PANAFEST's Reparations Day. He said he never travelled without the 'weaponry' of books, and he gave a Ghanaian chief on the platform with him a copy of Amos Wilson's *Blueprint for Black Power: A Moral, Political, and Economic Imperative for the Twenty-First Century* (1998). In this book Wilson, an 'Afrikan Psychologist', demands the creation of an African American, Caribbean and Pan-African 'bloc' to free all 'Afrikans' from the 'networks' of 'White and Asian power'. Elsewhere Wilson has written about the way in which European historiography's purpose is to create historical 'amnesia' in Africans.[14]

Be that as it may, Jeffries then warmed to his main theme. He said that 'a war was going on', and that Africa must be rescued from yet more European, Asian and Arab 'bloodsucking'. He mentioned Maat as the clearest indicator that Africa was civilised before Europe. He talked about 'the mind of the oppressed' as manifested in a 'post-slavery colonial trauma syndrome'. This 'illness' fed an 'internalised self-hatred' that expressed itself in dysfunction, crime and drug use. Mention was made of 'medical evidence' that the syndrome could be transmitted 'genetically'.[15]

Both Jeffries and Small intermix ABPsi and ASCAC ideas with the radical politics of post-civil rights urban black America. Their primary focus is on the slave forts. For a number of years they have been trying to persuade the Ghana government to give into their care a slave fort at Anomabo. The idea behind this project is to honour the Pan-African intellectual Dr Aggrey, who was from Anomabo and who lived and taught in South Carolina, and the Afrocentric forefather John Henrik Clarke. A proposed Dr Aggrey Foundation is intended to focus diasporic attention on an Afrocentric centre in Anomabo fort, and this in turn is designed to anchor a 'Golden Triangle' of diasporic pilgrimage involving Anomabo, Accra and Kumase. Both Nobles and Akbar are to be involved in this project.

The transatlantic slave forts, most notably Elmina and Cape Coast, are conflicted and contested sites. In the 1990s the government of Ghana and the Smithsonian Institution worked together to rehabilitate Cape Coast and Elmina and to install museums in both forts. To many African Americans, newly whitewashed fort walls equate to the malign 'whitewashing' of the true history of the Atlantic slave trade. The slave dungeons are sacred spaces to African Americans, in which the 'pain and anguish' of the slave trade and the Middle Passage can be addressed and defused. The healing rituals involved in this cannot even be done by Ghanaians, because only those who were 'born under the lash of slavery and oppression' and have lived in a racist society like the United States can truly understand the import of what is going on. Museum plans met with a similar criticism, and for many African Americans the link with the Smithsonian Institution has utterly compromised the scheduled and achieved outcomes.[16]

Nobles and Akbar, both of whom have attended PANAFEST and are frequent visitors to Ghana like Jeffries and Small, have their own projects as well as being involved in those of others. While sharing in many of the precepts and goals of Jeffries and Small, Nobles and Akbar have a distinct approach rooted in their professional psychological training and ABPsi membership. Since 1995 Nobles and Akbar have created and run the US-based Enyimnyam organisation (Twi: 'the radiance of the face'; cf. *obi a n'ani agye a ma ada adi wo n'anim hwebea mu*). This was 'a special development project'. It was to put into practice its founders' 'life work' of 'illuminating the spirit', and by this means 'extend the splendor' of African peoples by sharing 'radiance' between the Ghanaian and African American communities.

African Americans travel with Nobles and Akbar to Ghana, and there they witness the slave dungeons of the Atlantic slave trade and interact with Ghanaians to 're-connect with our African selves'. In July 2006 the Enyimnyam organisation organised a tenth anniversary 'Return to the Splendor' tour around Ghana. The objective of this tour was to build on the healing mission of ABPsi. African American visitors were to be 'reconnected' with the culture that had been 'robbed' from them and would find 'new inspiration and invigoration from the first-hand experiences that can only happen in the Motherland and most gently in the wonderful land of Ghana'. The psychological orientations of this tour were to have participants encounter the sites of their cultural rupture and alienation from Africa and then achieve healing and peace in encounters with Ghanaians and their vibrant 'traditional' culture.[17]

The Enyimnyam itinerary promised a visit to 'the shrine of Nana Abbas'. The locally and internationally famous Black and White shrine of Nana Abass at Medoma, off the Kumase–Mamponten main road, merits a fuller discussion than can be given here. It is perhaps the best-known 'neo-traditional' Akan shrine in Ghana. Nana Abass was born in Agona, the Asante division whose chiefship was awarded to Komfo Anokye by the first Asantehene Osei Tutu. As a child he was 'chosen' by the *mmoatia* ('little folk' in the Asante forest) to serve the old gods. He resisted their call, becoming a Muslim for a time, but then settled in Medoma at their direction. There he drew water from a rock in a notoriously dry area and created the Black and White shrine.

The Black and White shrine is dedicated to all the *abosom* ('gods') of the pre-colonial Asante pantheon. Nana Abass rejects Christianity because of its 'brainwashing', and he equates it with a salvationist quietism that does nothing 'to sustain the society and posterity' of Asante and Ghana. He operates a large 'hospital' at Medoma where, like pre-colonial *akomfo*, he treats such ills as childlessness, infertility and witchcraft. He also treats the 'schizophrenia' produced in Ghanaians by Western modernity. Nana Abass is a community activist, organising and paying for self-help programmes in Kumawu and other Asante towns. To the experienced observer his religious practice is clearly based on received Asante models, but it has been reconfigured to address the current concerns of African Americans and Ghanaians.[18]

Cheryl Grills is a Professor of Psychology at Loyola Marymount University in Los Angeles. A member of ABPsi and a colleague of Nobles and Akbar, she is an activist who uses Afrocentric perspectives in therapeutic treatment.[19] Dissatisfied with efforts to create a distinctive African psychology, she explored religious and healing contexts among the Wolof and Yoruba. She met Nana Abass at the Akonnedi shrine at Larteh in Ghana and visited Medoma with her students. On her first visit one of the 'spirits' conduced by Nana Abass slapped her across the face for exhibiting impatience. She immediately apprenticed herself to Nana Abass.

Grills brought Nana Abass to California in the mid-1990s where he sanctified a shrine to the *abosom* in her backyard. The clientele built up by word of mouth. Two-thirds of it was African American. The remainder was made up of Cubans and other Latinos, West Indians and a few whites. The 'spirits', Grills says, pick out African Americans because they have what the Akan call *mogya* (blood), a physical and metaphysical substance that enables a diasporic 'genetic memory' of Africa. This idea of a genetically transmitted history, manifested in speech, behaviour, music, cuisine and the rest, is a salient idea in Afrocentric and ABPsi thinking. Grills is also a convinced supporter of the ritual conducted by Nobles and Akbar at the 'Door of No Return' in the slave forts, for this is the historical point of rupture with Africa.[20]

In July 2004 Nobles, Akbar, Hilliard, Jeffries and Small visited Medoma. They came to implement a decision agreed by a gathering of Panafricanists in Atlanta. This was to place a bust of the Afrocentric forefather John Henrik Clarke within the Black and White shrine and have Nana Abass consecrate it as *abakosem sunsum* (i.e. the essence or incarnation of true history). In attendance was a group of African American visitors from the African Studies Program at SUNY at Albany. Nana Abass danced before the image of *adiepu* (originally *atipo* from the Gyaman Akan of the Ivory Coast) and he covered it with *hyire* (white clay; associated with good fortune). People were asked to dance, after which Nana Abass spoke the message he had received. This was that the spirit of the dead Clarke was still with the celebrants and was urging a continuation of the struggle against the long legacies of the Atlantic slave trade. At a later point in the day Nana Abass was possessed by *ntantanta*, a spirit that can be interrogated about the future. The audience was now predominantly Asante, and many of the questions were about how to obtain visas for Europe and the United States.[21]

'Knowing the truth of history will develop Ghana'[22]

In 1995 tourism became Ghana's third highest foreign currency earner. Government noted the 'special sub-segment' of 'the heritage-seeking visitor', most of these being African Americans returning to Africa. Plans were set in train to increase this sector. The primary attraction for them was the Atlantic slave trade and its sites.[23] Revenue played a role in attempts to increase African American tourism but so too did politics.

By the later 1990s Rawlings, in power since 1981, was increasingly unpopular. It was widely thought that his National Democratic Congress government would lose the 2000 national election to the resurgent New Patriotic Party led by J. A. Kufuor. Kufuor was a very well-connected Asante from Kumase. The Asante were mostly and sometimes vociferously anti-Rawlings. Stories circulated that once out of office Rawlings would face criminal charges and a jail term for corruption and mismanagement.

The zeal with which Rawlings embraced African-American tourism must be seen in the light of Ghana's politics. He was trying to create a constituency that would bring in cash and investment, but that might also provide vocal international support if and when he faced any sort of judicial investigation after the 2000 election. One highlight of Rawlings' embrace of African-

American visitors was when Accra hosted ABPsi's 32nd annual convention in 2000. Hundreds of members attended.[24] This was the first time that the ABPsi had met in Africa.

Rawling's opening speech of welcome, a lengthy address, was entitled 'Sankofa, The Healers' Journey'.[25] It declared that Africans were frustrated and angry because of all the failures that had followed independence. It argued that economic cooperation with African American lobby groups such as Rev. Jesse Jackson's Rainbow/Push coalition, which had visited Ghana, would aid in the African Renaissance of the twenty-first century. It defined the concept of *sankofa* as 'going back for it', meaning that the best in tradition had to be retrieved for present and future use.

Rawlings said that tradition was not enough. Africans and all their African-American 'brothers and sisters' must pursue a political 'realism' beyond culture in order to build the Ghanaian and African 'nation state'. The villains in the way of this outcome were, as ever, Europe and the United States. Their crimes, beginning with the Atlantic slave trade and still going on in the present era of hegemonic World Bank programmes, had inhibited development and colonised the African mind. Development, once achieved, would liberate the oppressed African psyche. African Americans, said Rawlings, were needed in Ghana to invest in local development to help kick-start true decolonisation. In a sense the President's priorities stood the ABPsi agenda on its head.

In fact African Americans, and others, had already found a mechanism that met the President's requirement. As we have noted, by 2000 Nobles, Akbar, Hilliard and both Jeffries were all invested with the stool and title of Nkosuohene in various parts of Ghana. The word *nkosuo* means 'progress'. In Asante especially it has long been used to mean responsible advancement through combined or communal effort. In 1985 this concept was selected by Asantehene Opoku Ware II (1970–99) to name the new stool that he was obliged by custom to decree into existence to commemorate his reign. He later urged all Asante settlements to acquire and appoint such 'development chiefs'.

By the 1990s the idea had spread throughout and beyond Asante, and many Ghanaian towns and villages enstooled an Nkosuohene. Many communities sought an expatriate in the hope that he (or as Nkosuohemaa, she) would bring investment and other socio-economic benefits. African Americans were honoured and flattered to be appointed to such stools.

Leonard Jeffries was one of the earliest such appointees. He was given his stool by Agogohene Akuoko Sarpong, one of the handful of Asante chiefs who supported Rawlings and held national office under the NDC. Akuoko Sarpong saw in Nkosuo stools a way in which to bring money into Ghana and simultaneously to fund the development powers of local chiefs like himself. In Asante a fierce if covert battle ensued over the control of

Nkosuo appointments between the NDC and the anti-NDC Kumase royal establishment. In the middle of this were villagers who simply wanted to improve their lives.[26]

Nkosuohenes were, to say the least, a mixed success. Whether from idealism or some other motive, the institution inspired over-ambitious projects that never really got off the drawing board. Molefi Kete Asante himself, as Nana Okru Asante Peasah of Tafo in Akyem Abuakwa, sponsored a 'cultural center' in that 'ancient Ghanaian city'. Its purpose was to honour 'Africans Involuntarily Uprooted from the Continent', and it was dedicated to 'the goals and missions of the greatest thinkers of Africa'. This was an eclectic list of Ghanaian, African and African American persons: Yaa Asantewaa, Nkrumah, Efua Sutherland, DuBois, Azikiwe, Garvey, Malcolm X, Martin Luther King, Queen Mother Moore, Biko, Rodney, Cabral and Blyden.

There were plans for a theatre, art museum, children's library, traditional medicine centre, broadcasting facilities, seminar rooms, performance space and an Institute for research 'in Afrocentric theory and practice'. This was to cost US$1 million, which was to be raised by donations and subscriptions. Involved in the project was Kwame Botwe-Asamoah, himself an Akyem, who worked in the Africana Studies Department at Pittsburgh University, and who received a PhD for a dissertation on Nkrumah from Asante's department at Temple University. Whatever prompted schemes like this, the gap between their soaring vision and halting implementation confused, frustrated and even alienated Ghanaians in search of material betterment.[27]

As Abono Nkosuohene, Akbar was confronted by a difficult and even devious village chief and a complex dispute with neighbouring Kuntanase over rights in land. Hilliard and Leonard Jeffries too faced a variety of problems. Nobles, however, has an active and productive relationship with local people as Nkosuohene of Akwasiho which is, perhaps significantly, in Kwawu rather than in neighbouring Asante. In 2001 Nobles launched a soap-making enterprise that brought jobs to the village. A dried pepper and batik-making business has followed. He has also worked to install solar energy panels to provide power.

However, priority has been given to education, with Nobles supplying everything from pens and pencils to computers for the village school named for him. The school library has books that have been contributed by Nobles and ABPsi and Enyimnyam visitors or 'ambassadors' he has brought with him to Akwasiho. Library desks have brass plaques giving the name of the donor. Among those honoured in this way are Nobles himself, Akbar and Cheryl Grills. Donated books are all titles on African and Afrocentric topics. According to the librarian the single most popular book among the children is J. A. Rogers' *Africa's Gift to America: the African-American in the Making and Saving of the United States*, in a revised edition of 1989 with an added chapter on 'Africa and Its Potentialities'.

Akwasihohene Nana Opoku Ofari Kosako II says that Nobles represents the return home of those stolen away. He himself has visited New Jersey where he saw a woman who looked 'just like my auntie'. He thinks that Nobles believes that Akwasiho is his own ancestral land, and is learning Twi to further his commitment to the place. Nana says that the Atlantic slave trade broke the wholeness of the African world but that its unity is now being restored by people like Nobles. There is no doubt that Akwasiho's Nkosuohene is a much-admired man. However, those schoolchildren who have read the book by Rogers and others in the same vein say that they want to visit and live in the United States. Questioned further they talked of professional ambitions but also of the idea that America was the land of *di*, which means literally 'to eat' but also means the whole process of unlimited consumption. There are contradictions here that can be replicated everywhere there is an overseas occupant of an Nkosuo stool.[28]

The NDC did lose the 2000 Ghanaian election. Kufuor became President and head of an NPP government. The new Asantehene Osei Tutu II, enstooled in 1999, moved to restrict access to Nkosuo stools in Asante. At the same time relations cooled between the new regimes in Accra and Kumase and African Americans who were identified in Ghana with Rawlings and the NDC. One important Kumase insider complained of the African American presumption of rights to talk with the Asantehene, saying that Osei Tutu II was not a 'cultural museum piece'. Others in Kumase express private views of African Americans that are damning. These range from the descriptively dismissive – 'Christmas trees', because of their propensity to wear *kente* with 'pan-African' dress, or 'Michael Jordan', because of their 'African' attire being completed by the wearing of Nike or other sports shoes – to the more considered. Some call African Americans 'ghosts' (*asamanfo*), not in the sense of 'ancestors' but of those departed to the United States. 'We sold them', said one important Asante chief, 'so what are they doing back here?'[29]

If pressed to describe the current view of Ghanaian chiefship and citizenry of the now familiar presence of African Americans I would say that they are seen as one among a number of development possibilities. The Asantehene, emulated by the Okyenhene of Akyem Abuakwa, has moved the goalposts. The object of chiefship now is to foster a series of development initiatives, controlled by themselves, to which Ghanaian as well as international donors are solicited to contribute. African Americans might play their part in this, but in a supportive role and by invitation. The clearest indication of this shift since the Rawlings years can be seen in two things. First, in 2001 Asantehene Osei Tutu II inaugurated the Golden Development Holding Company Ltd, offering a public flotation of 60 million ordinary shares. He was doing this, he said, because 'we cannot always rely on donations from benevolent organizations and individuals', and anyway Asante must 'take its destiny into its own hands'.[30] Secondly, in 2003

Osei Tutu II signed a Development Grant Agreement under the rubric of the World Bank's 'Promoting Partnerships with Traditional Authorities Project'. By this means Asante became the first traditional authority in Africa to receive direct World Bank funding for development.[31]

At the time of writing African Americans still visit Ghana in numbers. They remain very much interested in Elmina, Cape Coast and other forts and sites associated with the Atlantic slave trade. They are now a familiar part of the landscape. Afrocentrism as an ideology has had only a limited impact in Ghana. Books such as the Ghanaian O. Kwame Osei's *The Ancient Egyptians Are Here*, published in Kumase in 2001, are few in number and have a limited local appeal.[32] Unsurprisingly, those most interested in Afrocentric ideas are a scattering of intellectuals (many of whom seek and find jobs in American universities) and those involved in the tourist industry itself. Few African Americans have settled permanently in Ghana, and pleas by them for dual citizenship have gone unheard in Accra.

It is difficult to know what ordinary Ghanaians make of ABPsi ideas, as distinct from their admiration for some of the African Americans who endorse them. The truth, sad or predictable depending on one's point of view, is that for the most part Ghanaians do not have the luxury of thinking about their spiritual or historical status. And if and when they do, as is well documented, they tend to embrace Pentecostal Christianity. A conversation with Ghanaian medical practitioners revealed a divided attitude towards ABPsi views. Some thought them an admirable effort to probe and understand the underlying reasons for African underdevelopment and white racism. Others thought that the whole enterprise was wholly American rather than African in its concerns.[33] One doctor and intellectual summed up by saying that at bottom ordinary Ghanaians of his acquaintance could not understand why mainly middle-class African Americans would quit their economic comfort zone to come to Ghana. Ghanaians, and especially the young, he said, wanted passionately to go in the other direction.

Endnote: Ghana's Slave Trades, Ghana's Future

In 2004 the Asante historian A. A. Perbi published a history of indigenous slavery in Ghana. In the past, in both matrilineal and patrilineal Ghanaian societies, she noted, domestic slaves were eventually integrated into the kin of their owners via adoption or marriage. However, this was 'a gradual process', and one that 'did not necessarily confer equality of status with their owners or members of the family'. People who owed their position to birth rather than adoption 'guarded their birthright jealously'.[34]

Private conversation in any village today illustrates the legacies of traditional jural inequities. Akan people situate themselves in kin structures in terms of belonging to the free and hence superior 'right' (*nifa*), or the once unfree and therefore subordinate 'left' (*benkum*). They might say of someone else, 'we are both *oyoko* [i.e. members of the Oyoko clan], but I am more *oyoko* than him [or her]'. This type of differentiation is proverbial: *abusua nyinaa ye abusua, nanso yehwe mmetema so de*, 'Every member of a matriclan is matriclan, but we discriminate in favour of those who are nearest'.[35]

However, allusive references mask an underlying historical tension. Everyone might be aware of who among their kin or neighbours is the descendant of domestic slaves, but this is only referred to in the indirect manner described. Historically, for example, it was a maxim of Asante society, one of the basic 'seventy-seven laws' supposedly promulgated by Komfo Anokye, that on pain of death 'nobody is to reveal the origins of another'. This was because Akan societies like Asante were built from the outset on the acquisition of domestic slaves, and continued to accumulate 'wealth in people' via this mechanism until the colonial era.[36]

For the most part Akan societies have come to terms with this aspect of their past. The same cannot be said for contemporary manifestations of 'slavery'. Ghanaians are very concerned about this issue today, and especially as it affects children. In recent years civil disorder in the neighbouring Ivory Coast has generated a steady flow of refugee youth eastwards into Ghana's Ahafo region. Some find work on cocoa or food farms, while others are employed as domestic servants. Ghanaian children too are involved, either through family poverty or exploitation by powerful kin. This situation has led to a widespread outcry in Ghana about 'children in slavery'. Such protest makes use of contemporary human rights discourse.

In 2007 a public discussion in Goaso in Asunafo North District of Ahafo addressed the topic of 'Making the Domestic Servant Institution a Job Creation Avenue'. All speakers deplored the mistreatment of children in domestic service and demanded that 'they must be respected and protected' against any and all 'inhuman acts'. If this was not done, such children might be criminalised and society would pay the price. They also demanded that buyers be prevented from purchasing cocoa and other crops from farmers who used child labour. Similarly, in 2007 at Kpando in the Volta region of eastern Ghana, the UN's World Day Against Child Labour was observed, with all government and church speakers equating child labour with a sinister 'resurrection' of domestic slavery in a new form.[37]

Today domestic slaveries, past, present or even putative, are part of Ghana's official discourse and public consciousness. Such concerns appear to impact less on visiting African Americans, or at least on those persons discussed in this essay. They express a marginally greater interest in the much-publicised institution of *trokosi*, an Ewe shrine 'custom' that has been attacked by Ghanaian Christians as a form of slavery involving young girls, but whose defenders assert its value in terms of 'tradition'. Be that as it may, visiting African Americans in Ghana are overwhelmingly, and quite understandably, interested solely in the historic Atlantic slave trade. Some even deny the very existence of domestic slavery in Ghana's past, let alone its present.

It has been noted that President Rawlings, as the Ghanaian head of state in the 1990s, encouraged African-American interest in the Atlantic slave trade from a mixture of personal conviction and political calculation. After 2000 and the election of President Kufuor, it seems there occurred a gradual shift in the Ghana government's view. After 2004, when Kufuor won re-election, the nature of this change became more apparent. In brief, the present NPP government seems to value African Americans as cultural kin or potential investors, but is at pains to distance itself from their political agenda and more strident demands.

In February 2007 Ghana's Minister of Tourism and Diasporan Relations (and note the coupling of portfolios) launched the *akwaaba anyemi* programme. This meant, in Twi, 'Greetings, my brother (or sister)' and it addressed a vexing issue of long duration for African Americans. Many African-American visitors to Ghana have complained over the years that local people refer to them as *oburoni*, or 'white man'. The term is used because to Ghanaians, African Americans have black skins but are stranger-visitors and, most importantly, have all the trappings and signs of Western wealth.

The Minister said this change was necessary, and he went on to announce a project subsumed within the *akwaaba anyemi* programme. This was a 'Pan-African project', aimed at African-American churches, schools and universities, that sought to deliver on 'African unity' and 'African strength' in the twenty-first century. The Minister was at pains to declare that this was 'not a tourism product' and 'if we see it as a tourism product it will fail'. Fostering 'unity' and 'strength' through understanding the 'true and full history' of African peoples would lead to full 'emancipation' for everyone of African descent. This project was to be launched with a 'healing concert' at Elmina Castle, at which 'traditional priests' would 'heal our wounds from the past'. Finally, he declared that peoples of African descent must forgive one another, and especially now in the 200th anniversary year of Britain's abolition of the Atlantic slave trade.[38] Whatever might be said about the practicalities of all this, it privileges cultural affinity over tourism, and generic future solidarity rather than any concrete political agenda in the here and now.

For those African Americans mentioned in this paper worse followed. In March 2007 President Kufuor, an Asante aristocrat, spoke at a ceremony at Elmina Castle that was held to commemorate both the 200th anniversary of Britain's abolition of the Atlantic slave trade (in 1807) and the 50th anniversary of Ghana's independence (in 1957). In his speech Kufuor dissociated himself completely from a fundamental aspiration of the African-American diaspora.

He said that since Africans had themselves played a part in the Atlantic slave trade, the payment of reparations was neither necessary nor the best approach to the facts and legacies of that trade. Instead, he asked for 'genuine remorse' on all sides, and stressed the ideas of mutual 'respect', 'human dignity' and 'common humanity' as the tools of reconciliation. He said the World Bank's and the Western governments' New Partnership for Africa's Development (NEPAD) was the way ahead, 'seeking to reconnect with those in the diaspora and to correct the historic *mistake* epitomised by the slave trade'. Above all, stated Kufuor, 'let us re-dedicate ourselves to show courage and energy to fight injustices in *our modern world*'.[39]

Kufuor spoke in the presence of the British Deputy Prime Minister, and he joined in a video link with British Prime Minister Blair. As is well known, Britain has resolutely refused to offer a formal apology for the Atlantic slave trade, fearing that this might create a legal basis for a claim to the very reparations that Kufuor now disowned. It is apparent that Kufuor's statement was not born of opportunism or even politeness. He meant what he said, and was severally taken to task by the Ghanaian media for saying it.[40]

Kufuor's refutation of reparations and support for NEPAD is at the opposite end of the political spectrum from Rawlings's speech to the ABPsi in 2000. At present, it remains to be seen how African Americans will respond to this change, just as it is unclear if Kufuor's speech is the last word on Ghana's view of African Americans and their agenda. Clearly, in Ghana now there are present problems and future hopes that take priority over any past issue, even one as important in global history as the Atlantic slave trade.

References

Reference to websites and texts available electronically on the www is contained in relevant footnotes. All internet addresses were checked and working on 3 March 2008.

Akbar, N., 1985. *The Community of Self.* Jersey City, NJ: New Mind Productions.
Akbar, N., 1994. *Light from Ancient Africa.* Jersey City, NJ: New Mind Productions.
Akbar, N., 1996. *Breaking the Chains of Psychological Slavery.* Jersey City, NJ: New Mind Productions.
Akbar, N., 1998. *Know Thy Self.* Jersey City, NJ: New Mind Productions.
Akyaw, K. O., 2000. *A Profile of Nana Abass (Akwantimfi Gyeaboo).* Kumase: Fickle Productions.
Akyeampong, E., 2000. 'Africans in the Diaspora: The Diaspora and Africa.' *African Affairs*, 99(395), pp. 183–215.
Akyeampong, E., 2001. 'History, Memory, Slave-Trade and Slavery in Anlo (Ghana).' *Slavery and Abolition*, 22(3), pp. 1–24.
Appiah, P, Appiah K. A. and Agyeman-Duah, I., n.d. *Bu Me Be: Akan Proverbs.* Accra: The Centre for Intellectual Renewal.
Asante, M. K., 2007. *The History of Africa: The Quest For Eternal Harmony.* New York and London: Routledge.

Asante, M. K. and D. D. Turner, 2002. 'An Oral History Interview: Molefi Kete Asante.' *Journal of Black Studies*, 32(6), pp. 711–34.

Benson, S., 2003. 'Connecting with the Past, Building the Future: African Americans and Chieftaincy in Southern Ghana.' *Ghana Studies*, 6, pp. 109–33.

Benson, S. and McCaskie, T. C., 2004. 'Asen Praso in History and Memory.' *Ghana Studies*, 7, pp. 93–113.

Bruner, E. M., 1996. 'Tourism in Ghana: The Representation of Slavery and the Return of the Black Diaspora.' *American Anthropologist*, 98(2), pp. 290–304.

Bruner, E. M., 2005. *Culture on Tour: Ethnographies of Travel*. Chicago and London: University of Chicago Press.

Christaller, J. G., 1990 (1879). *Three Thousand Six Hundred Ghanaian Proverbs (from the Asante and Fante Language)*, trans. K.R. Lange. Lampeter: Edwin Mellen Press.

Grills, C. and Longshore, D., 1996. 'Africentrism: Psychometric Analyses of a Self-Report Measure.' *Journal of Black Psychology*, 22(1), pp. 86–106.

Hasty, J., 2003. 'Rites of Passage, Routes of Redemption: Emancipation Tourism and the Wealth of Culture.' *Africa Today*, 49(3), pp. 47–78.

Hasty, J., 2004. 'Forget the Past or Go Back to the Slave Trade! Trans-Africanism and Popular History in Postcolonial Ghana.' *Ghana Studies*, 6, pp. 131–57.

Howe, S., 1998. *Afrocentrism: Mythical Pasts and Imagined Homes*. London and New York: Verso.

Imakhüs, 1999. *Returning Home Ain't Easy But It Sure Is A Blessing*. Cape Coast: One Africa.

Longshore, D., Grills, C., Annon, K. and Grady, D., 1998. 'Promoting Recovery from Drug Abuse: an Africentric Intervention.' *Journal of Black Studies*, 28(3), pp. 319–33.

McCaskie, T. C., 2007. 'The Life and Afterlife of Yaa Asantewaa.' *Africa*, 77(2), pp. 151–79.

McCaskie, T. C. 2008. '*Akwantemfi* "in mid-journey": an Asante shrine today and its clients.' *Journal of Religion in Africa*, 38(1), pp. 57–80.

Nobles, W., 1986. *African Psychology: Toward Its Reclamation, Reascension and Revitalization*. San Francisco: Institute for Advanced Studies.

Nobles, W., 2006. *Seeking the Sakhu: Foundational Writings for an African Psychology*. Chicago: Third World Press.

Oduro-Mensah, D., 2007. *Akanism and Hebrewism: Akan-Mesopotamian Links and Earlier Civilization*. Accra: Woeli Publishing Services.

Perbi, A. A., 2004. *A History of Indigenous Slavery in Ghana: From the 15th to the 19th Century*. Accra: Sub-Saharan Publishers.

Rattray, R. S., 1916. *Ashanti Proverbs*. Oxford: Clarendon Press.

Singleton, T., 1999. 'The Slave Trade Remembered on the former Gold and Slave Coasts.' *Slavery and Abolition*, 20(1), pp. 150–69.

Wilks, I. 1993 (1977). 'Land, Labor, Gold, and the Forest Kingdom of Asante: A Model of Early Change.' In I. Wilks, ed., *Forests of Gold: Essays on the Akan and the Kingdom of Asante*. Athens, OH: Ohio University Press, pp. 41–90.

Wilks, I., 1998. 'Unity and Progress: Asante Politics Revisited.' *Ghana Studies*, 1, pp. 151–79.

Wilson, A., 1993. *The Falsification of Afrikan Consciousness: Eurocentric History, Psychiatry and the Politics of White Supremacy*. New York: Afrikan World Infosystems.

Wilson, A., 1998. *Blueprint for Black Power: A Moral, Political, and Economic Imperative for the Twenty-First Century*. New York: Afrikan World Infosystems.

Notes

1 Elmina Castle Visitors' Book, entry by 'African-in-America', dd. 20 November 1990. This essay arises from joint and individual research conducted by Susan Benson of Cambridge University and myself; see Benson and McCaskie, 2004. Dr Benson died suddenly in 2005. This essay makes use of her work at her specific request and is dedicated to her memory. Our work would not have been possible without Isaac Abban and Sly Hutchinson and thanks are due to both.

2 Asante, 2007, 38; see further Asante and Turner, 2002.

3 Nobles, 1986; 2006; for ABPsi see www.abpsi.org/about_abpsi.htm; for Wade Nobles see www.iasbflc.org/nobles.htm.

4 Akbar, 1994; see too Akbar, 1985; 1996; 1998; for Na'im Akbar see http://www.africa-within.com/akbar/akbar_bio1.htm; for a short critique of Nobles and Akbar see Howe, 1998, 265–66.

5 See www.ascac.org/pdfs/2007ReturnToTheBlackLand.pdf.

6 See www.africawithin.com/small/small_bio.htm.

7 See www.ascac.org/bios/rjeffriesbio.html.

8 See www.africawithin.com/jeffries/reclaiming_nile_valley.htm.

9 Fort St Anthony, Axim, Visitors' Book, entry by 'African pilgrimage '92 with Dr. Leonard Jeffries', dd. 30 July 1992 (emphasis in the original).

10 Government of Ghana, Ministry of Tourism, *National Tourist Development Programme 1996–2010* (Integrated Tourism Development Programme GHA/92/013, Final Report, 1996), pp. 85–86.

11 See for example, Bruner, 1996; 2005; Hasty, 2003; 2004; Benson, 2003; Akyeampong, 2000; 2001; Benson and McCaskie, 2004; Perbi, 2004; Singleton, 1999.

12 Benson/McCaskie, Fieldnotes, dd. Asen Manso and Cape Coast, July 2003.

13 Idem.

14 Wilson, 1993; 1998.

15 Benson/McCaskie Fieldnotes, dd. Cape Coast, July–August 2003.

16 See University of Cape Coast and the Smithsonian Institution, *Ghana: The Chronicle of a Museum Development Project in the Central Region,* and Imakhüs, 1999.

17 See www.iasbflc.org/return to splendor.htm.

18 See Akyaw, 2000, Benson/McCaskie, Fieldnotes, dd. Kumase, December 2000, July–September 2001, December 2001, July 2003 and July–August 2004 and McCaskie, 2008.

19 See Grills and Longshore, 1996; and Longshore et al. , 1998.

20 In 1999 Professor Grills received a grant from the Centre of Consciousness Studies at the University of Arizona to study 'Akan Conceptualizations of Consciousness'; see Benson/McCaskie, Fieldnotes, dd. Medoma, July 2002.

21 Benson/McCaskie, Fieldnotes, dd. Medoma, July 2004.

22 Fort St Anthony, Axim, Visitors' Book, entry by 'Afrikan exile in Amerika', dd. 7 August 2000.

23 See Government of Ghana, Ministry of Tourism, *National Slave Routes Project: Rapid Assessment of Slave Sites in Ghana,* revised edition, 2002.

24 By one estimate, as many as 800.

25 See *Psych. Discourse,* News Journal of ABPsi, 31(8) (2000), pp. 2–6; the address is available online at http://pzacad.pitzer.edu/~hfairchi/PsychDiscourse/2000%5C3108html.

26 See Wilks, 1998; McCaskie, 2007; and Benson/McCaskie, Fieldnotes, dd. Accra, Kumase and Agogo, July 2002.

27 Benson/McCaskie, Fieldnotes, dd. Akyem Abuakwa, July–August 2004; for the scheme see www.asante.net/tafo/index01.html; for Botwe-Asamoah see www.pitt.edu/~bjgrier/asamoah.htm.

28   Benson/McCaskie, Fieldnotes, dd. Accra, Kumase and Akwasiho, December 2001.
29   Benson/McCaskie, Fieldnotes, dd. Kumase, July–August 2004.
30   *Prospectus: Golden Development Holding Company Ltd.*, Databank Brokerage Ltd. (Lead Manager), dd. Kumase (2002).
31   World Bank, IDA Grant H056 GH, 25 June 2003.
32   See now too Oduro-Mensah, 2007: I am grateful to Kate Skinner for drawing my attention to this book.
33   Benson/McCaskie, Fieldnotes, dd. Accra, July 2002.
34   Perbi, 2004, 200.
35   See Appiah et al. (n.d.), 245; see further Rattray, 1916, 124, and Christaller, 1990, 59.
36   See Wilks, 1993 for slavery and Asante origins.
37   See www.ghanaweb.com, Regional News, 'Speakers Call For Law To Protect Domestic Servants', 14 August 2007; and www.ghanaweb.com, Regional News, 'Child Labour, Modernized Form Of Domestic Slavery, Imperialism', 14 June 2007.
38   www.ghanaweb.com, General News, 'Jake Defines "Joseph Project"', 16 February 2007.
39   www.ghanaweb.com, Regional News, General News, 'Reparation For Slave Trade Not The Best Approach – JAK', 26 March 2007 (my emphasis).
40   www.ghanaweb.com, General News, 'Kufuor Punches The Hornet's Nest On Reparation', 29 March 2007.

4

After Abolition: Metaphors of Slavery in the Political History of the Gambia

Alice Bellagamba

Beyond Slavery: A Trajectory of Historical Metamorphosis

On a small island at the mouth of the River Gambia constantly menaced by erosion, the ruins of Fort St James – which UNESCO inscribed on the World Heritage List in 2003 – testify to the secular engagement of this area of West Africa with the traffic in slaves and with slavery as a social institution (Curtin, 1975; Meagher and Samuel, 1998; Wright, 2004). From the second half of the fifteenth century slaves were traded from the Senegambia to the Iberian Peninsula. By the sixteenth century the whole region participated in the transatlantic slave trade (Barry, 1998; Hair, 1980; Klein, 1990). The age of enslavement did not end with the closure of the Atlantic markets in the first half of the nineteenth century, as slavery had become a part of the economy of local societies. This institution began to die only in the 1890s. The first ordinance banning slave raiding and slave-trading from the territories of the River Gambia was promulgated in 1894 after the establishment of the British Protectorate. Colonial officials believed that the outlawing of the traffic in slaves would facilitate a smooth transition towards freedom in the long run (Bellagamba, 2005; Klein, 1998; Swindell and Jeng, 2006). The subsequent story was more complicated. Masters lamented their lost privileges. Conversely, slaves began their fight for upward mobility. Eventually, the legal status of slavery was completely abolished in 1930. Calling somebody a slave became a criminal offence, a piece of legislation which was included in the Laws of the Gambia (Ames, 1967) at the time of independence. 'Is it your father or your mother who bought me?' a descendant of slaves may currently say when annoyed by attempts at recalling in public his or her servile origins.[1]

As a social relationship slavery has survived its legal ending, though in circumscribed niches. Throughout the twentieth century, 'slaves' and 'masters' engaged in a complex process of reformulation of their reciprocal social and moral obligations (Cooper, 2000a; Klein, 2005b).[2] From the point of view of slaves, there were two options. Both were practised diversely in different areas of the country. The proportion is difficult to calculate given the lack of consistent colonial evidence on this point.

First and foremost, slaves could demand their freedom and did so in a variety of ways: by running away from their masters, by paying the redemption price established by the British legislation, by denouncing mistreatment and requesting certificates of freedom from colonial officials.[3] Involvement in commercial groundnut cultivation, constantly expanding along the river since the second half of the nineteenth century, rural–urban and transnational migrations, and education have sustained former slaves' efforts at building up new social identities for themselves and their children. This process has been accompanied by attempts to drop into oblivion their servile memories. To a certain extent the rest of society has complied with such strong desires for forgetting. The Gambia is a highly interconnected social environment where nobody really wishes to expose in public the distasteful details of other people's lives. Slave origins simply became a topic that encourages neither open discussions nor conversations.

The second option was to cultivate social proximity with former masters and might well have resulted from a lack of other practicable alternatives. In these circumstances, freedom meant renegotiated belonging to the social units into which slaves had been originally incorporated, rather than radical detachment. From the 1930s slaves gradually stopped working for their masters except for ceremonial occasions and small domestic tasks also performed by other categories of social dependents, such as juniors, women and strangers. Masters abandoned their customary responsibility for feeding, housing and taking care of their slaves in all phases of the life cycle. Despite enduring conflicts and tensions, the process has entailed a growing mutual respect and even affection between the two social categories, which reciprocally consider themselves as kin. In a number of settlements, whose foundation predates colonisation, historical slavery has been transformed into an openly recognised alliance between descendants of slaves and representatives of the former masters' class. The Mandinka verb *songma* – to accept – is used to underline the voluntary nature of this relationship, which is usually renewed for each newborn either on the side of 'slaves' or of 'masters' with a small ceremony.[4] The resulting bond is better conceived of as a form of family heritage to whose continuity both sides commit (Bellagamba, 2005, 34).

Today 'slaves' work for their 'masters' only on special and ceremonial occasions. Their labour is represented as a form of assistance and it is adequately compensated. They even chose who their 'master' should be, in the sense that a master who does not meet their expectations in terms of rewards and patronage can be abandoned in favour of a more powerful and generous personality. Being 'slave' or 'master' (and I deliberately put the two categories in inverted commas to stress the distance from their late nineteenth-century use) is conceived of as a hereditary condition. 'They believe in slavery' is the way in which such attachment to past hierarchies and social distinctions is described by Gambians who, on the contrary, consider slavery as a traditionalist vestige to be definitively consigned to the past. From a scholarly point of view, caution is necessary when dealing with the ambiguous and controversial developments of slavery after its legal abolition (Klein, 2005a, 2; Lovejoy, 2000).

Furthermore, the narrative of emancipation is supplemented by a second and suggestive story that unfolds beside and together with it. Processes transforming slavery into a reciprocal act of acceptance between masters and slaves probably intensified by the 1950s, thanks to the favourable economic conjuncture that lasted till the late 1960s. At the same time, political rhetoric captured the fresh and still-lived social memory of historical forms of enslavement and gave it a metaphorical afterlife. Thus the trajectory of slavery as a political trope of subjugation (Akyeampong, 2001, 2; Araujo, 2007; Bako-Arifari, 2000; Mbembe, 2002; McDougall, 2005) originated in its gradual death as a system of political domination and labour exploitation. The following pages attempt to explore this process of historical metamorphosis.

Twice at least, notably in the late 1950s and in the 1990s, slavery emerged into the Gambian public sphere. Such surfacing was only marginally related to the on-going processes of social adjustment in which 'slaves' and 'masters' had been reciprocally engaging since the 1894 ordinance against the traffic in slaves. In the first place it referred instead to colonial dominion and then to the persistent economic and social marginality of the Gambia and other African countries in the world economy decades after the achievement of independence. Democracy was at the top of the political agenda in both historical periods. The struggle for self-government and independence was begun in the 1950s and eventually achieved in 1965 and in 1970. This political era closed on 22 July 1994 when a small group of low-ranking officers of the Gambian army overthrew the democratically elected civilian government. Return to democracy in 1996 saw the head of the military junta becoming the President of the Second Republic, an office he still holds.

By practising an effort of contextualisation, I will try to assess the diverse use of the slavery metaphor in the two historical periods. The historical past they evoked was diverse, though similar in producing images of deprivation, social vulnerability and unjust subordination. Centuries of traffic in slaves and of life in slavery have in fact left the Gambia with a controversial and complex legacy made up of shifting discourses, practices and social activities associated with different historical periods. This legacy has an inner dimension made of remembrances of the late nineteenth century, a period in which slavery and the slave trade were described by colonial officials as still endemic in many areas of the country (Bellagamba, 2005, 15; Klein, 1977).

I would qualify this inner level as neither public, in the sense of being displayed on the national and international stage, nor completely private. Often enough such social memories work as public secrets, that is, knowledge widely shared within society but hardly articulated except for comments, gossip and fragments of recollections and oral traditions that might spontaneously surface in daily conversations. For a while, when the mask cracks, this knowledge becomes visible and discussed. Then manners, courtesy and self-control bury it again in the underground of social life, together with the painful emotions associated with this kind of remembrance (Roth and Jansen, 2000; Schulz, 2000, 71–72; Taussig, 1999).

In addition to this there is an 'extraverted' and more visible heritage of slavery made up of new museum exhibitions, renovated ruins of European buildings such as Fort St James, cultural festivals, movies and African-American tourism. This is the legacy that the government has appraised since the 1990s. I borrow the idea of 'extraversion' from François Bayart (2000) so as to stress the cultural reproduction of these recent discourses on slavery at the frontier between the Gambia and the rest of the world, and on a stage which is potentially global. By recalling the involvement of the River in the transatlantic slave trade, they connect the country to the long history of African forced and voluntary displacement towards Europe and the Americas, which I will critically comment upon in due course.

Debating Subjection and Freedom in the Late Colonial Period

People would provide a horse for the commissioner to travel. The town youths would assemble and carry his luggage from one post to the other, wherever he was going they would carry his luggage up to that point. At times also, some white men had those animals – you know baboons and monkeys – they had baboons and monkeys! Thus, if your turn to carry the loads coincides with those animals, you would carry them on your head. It would excrete and urinate on your head. That was a very sad and sorrowful situation, this was how we were.[5]

In this vivid way, Amadou Bansang Jobarteh talked of the experience of being a young man in rural colonial Gambia. As an elder he still felt the resentment of those days. The list was long: young men like him were controlled by the district chiefs, subordinated to the authority of family elders, mobilised for communal labour and for the personal needs of British officials. At the beginning of the 1960s, as the majority of his generation, Amadou joined the propaganda activities of the newly established Protectorate People's Party (soon renamed People's Progressive Party, the PPP). Later he established himself near the capital city of Banjul and became the bard and the praise-singer of one of the strongest political personalities of independence times.[6]

For learning about the metaphor of slavery in the anti-colonial struggle, remembrances of men like him are precious. The official narrative – both in the guise of scholarly analyses (Hughes, 1975; Hughes and Perfect, 2006) and of the 1992 volume published by the PPP party (PPP, 1992) – are silent in this respect. Amadou's recollections supplement officialdom, by recalling the challenges of an epoch that looked at the future as a time of progress and prosperity. As a matter of fact, politics as mass phenomenon was a development of the late 1950s linked to the launching of the PPP. The few political parties established before then got their support from Bathurst, the capital of the colony, while the Protectorate, administered as it was under a system of indirect rule, remained marginal to this early political debate.[7] District chiefs, who had gained a certain number of seats in the Legislative Council of the Colony after the Second World War, represented their rural subjects in the face of the colonial government. The situation was nonetheless evolving rapidly, and migrants from the Protectorate to the Colony played a major role in shaping the participation of rural areas in the political activities of the PPP.

Mobility to Bathurst had begun early in the twentieth century, mostly on a seasonal basis, as labour was needed during the commercial season when groundnuts were shipped to Europe (Swindell and Jeng, 2006, 120ff.). During the Second World War, government departments began to employ people permanently for the construction and maintenance of new infrastructure. By the end of the conflict flocks of young and illiterate rural men cultivated the aspiration of coming to town where they could get a salaried job that would emancipate them from the restraints of rural life.[8] Elderly men of this generation, like Amadou, could recall the efforts of their mates in travelling from the Upper River to Bathurst on foot, as the boat ticket was too expensive for them (Bellagamba, 2006a, 102). A few young men even attempted stowing away on ships going to Great Britain.

Periodically, the government forced the return of the Bathurst migrants to the home villages for fear of manpower shortages during the rainy season, and invited the chiefs to control the youth of their districts. Most were Mandinka as they were the support base of the PPP in the beginning.[9] A good number came from Baddibu, a region on the north bank of the river seriously affected by famine during wartime. Some belonged to good and respected families but did not have the chance to attend one of the few schools in the Protectorate. Families selected only a restricted number of children for Western-style education, following criteria which were cultural, religious (since the majority of rural schools were run by Catholics) and economic. The rest could find in trade, agriculture and migration to the commercial settlements along the river their space for achieving social maturity. Some others were probably the sons of slaves, though colonial records do not offer evidence to support such assumptions and oral sources provide little information.[10] The option of flight remained the favourite strategy for overcoming the social stigma of servile identity. Each generation of slaves' descendants had the opportunity to leave or stay in the areas where their forefathers and fathers had lived in bondage. In the 1950s parents born in slavery in their masters' houses or captured as children in the late nineteenth century might well have been content with having acquired land to cultivate on their own, control of the product of their labour and a voice on their children's future. Their sons, in turn, rebelled and wished for something more. Parents themselves supported the geographical mobility of youth as a means of economic and social advancement for the whole family.

Cultural associations, which the colonial administration encouraged, organised the social life of rural migrants in Bathurst and assisted them in times of need.[11] The proto-PPP began exactly like this. Initially called Protectorate People's Society (PPS), it then became a party and was renamed Protectorate People's Party (changed subsequently to Progressive People's Party and finally to People's Progressive Party) immediately before the first 1960s national elections. The founders of the association were young and literate men belonging to the rural elite or to an emerging class of educated government clerks (Hughes and Perfect, 2006, 136), who had moved to the Colony looking for jobs in the civil service or for opportunities of a scholarship abroad. Some were members of families whose prestige predated colonisation. Others were the sons of colonial parvenus enriched by their successful engagement in the commercial and agricultural economy of the Protectorate. This group of young men had to face 'the economic ascendancy and the social disdain' of the African elite of Bathurst (Hughes and Perfect, 2006, 134–35) and to witness the humiliation of their illiterate rural companions, who tried to enter the town's low-wage labour market. In 1957, they pursued the objective of awakening the political awareness of rural Gambians. Constitutional developments were just around the corner and the meetings of the association became the proper context to propagate the idea that Protectorate people were in the best position to promote and safeguard their own interests. They did not need Bathurst politicians and political parties, as they had their own literate representatives. Colonial officials and a certain number of district chiefs shared the same opinion, at the beginning at least (PPP, 1992, 11). In 1959 the colonial government conceded the electoral franchise to the Gambia. As for the Protectorate, the Colonial Office preferred to give the right to vote only to yard-owners, but the Governor of the Gambia opted for universal suffrage (Hughes and Perfect, 2006, 132).

By 1960 the PPS had evolved into a strong rural party. Having achieved the result of committing the migrants' community of Bathurst to having rural Gambians properly represented at the national level, it launched its propaganda activities in the Protectorate. Youth in particular responded with great enthusiasm. The agenda of the new party was simple but resonated with the feelings of exclusion and oppression of rural Gambians. The countryside needed development after years of neglect in favour of the Colony. In the nation-to-be they could not be subordinated to the political agenda of the African elite of Bathurst. Protectorate society had its internal hierarchies, as I stressed, but the PPP transcended rural status distinctions in winning the 1960 and 1962 elections. Cohesiveness prevailed over existing and emerging fractures.[12] Wealthy farmers, traders, notables, cattle-owners and even a certain number of district chiefs led their clienteles to support the party.[13] Subordinate categories, such as former slaves, women, youth and members of professional endogamous groups joined the flow. In these circumstances, they acted as clients but did not drop their desire for social emancipation.[14]

'Breaking the rope of slavery' became the political slogan of the party activists.[15] The slavery they talked about stood as a metaphor for contesting colonial rule though it took its cue from the history and lived experience of generations of slaves. In the PPP rhetoric all rural Gambians were slaves and risked remaining so if they dared not raise their voices. They toiled in the groundnut fields, they struggled with debts and with the requests of colonial officials and of district chiefs who backed their authority with coercion. Such domination could be equated to slavery and slavery indeed offered the most appropriate trope to contest the backwardness of the Protectorate against the more privileged economic, political and social status of the Colony. Bathurst had services, schools and a European style of life. Although substantially contributing to the economy of the country, rural areas had been neglected for decades. Subjugation to the colonisers and to their African allies could be overcome only by asserting the rights of the rural citizenry in the new national space.

'We have been slaves of the British. Should we now become slaves of the African elite of the colony?' was the kind of discourse circulating among party supporters.[16] Born and growing up in communities where master–slave bonds were part of daily life, even if the legal position of slave had been formally abolished, the PPS/PPP founders were familiar with the implications of a servile identity. They were not radicals and would never be, but they knew that the times were ripe for change. The official history of the party, for instance, insists on the egalitarian style of the PPS. From the beginning the association opted for internal democratic procedures, which could give voice to the aspirations and thoughts of each of its members regardless of social origin. This was a break with custom and established norms of behaviour. In rural society former slaves and descendants of slaves abided by the decisions of family elders, being passive political players like youth and women.[17] They rarely made their voices heard in community and public meetings. Silently they would follow communal discussions but did not intervene if not directly invited to do so. Public deference, together with humble manners and modest clothing, was part of the subordinate role that rural society ascribed to the slave category and to which they conformed by internalising the dominant ideology of their masters (Klein, 2005b, 833).

On the eve of the first elections, the choice of the PPP leader sounded equally innovative. Young men with good family origins had participated in the creation of the PPS/PPP. Yet the man who became the head of the party and lately the first President of the Gambia, although being the son of a very rich and successful trader, belonged to the endogamous professional group of leatherworkers. Arnold Hughes and David Perfect (2006, 137) list some of the reasons behind his ascent to leadership: he had a university degree; he was in a high position in the civil service, as head of the veterinary department; he knew the rural areas and rural people knew him. In their eyes, his social origins must have carried significance too. Like praise-singers and smiths, leatherworkers occupied an intermediate position between freeborn and slaves. A man with such a background could undoubtedly attract the consensus of all the PPP constituents irrespective of social origins. At least this was the opinion of those who supported his candidature within the party. Former slaves and descendants of slaves must have seen in such political talks a further chance to counter their social marginality.

At the beginning of my fieldwork, when questioned about the social trajectories of former low-status social categories, elderly men and women like Mama Baldeh, who was the daughter of a renowned colonial chief, kept repeating: 'they are ruling today'.[18] Beside the social origins of the first President of the Gambia, such assertions pointed to a more complex history of exit from slavery that needs to be reconstructed in depth. The general outline is in fact clear but details on specific trajectories of emancipation are concealed by the practice of the public secret, which characterises what I have defined as the inner legacy of slavery. Internal and international migrations undoubtedly played a role, along with the democratisation wave of the late 1950s and early 1960s.

Unlike what happened in Guinea Conakry or Mali, where Sekou Toureh or Modibo Keita directly addressed the aspirations for change of their slave constituents (Bayart, 2007; Berndt, 2007; Klein, in this volume), the PPP had no clear programme for social development. Its claims for freedom and for the acquisition of formal citizenship were coupled with a conservative agenda, which was directed at reassuring colonial officials, Protectorate elders and notables that the social order consolidated in decades of colonial rule would not break down with the achievement of independence. By restraining the influence of district chiefs, by offering new chances for political participation and visibility, by nurturing a diffuse awareness of civic and political rights, democracy interfered with local hierarchies. The PPP manipulated these reconfigurations in power relations to suit its electoral needs and undermine the rural elites' ability to form a political opposition. Former slaves, on their side, knew well how to work hard (Klein, 2005b, 845). The favourable economic juncture of the late 1950s and 1960s allowed them to improve their living conditions. They invested in the education of their children, who joined the expanding ranks of the civil service in the capital city. Some migrated abroad and decided not to return to the home villages, where their improved economic status would not easily translate into a new and emancipated lifestyle. As for the rest of rural Gambians, the aspirations to generalised socio-economic improvement that sustained the political mobilisation of the early 1960s were soon to be disillusioned. Becoming a ruling party, the PPP shifted to a more inclusive policy towards the African elite of the capital city (Hughes and Perfect, 2006, 171). Rural–urban exodus intensified as the country's economy began to show its structural weakness during the droughts and the petrol crisis of the 1970s (Nyang, 1977). The disparity between the Colony and the Protectorate that had inspired the PPP's early mobilisation reproduced itself in the guise of a widening socio-economic gap between the capital city and the provinces (Sallah, 1990; Wright, 2004, 233). Politicians neglected their rural constituents who, in turn, found themselves increasingly dependent on the patrimonial policies of the PPP elite. Contracts for party supporters came at the time of elections along with promises of services and positions in government. Loyal militants had to fight to maintain their visibility in the face of new and emerging constituents.

Before the 1994 coup international observers praised the Gambia for the results achieved with the 1985 plan of structural reforms, whose social costs had nonetheless been high. Lack of services and deteriorating infrastructures, the progressive impoverishment of rural households (Haswell, 1975; 1992), high mortality rates among women and children, and the youngest sections of the population being either underemployed or unemployed were part of the legacy consigned by the First Republic to the military government. Along with their families, who urged them to become socially responsible and economically productive, youth thought of international migrations as the way to counter their social exclusion. Members of the elite and the civil service sent their children to Great Britain or the USA to acquire educational qualifications, as the country lacked a university, which was to be launched by the new government. Common people shared the same dream of exit for their children.

Roots Festival and the Public Reappraisal of the Atlantic Slave Trade in the Gambia of the 1990s

Following the declarations of insecurity pronounced by the British High Commissioner in the aftermath of the 1994 military coup, the 1995 tourist season turned out to be almost a complete failure, with heavy consequences in terms of employment (Edie, 2000, 183). In an urgent effort to counter the economic decline, a few months before the 1996 presidential elections that would sanction the return to civilian rule the National Council for Arts and Culture launched the first 'Roots Home Coming' festival.[19] The celebration aimed at marketing the Gambia as a privileged destination for Afro-American tourists in order to promote links of friendship and economic and social cooperation between the two shores of the Atlantic.[20]

In the genealogy of the festival, two different events seem to dominate. On the one hand, the launching in 1993 by UNESCO of the Slave Route Project promoted a renewed interest in the monuments and historical sites relating to the traffic in slaves along the Western coast of Africa. Initiatives in Ghana and Benin predated those of the Gambia (Bruner, 1996; Hasty, 2002; Singleton, 1999) and representatives of the Gambian cultural sector participated in joint workshops with their Ghanaian colleagues. On the other hand, in the late 1960s Alex Haley visited the country in search of information about his African ancestors (Ebron, 1999; Haley, 1973; Wright, 1981). This fascinating story saw him interacting with Gambian intellectuals and government officials, and with Mandinka elders and bards who told him the genealogy and vicissitudes of the Kinteh family.

Haley identified the community of Juffureh (located at the mouth of the River in proximity to the old French commercial post of Albreda) as the home-village of his ancestor Kunta Kinteh. The publication of the novel *Roots* (1976), and the subsequent TV series based on the book, gave impetus to several initiatives at the national and local level. Gambian cultural officials carried out historical research on the European commercial posts along the River. The government helped the villagers of Juffureh to refurbish the settlement and to establish an arts and crafts market. In the course of the 1980s, as the Gambia tried to diversify its economy by developing the tourist industry, the village and the nearby locality of Albreda became privileged destinations for the daily excursions organised by the tourist resorts in proximity of the capital city.

Capitalising on Haley's heritage, the 'Roots Home Coming' festival was to become a regular contact between the Gambia and Africans in the diaspora, who came to Africa both to commemorate the suffering of their ancestors and in search of a taste of African life. The 1996 celebration was accompanied by a number of other events. One was the restoration of the ruins of Fort St James and the request to have this historic site placed on the UNESCO World Heritage List. Another was the creation of a new museum in Albreda explicitly dedicated to the traffic in slaves and situated in a renovated commercial house. The exhibit illustrated the historical connections between the Gambia and America created by the Atlantic slave trade. During the first Roots festival, the National Council for Arts and Culture also awarded a prize to Yacubu Saheed (1996), a Nigerian teacher, for his play *Chains*, on the contemporary vestiges of the Atlantic slave trade. In the following year, together with the newly established Gambian television company, the NCAC supported the production of a TV movie based on the play. The Roots festival had been intentionally designed for Afro-Americans so that they would appreciate the cultural richness of the country and sustain the feeble national economy with their investments. *Chains* attempted to become the vehicle of an explicit political critique whose targets were the rich Western countries, the African ruling elite and the masses of African youth who, disillusioned by politics and politicians, had given up hope in the future of their home-countries. This resonated with government propaganda against the disengagement of the youngest generations.

Babylon, the Youth and the Gambian Government

'Africans are chained to dreams of Babylon, they are the "willing slaves" of the West and the slavery of today is even worse than the forced slavery of before.' So the author of *Chains* commented in an interview released on the occasion of the official launch of the movie in 1997 (National Council for Arts and Culture, 1997, 3). Evocative of slavery in its references to the Hebrews' exile and their servitude in a foreign land, Babylon is the suggestive name that Gambian youth and their coevals from other West African anglophone countries have adopted to talk of Europe and North America as the privileged destination of their attempted migrations.[21]

When and how the image reached the Gambia is difficult to judge. Possibly it happened in the 1980s with reggae music, Bob Marley's songs, the spread to the Gambia of Rastafari culture and the beginning of international migration as a mass phenomenon, or perhaps even before through the contacts between expatriate Gambians and other West African migrants in Europe and the United States.[22] In any case, the biblical reference is loaded with ambivalent feelings of desire and dispossession – Babylon representing the land of plenty where successful migrants build up their fortunes – as well as being the context in which they experienced racism, exclusion and poverty. Both themes recur in *Chains* with a strong emphasis on the latter.

Two temporalities overlap in the narrative. There is the past, which has the flavour of myth, lacking any reference to when and where the events took place. In this past the audience is confronted with a group of white slave traders raiding a village by the river and deporting its inhabitants. Reference to the *Roots* novel and serial is evident and for those who are familiar with the River Gambia, the locality strikingly resembles Juffureh and surroundings. And there is the present, dominated by the biography of Salifu, a young and educated man who is critical of the structural adjustment policies imposed by international donors on the national economy of his country. Salifu wishes the political class to resist the international pressures. Disillusioned by the way the government agrees to implement reforms that will impoverish its citizenry, Salifu resigns from his position in the civil service and explains to his wife and friends his decision to leave the country to try his fortune in the USA:

> What are we all if not slaves? You must either be a slave of one thing or another. I would rather be a slave for the white man, get something out of it and still feel relevant in the society than do the same for these African leaders, whose sole aim seems to be only the continuous impoverishment of their people. (Saheed, 1996, 36)

After a long sequence of misadventures, which see him dwelling in marginality and alienation, Salifu dies in loneliness. Babylon betrayed his dreams and consumed his life. The story ends with the bitter comment of his best friend, whose words metaphorically associate the Atlantic slave trade of the past with the contemporary flux of Gambian, and more generally African, young men and women to the West. The position of the River Gambia in the world order remains the same, that of a provider of manpower.

> The whole tragedy of our continent seems to be reflected in Salifu's life. Whenever I think of him I'm filled with an uncontrollable anger but I do not know against whom this anger is directed. Is it for myself for all the compromises I made in my life? Is it for the white slavers of centuries ago, whose actions set in motion the tragedy we witness today? Or is it against a system that still lures us into willing slaves, chews all the goodness out of us and then spits us out? I can't tell. (Saheed, 1996, 48)

By espousing a narrative of victimisation centred on the enduring draining of human and material resources from Africa, *Chains* strongly evoked global discourses on the credit of the continent towards the West.[23] By highlighting the continuing marginality of African countries in the world economy and the inefficiency of their ruling classes, it captured feelings of deprivation and loss common to Gambian society as much as to the African Diaspora. Notably, the author of the script, like many other Nigerians and Ghanaians, worked as a teacher in the Gambia in the 1990s. He belonged to that category of migrants who circulated within the circumscribed space of anglophone West Africa and never reached either Europe or Northern America.

Last but not least, the political developments in the Gambia imbued the movie with specific and historically situated meanings. Behind the character of the corrupt politician, whom Salifu vehemently attacked, youth and Gambian society at large could see the representatives of the PPP regime. Commissions of Inquiry established by the military junta had revealed the misuse of public resources and the corrupt habits of civil servants and members of government, thus substantiating popular resentment towards the toppled elite (Edie, 2000; Hughes, 2000; Wiseman, 1998). By staging the failure of Salifu, *Chains* called for a renewed wave of patriotism during a period in which the government of the Gambia was not even as much committed as it is today to reduce illegal emigration to Europe and North America.[24] Instead, the military junta and the civilian government established after the 1996 elections pursued the more immediate objective of re-engaging young constituents in national politics.[25] They needed the support of youth to overcome the rise of an opposition front within the country and win the democratic transition. Far from being the green pastures they thought of, Babylon was built 'for its citizens' and offered nothing beside subjection to foreigners and aliens. Such was the public statement of a member of the junta a few months after the coup.[26]

As responsible citizens, youth had the concrete opportunity to engage in the development of their country. The message sounded particularly appealing to those categories of young men and women who were economically and socially vulnerable and would never succeed in their aspirations towards international mobility. After the military coup, concrete alternatives opened in front of them. Government requested their assistance to monitor its opponents within the villages. It asked youth to sustain the political and social innovations of the military junta by contesting the authority of elders, who had backed the previous regime.

In a process comparable to the gathering of youth around the PPP in the early 1960s, the young generation of the 1990s espoused the idea of a 'change of personnel' that could create opportunities for social advancement in terms of political offices, jobs, and material and social rewards. Such a desire for renovation coalesced in a popular initiative, the 22nd July Movement, whose young activists energetically espoused the cause of the new political order. Created in 1995 with the financial support of members of the junta, the movement was disbanded in 1999 (Hughes, 2000, 30) without many of its supporters having ever gained the social recognition they longed for.

International migration remains the privileged path to success for the youngest generations even if the narrative of youth's patriotism and return to the land continues to date. For some years the government has pushed for their re-engagement in agriculture. Even more than in the 1990s, the country's leadership has publicly denigrated the youngest sections of the population as lazy drug-addicts useless to their families and to the nation (Wright, 2004,

244). On their side, the Internet debates of opposition intellectuals have replied by critically identifying the oppressive practices of the incumbent regime and the ever-deteriorating economy of the Gambia as the major factors pushing the youngest generations abroad.[27] Metaphorically speaking, internal 'enslavement' contributes to the self-exile of youth to Babylon.

Bringing History to the Present

Metaphors have a provocative power; they move to action by transforming the ways in which a situation is perceived. Their force stems from their original embedding in history and experience and from their capacity to suggest innovative and imaginative links that lump together formerly disconnected and often remote domains of thought (Fernandez, 1974, 132). Culturally and socially entrenched in the long-term history of the River Gambia, slavery, enslavement and slave-trading have presented (and continue to present) politics and society with evocative images to antagonise contemporary forms of submission and exploitation. Such processes of resurgence exemplify the complex and creative returns of the past in the present and break the conventional historical periodisation between the pre-colonial, the colonial and the post-colonial (McCaskie, 2007; Shaw, 2001; Spear, 2003).

Throughout the twentieth century and still today the inner legacy of slavery has remained vivid within society. The reasons for this survival are manifold. Slavery constitutes the background of formal oral traditions, especially in the case of Mandinka bards, even if this part of their repertoire is rarely narrated in public. It proves instead useful in the context of private negotiations. When bards talk about the late nineteenth-century polities, they depict a world of raiding, military leaders and big traders who participated in the groundnut economy of the River thanks to the work of their slaves. Slavery, furthermore, has marked the social experience of generations of elderly men and women and has been the subject of disputes which, though mostly resolved within the confidential circles of the family, have contributed to keeping alive a debate on its social and cultural vestiges. Such a set of memories was even more emotionally overloaded at the time of the anti-colonial struggle, when the generation of slaves resulting from the slave raiding of the late nineteenth century was still alive.

Frederick Cooper (2000a, 9) sees freedom and slavery as historical and cultural constructs whose contents shift in time and contexts. The discourse of freedom in the late 1950s and early 1960s was constructed against the inner legacy of slavery, particularly in the rural areas where the social stigma attached to servile identities implied second-class belonging in key social networks. Instead of siding with former slaves, the political rhetoric of the PPP stretched the lived significance of life in bondage to cover the diverse experiences of forced labour, of colonial dominion and of peasants' subordination to the despotism of colonial district chiefs. Real and enduring differences between former 'masters' and 'slaves' were put aside. The latter continued their patient and individual battles for social recognition.

As a matter of fact, the political use (and abuse) of the slavery metaphor does not provide for its historical accuracy. As soon as they are created, metaphors enjoy an autonomous life, which sees them crossing diverse social domains and acquiring meanings that distance them from the contexts out of which they were originally produced. At each turn in history, this detachment from the material facts at the origin of historical metaphors may increase (Austen, 2001, 229).

The late twentieth-century public reappraisal of the memory of slavery, as I remarked, deals with a remote past whose traces are long gone.[28] It completely ignores the living and inner legacy of slavery and fills this void in concrete historical references by assembling fragments from different and disparate sources (Mbembe, 2002, 259). There is the legacy of Alex Haley and *Roots*, the biblical image of Babylon as spread in West anglophone Africa and the global narrative of Africa as a victim of the predatory attitude of Western and developed countries. Beside the Gambia, such discourses could fit any other contemporary West African country. Yet, despite their extraverted nature, they are able to address the public secret of current times, which is as painful as the concealed memories of past enslavement. Babylon, the land that the narrative of successful returnees depicts to coevals and society as the place of material abundance and economic opportunities, is for others the context of enduring and dramatic humiliation. The failed migration projects of the anonymous young men and women who disappeared in Europe and North America or came back defeated and longing for reintegration within their families and communities are not easily commented upon even in confidential circles.[29]

Thus, nurtured by contemporary suffering, the metaphor of slavery remains vital, socially attractive and ready for transmogrification. I give just two examples of its recent coming back to the public stage. On the occasion of the 2006 presidential elections, an extremely critical article appeared on the Internet. Its style revealed the familiarity of the author with the political history of the country. By calling the current government a slave-master regime it recalled the discussions that animated the late 1950s. The main topic of the article were the relationships between the country's leadership and the civil service, as since the end of the PPP regime civil servants have been kept in a state of constant fear for their jobs.[30] During the 2007 rainy season, government repeated its 'back to the land call', asking the national community at large to assist in the cultivation of presidential farms in rural areas. For the government of the day and its supporters such efforts were meant to reinvigorate the national economy. For opponents, this new form of enslavement exposed the long record of abuses in human and civic rights that has characterised the country since the military coup (Ceesay, 2006; Hughes and Perfect, 2006).[31] As it is premature to say whether such debates will ever develop into innovative forms of political participation that might ultimately open an alternative future, my narrative ends up waiting for the next metaphorical rising of slavery in the political life and discourse of the Gambia.

References

Ames, Sir Cecil G., ed., 1967. *The Laws of The Gambia, in force of the 1st day of July, 1966.* Bathurst, The Gambia: The Government Printer; London: Sweet and Maxwell.

Akyeampong, E., 2001. 'History, Memory, Slave-Trade and Slavery in Anlo (Ghana).' *Slavery and Abolition,* 22(3), pp. 1–24.

Araujo, A. L., 2007. 'Political Uses of Memories of Slavery in the Republic of Benin.' *History in Focus,* Issue 12: Slavery, http://www.history.ac.uk/ihr/Focus/Slavery/articles/araujo.html.

Austen, R., 2001. 'The Slave Trade as History and Memory: Confrontations of Slaving Voyage Documents and Communal Traditions.' *William and Mary Quarterly,* 58(1), pp. 229–44.

Bako-Arifari, N., 2000. 'La Mémoire de la traite négrière dans le débat politique au Bénin dans les années 1990.' *Journal des Africanistes* 70(1–2), pp. 221–32.

Barry, B., 1998. *Senegambia and the Atlantic Slave Trade: Senegambia before the Colonial Conquest.* Cambridge: Cambridge University Press.

Bayart, F., 2000. 'Africa in the World: A History of Extraversion.' *African Affairs,* 99(395), pp. 217–67.

Bayart, F., 2007. 'Les Chemins de traverse de l'hégémonie coloniale en Afrique de l'Ouest francophone. Anciens esclaves, anciens combattants, nouveaux musulmans.' *Politique Africaine,* 105, pp. 201–40.

Bellagamba, A., 2005. 'Slavery and Emancipation in the Colonial Archives: British Officials, Slave Owners, and Slaves in the Protectorate of the Gambia (1890–1936).' *Canadian Journal of African Studies,* 39(1), pp. 5–41.

Bellagamba, A., 2006a. 'Personal Memories, Historical Recollections and Political Activism in Contemporary Gambia. Anthropological Perspectives on Social Memory.' In P. Hautaniemi, H. Jerman and S. MacDonald, eds, *Anthropological Yearbook of European Cultures,* 15, pp. 93–116.

Bellagamba, A., 2006b. 'Before It Is Too Late: Constructing an Archive of Oral Sources and a National Museum in Independent Gambia.' *Africa Today,* 52(4), pp. 29–54.

Berndt, J., 2007. 'Speaking as Scholars: The First Generation of Slave Moodibabe in Gimbala, Northern Mali.' Paper presented at the international Workshop 'Looking for the African Voices: Narratives of Slavery and Enslavement', Rockfeller Foundation, Bellagio, 24–28 September 2007.

Bruner, E., 1996. 'Tourism in Ghana. The Representation of Slavery and the Return of the Black Diaspora'. *American Anthropologist* 98(2), pp. 290–304.

Ceesay, E., 2006. *The Military and Democratization in The Gambia: 1994–2003.* Victoria, BC: Trafford Publishing.

Cohen, R. and Middleton, J., eds, 1970. *From Tribe to Nation in Africa: Studies in the Incorporation Process.* Scranton, PA: Chandler.

Cooper, F., 2000a. 'Introduction'. In F. Cooper, T. C. Holt and R. J. Scott, eds, *Beyond Slavery. Explorations of Race, Labor, and Citizenship in Postemancipation Societies.* Chapel Hill, NC, and London: University of North Carolina Press, pp. 1–32.

Cooper, F., 2000b. 'Conditions Analogous to Slavery. Imperialism and Free Labor Ideology in Africa'. In F. Cooper, T. C. Holt and R. J. Scott, eds, *Beyond Slavery. Explorations of Race, Labor, and Citizenship in postemancipation societies*. Chapel Hill, NC, and London: University of North Carolina Press, pp. 107–56.

Cooper, F., 2001. 'What Is the Concept of Globalization Good For? An African Historian's Perspective.' *African Affairs*, 100, pp. 189–213.

Curtin, P., 1975. *Economic Change in Precolonial Africa. Senegambia in the Era of the Slave Trade.* Madison, WI: University of Wisconsin Press.

Davidheiser, M., 2006. 'Joking for Peace. Social Organization, Tradition and Change in Gambian Conflict Management.' *Cahiers d'Études Africaines*, 184, pp. 835–60.

de Bruijn, M. and Pelckmans, L., 2005. 'Facing Dilemmas. Former Fulbe Slaves in Northern Mali.' *Canadian Journal of African Studies*, 39(1), pp. 69–95.

Ebron, P., 1997. 'Traffic in Men.' In M. Grosz-Ngate and O. H. Kokole, eds, *Gendered Encounters: Challenging Cultural Boundaries and Social Hierarchies in Africa*. New York and London: Routledge, pp. 223–44.

Ebron, P., 1999. 'Tourists as Pilgrims: Commercial Fashioning of Transatlantic Politics.' *American Ethnologist*, 26(4), pp. 910–32.

Edie, C. J., 2000. 'Democracy in The Gambia: Past, Present and Prospects for the Future.' *Africa Development* XXV(3–4), pp. 161–99.

Fernandez, J., 1974. 'The Mission of Metaphor in Expressive Culture.' *Current Anthropology*, 15(2), pp. 119–45.

Fletcher, A. J., 1978. 'Party Politics in the Gambia.' Unpublished PhD thesis, University of California.

Gailey, H. A., 1964. *A History of The Gambia*. London: Routledge and Kegan Paul.

Gamble, D., 1955. *Economic Conditions in Two Mandinka Villages: Kerewan and. Keneba*. London: Her Majesty's Stationery Office.

Gilroy, P., 2005. 'Could You Be Loved? Bob Marley, Anti-Politics and Universal Sufferation.' *Critical Quarterly*, 47(1–2), pp. 226–45.

Gray, J. M., 1966 (1940). *History of The Gambia*. London: Frank Cass.

Hair, P. E. H., 1980. 'Black African Slaves at Valencia, 1482–1516: An Onomastic Inquiry.' *History in Africa*, 7, pp. 119–39.

Haley, A., 1973. 'Black History, Oral History and Genealogy.' *The Oral History Review* 1, pp. 1–25.

Hasty, J., 2002. 'Rites of Passage, Routes of Redemption: Emancipation Tourism and the Wealth of Culture.' *Africa Today*, 49(3), pp. 47–76.

Haswell, M., 1953. *Economics of Agriculture in a Savannah Village*. London: Her Majesty Stationery Office.

Haswell, M., 1975. *The Nature of Poverty. A Case Study of the First Quarter Century After World War II*. London: MacMillan.

Haswell, M., 1992. 'Population and Change in a Gambian Rural Community, 1947–1987'. In M. Haswell and D. Hunt, eds, *Rural Households in Emerging Societies*. Oxford: Berg, pp. 141–71.

Hughes, A., 1975. 'From Green Uprising to National Reconciliation: The People's Progressive Party in the Gambia, 1959–1973.' *Canadian Journal of African Studies*, 9(1), pp. 61–74.

Hughes, A., 2000. 'Democratization under the Military in the Gambia: 1994–2000.' *Commonwealth and Comparative Politics*, 38(3), pp. 35–52.

Hughes, A. and Perfect, D., 2006. *A Political History of The Gambia, 1816–1994*. Rochester, NY: Rochester University Press.

Jewsiewicki, B. 2004. 'Héritages et réparations en quête d'une justice pour le passé ou le présent.' *Cahiers d'Études Africaines*, 173–74, pp. 7–24.

Klein, M. A., 1977. 'Servitude among the Wolof and Sereer of Senegambia.' In Kopytoff and Miers, eds, 1977, pp. 335–63.

Klein, M. A., 1990. 'The Impact of the Atlantic Slave Trade on the Societies of the Western Sudan.' *Social Science History*, 14(2), pp. 231–53.

Klein, M. A., 1998. *Slavery and Colonial Rule in French West Africa*. Cambridge: Cambridge University Press.

Klein, M. A., 2005a. 'The Persistence of Servility.' *Canadian Journal of African Studies*, 39(1), pp. 1–4.

Klein, M. A., 2005b. 'The Concept of Honor and the Persistence of Servility in the Western Sudan.' *Cahiers d'Études Africaines*, 45(179–80), pp. 831–51.

Kopytoff, I. and Miers. S., eds, 1977. *Slavery in Africa*. Madison, WI: University of Wisconsin Press.

Lovejoy, P., 2000. 'Identifying Enslaved Africans in the African Diaspora.' In P. Lovejoy, ed., *Identity in the Shadow of Slavery*. London and New York: Continuum, pp. 1–29.

Mahoney F., 1963. 'Government and Public Opinion in The Gambia, 1816–1901.' Unpublished PhD dissertation, University of London.

Mbembe, A. 2002. 'African Modes of Self-Writing.' *Public Culture*, 14(1), pp. 239–73.

McCaskie, T., 2007. 'The Life and Afterlife of Yaa Asantewaa.' *Africa*, 77(2), pp. 151–79.

McDougall, A., 2005. 'Living the Legacy of Slavery. Between Discourse and Reality.' *Cahiers d'Études Africaines*, 45(179–80), pp. 957–86.

Meagher, A. and Samuel, A., eds, 1998. *Historic Sites of The Gambia. An Official Guide to the Monuments and Sites of The Gambia*. Banjul, The Gambia: National Council for Arts and Culture and Roc International.

Meillassoux, C., ed., 1975. *L'Esclavage en Afrique precoloniale*. Paris: Maspero.

National Council for Arts and Culture, 1997. *Roots News 1997*. Banjul, The Gambia: New Type Press.

Nyang, S. 1977. 'Ten Years of Gambia's Independence. A Political Analysis.' *Presence Africaines*, 104, pp. 28–45.

PPP, 1992. *The Voice of the People. The Story of the PPP 1959–1989*. Banjul, The Gambia: Baroueli Publications.

Rochmann, C., ed., 2000. *Esclavage et abolitions. Mémoires et systèmes de représentation*. Paris: Karthala.

Roth, M. and Jansen, J., 2000. 'Introduction: The Social Life of Knowledge.' *Mande Studies*, 2, pp. 1–6.

Saheed, Y., 1996. *Chains*. Banjul, The Gambia: N.P.C.S.

Saine, A., 2000. 'The Gambia's Foreign Policy Since the Coup: 1994–1999.' *Commonwealth and Comparative Politics*, 38(2), pp. 73–88.

Sallah, T. M., 1990. 'Economics and Politics in The Gambia.' *The Journal of Modern African Studies*, 28(4), pp. 621–48.

Savishinsky, N., 1994. 'Rastafari in the Promised Land: The Spread of a Jamaican Socio-religious Movement among the Youth of West Africa.' *African Affairs*, 37(3), pp. 19–50.

Sayad, A., 2004. *The Suffering of the Immigrant*. Cambridge: Polity Press.

Schulz, D., 2000. 'Seductive Secretiveness: Jeliw as Creators and Creations of Ethnography.' *Mande Studies*, 2, pp. 55–80.

Shaw, R., 2001. 'Cannibal Transformations: Colonialism and Commodification in the Sierra Leone Hinterland.' In H. L. Moore and T. Sanders, eds, *Magical Interpretations, Material Realities: Modernity, Witchcraft and the Occult in Postcolonial Africa*. London and New York: Routledge, pp. 50–70.

Singleton, T. A., 1999. 'The Slave Trade Remembered on the Former Gold and Slave Coasts.' *Slavery and Abolition*, 20(1), pp. 150–69.

Spear, T., 2003. 'Neo-traditionalism and the Limits of Invention in British Colonial Africa.' *Journal of African History*, 44, pp. 3–27.

Swindell, K. and Jeng, A., 2006. *Migrants, Credit and Climate. The Gambian Groundnut Trade, 1834–1934*. Leiden: Brill.

Taussig, M. T., 1999. *Defacement: Public Secrecy and the Labor of the Negative*. Stanford, CA: Stanford University Press.

Wallerstein, I., 1960. 'Ethnicity and National Integration in West Africa.' *Cahiers d'Études Africaines*, 1(3), pp. 129–39.

Weil, P., 1968. 'Mandinka Mansaya. The Role of the Mandinka in the Political System of the Gambia.' Unpublished PhD dissertation, University of Oregon.

Wiseman, J. A., 1985. 'The Social and Economic Bases of Party Political Support in Serekunda, The Gambia.' *The Journal of Commonwealth and Comparative Politics*, 23(1), pp. 3–29.

Wiseman, J. A., 1998. 'The Gambia: From Coup to Elections.' *Journal of Democracy*, 9(2), pp. 64–75.

Wright, D. R., 1981. 'Up-rooting Kunta Kinte. On the Perils of Relying on Encyclopedic Informants.' *History in Africa*, 8, pp. 205–27.

Wright, D. R., 1991. 'Requiem for the Use of Oral Tradition to Reconstruct the Precolonial History of the Lower Gambia.' *History in Africa*, 18, pp. 399–408.

Wright, D. R., 2004. *The World and a Very Small Place in Africa: A History of Globalization in Niumi, the Gambia*. Armonk, NY: M. E. Sharpe.

Notes

1   Recording with Bambi Jobarteh, Bansang 22/12/1992 and 10/01/1003. Recording with Maudo Suso, Talinding, 13/06/2000. Maudo's text belongs to a set of narratives devoted to the historical memory of slavery which I collected in 2000 along with Bakary Sidibe, creator of the Gambian Cultural Archives and former Director of the National Council for Arts and Culture. I hereby thank him for his friendship and patience in supporting my research efforts over the years. Fieldwork was carried out in the frame of MEBAO (Missione Etnologica in Bénin e Africa Occidentale). This is a national co-ordinated research project jointly financed by the Italian Ministry of Foreign Affairs and the Department of Human Sciences for Education 'Riccardo Massa' of the University of Milan-Bicocca, which I have directed since 2000.

2   Relative to emancipation, evidence in the colonial archive is scanty and fragmented. The interest of colonial officials in documenting the topic of slavery had already waned at the beginning of the twentieth century. We find references to the social stigma of slave origins, a few court cases on disputes between masters and slaves, and some notes on the transformation of slavery into a hereditary social condition that began to be reproduced by selective marriage practices after abolition. David Gamble, who worked as a government anthropologist in the Gambia in the 1950s and 1960s, assembled part of this information in a dossier on slavery, which is currently available at the National Archives of the Gambia. See National Archives of the Gambia, NGR1/19, Dr Gamble's file on Slavery (previously CSO 76/19).

3   Records of the late nineteenth century, and relating to the north and south bank regions just annexed to the Protectorate, spoke of the running away of recently acquired slaves and of the worries of the British administration about the resulting social disturbances. See National Archives of the Gambia, Banjul, Annual Reports on Provinces 32/1, Travelling Commissioner's reports, North Bank 1893–1898.

4   I base these remarks on my ethnographic familiarity with the social structures of the Upper River Gambia where I have been carrying out research since 1992. The notion of 'acceptance' recognises a certain agency on the side of slaves and of their descendants. It also speaks of a temporary achieved agreement between the two social parties. Acceptance, however, may also be the by-product of a lack of opportunities and even of a sort of fatalism. I offer an example drawn from another social domain. A wife accepts a husband's mistreatment as she knows that her family will never agree to her

divorce. She does not like the situation she lives in but she practises acceptance, which demands the public silencing of her personal feelings. Mark Davidheiser (2006) has recently stressed the high social value attached to concepts of patience and forbearance in Gambian society.

5 Recording with Amadou Bansang Jobarteh, Kembuje, 12/06/1998. Born in 1915 in the commercial settlement of Bansang, Amadou Bansang was a bard and an internationally renowned kora player with a vast historical knowledge on the Upper River and the coastal regions of the Gambia.

6 This personality was Sanjally Bojang. For biographical details see Hughes and Perfect, 2006, 135–36.

7 Established in 1816 at the mouth of the River as a military post to suppress the Atlantic slave trade, Bathurst became a commercial base for a number of British merchants who left the Island of Gorée after its return to France. Wolof artisans from the French Colony of Senegal joined the settlement as well. During the nineteenth century the town grew thanks to the resettlement of liberated Africans from Sierra Leone to the Gambia (Gray, 1966; Mahoney, 1963). Gradually an educated and prosperous African elite engaged in trade and professions emerged and made its voice audible in the government of the town. Created during the 1890s, the Protectorate had a completely different historical trajectory. It also differed from the Colony as far as ethnic composition was concerned. Mandinka and other Mande-speaking groups formed the majority of the Protectorate population, followed by the Fulbe, the rural Wolofs and the Diola. For historical details on the development of Bathurst see Gailey, 1964; Gray, 1966.

8 National Archives of the Gambia, ARP5, Development and Welfare in the Gambia, Chapter 12, Labour, Bathurst, The Government Printer, 1943. Compiled during the war and then supplemented with further notes and information, the report offers a picture both of the changes occurring within society and of the policies of the colonial administration.

9 The PPP began as a Mandinka party, as the majority of Protectorate Gambians were Mandinka. Yet the party rapidly gained the support of other ethnic groups, including the Diola of the coastal regions. On such developments see Fletcher, 1978; Hughes, 1975; and Nyang, 1977. Ethnic issues have become particularly sensitive since the military coup, the partisan rhetoric of the ruling party insisting on depicting Mandinka as tribalists who under the PPP regime dominated the political life of post-colonial Gambia at the expenses of other ethnic groups.

10 Among the remarks from oral sources is the fact that descendants of these former slaves did not seem ready to overtly declare their social origins. In some cases they do not even know the servile status of their grandparents and parents. See, for instance, recording with Bakoyo Suso, Dippakunda, 2/05/2000 and with Maudo Suso, Talinding, 13/06/2000.

11 National Archives of the Gambia, ARP5, Development and Welfare in the Gambia, Chapter 12, Labour, and Chapter 15, Social Welfare, Bathurst, The Government Printer, 1943.

12 The 1960s literature on the African State was very preoccupied with the role played by ethnic and tribal divisions in electoral competition (for instance Cohen and Middleton, 1970; Wallerstein, 1960), but class and status distinctions were overlooked, probably due to ignorance of the role that the distinction between freeborn and slaves still played in many parts of the continent. Functionalist anthropology usually ignored the topic of slavery and therefore gave the debates of the late 1950s and 1960s a cohesive image of the African rural landscape. Awareness of slavery was to come only during the 1970s, with the pioneer works of Claude Meillassoux (1975) and Igor Kopytoff and Susanne Miers (1977).

13 The position of the district chiefs in national politics was complicated. First, the newly established PPP looked for their support. Then during the 1962 elections the party adopted an open anti-chief stance. Chiefs, on their side, withdrew their support from the party immediately after the 1960s elections, probably in order to defend their position at the national level. Hints are in Gailey, 1964, and in Hughes and Perfect, 2006. See also n. 15.

14 For rural Gambians there was not much alternative to the rising tide of PPP political mobilisation. The United Party (the other important political organisation of the time) was strong in the Colony and in the Upper River, where it had sustained the early grievances of peasants, traders and cattle-owners against the abuses of district chiefs. But the UP position was to evolve in a more conservative direction after the 1960 elections in an effort to capture the support of district chiefs. The first Constitution had reserved eight seats to the chiefs in the House of Representatives, thus enabling them to strongly influence the national political sphere. The number of seats was reduced to four in preparation of the 1962 elections, which saw the PPP win control of the country.

15 As shown by Frederick Cooper (2000b, 138), after the Second World War the group of African delegates led in Paris by Félix Houphuët-Boigny focused attention on slavery and forced labour in the French parliament. This led to the abolition of forced labour in French West Africa in 1946. In the Gambia the colonial administration had already questioned the legitimacy of the institution of forced labour in the mid-1930s but then decided on the more neutral expression of communal labour. Hidden by such cosmetic change, the practice of forced labour continued until independence.

16 Recording with Farli Kurubally, Seineh Darboe, Fode e Bakary Sidibe, Talinding, 3/08/2002 and 7/08/2002.

17 For details on the social structures of rural Gambia in this specific historical period see Gamble 1955; Haswell 1953. Peter Weil (1968) had the chance to observe the developments that followed the achievement of independence.

18 Recording with Mama Baldeh, Bansang, 19/01/1993 and 6/12/1994.

19 The National Council for Arts and Culture is the government body responsible for preserving national heritage and promoting cultural activities. I described the trajectory of this institution since independence in Bellagamba, 2006b.

20 For some information on the recent festivals, see the official website of the initiative http://www.rootsgambia.gm.

21 I owe this insight to conversations with Paolo Gaibazzi on the research he carried out between 2006 and 2008 on youth, international migration and the Soninke communities of the Upper River Gambia.

22 On the spread of the Rastafari movement in anglophone West Africa see Savishinsky, 1994. On Bob Marley and his message of liberation see Gilroy, 2005. Different observers have commented on the development of youth counter-cultures in the Gambia, especially as far as the coastal and tourist areas are concerned. See for instance Ebron, 1997.

23 In a recent collection of essays, Bogumil Jewsiewicki (2004) provides an assessment of these debates and of their current political relevance.

24 The engagement of the Gambia in the struggle against illegal migration came to the fore in the course of 2005 and 2006, when the Gambian and Senegalese shores became one of the major departing points for the boats of emigrants trying to reach the Canary Islands. In the months that followed the repatriation of the clandestine migrants, the Spanish government funded both the Gambia and Senegal to develop specific programmes for the reinsertion of returnees. In the Gambia rumours spread of the funds having been misused to reinforce the repressive apparatus of the state. See for instance 'Spain probably funding Gambia torture unit', 22 September 2006, afroInews, http://www.afrol.com/articles/22860.

25 Wiseman (1985) commented on the disillusioned attitude of Gambian youth towards politics at the time of the First Republic. Youth radicalism and dissatisfaction against the PPP government led to an aborted coup in 1981, followed by the rapid restoration of the status quo thanks to the intervention of the Senegalese army (Hughes and Perfect, 2006, 210ff.)

26 'Time is running out', *Daily Observer*, 13/10/1994.

27 For instance, 'The Dilemma of Gambian Youth' by Baboucar Caeesay, Foroyaa Newspaper Burning Issues, Issue no. 77/2005, 3–5 October 2005.

28 In a critical essay, Donald Wright (1991) has questioned the utility of oral traditions for reconstructing the history of the River Gambia and showed how far they have been influenced by the political developments of the twentieth century. As a matter of fact, oral traditions provide useful insights for discussing how slavery and the trade in slaves were practised along the River in the late part of the nineteenth century. They are, however, completely silent on the previous centuries of Atlantic connections apart from a few remarks which seem indeed the by-product of recent exposure to media and global discourses on slavery.

29 Another critical point relating to the emigration trend of the past decades has been explained by several observers of the Gambia's foreign policy of the 1990s (for instance Saine, 2000). Neither the military government nor its civilian successor has ever tried to part with the neo-liberal policies embraced by the previous leadership of the country with the Economic Recovery Program in 1985. Thus emigration as an epochal process is embedded in a number of public secrets or 'lies' to use the more direct expression of Abdelmalek Sayad (2004), which hide the actual economic position of the Gambia in the world order behind the public rhetoric of containing youth's dreams of exit. For an overview of the economic agenda of the military government see the programmatic document produced in the aftermath of the coup, in which the junta explains its agenda for the development of the country in detail (Vision 2020, Foreword, 1996, http://www.statehouse.gm/vision2020).

30 'Is Jammeh a slave-master President', AllGambian.net, 22 December 2006.

31 'Slave Labour at President Jammeh's Farm (The Verdict)' by Adama Hawa, *The Gambian Echo*, 22 September 2007.

5

Islamic Patronage and Republican Emancipation: The Slaves of the Almaami in the Senegal River Valley

Jean Schmitz

The only solution proposed by President Wade when faced with the Senegalese boat crisis in the summer of 2006 was the REVA (Retour vers l'Agriculture) Plan for agricultural development. The Senegalese interviewed on the Plan's objectives responded briefly and negatively. Their lack of enthusiasm bespoke a situation familiar to all and yet difficult to explain to international donors: disregard for agricultural work inherited from the time when this activity was restricted to 'slaves'. This essay attempts to write the regressive history (Bloch, 1955) of this unspoken knowledge and to reassess its sociological import. The question of internal slavery was until recently taboo in Senegal. Moreover, the focus on a certain reading of Atlantic slavery, of which the recent operations associated with Gorée Island constitute a good example, 'magically' cleared Senegal from all suspicion of compromise with slavers, seen as unquestionably 'Western' (Schmitz, 2006; Thioub, 2002; 2005). This essay aims at breaking this cultural silence by questioning the effects of this censorship of the internal history of Senegalese slavery.

The essay focuses particularly on two strategies of emancipation of Muslim slaves in the Senegal River valley. The first section looks at the integration of slave descendants into the larger cohort of the rural poor, including fishermen and FulBe (or Peuls) herders, through the local reconfiguration of dependent relations and the acquisition of land via patrimonial practices.[1] Far from being a new phenomenon, this process of land appropriation recalls the trajectories of change promoted through Islamisation and leading to the establishment of the Fuuta Tooro imamate at the end of the eighteenth century. Hence this pattern of emancipation is situated in the *longue durée* of Senegambian regional history, challenging the widespread tendency of historians of African slavery to attribute emancipation solely or primarily to European action. The second part outlines patterns of social mobility characteristic of colonial times, which saw slave descendants joining the Senegalese Rifles (*tirailleurs sénégalais*) and

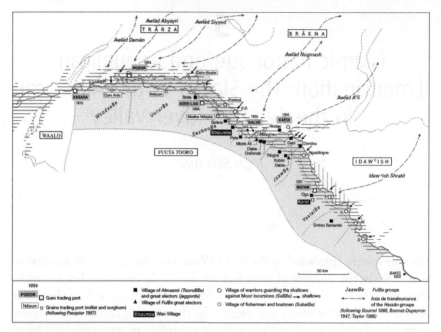

Figure 5:1 The Islamic state of Fuuta Tooro at the end of the 18th and 19th centuries: *Almaami* and electors

taking up school teaching positions thanks to the patronage of some former masters. While this second pattern is anchored in opportunities that became available through colonial intervention, close examination of individual cases reveals considerable cultural continuity with pre-colonial emancipation strategies. In particular, it is by *relying on* the patronage of former masters, rather than by severing all ties of dependence, that a section of ex-slaves was able to overcome slave status.

Engaging critically with the 1980s debate on the paradoxes of belonging and exclusion of African slavery (Cooper et al., 2000; Kopytoff, 1988), the present chapter sheds light on change and continuity in avenues of emancipation in the Senegal River valley since the late eighteenth century. Instead of considering slaves individually, it examines the ways in which the relative strength of the stigma attached to slave status resulted from the nature of the ex-slaves' relationships with ex-masters and freemen in general (Elias and Scotson, 1965). In the contexts considered here, the maintenance and renegotiation of dependence is key to the slave's social mobility. Thus, the essay examines examples of the transformation of slave–master relations into patron–client relations. The particular avenues and cultural idioms for renegotiating dependence changed across time. Yet, ultimately, they led to the acquisition of a new status for former slaves, within new social networks (e.g. Islamic brotherhoods, the military, schoolteachers). On the basis of research conducted since the 1980s in Mboumba and Meri,[2] coupled with information collected in 2006 at the Ceerno WanwanBe's enthronement in Kanel and new research carried out in 2007 among schoolteachers in Dakar, this study begins to unveil some of the processes hidden behind the conventional silence that surrounds Senegalese trajectories of slavery.

Islamic Patronage and Pre-colonial Emancipation: Patrimonialism, Clientelism and the Integration of Slaves into the Rural Poor

In February 2006 I was invited to assist at the enthronement of the last Ceerno WanwanBe[3] from the Wan family, which had supplied numerous imams (or *almaami*) of the Fuuta Tooro nineteenth-century Islamic state, as well as several colonial canton chiefs (*chefs de canton*). In the procession of castemen at the ceremony I was surprised by the absence of representatives of slave groups (*maccuBe* or *gallunkooBe*) from Kanel, one of the two capitals of the Wan family in the Matam District. Having worked near Mboumba in the district of Podor (west of Matam), where the almaami of the nineteenth century were settled in the 1980s, I knew that slave descendants formed the majority of cultivators of the village's irrigated perimeters (fig. 1). Here, in the 1980s, I conducted

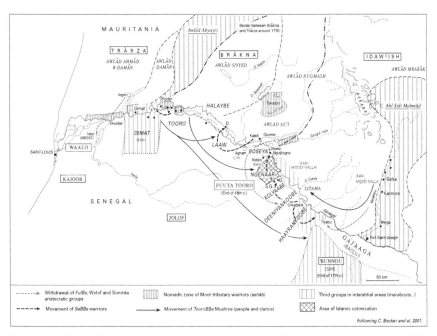

Figure 5:2 Reconfiguration of space in the Senegal valley: the movements of *SeBBe* warriors (end of 18th–beginning of 19th century)

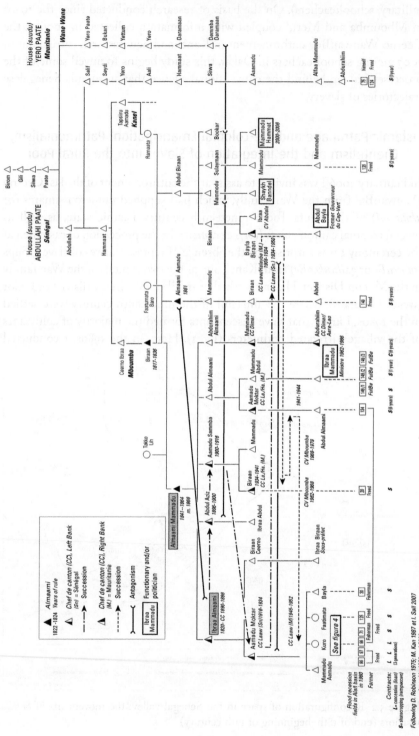

Figure 5:3 Genealogy of the *almaami*, canton chiefs (*chefs de canton*) and politicians of the Wan dynasty of Mboumba

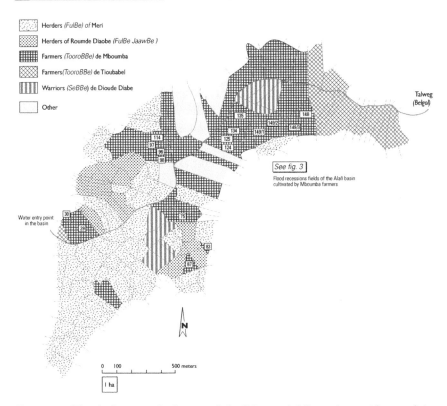

Herders *(FulBe)* of Meri
Herders of Roumde Diaobe *(FulBe JaawBe)*
Farmers *(TooroBBe)* de Mboumba
Farmers *(TooroBBe)* de Tioubabel
Warriors *(SeBBe)* de Dioude Diabe
Other

Talweg *(Belgol)*

See fig. 3

Flood recessions fields of the Alañ basin
cultivated by Mboumba farmers

Water entry point
in the basin

N

0   100   500 meters

I ha

Figure 5:4 Flood plains in the basins of the Meri and Mboumba: residence of the
field owners

with other researchers a monographic study (Boutillier and Schmitz, 1987) of
four villages of the Laaw region (district of Podor), which hosted all the main
status groups. Aside from Mboumba, headed by the *tooroBBe*, we worked in
Meri, a village of sedentary Fulani *(FulBe)*, in Dioude Diabe, composed of
seBBe warriors, and in a village of *sulbalBe* fishermen. The intensive survey of
the configuration of these relations (Jézéquel, 2003) allowed us to reconstruct
exhaustive biographies, genealogies and social networks for the ensemble of
landlords and farmers – freemen or slaves, fishermen or *tooroBBe* – of a vast
area farmed by men from different villages.

The absence of former slave groups at the enthronement suggested a
possible realignment of local dependent relationships. Yet the absence was not
openly commented upon at the event, in line with the generalised silencing
of the subject of slavery. This silence can partly be attributed to the politics of
denial led by development institutions: as much as the development discourse
depoliticises (Ferguson, 1990), it de-socialises, reducing complex social statuses
to the single category of 'peasant'. While the first hydro-agricultural perimeters
on the banks of the Senegal River were created at the request of Mauritanian

masters who needed resources to feed their freed slaves, or *harâtîn*, the redistribution of irrigated parcels that followed the 1973–74 drought did not take status into consideration. In spite of this, 'slaves' turned out to be an over-represented constituency on the village's irrigated perimeters (Boutillier and Schmitz, 1987). Taking a more historical perspective, one could ask to what extent the Roume decree of 1903, aimed at the elimination of slavery (Lovejoy and Kanya Forstner, 1994), was actually responsible for slavery's partial dissolution through seasonal migration and, for those who didn't migrate, through sharecropping. The following cases highlight axes of emancipation that owed less to colonial decrees and more to internal readjustments of dependent relations.

The Case of Mboumba

Seasonal migrations in the Wolof peanut basin are known generally to Senegambians as 'navetanat' (from the Wolof *navetaan,* 'rainy season cultivators') or, to the Haalpulaaren of the Senegal valley, as *demal gerte* ('cultivating peanuts' in Fulfulde). If the introduction of this type of contract by slave traders from the upper river region dates back to the mid-nineteenth century (Manchuelle, 1997; Searing, 2002), its diffusion to the whole of Senegambia was a colonial policy of the period from 1920 to 1950 (David, 1980). This seasonal migration polarised the *maccuBe* and the majority of the other social categories of the two Fuuta, the Fuuta Tooro (Senegal valley) and the Fuuta Jaloo in Guinea, from where the nineteenth-century *Jihâds* had started. This statement can be verified through the biographies of farmers and users of a large flood-recession farming area located at the intersection of the lands of four villages in the department of Podor. The biographies of migrants show that, at the beginning of the century, most young men participated in seasonal migrations to the peanut basin regardless of their social status, free or *maccuBe*. A large number of *maccuBe* settled in the peanut basin and founded new villages (such as Diofior), but many continued practising wet season migration until the 1970s, alternating groundnut cultivation (or *demal gerte*) with weaving in the dry season *(noraan)* in the Sereer country of southern Senegal. Weaving was a substantial source of revenue for the *maccuBe sanyooBe*,[4] especially since weaving jobs moved into town, to the extent that they were earning more than free people in the 1950s (Diop, 1965). Thus, as shown by the following two examples, weaving opened the path to the city.

Baba Diouf, a former slave and younger brother of the district head of Madina Gounass (Pikine), learned to weave from his landlord-patron (*jatigi*), a friend of his father settled in Grand Thies, and then practised this craft in Dakar in the neighbourhood of *La gueule tapée* close to the Medina.[5] In this neighbourhood a rotating credit association was created that collected contributions of members of age groups (*fedde*) from a neighbourhood of

Mboumba and financed two or three *chambres*[6] (*suudu*) and evening meals. Later the *chambres* were transformed into villagers' 'guest-houses' (*galle*) in Guediawaye, near Pikine, one of the extended suburbs of Dakar. Gradually, with the arrangement of marriages and the formation of families settled in individual compounds (*galle*), the villagers' guest-houses disappeared and new migrants were hosted in familial compounds, with the family-head fulfilling the role of *jatigi*.

If weaving paved the way to the city, finding a job depended on patronage. Amadu Dawuuda Diouf, elder brother of Baba, started off as a weaver, then found a job as a sweeper in the Dakar Townhall (SOADIP). In 1966 he worked as collector of market duties, and eventually became neighbourhood head (*chef de quartier*), all thanks to a powerful patron, the minister Ibraa Mamadu Wan. Amadu lived in *La gueule tapée*, a working-class neighbourhood, and in 1970 he moved to Madina Gounass[7] in Guediawaye. Diversifying his alliances, he militated in favour of Wolof politicians, including Kabirou Mbodj, who was then a political leader in Pikine. Amadu was one of the few former slaves who became a delegate of the Madina Gounass district from 1976 to 2004, when he died, still a member of the Socialist Party (PS).

The comparison of migratory biographies of freemen and *maccuBe* is instructive. The year-long occupation of slaves postponed their definite settlement in town, a preliminary condition for their entrance into the most profitable migratory strategies. Instead, from the 1930s, freemen abandoned seasonal migrations to settle in Dakar, before starting to practise international migration. From the 1950s they had stable jobs in Dakar. Then, in the 1960s, they started practising inter-African migrations as traders, hawkers and diamond traders (*diamantaires*) in the Ivory Coast, Cameroun, Gabon, Congo and Zambia. Then, in the 1970s, they began travelling to Europe: France, Germany, and now Italy and Spain. The 'rank effect' that delayed the ex-slaves' access to profitable migrations equally hit the rural poor, who lacked stable 'moorings' in towns. This is the case for free *SulbaBe* fishermen, environmental refugees on the Senegal river, where they have been practising irrigated cultivation since the drought of 1975 while migrating to the estuaries of southern Senegambia to fish shrimps (*gambas*) in the dry season (Schmitz, 2007). This is also the case for *FulBe* herders who had to abandon their transhumant trajectories in Mauritania after the events of 1989. Many sharecroppers and daily labourers on the flood-recession lands and irrigated perimeters came from these two categories. Thus the fate of 'slaves' was not necessarily the worst possible condition, for they shared these activities with other groups, such as herders or fishermen. This would explain why a large number of descendants of slaves and freed slaves did not relocate to the peanut basin from the beginning of the twentieth century or take up maritime fishing when this activity boomed in the 1980s–1990s.

A second pattern of emancipation, sharecropping or *rempeccen*, started being practised at the beginning of the century (Leservoisier, 1994). Share-cropping effectively blurred the frontiers between status groups by attracting various poorer sections of the population whose mobility was restricted to rural areas. Thus, of the ten floodland-fields owned by the Wan family (fig. 3) and cultivated by sharecroppers from various villages (fig. 4), six were given to slaves or freed slaves, and the other four to *SubalBe* fishermen (two) and *FulBe* herders (two).

The genealogies collected among slave descendants of Mboumba force us to reconsider the attribution of the transformation of slaves into clients to colonial abolition at the beginning of the twentieth century (Leservoisier, 1994; Lovejoy and Hogendorn, 1993). In fact, this transformation resulted from the autonomous strategies of the masters, the Wan Almaami, and probably started in the second half of the nineteenth century. In the nineteenth century Mboumba was the residence of Ibraa Almaami (1820–96), a warlord who remained on the frontline of the political scene for almost half a century due to his ongoing struggle with Abdul Bookar Kan, based in the eastern village of Dabia (Robinson, 1975a). Besides the support of the French in Saint-Louis, he could count on a cohort of loyal slaves, his *jaggorde*, each of whom received a horse and were armed with guns (*jom fetel*).[8] Thanks to them, to the SeBBe warriors from the village of Dioude Diabe, and to some Moorish allies that included the Twabir and the emir family of the Awlâd Nugmash (Taylor, 1995), he was able to fight his rival (Schmitz, 2000b). But all these warriors also partic-ipated in slave raiding and protected Moorish raiders from the retaliations of the French army. The fortified village of Mboumba attracted not just margina-lised individuals but also traders and adventure-seekers hoping to profit from ongoing raiding and pillage.[9] The Wan, as village chiefs, allowed the marriage of the daughters of their *maccuBe* to people who thereby became integrated into local communities. The following are two examples of this pattern:

- Aamadu Diouf's grandfather, Hammat Diouf, chief of the neighbour-hood of Madina Gounass, where the Mboumba community of Pikine was concentrated, was a Seerer hawker from Fatick who often stopped in Mboumba. When he finally settled there, the Wan family which hosted him gave him a slave wife, Ramatulaay Soh.
- The father of Ablaay Sih did not accept being called 'slave'. As he didn't own any land, he took some in *rempeccen* from several families, and cleared new fields in Lewe. Indeed, his parents were not strictly speaking 'slaves'. His father had reached Mboumba to trade, attracted by the village's reputa-tion for abundant wealth from the raids. Accepted as a stranger (*arani*) in the Bambara neighbourhood, he married a young Bambara woman. His mother was the daughter of a certain Abdoulaye, who had come to

Mboumba hoping to find his kidnapped sister and had remained there, marrying a slave girl named Kuumba Njaay, who had been kidnapped very young.

Marriages between free foreigners and local slave girls, organised or encouraged by local chiefs, created a large constituency of people of mixed status whose descendants could claim free status. Hence, these marriages opened potential paths to emancipation that, when accompanied by access to land and resources, would become concrete avenues of social mobility. The Wan's patronage also underpinned this aspect in the form of patrimonial support.

Ibraa Almaami provided land to his followers, as shown by four types of contract regulating the tenure of fields, starting from the most favourable conditions (gift, loan), and ending with the most precarious (sharecropping and piecework). Only the house of the powerful canton chief of Laaw (1916–34), Aamadu Moktar Wan, granted land in the form of gift (*dokkal*) or loan (*lubal*), both free except for the payment of the Qu'ranic dime (*asakal*). Two liberated slave ancestors benefited particularly from lands given or lent to them by the Wan. It was probably the Almaami himself who granted a first set of fields to two brothers, Aamadu Sirandu and Muttar Sirandu, sons of the same mother, Sirandu.

To thank Aamadu Sirandu for his role in the construction of the mosque of Mboumba, Ibra Almaami granted him two fields (29 and 30, fig. 4) in 'definitive donation' (*dokkal pandugal*). However, these fields were located in the domain of the Soh of Meri. Ibra Almaami had wished to give Aamadu a field situated far from the small hills where the wild boars that ravaged the harvests lived. This is why he asked his 'friend', the village chief of Meri, ArDo Demmba Ciigel Soh, to give him these fields. The latter acquiesced to his request in the hope of gaining Ibra's support and being re-elected village chief (Schmitz, 2000b). This was the main method of land allocation by the Almaami. The Wan did not own fields in this part of the floodlands. The landlords and chiefs (*jom leydi*) of the floodlands were the SaybooBe, who carried the honorific title of Soh, and among whom the Jom of Mboumba and Ardo of Meri were recruited.[10]

A second lot of land was apparently given later, most likely in the form of a loan (*lubal*), by Aamadu Moktar Wan to Al-Hâjj Sih, a slave who studied the Qu'ran and performed the pilgrimage.[11] At the same time, between the Wan and the Sih was established a milk kinship (*ennDam*),[12] possibly characterised by greater egalitarianism and affection than competitive agnate relations (Schmitz, 2000a). The milk kinship obfuscated the memory of the slave–master relation (*khilifa/jiyaaDo*). The only remaining mark of the earlier slave–master relation is evident in the domestic services carried out by ex-slaves at their ex-masters' family celebrations (baptisms, weddings). The code of honour (*teddungal*) imposes this with no exception.

The process of 'clientisation' examined above, sometimes metaphorically sealed by fictive milk kinship, shows that emancipation is not only a sociological phenomenon but also a cultural one, situated in a universe of meanings that Igor Kopytoff calls 'African' (Kopytoff, 1988, 492; Kopytoff and Miers, 1977). However, Islam's preponderant role forces us to question the meaning of 'Africanity' in relation to this model of slavery and emancipation, or at least to examine more closely the influence of Islam in this model. As we have seen, the building of a mosque or knowledge of the Qu'ran functioned as tokens for the emancipation of slaves who were also, at the same time, clients and warriors.

'Lack of Islam' is at the heart of the negative characterisation of the slave as belonging to the world of impiousness and pagan ignorance (*jâhiliyya*). If, according to Roger Botte, 'the Muslim / non-Muslim distinction set the basis for the free / un-free opposition' in the Fuuta Jalo (Guinea) (1990, 40), the same holds for the Fuuta Tooro (Senegal River valley). Colonial abolition at the beginning of the twentieth century refers to a Euro-American notion of identity rooted in the freedom–slavery dyad, whereby the slave's liberation breaks the relation with the master, 'owner' of the slave-chattel (Kopytoff, 1988, 488). Instead, in the Islamic (*and* African) world, the dissolution (*deliaison*)[13] or undoing of all social ties is synonymous with wandering, exposure, lack of protection and social death.[14] Similarly, among the Haalpulaaren, slaves are sometimes characterised as *majjuBe*, 'misplaced people who have lost their way', a term close to *maccuBe* (Wane, 1969, 67).[15] 'Proper' emancipation must pass through the establishment of clientelist relations (*mawlâ*), generally euphemised as 'friendship' (Touati, 1996).[16]

The example of land tenure contracts highlights the incredible internal diversity of the generic constituency of 'slaves'. Subtle nuances of status derive from specific combinations of the statuses of the parents of slaves and previous generations, as well as from the particular nature of the relations with masters. As exploitation and protection are inextricably connected, the slave is also a client, blurring the frontier between freedom and servitude (Searing, 2002, 149). Slaves who were privileged, for military or religious reasons, received land in *lubal*, while the wide majority cultivated land through sharecropping tenancies, sharecropping being the primary means of clientisation for allotment slaves (Meillassoux, 1986).[17] Finally, even today, the lowest place in the social hierarchy is reserved not to sharecropping tenants but to casual labour paid on a daily basis (*dawol/dawi*). These are usually foreigners whose names we do not even know: before the 1989 events they were *harâtîns* from Mauritania then, after their expulsion, they were replaced by Fulani 'refugees'. The latter, victims of the stigma that the natives inflict upon the most recent immigrant categories (Elias and Scotson, 1965), are currently being stereotyped almost as negatively as those who preceded them, even though they speak the local language. Hence, belonging to a network of clientage, even as a slave, is a better position than being a stranger (*arani*) in a village (*wuro*) or a territory (*leydi*).

Paradoxically, clientisation kept in the village a large number of slave descendants by playing on internal micro-differences. The result is that these slave-clients are the last to become aware of changing avenues of social mobility. Dependants reaped some benefits from patron–client relations with former masters, but at the same time these relations kept them from joining 'faster tracks' of emancipation and mobility. Today, it is the date of entry into migratory networks that determines a person's position in the new social hierarchy that became established in the Senegal valley in the 1970s, and spread to the whole country in the mid-1990s.

Land and Marriages in Meri

As the situation of the slaves in Mboumba may appear exceptional as a result of Mboumba's particular political and economic situation, it will be helpful to compare it with the more characterisitc condition of slaves in the neighbouring village of Meri, inhabited primarily by sedentary Fulani. The emancipation decrees of the beginning of the twentieth century (1905), coupled to the policy of distribution of land to the tiller, caused a generalised flight. But, in contrast to other slave exoduses that left a clear trace in the archives (Klein, 1998), in the case of the Senegal valley we find a series of contradictory movements reflected in the complexity of the terminology. The term *maccuDo* (plur. *maccuBe*) is used most often to refer to the slave, the person 'owned' (*jiyaaDo*, plur. *jiyaaBe*[18]), but sometimes it is also used to designate liberated slaves. This ambiguity is further increased by the fact that legal emancipation does not terminate the relationship between master and slave. The attribution of land and the arrangement of a marriage are essential complements of the legal act of ransom (*cootigu*). Yet, rather than terminating the relation with the master and his family, land and marriages allow its renegotiation. These considerations become particularly appropriate when seen in the context of the three main axes of flight from the region surrounding Meri discussed below, starting with the most distant.

At the beginning of the century, the majority of slaves seem to have gone towards the Sine Saloum and the Petite Cote in the south, separated from the Senegal valley by the desert zone of the Ferlo. These trajectories corresponded to two types of activity that offered alternatives to the stigma of servility: the culture of groundnuts in the Sine Saloum, and artisan maritime fishing in the region around Mbour.

Other directions, which remained confined to the Senegal valley, were also important. We reconstructed the lineage of an ancestress, Nilan Faay, going back eight generations.[19] This woman, to whom the people of Meri attributed

Sereer origins, is said to have sought refuge in the village in the aftermath of a famine. Her sons, unable to find a bride among the free, married *maccuBe* women. As the Sereer country and the Gambian border were areas where the Haalpulaar'en captured slaves, we cannot exclude a possible slave origin of Nilan Faay. In any case, we can trace twenty-two lineages descending from this woman. Today, the majority of her descendants live not too far from the village of Meri, nine in the neighbouring village of Gollere and seven in the region around the river.

The third trajectory was towards an area of rain-fed agriculture that forms a thin strip along the borders of the floodplains. Fields in these lands are farmed in the rainy season (*jeeri*) and pressure for their occupation is less intense than on the floodlands (*waalo*). It is in this liminal space that six other slave lineages settled and were able to form herds of sheep and goats, and then of cattle. Because the large compounds in which the slaves settled on *waalo* lands lived were called *gallo*, a Wolof term, they were given the name *Gallunk-ooBe*, which today is commonly used in substitution of *MaccuBe* to refer to slave descendants.

Because the slave belongs to the master of his/her mother, the main status distinction between slaves and freemen consists in the constitution of agnatic families. Six out of eight genealogies of freed slaves from Meri that we managed to reconstruct in the 1980s were still arranged matrifocally (children of the same mother or clusters of married brothers and brothers-in-law), and their members did not own any floodland fields but only exploited them temporarily as sharecropping tenants whose landlords were not their past masters. The only two that managed to constitute agnatic families descended from ancestors who had been bought by their masters, the Soh of Meri, the principal landowners (*jom leydi*) from which the village *arDo* are recruited. The Soh arranged their clients' weddings in parallel to their own. They are divided over three lineage segments or 'houses' (*suudu*) – Dikki, Amar and Cabballe – which intermarry, forming a highly endogamous network. Let us take the example of Maalik Demmba Jah, bought three generations ago by ArDo Demmba Ciigel of the house of Cabballe (the same which provided a parcel of land to Ibraa Almaami). Maalik took the name of his master and received a parcel of land. He married a slave of the Amar house, Tako, who gave him a son, Abdul. Abdul also married a slave attached to the Cabballe Soh, called Surbu. Being doubly linked to the Cabballe Soh, by kinship (marriage with their slaves) and land, he set up a compound (*galle*) in which his six married and unmarried sons live today. The strong tie with the master had two main consequences. On the one hand, this compound is among the few established right next to the master's residence. On the other, Saydu, Abdul's son, became the sharecropping tenant of two floodland fields of the masters.

As in other parts of Senegambia where slaves have become clients, particularly in the Wolof country, the main remaining stigma of slavery concerns marriage practices[20] that transform the group of slave descendants into a 'pseudo-caste' (Searing, 2002, 150). However, what defines the process of clientisation in the Senegal valley, both among the slaves of Mboumba and the slaves of Meri, is the particular function played by the slaves' acquisition of land rights through their masters' patronage. Land tenure rearrangements also characterised the emancipation of the warrior slaves of the dynasty of the *satigi* peuls or *FulBe* of the sixteenth–eighteenth century which had preceded the Islamic Almaami (*TolroBBe*). The earlier trajectory of emancipation discussed below helps us to set the cases of Mboumba and Meri in a longer historical perspective.

Land Acquisition and Emancipation of Warriors of the Ancient FulBe Dynasty of the SeBBE KoliyaaBe (End of Eighteenth–Nineteenth Century)

Earlier examples of clientisation exemplify the support from which the *SeBBe KoliyaaBe*, the warrior slaves of the *Satigi FulBe*, benefited when they allied themselves to the *TolroBBe* at the end of the eighteenth century. They formed communities assigned to guarding the shallows (*juuwde*) over the entire length of the Senegal river and, in compensation for their services, they received lands and titles, as in the village of Juuwde Jabbe near Mboumba (Kane, 1973, 2004).[21] The river was used as a natural barrier (Johnson, 1974, 111): communities of SeBBe warriors were established near the shallows to prevent the passage of Moors or, at least, to recover the loot when the latter returned from their raids (Johnson, 1974, 163; Wane, 1969, 41). The Moors in question were usually tributaries (*znâga*). Their raids were aimed at capturing either cattle or women and children: in the latter case, the main objective was to obtain a ransom for the prisoners' rescue (Searing, 2004).

Let us consider the case of the *SeBBe KoliyaaBe* slave warriors who lived in Orkadiere (fig. 2) in the Damnga region, the capital where the last Satigi sought refuge after leaving Gorgol. As shown by Shaykh Muusa Kamara,[22] the *SeBBe KoliyaaBe* moved in two directions, eastwards towards the Gajaaga-HayrankooBe frontier, and westwards towards the area that was subsequently named Ngeenar. Allied to Abdul Almaami, the *KoliyaaBe* followed him into central Booseya (in Tilogne and then in Kobilo) and in the country's hinterland, until he ordered them to build a fortified camp (*ribât*) along the river on the site called Nguijilogne, where they blocked the shallow (*juuwde*) through which the Moors crossed the river. They moved, physically, from Sintiou Garba (SG, see fig. 2) and Diandiouli (D, fig. 2) to Nguijilogne (fig. 1 and N, fig. 2), and at the same time changed their status of warrior slaves. In fact, by acquiring land and forming alliances with other groups, they became *SeBBe*, a 'free' category.

They initially gained access to land thanks to the personal tie of friendship (*cehilagal*) between Almaami Abdul, founder of the imamate, and Siree Daara Jah of the *KoliyaaBe*, who became chief of Nguijilogne. In compensation for his services, Siree Dara received lands in various parts of the Ngenaar, next to where the warriors had stopped – Diandiouli, Sintiou Garba – as well as in Tilogne and in Navel, near Matam. A legend narrates that Siree Dara carried the Almaami on his back across a branch of the river. Loyal to the Almaami until the end, Siree Dara eventually died in Bunngoowi, during the Kajoor expedition (Kamara, 1998, 201). Siree Daara merely received these lands in usufruct, as implied by the literal meaning of his title *jaagaraaf*. However, repeated renewals of the alliance with the Almaami of the Fuuta deleted the memory of the originally servile status of the *SeBBe*, as well as of the original nature of the tenure contract. These two processes of forgetting proceeded in tandem. After one or two generations, the surreptitious transformation of the tenure regime from usufruct to ownership ceased being contested, implicitly sanctioning the *KoliyaaBe*'s emancipation.[23] But this would not have been complete without a politics of alliance with the other three 'free' groups: the *TooroBBe*, the *FulBe*[24] and the *SubalBe* 'fishermen'. In the last two cases, the alliance was sealed with groups outside the Senegal valley, Somono fishermen also originally from the Niger River and *FulBe* herders from Mali (Kamara, 1998, 224). But the most important alliance was with the Njaay TooroBBe, among whom imams were selected through hereditary succession (Kamara, 1998, 221–24). In fact, this alliance allowed the *KoliyaaBe* to embrace Islam, overcoming the barrier that, in those times, denied slaves access to Islam.

The cases discussed above show that in Haalpulaar'en localised Islamic communities the distinction between citizen (*jom wuro*) and stranger (*arani*) is articulated in complex ways with the distinction between master (*khilifa*) and slave (*jiyaado*). In this first model, which can be qualified as Islamic, emancipation stemmed from adherence to Islam and the multiplication of the local and supra-local networks of clientage of Islamic micro-states. Emancipation implied the progressive integration of the stranger/slave into the community of Islamic freemen. It took place through various forms of alliance and land acquisition achieved through clientelistic strategies. This pattern of emancipation is clearly in continuity with the more recent examples of Mboumba and Meri, considered at the beginning of this section. The following section considers avenues of emancipation characterised by both continuity and change.

'Republican' Emancipation: Veterans, Schoolteachers and Political Activists

The trajectories illustrated in this section take advantage of new opportunities and discourses introduced during French domination. We suggested above that, in the long run, 'clientisation via land acquisition' had a perverse effect. The *GallunkooBe* continued practising seasonal migrations throughout the whole year, and it took them a long time to settle into town, the preliminary step in the more successful strategy of international migration. But not all of them followed this pattern. Many slave descendants from Mboumba came to town at an early stage to go to school, achieving excellent results. They were so successful that today they sit at the head of a council of dignitaries, or *batu*, which manages from Dakar the development activities (irrigated perimeters, etc.) of the 'transnational village' and organises the celebration of the prophet's birth (*mawlud*) in Mboumba. The most active in this group are the leaders of left-wing associations in Senegal's political chessboard. This second cohort may at first appear to belong to a 'Western' emancipation model, which requires a complete break of relations with former masters. However, it is often through these relations that ex-slaves were able to pursue strategies of social mobility, though the avenues they utilised belonged to the colonial reconfiguration of opportunities.

It is illustrative to draw up a list of the 16 professionals originally from Mboumba, ten of whom became teachers and schoolmasters, while the other six succeeded in the *écoles normales*. Most of them did not marry Mboumba women. The ten teachers who did their primary schooling in Mboumba belong to the '1954 generation', which marks the stable opening of the school. They are:

> H. Thiam, director of the Thierno Salif Ndongo School in Pikine and General Secretary of the *batu* council of Mboumba, which contains most of the natives of Mboumba who made their fortunes outside the village, primarily in Dakar
>
> D. Y. Sy (whose brother is a teaching inspector in Physics), secretary of the society for the development of Mboumba within the *batu* and General Secretary of the LD/MPT (*Ligue Democratique / Mouvement pour le Parti du Travail*)
>
> K. Diagne, teacher in Damaguene and member of the executive bureau of the LD/MPT party.
>
> A. Dia, school director in Podor (regional capital of the Senegal River region)
>
> B. Sire Ndiaye, school director in Tambacouda (eastern Senegal)
>
> O. Diallo, director and then bursar in the high school of Diofor (Saloum), which contains many people from Mboumba

I. Sall, schoolteacher in *Parcelles Assainies* district of Dakar

D. Y. Sy, teacher of mathematics

Idi Karas Bookum, who from his position of Director of the Ministry of Education supported other *jawamBe*, a caste of advisors of people in power

I. Bokoum

S. Bokoum

The six teachers who studied at the *écoles normales* followed different career paths:

A. Sih, specialised educator

D. S. Thiam, specialised educator

S. Diouf, financial agent

H. Sy, stomatologist

S. Bokoum, post and telecommunications (PTT) officer, deceased

A. Koundoul, tourism professional

All of these professionals are of slave descent. Their careers attest to the patterns of social mobility discussed below.

'Noble' Tutors and Patrons: Military Paternalism, Schoolteachers and Party Militants

In order to understand the attraction of the school for former servile groups we must look at the broader context of the *GallunkooBe*'s relations with their old masters, or with some personalities of the Wan 'administrative dynasty'. The Wan, who provided the political personnel of the regime of Senghor, the first President of Senegal, were the main promoters of their slaves' mobility in the schooling sector. Within this emancipation axis, the interactions between the Wan and the *GallunkooBe* reveal the existence, among the former, of 'initiates' (Goffman's 'wise' persons, 1963, 41), who had endured forms of stigma similar to those directed against the *GallunkooBe*. These personal experiences motivated them to transform the patron–client relationship with descendants of their slaves into active tutoring in the latter's favour. Shared experience of stigma – be it collective, such as the racism experienced by the *tirailleurs sénégalais* during the two world wars, or personal and linked to family conflicts – allowed these two groups to overcome status divisions and express their claims and expectations through a common idiom.

One of the three characters who would play an important role in the establishment of Mboumba's primary school and in creating stimuli for students to continue their studies at the *écoles normales* was Doctor Ibraa Mammadu Wan, who descended from Ibraa Almaami and served repeated mandates as Minister of Education and National Deputy. The other two, Mammadu

Hammat Sulaymaan, veteran and education activist, and Shaykh Banndel, the school's first teacher, both belonged to a powerless branch of the Wan family (fig. 3). The first successful representative of this branch was Bayla Biraan, who worked as colonial interpreter before joining the army and becoming one of the principal canton chiefs of colonial times.

Mboumba school is one of the oldest in the region. It was opened in 1893, two years before the death of Ibraa Almaami, who had been a loyal ally of the French in the years of his rivalry with Abdul Bookar Kan (Robinson, 1975a). Thereafter, it functioned intermittently until it was closed down when Bayla Biraan replaced Amadu MoktarWan as canton chief in 1934, and the regional school was established in Podor. In the 1920s, Bayla Biraan took the initiative in a number of 'colonial development' activities (Wilder, 2005, 80), such as irrigation works and the school farm in Toulde Boussobe (Sall, 2007, 590), but he did not make any progress on schooling. The early opening of the primary school of Mboumba signals the will of the *Tooroodo* section allied with the French (represented here by the Wan) to learn the language of the coloniser at the expense of Arabic.[25] The Wan's lesser sympathy towards Islamic learning echoes Ibraa Almaami's opposition to the radical reform movements supported particularly by al Hâjj Umar.[26] This investment in French schooling runs counter to the leitmotif of the Islamic elite's disregard for French schools, to which they sent their slaves (Jézéquel, 2003). On the contrary, some *Tooroodo* elites tried to keep French schooling to themselves, as a condition for the continued supremacy of the dynasties of canton chiefs, who sent to French schools the youths destined for succession (Sall, 2007, 550).[27]

We have to wait more than half a century and another world war before other social strata would gain access to schooling thanks to Mammadu Hammaat Sulaymaan and to the man who would become its first teacher, Cheikh Banndel Wan. Mboumba's school opened definitively in 1954,[28] probably due to Mammadu Hammaat's personal trajectory marked by his peculiar position within the Wan family and his military career.

Mammadu Hammaat studied at the Mboumba school from its very opening. He then continued his studies in the regional school of Podor, while also pursuing Islamic education. In 1933 he joined the army in France (Toulon) where he met Captain Charles Ntchorere, who directed the *Ecole des Enfants des Troupes* de Saint-Louis (rue Blanchot). Created in 1920, this school trained the officers of the *tirailleurs sénégalais* in the last years of colonialism and after independence (Echenberg, 1991, 118–19; Mann, 2006, 170–71). Captain Ntchorere and the training at the Saint-Louis military school would have a determinant influence on the life of Mammadu Hammaat even after his return to Africa in 1938, where he was assigned to serve in Niger and Senegal during the Second World War. A brief look at Ntchorere's career and ideas will allow us to contextualise Mammadu Hammaat's experience and future role in Mboumba.

Captain Charles Ntchorere, following the policies initiated by Gouraud in 1920 (Echenberg 1991, 67–68, 87, 166–68), wrote articles in favour of the promotion of African officers. He had also directed the School of Kati in Mali. Here a 'mobile military culture' developed, characterised by an ambivalent attitude towards issues of 'race',[29] which turned out to benefit the larger Bamankan-speaking community whose internal soldier-officer hierarchy was regulated by the paternalism characteristic of the *tirailleurs sénégalais*[30] (Mann, 2006, 162–63). In the Second World War Ntchorere distinguished himself through his heroic resistance against the German offensive on the Somme in June 1940, at the head of the *tirailleurs* of the 53rd RICMS (*Régiment d'Infanterie Coloniale Mixte Sénégalais*). Captured, he was able to save his men from immediate massacre, but was killed when he insisted 'on being treated as an Officer of the French army rather than being discriminated against as an African' (Mann, 2006, 128).[31] Ntchorere and his men fell as victims of the 1940 massacres of Africans, which were a fundamental element of the 'racial war' conducted by the Wehrmacht between 1939 and 1945 (Scheck, 2006, 28).[32] Although inclusion in the military 'civilisation'[33] was only partial, and African soldiers occupied a liminal position between citizens and subjects, they were exempted from the *code de l'indigenat* (Mann, 2006, 201, 208). Moreover, in the military the free/slave status distinction was 'diguised' by dominant logics of promotion or stigma geared on the civilised/savage opposition and on an ethnic framework of reference.

During and after the war, Maamadu Hammaat's military career brought him to Niger and the Ivory Coast before he returned to Dakar in 1954 and became chief of the *Bureau des Douanes*.[34] His house in Pikine Tally Bu Mak hosted a large cohort of river diaspora, and his famous hospitality gave him the title of *karasire*. He remained in Dakar until his retirement in 1970 as Chief of Personnel. Being related, through his paternal grandfather,[35] to the two principal branches of the Wan of Mboumba and Kanel, he was able to entertain his relatives from the two villages that had been rivals in the nineteenth century. The Wan of Mboumba monopolised the title of Almaami and then the posts of canton chief, leaving those of Kanel often in the position of dissidents. The former role is well represented by the figure of Ibraa Almaami. The dissident role is typified by Alfaa Umar Ceerno Bayla of Kanel, who became al Hajj Umar's lieutenant (Robinson, 1985). Linked to Mboumba through his father (*gorol*), and to Kanel through his mother (*dewol*), Mammadu Hammaat neutralised the characteristic rivalry between agnates through ties of 'milk kinship' (*jokkere ennDam*) (Wane, 1969), to the extent that the family ceremonies of the two branches of the Wan took place at his home. He was also able to straddle the divide between the opposed factions of Diaists (followers of Mammadu Dia[36]) and Senghorists that split the Fuuta in two for a long time.

From his army experience he derived an attitude of 'active patronage'[37] that partly explains the energy he put into his efforts to achieve the reopening of Mboumba's school as soon as he returned to Dakar in 1954.[38] Before his intervention, the school of Mboumba offered courses only for the first cycle of primary school up to CE1 (first year of the elementary course). To continue their studies students had to go to Kaskas or Podor or Saldé, and only free people, who could find a host and pay the health fees, could afford to send their children. The *msikineeBe*, the poor, could not send their children to school. When Mammadu Hammaat went to Mboumba and found the school closed, he put pressure on the authorities for a teacher to be appointed.[39] He also bought school uniforms in *mulis* cloth (from Mulhouse) for the students. Being a real democrat, with no regard for background and no interest in political games, he obtained a complete primary cycle for the Mboumba school.[40] The general gratitude of the people was shown in his election as Ceerno WanwanBe in 2000.

Cheikh Banndel Wan,[41] another key figure, was the first teacher of the primary school, where he taught for twenty years from its opening in 1954. His dedication to teaching and the support he offered to the sons of his friends is related to the fact that he had been an orphan since an early age[42] and belonged to a powerless branch of the Wan family. The sociability model that prevailed in the school differed radically from the one of the age groups (*feDDe*), where status divisions and the stigma attached to slaves and castemen were learned through the informal training of youths paired by age (*fasiraaBBe*, cf. N'gaïde, 2003).

The two following personalities trained in Mboumba illustrate the post-war generation marked by the general availability of schooling (Atlan, 2001) and the appearance of political parties geared towards cultural questions, such as the PRA[43] in the 1960s and the LD/MPT[44] today. The African experience of the military in the Second World War created a deep anti-colonial culture, to which, according to the testimony of Abdoulaye Ly,[45] founder of the PRA, these parties contributed. Engagement in these two parties is exemplified by the experiences of two schoolteachers, Ablaye Sih with the LD/MPT and Hammat Thiam with the PRA.

Ablaye Sih,[46] born in 1949 (or 1947) and brother of the LD/MPT party secretary, went to school in Mboumba with Cheikh Banndel Wan, who was a close friend of his father. Cheikh Banndel gave him his first schoolbag and nicknamed him 'Pascal' because of his skill in mathematics. He advised his father to send him to Dakar, to Mamadou Saada Wan's house. His father had fought in both world wars, ending his military career as corporal. He had a friend named Yero Tedi Sih, who was also among the few who came back alive to the village. When they returned, the two ex-soldiers revolted against the division of chores between the maccuBe and the Wan, which was a vestige of the old slave–master relations: 'whenever some work had to be realised, the maccuBe dug and the Wan paid'. Ablaye Sih entered the Blaise Diagne high school in Dakar in 1962. His unruliness at the time pushed him to register at the *école normale* before completing second grade in the *Lycée technique* of La Gueule Tapée. He followed an erratic path before sitting the professional educators' exam in 1977–1980. He wrote a manifesto article in defence of professional educators, *'Laissé pour compte, je demande la parole'* ('Left behind, I ask permission to speak'). He then obtained a grant to take a psychology degree in France. Today he follows the victims of the boat *Le Joola* which sank a few years ago, and the young would-be migrants who, since 2005, have been trying to reach Spain by boat through the Canary Islands.

Born in 1947, Hammat Thiam[47] went to school in 1960 in Thiés, where he lived in the house of a friend of his father who worked at the *Bureau des Postes et Telecommunications* (PTT) and was a member of the PRA. Thanks to Doctor Ibraa Mammadu Wan, he registered at the school of Soumbedioune, a fishermen's neighbourhood in Dakar. He lived at the house of a friend of Cheikh Banndel, Ammadu Ibraa Wan, also a member of the PRA. When he was expelled from school in sixth grade, another friend of his father, Suleymann Rasin Wan, helped him to be accepted in the school Al Hadj Malick Sy. From the sixth grade to the third grade he lived without a grant at the home of his tutor, who provided him with electricity, while his clothing was paid for by his father who was a weaver. Hammat had to walk from his home to the school four times a day, which is why he often stayed over at the place of his weaver friends. When he passed the sixth grade exam, he could not get his school report signed and was called into the director's office, where he stated: 'As my parents are illiterate, I am my own father and my own mother'. To prepare for his final exams (BEPC), he was accepted in the Van Vollenhoven high school, the best high school of Dakar, frequented almost exclusively by French pupils: 'out of 55 students in second grade, four of us were black'. Unable to succeed here, he passed the elementary school teacher examination and then worked in the hinterland of Senegal, before returning to Dakar in 1975. From 1991 onwards, he was director of the Madina Gounass district school in Pikine.

In a supposedly 'Western' model (Kopytoff, 1988) of slavery, the attainment of freedom presupposes a clear break with all ties of dependence. In the cases examined here, cutting relations with the master's family would have decreased the individual's social capital, that is, it would have reduced the relationships through which a change of status could be achieved. Hence maintaining these relations, which, for Hammat's father, are shaped within his age group (*fedde*) and his political party, was vital to his son's introduction in town and school. The son truly achieves liberation when he repays his debt to his father, who was able, in spite of his servile status, to exercise the paternal role towards his offspring – one of the main functions denied to him as slave even after abolition: 'As soon as I earned a salary, I told my father to stop working on the fields'. The same could not happen in the case of Hammat Thiam's best friend whose father, who struggled for his son to attend school, died before the son earned his first salary.[48]

Whether through the fight against racism experienced during the two world wars; through militancy in a nationalist or left-wing party; or through the defence of one's profession, emancipation presupposes a cultural transformation of ideals of success and registers of stigma. The political engagement of ex-servile groups no longer coalesces around the issue of slavery, but reflects an engagement with more encompassing goals such as anti-colonial struggle and political activism.

Conclusion

Let us return to the question raised in the introduction concerning the invisibility of slavery and the silence of the actors concerned. In Senegal, or even the whole of Senegambia, slaves failed to achieve a political voice or unfold a 'visibility strategy' through political mobilisation or associational activism in organisations such as *SOS Esclaves* in Mauritania or Timidria in Niger (Botte, 1999; 2000b).[49] It is only recently that professional historians have begun to tone down the importance of Atlantic slavery and the myths of Gorée in Senegal and Juffreh in Gambia, and to reconsider the role of internal slavery and the trans-Saharan trade (Thioub, 2002; 2005).

This essay has discussed two emancipation strategies. The first corresponds to the emancipation of the *GallunkooBe*, who remained where they were but renegotiated the relationship with their masters through clientelistic and patrimonial practices. The second is the path followed by the military and the schoolteachers who taught French, a language that, in Africa as well as France, conveyed abolitionist and emancipatory values (Botte, 2000a; 2000b; Peabody, 1996).[50] The third way out of slavery is through religious piety. Indeed, emancipation here matters more as an avenue of conversion to Islam than as a fight against slavery. The most durable stigma of slavery is cultural. While the moral debasement of slavery (absence of honour, depravation, etc.) has been much debated (De Bruijn and Pelckmans, 2005; Klein, 1998; 2005), the servile *macula*, or stain, has a primarily religious connotation. Both in the *ulama* and in cultural conventions attributed to Islam but not founded on textual tradition (Clarence Smith, 2006, 20), the slave is situated outside *dar-al-Islam* in the space of *kufr* (idolatry) and *jahiliyya* (impiety) (Robinson, 2004). This denial is exemplified by the ritual line preventing any Muslim from joining a prayer led by a slave Imam (Botte, 1994, 132; Schmitz, 2006).

At the micro level, the enthronement of Ceerno WanwanBe on 11 February 2006 offered a snapshot of Haalpulaar society in the form of a procession of what Yaya Wane (1969), himself a native of the village of Kanel, qualified as 'castes'. On this occasion, I was struck by the absence of two components: first, the Tijaniyya brotherhood of Madina Gounass,[51] which assembles many migrants to African countries and, recently, to France; and secondly, the GallunkooBe who, though present, remained in the background. Reference to the 'pious strategy' of emancipation might explain the two absences at Ceerno WanwanBe's enthronement.[52] Emancipation through piety only succeeds away from regions of mutual knowledge such as villages of origin. It succeeds in translocal brotherhood networks. During the 1930s, the Tijaniyya attracted ex-slaves to the region of Kaedi on the Mauritanian bank (Hanretta, 2003). One of the main reasons for the success of the Muridiyya, founded by Serigne Amadou Bamba, is that after the 1930s it attracted many slaves as disciples (*taalibe*), to whom it gave new lands taken from the transhumant Fulani and brides received as *addaya* from other disciples (Klein, 1998, 200–03; Searing, 2002, 249, 261).[53]

As in the case of emancipation by the military and 'republican' schools, the brotherhoods' strategy superimposes a world of meaning that implies new indexes of promotion and stigma and erases local status divides. In the three cases, emancipation is not to be confused with atomised 'freedom' for, as we have seen, it borrows the paths of *in loco* clientisation and patrimonial practices from colonial paternalism or the Shaykh-disciple relation of transnational Sufi brotherhoods. Moreover, in the three models of emancipation, past status becomes invisible as a new status is assumed in a new hierarchical system/index. From the moment this new status is taken up, the 'slave' past is silenced.

References

Atlan, C., 2001. 'Élections et pratiques électorales au Sénégal (1940–1958).' Unpublished PhD thesis, EHESS, Paris.

Babou, C. A., 2007. *Fighting the Greater Jihad. Amadu Bamba and the Founding of the Muridiyya of Senegal, 1853–1913*. Athens, OH: Ohio University Press.

Bloch, M., 1955 [1931]. *Les Caractères originaux de l'histoire rurale française*. Paris: Colin.

Botte, R., 1990. 'Pouvoir du livre, pouvoir des hommes: la religion comme critère de distinction.' *Journal des Africanistes*, 60(2), pp. 37–51.

Botte, R., 1994. 'Stigmates sociaux et discriminations religieuses: l'ancienne classe servile au Fuuta Jaloo.' *Cahiers d'Études Africaines*, 34(133–35), pp. 109–36.

Botte, R., 1999. 'RimayBe, Harâtîn, Iklan: les damnés de la terre, le développement et la démocratie.' In A. Bourgeot, ed., *Horizons nomades en Afrique sahélienne*, Paris: Karthala, pp. 55–78.

Botte, R., 2000a. 'L'Esclavage africain après l'abolition de 1848. Servitude et droit du sol.' *Annales, HSS*, 5, pp. 1009–37.

Botte, R., 2000b. 'De l'esclavage et du daltonisme dans les sciences sociales. Avant-propos.' *Journal des Africanistes*, 70(1–2), pp. 7–42.

Boutillier, J. L. and Cantrelle, P., 1962. *La Moyenne Vallée du Sénégal (étude socio-économique)*. Paris: PUF.

Boutillier, J. L. and Schmitz, J., 1987. 'Gestion traditionnelle des terres (système de décrue/ système pluvial) et transition vers l'irrigation : le cas de la vallée du Sénégal.' *Cahiers des Sciences Humaines*, 23(3–4), pp. 533–54.

Clarence Smith, W. G., 2006. *Islam and the Abolition of Slavery*. London: Hurst; New York: Oxford University Press.

Conklin, A., 1997. *A Mission to Civilize. The Republican Idea of Empire in France and West Africa, 1895–1930*. Stanford, CA: Stanford Univesity Press.

Cooper, F., Holt, T. and Scott, R., eds, 2000. *Beyond Slavery. Exploration of Race, Labor, and Citizenship in Postemancipation Societies*. Chapel Hill, NC, and London: University of North Carolina Press.

David, P., 1980. *Les Navétanes*. Dakar: Éditions des Nouvelles éditions africaines.

De Bruijn, M. and Pelckmans, L., 2005. 'Facing Dilemmas: Former Slaves in Modern Mali.' *Canadian Journal of African Studies*, 39, pp. 69–95.

Dilley, R., 2004. *Islamic and Caste Knowledge Practices among Haalpulaar'en in Senegal. Between Mosque and Termite Mound*. Edinburgh: Edinburgh University Press.

Diop, A., 1965. *Société toucouleur et migration*. Dakar: IFAN (Initiations et études 18).

Echenberg, M., 1991. *Colonial Conscripts. The Tirailleurs Sénégalais in French West Africa, 1857–1960*. Portsmouth, NH: Heinemann.

Elias, N. and Scotson, J. L., 1965. *The Established and the Outsiders. A Sociological Enquiry into Community Problems*. London: Frank Cass.

Ennaji, M. 2007. *De sujet et le mamelouk. Esclavage, pouvoir et religion dans le monde arabe*. Paris: Mille et une nuits.

Ferguson, J., 1990. *The Anti-Politics Machine: 'Development', Depoliticization, and Bureaucatic Power in Lesotho*. Cambridge: Cambridge University Press.

Getz, T., 2004. *Slavery and Reform in West Africa. Toward Emancipation in Nineteeth-Century Senegal and the Gold Coast*. Oxford: James Currey.

Goffman, E., 1963. *Stigma: Notes on the Management of Spoiled Identity*. London: Penguin Books.

Hanretta, S., 2003. 'Constructing a Religious Community in French West Africa: The Hamawi Sufis of Yacouba Sylla.' Unpublished PhD thesis, Madison, University of Wisconsin.

Hilliard, C. B., 1997. '*Al-Majmû'al Nafis*: Perspectives on the Origins of the Muslim Torodbe of Senegal from the Writings of Shaykh Musa Kamara.' *Islam et Sociétés au Sud du Sahara*, 11, pp. 85–105.

Jézéquel, J. H., 2003. 'Histoire de bancs, parcours d'élèves. Pour une histoire configuration-nelle de la scolarisation à l'époque coloniale.' *Cahiers d'Études Africaines*, 43(169–70), pp. 409–33.

Johnson, J. P., 1974. 'The Almamate of Futa Toro, 1770–1836: a Political History.' Unpublished PhD thesis, Madison, University of Wisconsin.

Kamara, C. M., 1998. *Florilège au jardin de l'histoire des Noirs, Zuhûr al Basâtîn*, Vol. 1, *L'aristocratie peule et la révolution des clercs musulmans (Vallée du Sénégal)*, ed. J. Schmitz, trans. S. Bousbina et al. Paris: CNRS-Éditions.

Kamara, O., 2000. 'Les Divisions statutaires des descendants d'esclaves au Fuuta Tooro mauritanien.' *Journal des Africanistes*, 70(1–2), pp. 265–90.

Kane, M. and Robinson, D., 1984. *The Islamic Regime of Fuuta Tooro*. Ann Arbor, MI: African Studies Center, Michigan State University.

Kane, O., 1973. 'Les Unités territoriales du Futa Toro.' *Bulletin de l'IFAN*, sér. B, XXXV(3), pp. 614–31.

Kane, O., 2004. *La Première hégémonie peule. Le Fuuta Tooro de Koli Tengella à l'Almaami Abdul*. Paris, Karthala: Presses universitaire de Dakar.

Klein, M., 1998. *Slavery and Colonial Rule in French West Africa.* Cambridge: Cambridge University Press.

Klein, M., 2005. 'The Concept of Honour and the Persistence of Servility in the Western Soudan.' *Cahiers d'Études Africaines*, 45(179–80), pp. 831–51.

Kopytoff, I., 1987. 'The Internal African Frontier: The Making of African Political Culture.' In I. Kopytoff, ed., *The African Frontier: The Reproduction of Traditional African Societies.* Bloomington-Indianapolis: Indiana University Press, pp. 3–87.

Kopytoff, I., 1988. 'The Cultural Context of African Abolition.' In S. Miers and R. Roberts, eds, *The End of Slavery in Africa.* Madison, WI: University of Wisconsin Press, pp. 485–503.

Kopytoff, I. and Miers, S., eds, 1977. *Slavery in Africa, Historical and Anthropological Perspectives.* Madison, WI: University of Wisconsin Press.

Kyburz, O., 1994. 'Les Hiérarchies sociales et leurs fondements idéologiques chez les Haapulaar'en (Sénégal).' Unpublished PhD thesis, Université de Paris X-Nanterre.

Leservoisier, O., 1994. *La Question foncière en Mauritanie. Terres et pouvoirs dans la région du Gorgol.* Paris: L'Harmattan.

Leservoisier, O., 2003. 'Démocratie, renouveau des chefferies et luttes sociales à Kaédi (Mauritanie).' *Politique Africaine*, 89, pp. 167–80.

Leservoisier, O., 2005. '"Nous voulons notre part". Les ambivalences du mouvement d'émancipation des *SaafaalBe HormankooBe* de Djéol (Mauritanie).' *Cahiers d'Études Africaines*, 45(179–80), pp. 987–1014.

Loraux, N., 1997. *La Cité divisée. L'Oubli dans la mémoire d'Athène.* Paris: Payot.

Lovejoy, P. and Hogendorn, J., 1993. *Slow Death for Slavery: The Course of Abolition in Northern Nigeria, 1897–1936.* Cambridge: Cambridge University Press.

Lovejoy, P. and Kanya-Forstner, A. S., 1994. *Slavery and its Abolition in French West Africa: The Official Reports of G. Poulet, E. Roume and G. Deherme.* Madison, WI: University of Wisconsin Press.

Manchuelle, F., 1997. *Willing Migrants.* Athens, OH: Ohio University Press.

Mann, G., 2006. *Native Sons. West African Veterans and France in the Twentieth Century.* Durham, NC: Duke University Press.

Meillassoux, C., 1986. *Anthropologie de l'esclavage. Le ventre de fer et d'argent.* Paris: PUF.

Moitt, B., 1989. 'Slavery and Emancipation in Senegal's Peanut Basin: The Nineteenth and Twentieth Centuries.' *The International Journal of African Historical Studies*, 22(1), pp. 27–50.

N'gaïde, A., 2003. 'Stéréotypes et imaginaires sociaux en milieu Haalpulaar. Classer, stigmatiser et toiser.' *Cahiers d'Études Africaines.* XLIII(4), 172, pp. 707–38.

Osborn, E., 2003. '"Circle of Iron": African Colonial Employees and the Interpretation of Colonial Rule in French West Africa.' *Journal of African History*, 44, pp. 29–50.

Pasquier, R., 1987. 'Un Aspect de l'histoire des villes du Sénégal: les problèmes de ravitaillement au XIXe siècle.' In J. Boulègue, ed., *Contribution à l'histoire du Sénégal.* Paris: Cahiers du Centre de Recherches Africaines, 5, pp. 177–212.

Peabody, S., 1996. *There Are No Slaves in France. The Political Culture of Race and Slavery in the Ancient Regime.* New York, Oxford: Oxford University Press.

Roberts, R., 1984. 'Women's Work and Women's Property: Household Social Relations in the Maraka Textile Industry in the Nineteenth Century.' *Comparative Studies in Society and History*, 26(2), pp. 229–50.

Robinson, D., 1975a. *Chiefs and Clerics. Abdul Bokar Kan and Futa Toro, 1853–1891.* Oxford: Clarendon Press.

Robinson, D., 1975b. 'The Islamic Revolution of Futa Toro.' *International Journal of African Historical Studies*, 8(2), pp. 185–221.

Robinson, D., 1985. *The Holy War of Umar Tal.* Oxford: Clarendon Press.

Robinson, D., 2004. *Muslim Societies in African History.* Cambridge: Cambridge University Press.

Sall, I., 2007. *Mauritanie. Conquête et administration coloniales françaises (1890–1945).* Paris: Karthala.

Scheck, R., 2006. *Hitler's African Victims. The German Army Massacres of Black French Soldiers in 1940.* Cambridge: Cambridge University Press.

Schmitz, J., 1994. 'Cités noires: les républiques villageoises du Fuuta Tooro (Vallée du fleuve Sénégal).' *Cahiers d'Études Africaines,* 34(133–35), pp. 419–61.

Schmitz, J., 1998. 'Introduction'. In *Shaykh Muusa Kamara, Florilège au jardin de l'histoire des Noirs, Zuhûr al Basâtîn. 1. L'aristocratie peule et la révolution des clercs musulmans (Vallée du Sénégal).* Paris, CNRS Éditions, pp. 9–91.

Schmitz, J., 2000a. 'Le Souffle de la parenté. Mariage et transmission de la baraka chez les clercs musulmans de la vallée du Sénégal.' *L'Homme,* 154–55, pp. 241–78.

Schmitz, J., 2000b. 'Un Espace politique en damier: émirats maures et provinces haalpulaar de la Vallée du Sénégal.' In F. Pouillon and D. Rivet, eds, *La Sociologie musulmane de Robert Montagne.* Paris: Maisonneuve and Larose, pp. 11–133

Schmitz, J., 2006. 'Islam et "esclavage" ou l'impossible "négritude" des Africains musulmans.' *Africulture,* 67, pp. 110–15.

Schmitz, J., 2007. 'Des Migrants aux "notables" urbains: les communautés transnationales des gens du fleuve Sénégal.' In L. Marfaing and E. Boesen, eds, *Les Nouveaux urbains dans l'espace Sahara-Sahel: un cosmopolitisme par le bas.* Berlin: ZMO-Karthala, pp. 91–104.

Searing, J., 1993. *West African Slavery and Atlantic Commerce: The Senegal River Valley 1700–1860.* Cambridge: Cambridge University Press.

Searing, J., 2002. '*God Alone is King': Islam and Emancipation in Senegal. The Wolof Kingdoms of Kajoor and Bawol, 1859–1914.* Portsmouth, NH: Heinemann.

Spear, T., 2003. 'Neo-Traditionalism and the Limits of Invention in British Colonial Africa.' *Journal of African History,* 44, pp. 3–27.

Stewart, C. and Stewart, E. K., 1973. *Islam and Social Order in Mauritania: A Case Study from the Nineteenth Century.* Oxford: Oxford University Press.

Taylor, R. M., 1995. 'Warriors, Tributaries, Blood Money and Political Transformation in Nineteenth-Century Mauritania.' *Journal of African History,* 36(3), pp. 419–41.

Thioub, I., 2002. 'L'Ecole de Dakar et la production d'une écriture accadémique de l'histoire.' In M. C. Diop, ed., *Le Sénégal contemporain.* Paris: Karthala, pp. 109–53.

Thioub, I., 2005. 'Regard critique sur les lectures africaines de l'esclavage et de la traite atlantique.' In I. Mandé and B. Stefanson, eds, *Les Historiens africains et la mondialisation.* Paris: Karthala, pp. 271–91.

Touati, H., 1996. 'Le Prince et la bête. Enquête sur une métaphore pastorale.' *Studia Islamica,* 83, pp. 101–19.

Wane, Y., 1969. *Les Toucouleurs du Fouta Tooro (Sénégal). Stratification sociale et structure familiale.* Dakar: IFAN (Initiations et études africaines 25).

Wilder, G., 2005. *The French Imperial Nation-State. Negritude and Colonial Humanism between the Two World Wars.* Chicago: The University of Chicago Press.

Willis, J. R., 1978. 'The Torodbe Clerisy: A Social View.' *Journal of African History,* 19(2), pp. 195–212.

Willis, J. R., 1979. 'Introduction: Reflection on the Diffusion of Islam in West Africa.' In J. R. Willis, ed., *Studies in West African History. The Cultivators of Islam.* London: Frank Cass, pp. 1–39.

Notes

1   Editor's note: in this chapter, the French terms *clientélisation* and *patrimonialisa-tion*, which lack a direct translation in English, have a key analytical function. When possible, I tried to convey their meaning through paraphrases. In some places I have used the translations 'clientelisation' and 'patrimonialisation' (or patrimonial practices) to indicate, respectively, the transformation of slave–master relations into relations of a patron–client type; and the former slaves' acquisition of capital (mostly land) through the patronage of their former masters. These meanings are specific to this essay, and may differ from related English words in other contexts.

2   This long adventure would not have been possible without the friendship and social ingenuity of Abdoul Sow, research assistant at the IRD of Dakar and native of Meri.

3   Having worked on village-based Islamic republics in the middle Senegal valley during the 1980s, we were interested in attending the enthronement of the 28th Ceerno, Mamadou Oumar Baidi Wane in Kanel, capital of the Matam district and political base of a branch of the Wan. All the more so, as we had not been able to assist at the enthronement of the last Ceerno, Mamadou Hamat Souleymane, which took place on 8 July 2000 in the large village of Mboumba located further west in the Podor district, the other capital of the Wan *almaami*. *Ceerno* is a title of the Islamic *TooroBBe* aristocracy of the eighteenth century, which dominated the Fuuta Tooro under the leadership of an Imam or *Almaami* elected by a college of great electors (Robinson, 1975a), in the same way as were elected the village chiefs whose titles were *ceerno* or *elimaan* (Schmitz, 1994). The Wan of Mboumba were in the main responsible for the return to a dynastic and warrior form of power since the rule of Almaami Mammadu, who was re-elected several times between 1841 and 1864, and of his son Ibraa Almaami (Ibraa, son of Almaami Mammadu) who in the second half of the century was able to put an end to the imamate through his military strength.

4   The *navetanat* internal to the ancient Wolof kingdoms comported 'cascade' recon-figurations of servile relations (Klein, 1998, 198–220). First, slave runaways were substituted by *navetanes*. Then slave villages acquired autonomy and, in turn, hosted *navetanes*, as full emancipation necessitated the attainment of one of the four pillars of Islam: pilgrimage to Mecca (Klein, 1998, 220). At the same time, the amount of time (number of days and duration of a working 'morning') that the young bachelor (*surga*) had to spend working on the field of his landlord, or *jatigi*, was reduced. Beyond the Wolof kingdoms, the rainy-season migrations of slaves coming from the ancient Islamic states formed in the FulBe jihads, be they the Fuuta Tooro or Fuuta Jaloo (Guinea), were not much studied studies, except for the work of M. S. Balde in Guinea. The dry-season migrations have been studied even less. Concerning the Senegal valley, Abdoulaye Diop's work (1965) concentrates mainly upon migrations to Dakar and looks at *maccuBe* weaving only after the settlement in town. In the Fuuta Tooro, weaving has only been studied as a specialised activity of the *maabuBe* caste (Dilley, 2004, 63, 69; Kyburz, 1994). The historiography is richer on the Western Sudan (current Mali), where Richard Roberts (1984) has shown that the slaves' weaving and women's indigo dying of luxury cloths (*pagnes*) underwent a crisis following the flight of the former, but did not disappear, and even reappeared in towns.

5   The other neighbourhoods of Mboumba had their 'guest-houses' in Medina and Niaye Thioker.

6   *Chambres* are rooms or houses that provide cheap communal housing, food and support to migrants usually from the same community of origin. For a discussion of this institution among the upper-river Soninke, see Manchuelle, 1997, 123ff. and note 25 at p. 274; for the Toucouleur (as the Haalpulaaren were called in the 1960s), see Abdoulaye Diop, 1965.

7   It is symptomatic that Madina Gounass was located on the border between Pikine 'regular' and Pikine 'irregular' (Schmitz, 2007), constituting a liminal space or an 'internal frontier' (Kopytoff, 1987), the only place where the ex-slaves could take power. Similarly, the *villages de liberté* were the Sudanese (today's Mali) antecedent where a *tirailleur sénégalais* of slave origin could become chief (Mann, 2006, 90).

8   Galo Ba, the coaxer of villagers at the bus station of Dakar knows the names of some *jaggorde*: Muttar Sirandu Sih, Sarateyba Ndiaye, Sammba Numa Sall, Demmba Loli Kulibali, Demmba Soxna Ba (fieldnotes 19/03/07).

9   See Moitt, 1989, and Getz, 2004, 163–67, on the importance of the slave trade from the interior of Senegal (Maba wars) or from Sudan (Al-Hajj Umar, Tieba and Samori Toure wars), which from the 1860s to the beginning of the 1900s crossed the Senegal valley from the posts of Bakel, Kayes, Medine and then Podor and the Kajoor. It should be noted that in the nineteenth century the Fuuta Tooro produced cereals, using slave labour, which entered the circuit of the rubber trade of Moorish marabouts and were sold in Saint-Louis (Pasquier, 1987; Searing, 1993).

10 As was already mentioned by Cheikh Banndel Wan (see below) in an interview with David Robinson in the 1970s (Kane and Robinson, 1984).

11 Al-Hâjj Sih's field was divided in three (96, 97 and 98, see fig. 4) by two of his grand-sons. Golle Sih, who traded outside the village, had two children and cultivated field 98. Furthermore, for eight years, he worked as sharecropping tenant on Aamadu Moktar's Wan's field 134. His brother, Wopa Sih, farmed two other fields, 96 and 97.

12 The word comes from *ennDu*, which designates the breast, but the milk metaphor, *kosam*, is also in use. Milk kinship is at the basis of adoption and serves to designate alliance between 'casted' groups that do not intermarry, particularly between *FulBe* and *SulbalBe*, who engage in reciprocal exchanges. It is significant that in order to designate maternal relations in marriage we use the word *dewol*, the mother's lineage, which comes from *debbo* (woman). Similarly, paternal lineage (*gorol*) comes from *gorko* (man).

13 Here I borrow the term *deliason* from the Hellenist Nicole Loraux to draw a parallel between her reflection on the Greek notion of *stasis* – dissent, civil war – and Houari Touati's discussion of *siba* – insubordinaion, revolt – which come from the freed she-camel (*sa'iba*) consecrated to the rise of Islam. From these meanings originates the spatial category of *bilad sa'iba*, scarcely subdued territory where central power (*makhzen*) only exercises episodic control, a formula which aptly expresses Morocco's fortune.

14 See another interpretation in Mohammed Ennaji, 2007, 33–43.

15 According to Olivier Leservoisier (2005, 990), in Djeol in Mauritania this term was incorporated in the toponym of a site linked to slaves, *hayre majjuBe*, 'the mountain of the lost ones'.

16 Far from shattering the bond between the master (*sayyid*) and the slave (*'abd*), the emancipation of slaves (*'itq*) substitutes a genealogical link (*nasab*) for one based on contract and market exchange. The legal consequence of the filial tie is to allow the 'two parties to inherit from one another' (Touati, 1996, 108), but in fact it is only the master who inherits from the slave, not vice versa (Ennaji, 2007, 50).

17 Shifting dependency onto land only occurred in relation to floodlands because of the irregularity of floods. Control of the lowest areas of the flooded basins allowed the nobles to maintain supremacy over their dependants (Boutillier and Schmitz, 1987).

18 This word is a deformation of *jeyaaDo,* which comes from *jeyeede,* passive form of *jeyDe:* 'to be master of', or 'owner of'.

19 We follow the tradition reported by Abdul Sow.

20 In the Wolof kingdoms of the end of the nineteenth century the transformation of the servile relationship into one of clientage created tensions in the individual's life,

especially related to the lack of a man's paternal rights over his offspring. According to Searing (2002, 174–76), in the Bawol at the beginning of the 1900s the emancipation of a slave living with his wives and children, granted by the master, was conditional on the slave's payment of an annual tribute of part of his harvest to the ex-master and to his leaving 'one or several of his children at the service of his master or his mistress'. The cycle would repeat itself in the next generation; hence the transformation of slaves into clients is based on control of the slave's offspring, as ties of affection prevent the flight of the parents. This is particularly true in the case of slave mothers, as the children belong to the mother's master.

21 When the *TooroBBe* state became an immense protected zone, a cosmopolitan *dâr-al-islâm*, the Almaami Abdul-Kader Kan is credited for having taken a series of military measures to organise the defence of this region, and for the creation of mosques on the left riverbank (Robinson, 1975b). The *SeBBe* warriors had been living in the region on top of the Fuuta Tooro, where the *Satigi* had sought refuge at the end of the eighteenth century. The fixation of warriors on the shallows resulted from the downstream movement of the *SeBBe* warriors, as they became allied to the Islamic clergy. Instead, the *TooroBBe* went upstream, a movement that was at the same time spatial and social (fig. 2). The group of *TooroBBe* Islamic scholars was formed thanks to the religious and status conversion of Peul or Wolof lineages, which settled, learned Pulaar and studied the Qu'ran. The steps they followed in this double conversion are described by Shaykh Musa Kamara in his monumental micro-history (Kamara, 1998) and in the analysis that he makes of it in the *Al-Majmû'al Nafis* (Hilliard, 1997). But it is possible to go further, and consider the *TooroBBe* clerisy (Willis, 1978; 1979) as the result of an impressive social promotion of marginal groups and people of mixed origins (castemen, slaves) that occurred under the banner of an egalitarian Islam from the early eighteenth century at the moment of the foundation of the imamates of Fuuta Jalo (Guinea) and Fuuta Tooro. Subsequently, these groups would fill the ranks of the Jihâd of the nineteenth century (Dilley, 2004).

22 Kamara dedicates two chapters on this process of land appropriation, chapter 3 on the *KoliyaaBe* and chapter 4 on other 'warrior groups' (Kamara, 1998, 189–213).

23 As argued by Claude Meillassoux (1986, 121), true emancipation presupposes the reestablishment of honour, which implies the forgetting of the past situation. On the aspects of honour denied to the slaves, see De Bruijn and Pelckmans, 2005; Klein, 1998; 2005.

24 The memory of slave origins reappears at weddings with non-*SeBBe*. Here the number of cloth bands (*pagnes*) is greater when a *CeDDo* wants to marry a *Pullo* woman, or when the bride is a divorcee (*diwo*).

25 From 1856 Faidherbe created the school of hostages in Saint-Louis; he considered the French language a 'true instrument of conquest' (Sall, 2007, 658). In 1895 it became the school of the sons of chiefs. In 1857 the secular schools of Dagana, Podor (for the Fuuta Tooro), and Bakel (for the upper river) were created. But it is at the beginning of the 1900s that the three-level system was put in place: village schools with preparation classes, regional schools, and finally (1906) the *école normale* of Saint-Louis, where teachers were trained. It became the William Ponty School in Goree and was transferred to Thies in 1937.

26 In order to improve the knowledge of Arabic in the Fuuta Tooro, he went all the way to Fuuta Jaloo to look for schoolmasters. Among them was Moodi Aalimu, the master of Shaykh Musa Kamara, who settled in Bokkijawe at the heart of Fuuta Tooro (Schmitz, 1998, 17–21).

27 We can compare this with Qu'ranic education in Fuuta Jaloo, where the Muslim elite limited the slaves' access to Qu'ranic school (Botte, 1990; 1994).

28 This reopening was preceded by the mission of two French pedagogues, Terrisse and

Mahe, who taught youths how to read and write and introduced sound movies (Samba Saydou Diouf, 21/03/07). This precedent partly accounts for the subsequent success of Shaykh Banndel Wan.

29 In the sense of the republican *politique des races* formulated by the AOF Governor General William Ponty in 1909 (see Conklin, 1997, 109–18).

30 According to Gregory Mann (2006, 170), in Kati, where was based the 2nd regiment of *tirailleurs sénégalais*, Colonel de Martonne celebrated the history of the regiment at an annual ceremony that included ethnic performances – Lobi dances, Bamana processions – meant to highlight the cultural diversity of West Africans, and at the same time to promote their amalgamation. Born in Gabon, Ntchorere married a Malian woman and encouraged such unions among the children of soldiers at the school of Kati.

31 Despite his valour, he was identified by German soldiers and shot. The following day, a group of his men (about fifty?) were executed at a nearby village. Knowledge of the massacres of May and June 1940 spread like wildfire, but while in France the memory of these events was repressed, in Senegal the events of Thiaroye have been commemorated ever since. In Senegal the school of children of soldiers, which later became the military school of Saint-Louis (Bango) was named after Ntchorere, and in France a stele and a mausoleum were erected in Airaines near Amiens in 1965 (Scheck, 2006, 45–46, 182). The photos of these monuments illustrate the conclusion of Echenberg's book (1991).

32 This corresponded to a 'tradition of stigma' towards African fighters that started well before the Second World War (e.g. the 1904 colonial massacre of the Herero and Nama in today's Namibia, the French–German wars of 1870 and 1940, etc.). The massacre of about 3000 *tirailleurs sénégalais* imprisoned in 1940 is the missing link in a chain starting with the 1939 Poland Campaign and the integral 'racial war' fought by the Wehrmacht in the Balkans and Soviet Union and continuing until 1945 (Scheck, 2006, 28–30, 97–103, 123).

33 This inclusion is attested since the First World War, when in 1919 up to 49,000 soldiers were demobilised in a chaotic manner, and the soldiers had to go back home on foot. This process revealed the contempt in which the soldiers held their parents, the elderly in particular, whom they qualified as 'savage' and ignorant (Mann, 2006, 77). This 'cascade' transfer of stigma reveals what the soldiers themselves had experienced in the war.

34 He was closely related to the division commissioner Oumar Mahi Wane to whom he gave his daughter in marriage.

35 His grandfather Abdul Biraan was son of Biraan (whose father was Ceerno Ibra, the founder of the branch of Mboumba) and of Ramatulaay, the daughter of Tapsiiru Aamadu, an ancestor of the Kanel branch. See fig. 3 which elaborates the genealogy established by David Robinson (1975, 25).

36 Himself a former teacher, Mamadou Dia became Senghor's prime minister before being jailed for an attempted coup in 1963. On Mamadou Dia, see Atlan, 2001, and Jézéquel, 2003.

37 Gregory Mann (2006, 130) illustrates this type of personal patronage through the example of Michael Dorange, who after 1945 supported the education of the children of veterans at his expense and fought to obtain pensions for them.

38 Abdul Bayla Wane, Dakar 27/03/07.

39 According to Samba Saydou Diouf (21/03/07), Mammadu Hammaat sent a petition mentioning all the notables present at a meeting regarding the school to the District Commander (*commandant du cercle*). Thanks to the intervention of the teaching inspector Bernard Coulibaly, this strategy was successful.

40 Samba Saydou Diouf, 21/03/07.

41 Shaykh Banndel Wan was one of David Robinson's interlocutors towards the end of the 1960s and he spoke about the relations between Ceerno WanwanBe and Joom Mbummba, a Peul who carried the patronym Soh of the ancient landlords (Kane and Robinson, 1984, 91–95).

42 Ablaye Sih, 21/03/07. He was also known under the name of Mammadu Mammodu (Mammadu son of Mammodu). His father Mammodu Abdul (Mammodu son of Abdul) with his brother Bookar Abdul took part in the assassination of Abdul Aziz Wan by Demmba Daramaan (Sall, 2007, 221), successor of Ibraa Almaami as *chef de canton* in 1900 (genealogy fig. 3).

43 When Lamine Gueye in 1958 created the PRA (*Parti du Regroupement Africain*), a large consortium of African socialist movements, the UPS (*Union Progressiste Sénégalaise*) was its Senegalese branch. Led by Senghor, the UPS dominated politically until 1976. Opposed to the positive vote on the 1958 referendum, the PRA-Senegal split from the UPS, following the leadership of Abdoulaye Ly, Assane Seck and Amadou Mahtar M'Bow. Constituting itself as opposition party, it faced its first failure. In 1966 the PRA, weaker but still the only opposition party, joined Senghor's UPS (Atlan, 2001). At the local level these party struggles became crystallised as struggles between the factions 'A' and 'B'. In the Senegal valley, faction B, represented by the politician Ibraa Mammadu Wan (fig. 3), remained in power for a long time, opposing the minority faction A, represented by Abubakri Kan, who also belonged to a family of canton chiefs. As an opposition party, the PRA aligned itself with the latter (Hammat Thiam, 20/03/07).

44 Recruiting its members and militants from among teachers, the LD/MPT is led by Professor Abdoulaye Bathily, an emblematic historian of the 'Dakar School,' who became a politician and minister. This double career started at the military academy (*Prytané*) Charles Ntchorere of Bango, from which he was expelled for having joined a strike. This event led him to continue his studies in England.

45 According to Catherine Atlan (2001), Abdoulaye Ly, born in 1919 and son of a notable from Saint-Louis, followed a metropolitan schooling path: primary school in Saint-Louis, middle and high school Van Vollenhoven in Dakar, he was then sent to France to take a teaching degree. Conscripted in 1939, he returned to his studies after 1943, applying to do a thesis in history in 1946 in Montpellier and Paris. It was during the war that he had his most important experience: 'It is in 1939 that I realized what the situation of the colonized was: fighting for another nation… This has structured my anticolonial conscience. In this war I experienced the negation of the self…' and he adds 'I never really stopped fighting' (Atlan, 2001, 397).

46 Ablaye Sih, *Parcelles Assainies*, Dakar, 21/03/07.

47 Hammat Thiam, school director of Thierno Salif Ndongo, Pikine, Madina Gounass district, 20/03/07.

48 More than in relation to his childhood sufferings, the speaker expressed intense emotion with respect to his failure to reimburse the debt to his parents.

49 Except for the *EnnDam Bilali* movement, which is unknown outside the Haalpulaar'en.

50 From 1901, before the 1903 Roume abolition decree, the future general governor William Ponty recommended that all references to 'captives' or 'slaves' be erased from the census data, 'mentions that do not suit the ideals of civilization' (Conklin, 1997, 98). This ban on naming resulted in various euphemisms – domestic captives, servants, serfs – that remained in use after Independences (Cooper et al., 2000). We witnessed this in the 1970s/1980s when, during a census, the chief of the village of Doungel truncated the forbidden word 'maccuBe' which became 'mac.' (pronounced 'match').

51 Thanks to Hamidou Dia, doctoral PhD student of University Paris V, who was invited to the ceremony.

52 I would like to thank the Wane familiy who invited me to the enthronement, and in particular Dean Abdoul Bayla, Colonel Birane, Professor Sada Taminou, Souleymane and Abdrahmane.

53 See the discussion of this thesis in Cheikh Anta Babou's recent book (2007, 24–26).

6

Curse and Blessing: On Post-slavery Modes of Perception and Agency in Benin[1]

Christine Hardung

The process of democratisation that Benin[2] embarked upon in the 1990s, and similar political developments in Niger, Mali and lately Mauritania, ushered in the active participation of communities of slave descent in new modes of local politics. Former slave communities are now claiming their rights through non-governmental platforms and organisations, employing Western human rights discourses. In such contexts research on slavery must, on the one hand, contribute to overcoming biases and enabling former slaves to be perceived as legitimate political actors. On the other hand, it should not dismiss the fact that the ex-slaves' ideological attachment to the communities of former masters may well prove stronger than the resentment for their past economic and political subjugation.

This is the case of the GannunkeeBe, a Muslim community living in the two provinces of Borgu and Atakora in Northern Benin. Being Fulfulde speakers, the GannunkeeBe have until recently been considered part of the larger FulBe society. However, in the 1994 census (and this itself can be seen as an indication of the ongoing process of ethnicisation) they became listed under the separate ethnonym 'Gando', although some of them would have preferred being classified as 'FulBe', as today the term 'Gando' implies former slave status in the history of Borgu.

'Gando' is employed, in French, with much broader connotations than its Fulfulde equivalent, 'GannunkeeBe'. It is used as an umbrella term, referring both historically to the slaves of the Bariba[3] and the FulBe, and to their present descendants. The equation of 'Gando' with slaves or ex-slaves is not only widespread in people's perceptions in South Benin, but it also figures in parts of Borgu, particularly among the younger generations who are no longer aware of subtle lexical nuances. From the point of view of the GannunkeeBe,[4] however, this equation is based on a false generalisation. Just as Fulfulde language unites the FulBe and the GannunkeeBe and makes them appear as one single ethnic group to outsiders, the fact that all GannunkeeBe speak Fulfulde also erases status differences among them: not all of today's GannunkeeBe are of slave descent. Yet speaking Fulfulde and not being FulBe makes all GannunkeeBe appear to be descendants of slaves. This includes those who do not think of themselves as in any way connected to slavery, and who claim that their forefathers were foreign migrants, or were *wasangari* (mounted warriors) who lost connection with their original lineage.

In their own vision of belonging, a significant number of GannunkeeBe trace their ancestry to their peasant neighbours, particularly the Baatombu, and in certain regions (such as Nikki/ Kalale) to the Bo'o, and stress in specific contexts their Baatombu or Bo'o identity. Others also try to avoid reference to their slave ancestry and define their identity generically as FulBe when talking to outsiders. This transformation or switching of identity throughout a person's life, or even just to suit the circumstances, is characteristic of this community. Besides, the GannunkeeBe who are descendants of slaves of the FulBe are often perceived as FulBe outside their home regions. Their habitus, their dressing style and their sense of taste affiliate them to the FulBe, and only those originating from the Northern Provinces may be in a position to recognise the subtle differences that point to the GannunkeeBe's distinctive status.

Apart from a small percentage of the population working in urban areas, the GannunkeeBe are primarily farmers, often combining farming with petty trade, weaving and livestock breeding. Today they constitute a prosperous community, roughly equal in economic status to their former masters. Unlike other regions, the FulBe of present-day Benin never controlled land tenure[5] to the extent of being able to deny access to land to their slaves, the *maccuBe* (also known as *jeyaaBe*), after their manumission. Whereas abolition in other communities of the Sahara-Sahel was accompanied by conflicts over the terms of land ownership and use, the freed *maccuBe* of present-day Benin rarely experienced landlessness. Thus they did not depend on the relationship with their masters to secure access to land.[6] Moreover, the GannunkeeBe successfully made a virtue out of the necessities of their slave past, which obliged them to undertake almost every type of labour for their masters. Unlike the latter, whose economic opportunities were restrained by a code of conduct related to the ethos of being FulBe (*pulaaku*), the GannunkeeBe's entrepreneurship and openness to various kinds of economic activity allowed them to adapt more flexibly to local and global transformations.

Judging by the developments of the recent past, the GannunkeeBe seem to have been able to emancipate themselves not just economically, but also politically. Politically active GannunkeeBe made their voice heard within the FulBe community in the *Laawol Fulfulde* movement, the first collective mobilisation of the FulBe of Northern Benin initiated primarily by FulBe intellectuals at the end of the 1980s. The first step in their disengagement from the FulBe occurred in 1997, with the founding of the first association of Gando farmers, *jiDi waDi*. This organisation adopted what was initially a consciously apolitical stance in its statutes, *inter alia*, to avoid confrontation with the FulBe. But the immediate reaction of the FulBe elite to the creation of *jiDi waDi* revealed that this small association was perceived as anything but apolitical, and that the explosive potential of an exclusive 'Gando organisation' was feared. Later on, the GannunkeeBe formed their own independent organisations and joined new political formations based on shared interests that sidestepped the boundaries of GannunkeeBe and FulBe identities. Over the last few years, they have progressively gained access to political resources, particularly in local political arenas (see Hahonou, in this volume). In fact, they gradually achieved more than the FulBe themselves. Except for an influential elite minority who attained higher education degrees, the majority of FulBe perceive themselves primarily as cattle breeders, even though they also farm land. Having been more sceptical about literacy and schooling than their former slaves, they often have to rely on the intermediation of the GannunkeeBe, especially in dealing with state institutions. This in turn has opened up new opportunities for the GannunkeeBe.

At the national level, Benin's GannunkeeBe do not appear to be more marginalised than their former masters. Unlike other FulBe groups, the Borgu FulBe largely abstained from assuming public functions or asserting themselves politically and socially. They therefore occupy a marginal political position[7] among the societies of Northern Benin, which dates back to pre-colonial times (Bierschenk, 1997, 6). For the FulBe of Benin, 'weakness' or 'fragility' is not a negative trait per se, but a constitutive element of their feeling of ethnic superiority (Boesen, 1999). In order to understand today's relationships between the descendants of slaves and their 'powerless powerful' former masters, it is important to take into consideration the spiritual, as well as economic and political, dimensions of power and to look at how power asymmetries are manifested in specific beliefs and ideologies.

Social relations between former free and bonded communities have changed. In political and economic terms, the descendants of slaves detached themselves from their former masters, some a considerable time ago. Nonetheless, the belief in the intrinsic superiority of the FulBe persists among some individuals and groups of unfree origin. Why do some people of slave descent remain committed to the notion of a universal order based on inequality, while others do not share this worldview? How does the notion of *lamaare FulBe*, 'the supremacy of the FulBe', become legitimised, and under what conditions does it lose significance?

This essay addresses these questions by exploring a particular aspect of the complex relationship between GannunkeeBe and FulBe, namely, the ex-slaves' perspectives on their former FulBe masters' power to curse and to bless. It also addresses methodological issues related to changing interpretations of the ideology of hierarchy through an analysis of day-to-day negotiations and interactions. The spiritual power ascribed to the FulBe to utter or revoke a blessing underscores hegemonic mechanisms for the maintenance of hierarchical relations. At the same time, slave descendants adopt creative practices in their daily lives to circumvent social hierarchies. This, in turn, sheds light on the conditions under which the masters' power to curse ceases to be effective.

Cursing Power and Individual Agency

Cursing and blessing, as well as the belief in the efficacy of spiritual power, are rooted in religious thought, which posits the invisible world as 'distinct but not separate from the visible one' (Ellis and Ter Haar, 2007, 387). Curses, like blessings, are 'legitimate attributes of authority' (Douglas, 1988, 139) in the ideology of slavery, consolidating the slaveholder's position as classificatory father or mother figure. In the words of a person of slave descent, 'Being seized by his [the Pullo's] curse is like receiving a curse from your mother or father. Their curse falls upon you, because they have taken care of you (literally, suffered for you).'

In the eyes of more than a few GannunkeeBe, the curse (*yaa'oore*) uttered by a Pullo (Pl. FulBe) in a dispute is capable of destroying their entire economic and social existence.[8] Someone struck by the curse of a Pullo, so they say, 'can accomplish nothing, not even the minimum' (*goDDun waDataa baa seDa*). 'Everything perishes' (*butu waatan*), 'you will find nothing remaining' (*a heBataa koomi*). Expressions such as these reveal the encompassing destructive capacity of a curse. 'Their mouth bears poison' (*hunnuko maBBe nun woodi tooke*) is how an older man described the cursing power of the FulBe, equating its impact to that of the fatal poisoned arrows of the Bariba. Anyone in the vicinity of a larger sized FulBe and GannunkeeBe hamlet, located southeast of Kouande, knows the story of a man whose herd was so large that it had to be split in two for grazing purposes. One day, it is said, a quarrel arose between him and an elder of the family of his former *joomiraaBe* (masters). The man confronted his FulBe neighbour saying that he was no longer a *maccuDo* and the Pullo no more his *mawDo* (head, leader), as he now possessed more animals than him. If he wouldn't believe it, he ought to come and count his cows himself.[9] This enraged the Pullo. In response, the Pullo noted that he would not mind counting the herd, but he would begin by counting the man and his wives and children since they were, after all, his property. The Pullo said 'you will see' (*a yiian nun*). With these words, he invoked a curse upon the man, 'he spoke ill' (*o bati bone*). The fact that the curse 'bore its impact' (*bonka waDi*, literally: 'made the ill word') was first confirmed to the GannunkeeBe by the fate of the cattle. One animal after another died, only a single cow remained. All of the man's attempts to save his cattle were vain. The curse, literally 'the mouth', followed him (*hunuko tokkimo*) and most people believed that it would continue to follow him till his last days. To all the inhabitants of this locality and its vicinities, the consequences of the Pullo's curse were evident in the impoverishment of the man and his entire household. In the meantime, the man had become dependent on others even for tilling the fields and, in the weeks leading to the harvest, he had to rely on his brother's help to feed his family.

Local comments on this incident, different accounts of which circulated in the region, highlighted divergences in the GannunkeeBe's conception of their own identity. 'We have no ancestry', remarked an elderly woman of unfree lineage on the impact of the curse, which, in her eyes, had been invoked upon her impoverished neighbour. Children of FulBe slaves in Borgu were assigned to the owners of their mothers, a practice common to other slave-holding societies of the Sahel. The ideology of slavery denied the social recognition of a slave couple's descent, although in practice the couple certainly sought to maintain familial bonds. The GannunkeeBe today have long-standing ties of kinship. However, even today, in some contexts their affinal and agnatic relations are not perceived as equally valid as those of the FulBe. Descendants of slaves, who do not belong to a community of ancestry (*lenyol/boseru*), may see themselves, and be seen as, more vulnerable and at the mercy of the curse, due to their lack of ancestral protection.

Further comments on this dispute exemplify the extent to which contemporary judgement is shaped by an ideology that in fact belongs to the past. *Ceede makko nun*, 'he is his property' [literally: his money], is how one woman described the status difference between the conflicting parties, implying that this justified the reaction of the Pullo towards the Gannunkeejo (pl. GannunkeeBe). Yet other remarks were self-ironic. 'How can a cow want to count other cows?' commented a cattle owner of slave descent on the apparent 'commonality' of a cow and a *maccuDo* (pl. *maccuBe*), which together formed the *jawdi*, the wealth and comfort of the FulBe in the times of slavery. There was also a growing sense of bafflement, particularly among younger educated members of the community, who were not convinced that the loss of the herd was due to the curse. In their view it was clearly related to a cattle disease. That being said, they did not wish to deny the power of the curse entirely.

The curse leaves various courses of action open to both its utterer and its target. A curse is not irrevocable. Someone who has been cursed still has the possibility to plead for its revocation through reconciliatory gestures, such as gifts of kola nuts, a roll of white cloth or the like. Those who have pronounced a curse may take back their words, may 'forgive' (*o tuubi mo*). However, the above incident shows that reconciliation is not always possible or necessary in the view of the GannunkeeBe. In the same region, another widely reported case concerned a young Gannunkeejo, who is reported to have had an accident in a taxi on the very same day when he was struck by the curse of a Pullo, also following a dispute, and died a few days later.

The GannunkeeBe of this region rarely ascribe incidents as momentous as death or complete ruin directly to the curse of the FulBe. It is rare to meet someone with direct experience of such incidents, and most accounts are based on hearsay. The power of the curse is experienced as a normative force. It bears structural resemblance to the threat. 'The avoidance of dangerous conflicts,' according to Popitz, 'leads to no precedents being set and thus to a limited range of experiences, which eventually consolidates assumptions of actual power relations into conventions' (Popitz, 1992, 85). The mere fear of being cursed hinders many a GannunkeeBe from taking chances with a Pullo who might use the power of his words in a dispute.

Someone still subject to customary bonds may speak of a certain 'fear' (*kulol*) in relation to the cursing power of his former master. This points to an emotion, the existence of which is very rarely expressed in explicit terms: 'That is why we fear them (the FulBe)' (*gam majjum men kulla Be*). Despite a certain tendency to overstatement (which is no doubt present in such utterances and is a common feature of the communication forms of the GannunkeeBe and the FulBe), this fear is, at least in part, real. Fear of the curse, or in some cases only a certain apprehension, may induce compliant behaviour towards former masters in specific contexts. The extent of this fear varies at the individual level. While some just prefer to avoid open conflicts with the former masters (*joomiraaBe*), or simply give in to disputes, particularly those related to their herd, others feel more vulnerable to the malevolence of a Pullo. Some believe that adverse consequences may follow even just from failing to comply with a request to carry out some task for the FulBe. However, fear of the FulBe's cursing power is primarily related to the consequences it may yield for herding.

Today the GannunkeeBe own their herds, but they are not heir to the cultural legacy attached to the cows of the FulBe. The herds of the GannunkeeBe are the product of economic labour and toil. Their animals are acquired through purchase, just as the *maccuBe* themselves were purchased in former times. The cattle of the FulBe, on the other hand, are God-given (*na'i jippoDii*). The mark of this divine predilection, distinguishing the FulBe from all non-FulBe, is cow's milk (*kosam*). Milk is not only a primary source of nourishment and the main economic asset, but also carries symbolic significance. It is a substance that metaphorically represents the self-perception and public identity of the FulBe (Boesen, 1999, 74; Dupire, 1970, 151).

The GannunkeeBe's recognition of the privileged position of the FulBe with regard to cattle is not merely an expression of status difference. Although the

GannunkeeBe also herd cattle, and the FulBe are involved with farming, these strategies of subsistence are ethnically marked and seen as activities exclusive to each community. Both groups mutually define themselves on the basis of this economic specialisation. The GannunkeeBe often highlight a difference in the functions of their own and the FulBe's cows. They claim that their cows are 'neither cows for naming ceremonies, nor for weddings' (*na'i amen laBirtaa Di, koowiroytaa Di*). A Pullo's cows must have these functions or he will not be able to perform these ceremonies. By stating the social significance of cattle for their FulBe neighbours, the GannunkeeBe distinguish them from their own animals. Surely, they view their cattle as living beings tied to their existence, and they are familiar with the individual traits and inclinations of each animal. However, unlike the FulBe, they do not view their livestock as central to the constitution of their identity. Cattle are primarily seen as a trade asset, often purchased with a surplus made through farming and exchanged for textile products, and sold when required.

Today those GannunkeeBe who own few animals and live in proximity to the FulBe often join their cattle to the FulBe's herd for herding. However, there is widespread anxiety about the Pullo possibly misappropriating their cattle, by selling their animals and then claiming they got lost, or secretly substituting a male animal for a female. Since the GannunkeeBe have increasingly been taking up cattle breeding over the past decades, those with smaller herds tend to entrust their animals to the care of relatives or neighbours from their own community. But even this type of agreement is not devoid of quarrels and disputes, as the cattle owner feels in a better position to enter into a confrontation with the other party. To many GannunkeeBe, an open dispute over cattle with a Pullo is unthinkable.

Broadly speaking, GannunkeeBe herders, in particular those who have not entirely disentangled themselves from older patterns of social interaction, often find themselves in difficult situations. Access to wells for watering cattle is usually regulated on a first-come, first-served basis. Many GannunkeeBe herders, even in the presence of FulBe herders, follow this rule as a matter of course. However, a Gannunkeejo still attached to customary norms and values would usually let a Pullo go first. Similarly, if he saw a FulBe herd approaching while his animals are grazing in the bush, he would try to keep maximum distance from them to prevent the animals from mixing. He would maintain a defensive stance in his interactions with the FulBe, as far as the choice of pasture and watering sites is concerned.

While it is possible to avoid the FulBe while grazing, it is impossible to conceal one's herd. Although in most regions the FulBe are undisputedly the owners of the largest cattle herds, more and more GannunkeeBe have succeeded in forming large herds. Sometimes, the size of a Gannunkeejo's herd may even significantly outnumber that of his FulBe neighbour. This situation may cause considerable trouble to some GannunkeeBe whose herd is kept close to that of their former FulBe masters. A Pullo can be deeply affected by the mere sight of a neighbouring Gannunkeejo's herd, which outnumbers his own: 'it causes pain in his chest' (*ko naawimo gabaare makko*). Consequently, in certain circumstances, the GannunkeeBe may see their own herds as a potential threat, inasmuch as they fear disappointing their former *joomiraaBe*. Some owners of large herds feel compelled to keep their cattle out of FulBe sight.

Another way to deal with this situation is to confide part of the herd to a Pullo. This type of herding contract has advantages for both sides, albeit of unequal nature. The Gannunkeejo needs no longer fear that his growing herd may stir the jealousy or malevolence of the Pullo. The Pullo, in turn, obtains free access to the milk of the cows placed in his care, in addition to maintaining his reputation as the 'actual' cattle owner. Furthermore, it is common for the Pullo to receive every third newborn calf as payment for grazing the cattle. When a Gannunkeejo increases the size of a Pullo's herd, it is not necessarily out of fear of the latter's curse, but occasionally even out of friendship. However, such arrangements are rare and tend to be conducted discreetly, outside the knowledge of neighbours or relatives. Apart from those directly involved and selected household members, nobody else would know.

How should this non-confrontational approach towards former masters be understood in relation to the GannunkeeBe's contemporary engagement in local politics, which requires them to assume a confrontational stance towards the latter? Which groups continue investing in their relation with the FulBe and the social order based on inequality? Who has managed to disengage him/herself from former relationships and the ideology of FulBe superiority? And which groups of GannunkeeBe see their forefathers as perhaps less powerful than the FulBe but not as their slaves, and therefore retain more agency? These questions can only be adequately answered when addressed in a broader context.

Historical and Economic Aspects of Slavery in Pre-colonial Borgu

While in pre-colonial Borgu several cities, such as Kandi, Kouande, Parakou and Nikki, had become powerful regional centres, the Borgu was not politically centralised. A large number of settlements formed a conglomerate of unstable political formations ruled by individual local leaders, called *wasangari* (Alber, 2000, 80f.). These were horse-riding warriors, whose power depended on military might and superior technology, individual prestige and dynastic closeness to the rulers of Nikki. In this social system warlords depended on military alliance with other leaders. Slaves, besides their economic function, played a major political role. Through gifts of captives, and sometimes even entire slave villages, the *wasangari* gained the loyalty and support of powerful individuals and followers. The slaves of the *wasangari* lived in separate settlements (*gando*), which they farmed, periodically delivering cereals to their owners. On the other hand, with the exception of wealthy FulBe families, who had slaves doing everything for them, the *maccuBe*, the slaves of the FulBe, only alleviated their master's workload, even when they were primarily responsible for farming. The *yobu* also, domestic slaves of Baatombu farmers, merely contributed to the farming economy of their masters. Like most of the slaves of the *wasangari*, some *maccuBe* groups formed separate small settlements that produced independently and, when necessary, sent labour and supplies to their masters (*joomiraaBe*). Conditions and opportunities in these separate slave settlements differed from those available to *maccuBe* living attached to their masters' households. Yet, even when *maccuBe* hamlets were detached from their *joomiraaBe*'s camps, they were seldom distant and often remained under the latter's control. The *gando* (slave settlements of the Baatombu and *wasangari*) enjoyed some autonomy in their life and production, as they were further removed from the main centres where their masters lived.

The structure and location of settlements and households played an important role in the development of the relationship between GannunkeeBe and FulBe. It is not a coincidence that the GannunkeeBe's political mobilisation would start in the region of Nikki/Kalale. Large pre-colonial slave communities in this region favoured the development of a GannunkeeBe corporate identity. Moreover, this region is densely populated by GannunkeeBe who trace their origin to free migrants, or refugee *wasangari* defeated in dynastic disputes, Bo'o or Bariba, who sought shelter in these communities and subsequently married-in and/or adopted the local language. This, in Fulfulde-speaking society, automatically transformed them into GannunkeeBe (cf. Schmitz, in this volume). GannunkeeBe chiefs (*gando suno*) also had slaves, who were called *yoosiyooBe*, 'slaves of the slaves', an expression that reveals how these masters' status was perceived. Yet these families owned slaves and belonged to those in power.[10]

Today the majority of GannunkeeBe political leaders and intellectual elites descend from three large chiefly families from the Nikki/Kalale region. The GannunkeeBe from these families never acted as slaves of the FulBe and saw themselves as descending from free ancestors. Their offspring today do not fear the power of the FulBe's curse and confront them openly. In the context of the political mobilisation of the end of the 1990s, GannunkeeBe elites tried to encourage the political participation of those GannunkeeBe whose ancestors had been enslaved and could not easily overcome their bond to the FulBe. In the words of a GannunkeeBe leader:

> There are people today who understand themselves as *maccuBe*, even if they are not slaves anymore they cannot leave the FulBe. It is not easy to include

them, because they are under the influence of this idea that the FulBe will curse them and their lives will be destroyed if they do something against the FulBe's will. So even now it is very difficult for them to declare openly that they are not standing by the side of the FulBe anymore. Even for the intellectuals among them, there are only a few who raise their voice.

The endurance or change of past ideologies is also connected to physical mobility. The *maccuBe* who moved away from their masters and no longer live near them have been able to change their belief in the FulBe's cursing/blessing power. The old social order, reflected in spatial arrangements, was partly transformed as a consequence of colonial forced resettlements, but later migration movements played a much greater role. In some regions bonds of dependence and affection between the children of free and unfree persons remained, to the extent that sporadic exchanges still occur even across large distances. In other areas, departures completely eroded former dependent relations and slave origins lost their social significance or were forgotten. Thus, physical detachment from the old masters enabled a more radical transformation of hierarchical structures and ideologies. Economic factors, at a regional or household level, are also important determinants of change. In areas characterised by the early development of cotton production, like the largest part of the Borgu, wage labour rooted in impersonal relations counterbalanced the personal nature of relations and exchanges between the FulBe and their former slaves. The neutralising power of money eroded customary forms of patronage and did not introduce comparable patterns of unequal interactions between the free and the descendants of the unfree.

Today, groups such as the GannunkeeBe of Bagou in the Borgu province, where wage labour was introduced in the colonial period, are cattle herders and farmers who plant cotton on a considerable scale. They have abandoned the behaviour and strategies of some descendants of slaves in other regions of Northern Benin, particularly areas where cotton planting was introduced recently. Commenting on those who continue to 'follow the [orders of the] FulBe', the people of Bagou argue that: *Be keBay taw laawol* – 'they have not yet found the way', or *gite maBBe laaBay taw* – 'they cannot see with clear eyes yet'. Although vestiges of customary rules and attitudes persist sporadically, hierarchical structures have generally disintegrated, and with them the belief in the destructive potential of the curse. Thus, a cotton farmer asked rhetorically: 'The Pullo does not give you clothes anymore, he does not provide you with food anymore. [...] What harm then should his curse be capable of wreaking upon you?'

Negotiating Status and Choosing Identity

Historical and economic factors alone do not suffice to explain the relative resilience of the power of the curse and its consequences for the agency of the GannunkeeBe. Why do some descendants of slaves continue to recognise bygone patterns of dominance in daily actions and symbolic thought?

The FulBe may pronounce a curse, just as they may issue a blessing (*du'aare*). Cattle are the source of their power to bless. The FulBe's superiority and its recognition by the GannunkeeBe are also closely related to cattle ownership. A material fact is thus given spiritual weight. In the GannunkeeBe's worldview, the FulBe, by virtue of their cattle, act as intermediaries between the profane and the sacred worlds and are therefore endowed with supernatural powers. Here one may speak of a 'charismatic qualification'[11] attributed to the FulBe as a group in its entirety.

> FulBe, who have helped their *jeyaaBe* [slaves] to breed cows, are rare. It is in fact a result of the blessing that the FulBe have given us (*du'aneego nun FulBe hokki men*).[12] They have not given us our cattle [...]. Their blessing consists of requesting God to bless what you have. For is it not God who showers blessings? We partake of their blessing, because our cattle are in their hands. Till today we remain their *jeyaaBe*, but we do not undertake slave labour for them anymore. We remain their *jeyaaBe*, because we choose to be so.

It would be wrong to conclude that the ideology of power relations and its operationalisation can be solely explained by, or ascribed to, the institution of cursing and blessing. Yet this institution demonstrates most clearly the GannunkeeBe's belief in the legitimacy of *laamaare FulBe*, the supremacy of the FulBe. The charismatic authority attributed to the FulBe group as a whole underpins the belief in the binding nature of the old social order.

There are important inter-generational differences among those whose lives are closely intertwined with the FulBe. *Pullo laamiiDo nun* – 'the Pullo is *laamiiDo* (superior / chief)' – most older GannunkeeBe are convinced of this. *Pullo e wattiri lamaare* – 'The Pullo is acting as if he were *laamiiDo*' – this, on the other hand, is the view of a young man who refused to join a group on its way to a FulBe ceremony to fulfil the menial task of cutting and cleaning ritually slaughtered animals (*kuttol*). Many younger GannunkeeBe question the socio-economic foundations of dependence and their ideological legitimacy. If they recognise the authority of their former masters at all, this is based on the assumption that the FulBe live up to their socially ascribed roles, thereby leading their life as *dimo* (free human) and behaving in the prescribed manner. These roles presuppose the participation of the GannunkeeBe in the lives of the FulBe, and vice versa. When the actions of certain individuals do not live up to expectations, the GannunkeeBe's willingness to 'follow the [command of the] FulBe' is adjusted accordingly. Instances of how the FulBe disregard the rules, for instance by consuming wild meat, or asking money of someone of slave descent, are keenly registered and debated among the younger generations of GannunkeeBe.

> After a year of tilling the soil, by the grace of God, you now own two bulls. The very same one, for whom you slogged for five years, and who compensated you with a single bull for five years of your labour, is today knocking at your door asking for a loan. He is borrowing money from your hand! [...] If the Pullo now comes to you, can he then convince you that your cattle are going to die? Can he sell your cattle as he pleases?

There is a fundamental difference between the commonplace request for the performance of certain tasks, and the request for material support. The former request is in line with the traditional role of the *joomiraaBe* (masters) *vis-à-vis* the GannunkeeBe, whereas asking for money amounts to a complete turnaround of the balance of power.

It would be misleading and simplistic to describe the continuing belief in the superiority of the FulBe as merely a matter of generational difference, with the older generation perceiving themselves as *maccuBe* in the sphere of influence of the FulBe, and the younger generation rejecting this view. The quote on the FulBe's power to bless is from a conversation with young men from a settlement whose inhabitants live at close quarters with their former masters. Yet this quote also articulates a reclaimed sense of being *maccuBe* that expresses both an affirmation *and* a redefinition of status – 'We are their *maccuBe*, because we choose to be so.'[13]

The Comaroffs highlighted 'the choice of identities' as one of the key features to which the notion of freedom is reduced in a world shaped by the ramifications of neo-liberalism, post-colonialism and globalisation (Comaroff and Comaroff, 2004, 190). Is it not 'the choice of identity' that descendants of slaves are demanding, albeit under different circumstances? One might argue that in the ambivalent experience of their contemporary relationship to the FulBe there lies a sense of autonomy reflected in the collective memory of the unfree living conditions of earlier generations. For those still attached to the FulBe today, autonomy is inherent in the capacity to retain agency by accepting and defining on their own terms a hierarchical relation, with all its rules and ideological connotations. In particular circumstances, perceived powerlessness can thus be turned into perceived agency, and even power to choose. The most obvious reflection of this is to be found in the labour relations that some GannunkeeBe forge with the FulBe even today, be it in the form of paid work or symbolic prestations, which are reminiscent of the days of slavery.

Remembering their daily lives as slaves, the GannunkeeBe today reconfigure their past identity by representing the *maccuBe*'s relation to work as imbued with responsibility and self-dependency, rather than determined by force and bondage. A female elder once remarked casually that her family had in fact chosen to remain with their masters, when the *annasaraaBe*, 'the White', came and put pressure on the FulBe to liberate the *maccuBe*. I probed further. She replied that they couldn't possibly leave the FulBe, then began enumerating the variety of tasks they were in charge of, finally adding that slave holders would have surely died if they had stopped providing their nourishment. Here she emphatically used the phrase 'we, the *maccuBe*' (*minon maccuBe*). In my conversations, there were repeated references to a sense of responsibility and commitment towards the masters in the world of the *maccuBe*, which in turn indicated an awareness that masters depended on them. This belief shaped their work ethos and self-perception. FulBe slavery was primarily a form of labour (Hardung, 2006). Today the GannunkeeBe reverse the interpretation of their unfree labour as a monopoly over manual and physically exhausting work. By positing their labour as a gift to the masters, they are actually challenging their inferior position.

The pounding of grain at FulBe weddings, *untal*, was formerly done by female slaves. When GannunkeeBe women today perform the same task, they explain that they do so simply because the FulBe lack *enDam* (*gam dullere enDam*).[14] However, when women and young girls help with pounding at the ceremonies of GannunkeeBe relatives and neighbours, they describe their motivation as stemming from a sense of *enDam*, i.e. emotional empathy and closeness. Between themselves, GannunkeeBe women tell of how their former mistresses are 'forced' to ask them for help (*ko waDi ko untal laati tilay to Pullo*). 'The FulBe woman has money, she has cattle, she collects her *horBe*, she pays them money; she has to do it this way, because she has no one to do the work for her (*tilay gam o woodaa gaDanaDo mo*).' The woman quoted here used the word *horBe* (female slaves) in a contemporary context, which is an indication of the significance of *untal*, done for the FulBe. Even though the pounding of grain is paid work nowadays and definitely a source of financial gain, that is not the only reason why most women feel they cannot turn down the FulBe's request to work at their ceremonies.[15] Descendants of slaves portray FulBe women as dependent on *untal*, since they need external help for this task. The contemporary context has given a twist to the cultural significance of *untal* for the GannunkeeBe. Thus, forms of interaction rooted in the former hierarchy have been reinterpreted and rendered acceptable in the current context.

Not only do people of slave descent creatively reinterpret the social order, but they also re-create this order from within and appropriate symbolic elements from the world of the former master. One of these is the privileged position towards cattle. This is a matter of much debate, particularly among young GannunkeeBe, who question the extent to which differences should be seen as socially constructed or defined by divine laws. While some are willing to discuss these issues, not everyone finds such discussions appropriate. This is evident from the following debate among young GannunkeeBe:

S.: If you see how much you grow and sell, if you count all that we are doing, then we and the FulBe are the same (*enen e FulBe kam en fu go'o nun*). But the FulBe just like their cows more than we do.

B.: That's got nothing to do with like or dislike. The cows belong to them. They were already there for them (*Dun kan jiiDe bane, kamBe jey na'i. KamBe tawi*).

De.: Well, whom else should they belong to?

Do.: Patience, Demmo.

De.: Come on, why should the Pullo be more fond of a cow?

J.: So what about the GannunkeeBe now?

B.: When a Gannunkeejo acquires cows [...] he uses them [as trek oxes] for tilling his fields. The Pullo doesn't use them for his fields. [...] He never uses them for tilling the soil.

J.: So you till the fields that feed you and help you acquire your cows. If you get as many cows as the one who only looks after his cows and does not farm the land,[16] then would you still never celebrate a naming ceremony with the bull?

De.: Who me, sure, I have. I celebrated the naming ceremony of my child with the ritual slaughter of a bull.

S.: That's not true. I was there at the naming ceremony. It was exactly like it used to be done in the past. We went there. The ceremony was celebrated with a slaughtered sheep. Even if he has become rich and owns a lot of cattle, a Gannunkeejo always performs the naming ceremony with a sheep. It is only the Pullo who uses a bull. [...] As far as the cows go, it's always the Pullo. He is entitled to them.

B.: Allah has ordered our naming ceremonies to be performed with the slaughtering of a sheep. But nowadays they are killing bulls for it. That's not correct. Allah has decreed how things should be done.

D.: Bani, what are you saying!

B.: The FulBe slaughter the bull for their naming ceremonies, but that is not what Allah has deemed fit for our naming ceremonies. Allah has assigned to us the sheep, not the ox.

It is by no means self-evident that the descendants of slaves would sacrifice a bull at their naming ceremonies today, as the FulBe do. A well-known GannunkeeBe leader, respected by GannunkeeBe and FulBe alike, once wanted to conduct a wedding in his family that would include slaughtering a bull. Yet even this man did not do so without first consulting the chief of the FulBe. Only then was permission granted for slaughtering an animal for the wedding. 'They are celebrating like the FulBe', noted the GannunkeeBe from a neighbouring village who followed the event. It was apparent that there was a major difference to what was otherwise a common procedure at FulBe ceremonies.

Although in FulBe ceremonies the cleaning and cutting of the slaughtered animals (*kuttol*) is usually the task of the GannunkeeBe, it is noteworthy that at this ceremony they did not carry out this task themselves. The animal was slaughtered prior to the festivities and given to a Bariba butcher to be cut and cleaned. This meat was cut, in a sense symbolically fragmented and chopped up, and brought to the ceremony from the Bariba village in the form of pieces of meat. New ways of circumventing old rules are introduced, without openly violating them and at the same time accommodating them with present-day circumstances, thus gradually transforming the rules.

The contemporary continuity and change of power relations and related ideologies can ultimately be understood only by way of a paradox. It is precisely the creative negotiations over power relations and their symbolic forms that seem to contribute to the persistence of these relations and the social order that legitimises them. However, creative ways of dealing with superiority and inferiority may eventually reach their limits. Highlighting creativity and agency alone would amount to romanticising a relation historically based on the enslavement of people through physical and 'ideological violence' (Botte, 1999, 56). It would be wrong to assume that this manner of negotiating the relation always granted the individual freedom of interpretation and action. The institution of the curse clearly demonstrates the extent to which a sanction can have fundamental consequences for the opportunities of persons of unfree descent.

Understanding Ideologies of Hierarchy and their Transformations

An engagement with the condition of being a slave and its contemporary implications presupposes an understanding of what it means 'to be free' in that particular society or setting. For the FulBe, the notion of the free human (*dimo*) is closely related to the individual's wish not to be dominated by physical needs and emotions. In the quest to negate these there lies a moment of overcoming impulses and gaining self-control. This quest is driven less by how one is perceived by the outside world, and primarily by the desire to trust one's self-regulating capacity. Thus it expresses a fundamental experience of autonomy. 'To be free' is literally to 'own one's head', as individuals and communities (Boesen, 1999; Riesman, 1974; 1975, 54).

The term *maccuDo* (pl. *maccuBe*) is used today in contrast to *dimo*, a way of being that describes the free human. Research on the FulBe generally refers to this pair of concepts as opposites. However, in the times of slavery, *maccuDo* did not per se denote the unfree human being, but was a precise reference to a particular status group in the Borgu. This term referred to those persons who had been enslaved and sold to the FulBe, as well as to their descendants. Similarly, there were a number of other terms that precisely classified different bonded sub-groups, according to gender, age group, manner of enslavement, function and their relations to various slave-holding communities of the Borgu. The Western term 'slave' simply does not reflect the complexity of the multiple positions articulated in this institution.

The term 'unfree'[17] is perhaps most useful, since it includes the antonym 'free'. This dichotomy constitutes the foundation of a hierarchical configuration, in which the category 'unfree' always represents a relation – not what a slave is, but what he or she is not, is determined by the hegemonic ideology. Regardless of their status, the unfree are always characterised in the FulBe world order in terms of the lack or absence of those attributes, values and behavioural patterns that distinguish the free. When naming the 'unfree' there is always also an articulation of what it means to be 'free', thus containing the identity of the master.

In his comparative article on former slave communities of the Sahel, Botte (1999) refers to the symbolic violence that continues to operate in people's mindsets. He identifies an 'ideological discrimination' that the ideology of slavery operates through the qualifications employed to characterise ex-slaves in contemporary West Africa. These include various distinctive traits, such as somatic categorisations ('black'), physical appearance ('robust'), specific behavioural characteristics ('unclean', 'shameless', etc.), the opposites of which denote the free.

The predominant dichotomous model, in which individual components seem to relate to each other in terms of 'hierarchical oppositions' (Dumont, 1991, 238), is reminiscent of the Indian caste system, to which certain African systems of slavery bear more than merely structural resemblance.[18] This type of comparison requires a special engagement with one's own categories, just as Dumont (1966) calls for a revision of the Western academic perspective on early modern societies, which he critiqued as bearing an 'unavoidable sociocentrism'. In his collection of essays on individualism, Dumont stresses that representations of the caste system are deeply influenced by the cultural viewpoint of the West, which has elevated values such as egalitarianism and individualism to universal categories. He points out that the inherent 'aversion to hierarchy' (1991, 240) has in fact hindered the understanding of social hierarchy. Any study of the ideology of slavery must ultimately ask Dumont's question of how far one's own mindsets may stand in the way of comprehending a foreign hierarchical order. Yet researchers ought to bear in mind that Dumont himself was criticised for elevating the anthropological concept of hierarchy to an essential characteristic of community (Appadurai, 1992, 38ff.) and for explaining the caste system primarily in terms of ideology rather than examining the practices of its members (Mines, 1988, 569; Searle-Chatterjee and Sharma, 1994, 6).

Also relevant to our discussion are critiques of binarisms, which present complex social configurations in terms of a system of oppositions. A dichotomous model clearly exists in the imaginary of the FulBe and the GannunkeeBe and it is indisputable that this model also serves as a guiding principle of action in certain contexts. The GannunkeeBe and FulBe attribute opposite qualities and characteristics to each other, particularly with reference to their values, behaviours and emotional propensities. However, dual classifications have little relevance in themselves. Their meanings are always contextual. A person belonging to the higher ranks of Wolof society may exhibit 'griot-like' behaviour, and lower-ranking people may speak like noblemen. Thus, depending on the situation, each may be employing forms of speech contrary to their ascribed role. These roles are relational, and not absolute, categories. They are two extremes of what is in fact a continuum of possible speech styles (Irvine, 1990, 132). The relation of *dimo* and *maccuDo* can be understood along similar lines. In certain phases of social life, the permeability of norms is even institutionalised. During the period of *sukanaaku*, the time of youth, young FulBe may exhibit patterns of behaviour otherwise attributed to the *maccuBe*, such as playing the role of the *bardeeji* at celebrations alongside musicians, who are allowed to publicly mock and taunt (Boesen, 1999, 236ff.). Conversely, depending on individual motivations, the GannunkeeBe may behave in a manner that is usually deemed fit only for the *joomiraaBe*.

I would like to elaborate on the above observation using one of the central binary oppositions, the sense of shame (*senteene*) and its absence,[19] as the case may be. Normative attributes, such as restraint and self-control, generate categories of exclusion[20] that function as primary criteria to distinguish between the social roles of former masters and slaves. But what is the meaning of the much-repeated utterance, 'a *maccuDo* has no shame'? Of course, sometimes such comments are purely rhetorical statements, with no relevance to particular individuals. Yet if it is uttered with the purpose of qualifying the status of the slave category, it no doubt indicates a power relationship. In other instances, such a statement may mean that the GannunkeeBe are not subject to the same codes of conduct, implying that they have the freedom to be less restrained, more expressive and articulate. Social labels, such as the attribution of shame or lack of it to a set of persons, can be perceived as part of a system of interactions, through which both the free and the descendants of the unfree recognise each other in their different emotional and expressive potentials. The same binary opposition can therefore express hierarchy or complementarity depending on context.

This polyvalence is granted not only to higher-ranking speakers but also to the actions of those who are assigned a particular social label by a hegemonic discourse. This once more raises the question of how ideologies and their transformations can be interpreted and understood by outsiders, given the finely nuanced epistemological negotiations that occur between the free and the descendants of the unfree. Hence a FulBe woman may, for instance, speak of the 'unclean' characteristic of the *maccuBe* (*Be nyiDDi*),[21] which prevents her from relying on the assistance of GannunkeeBe women to help her prepare the sauces during her ceremonies. However, the very same woman may pay a visit to her 'companion' (*passiijo*), a Gannunkeejo, and unhesitatingly partake of a meal prepared by her host. Such apparent contradictions can be explained by the fact that relational categories[22] are, at the same time, lived personal relationships. Yet the relation between ideological and day-to-day levels of action is not straightforward. Past asymmetries in the forms of interaction and exchange have been transposed to present-day relations, in as much as these relations stem from former bonds, but different groups interpret them differently. After a market day, a young Pullo would definitely share his cycle pump with his GannunkeeBe friend, with whom he spends every day, so that he may inflate his tyres before biking back home. On the other hand, between two elders, who are never to be seen apart from each other, the Gannunkeejo is without doubt the one who takes charge of transporting the sack of millet that his FulBe companion acquired at a ceremony they attended together.

No doubt such daily acts are, taken in isolation, often inconspicuous, though all the more significant in that they express the ongoing relevance of past power relations. Yet viewing these acts as the expression of contemporary power relations would be misleading. Beneath the signs of an evidently close friendship between two people, as can be often found in neighbouring GannunkeeBe and FulBe hamlets, beneath the well-attuned ease with which they relate to each other, there seems to be an underlying awareness that one is acting, as the case may be, as a Pullo or a Gannunkeejo (i.e. simply following custom rather than accepting a relation of dominance and subordination). But if the latter were asked by some other Pullo to carry his sack of millet, which is quite possible, then he would perform this action with full awareness of the hegemonic patterns of interaction between *joomiraaBe* (masters) and *maccuBe* (slaves). These patterns, handed down over generations and ingrained in one's childhood memories, encounter the immanence of the present in expressions such as the following statement by a Pullo: 'You, Pullo, if they [the *maccuBe*] saw you, they called you *joomiraawo* (master), even though you were a small child. When I sit with them today, I can send them off to go anywhere I want, even if I am younger than them. Do you understand, that is the path of the forefathers, that they are holding on to?' (*Hinaa a faamii laawol baabiiBe nun Be jogi Don?*)

'Sending off' a person from a former *maccuBe* family with a task (indeed this notion points to a much more extensive set of rules in status relations) may well belong to the realm of everyday experience for this FulBe man. Former relations of dominance are preserved in these forms of interaction. However, the relation of subordination and superiority may well be an imagined one, which exists only in ideal form, regardless of its existence in the real world. In such cases, a Pullo may speak confidently of the services that he could bring the members of a *maccuBe* family to perform at his behest. But he would de facto no longer demand such services. Even if today the relation between the FulBe and the GannunkeeBe is a power relation, and not a relationship of dominance, the awareness of this relation is comparable to what Georg Simmel has called the 'subjective grounds' of dominance.

> If the Spartans did not develop a nobility among themselves and yet felt like noblemen, and if the Spaniards had the air of lords even though they no longer had any servants, these phenomena have their deeper significance in the fact that the reciprocal effects of the relationship of domination is the sociological expression or actualization of inner qualities of the subject. Whoever has these, is ruler by this very fact. One side of the two-sided relationship of domination has been taken out of it, as it were, and the reciprocal relation exists only in an ideal form; but the other side does not thereby lose its intrinsic significance for the relationship. (Simmel, 1950, 270).

For both the descendants of the free and those of the unfree, such processes take place deeply within the subject. This makes it difficult for outsiders to be able to recognise continuity and change in ideologies and hierarchies. This is particularly true where they are invisible, unlike in common types of social demarcation or in expressions of political emancipation. The relationship between the descendants of slaves and masters may have preserved its external form and yet have changed its substance. This brings us back to the blessing and the curse.

It is possible that a herder of unfree descent may have internalised a certain hierarchical order and the behavioural rules that go with it. Thus his actions may be guided by fear of the consequences of disobeying rules (the power of the curse) or at least by a certain cautiousness. Yet it is also equally possible that he is fully aware of this perception of the world and its rules and has incorporated them in his actions because they help protect his welfare and that of his herd and family (the power of the blessing). In the latter case, it is a matter of choice ('we are their maccuBe because we choose to'), whereas in the former it is not. In actual practice, of course, these different inner attitudes are extremely close to each other, so that it is difficult to distinguish what motivates an individual's action when he or she recognises the spiritual powers and the dominance of the FulBe in particular contexts.

Conclusions

A literacy course took place in a small village, in which both GannunkeeBe and their former masters from the neighbouring settlement participated. As an elderly FulBe man entered the room and there were no free seats, an old

GannunkeeBe man stood up to offer him his place. The Gannunkeejo sitting next to him pulled him back saying 'Stay seated, in this place everyone is equal'. The very same man, who insists on social equality in the area of knowledge and egalitarianism in his political activism, demanding his rights as a citizen in the process of democratisation, may abide by different rules and laws when it comes to cattle breeding. He belongs to those among the GannunkeeBe who adopt a direct and affirmative approach towards their former masters as far as communal politics go, yet are cautious about them as cattle owners and carefully avoid conflicts over cattle. The awareness of being a slave descendant is what counts here, disqualifying him from herding in the eyes of the masters. This is despite the fact that the FulBe have long since been forced to accept the reality that the GannunkeeBe are herders on a par with them. Thus, in order to live amicably with the FulBe, the man may adopt certain patterns of behaviour when dealing with cattle, drawing from the collective knowledge and strategies of former slaves. He is therefore actively shaping and transforming the relationship between the descendants of the unfree and the free, a relationship handed down through the ages via social hierarchy. Thus the avoidance strategies of the GannunkeeBe herdsmen and the tactics of cattle owners to increase their herd without invoking the malevolence of their former masters demonstrate that defensive acts may be active, not just passive, approaches.

In the search for a deeper understanding of the ideological transformations of the relations between slave descendants and their former masters, the different nuances in the self-perception of various slave groups and groups viewed as slave continue to play a significant role even today. Furthermore, the disentanglement from the old order varies not only from individual to individual but also across regions, reflecting historical and economic differences. Finally, this process is not a linear one, beginning with the legitimacy of ideologies supporting slave–master relations and ending with their dissolution. Several world orders co-exist in the same time and place. The individual making decisions and shaping alliances chooses from different frames of reference, each of which generates different options for her or his course of action.

References

Alber, E., 2000. *Im Gewand von Herrschaft. Modalitäten der Macht im Borgou (Nord-Benin) 1900–1995.* Cologne: Köppe.

Appadurai, A., 1992. 'Putting Hierarchy in Its Place.' In George E. Marcus, ed., *Rereading Cultural Anthropology.* Durham, NC, and London: Duke University Press, pp. 34–47.

Bierschenk, T., 1989. '"Vorwärts mit der Tradition der Fulbe!" Die Genese einer ethnisch-politischen Bewegung in der VR Bénin.' *Sozialanthropologische Arbeitspapiere* 20, Berlin.

Bierschenk, T., 1997. *Die Fulbe Nordbénins. Geschichte, soziale Organisation, Wirtschaftsweise.* Münster and Hamburg: LIT.

Bierschenk, T., 2004. *The Local Appropriation of Democracy. An Analysis of the Municipal Elections in Parakou, Rep. Benin 2002/03* (Working Papers of the Department of Anthropology and African Studies). Johannes Gutenberg University Mainz, No. 39.

Boesen, E., 1996. 'Fulbe und Arbeit'. In K. Beck and G. Spittler, eds., *Arbeit in Afrika*. Münster and Hamburg: LIT, pp. 193–207.

Boesen, E., 1999. *Scham und Schönheit. Über Identität und Selbstvergewisserung bei den FulBe Nordbenins*. Münster and Hamburg: LIT.

Botte, R., 1999. 'RiimayBe, Haratin, Iklan: les damnés de la terre, le développement et la démocratie.' In A. Bourgeot, ed., *Horizons nomades en Afrique sahélienne. Sociétés, développement et démocratie*. Paris: Karthala, pp. 56–78.

Comaroff, J. L. and Comaroff, J., 2004. 'Criminal Justice, Cultural Justice: The Limits of Liberalism and the Pragmatics of Difference in the New South Africa.' *American Ethnologist*, 31(2), pp. 188–204.

de Bruijn, M. and Pelckmans, L., 2005. 'Facing Dilemmas: Former Fulbe Slaves in Modern Mali.' *Canadian Journal of African Studies*, 39(1), pp. 69–95.

Diop, A., 1981. *La Société Wolof. Tradition et changement. Les systèmes d'inégalité et de domination*. Paris: Karthala.

Douglas, M., 1988 (1966). *Reinheit und Gefährdung. Eine Studie zu Vorstellungen von Verunreinigung und Tabu*. Frankfurt a.M.: Suhrkamp.

Dumas-Champion, F., 1985. 'Le Droit de maudire. Malédiction et serment chez les Masa du Tchad.' *Droit et Cultures*, 9/10, pp. 81–93.

Dumont, L., 1966. *Homo hierarchicus. Essai sur le système des castes*. Paris: Éditions Gallimard.

Dumont, L., 1991 (1978). 'Die anthropologische Gemeinschaft und die Ideologie.' In L. Dumont, ed., *Individualismus. Zur Ideologie der Moderne*. Frankfurt and New York: Campus, pp. 215–47.

Dupire, M., 1970. *Organisation sociale des Peuls. Étude d'ethnographie comparée*. Paris: Librairie Plon.

Ellis, S. and Ter Haar, G., 2007. 'Religion and Politics: Taking African Epistemologies Seriously.' *Journal of African Studies*, 45(3), pp. 385–401.

Guichard, M., 1998. 'Du Discours sur la faiblesse du pouvoir fulbe.' In E. Boesen, C. Hardung and R. Kuba, eds, *Regards sur le Borgou. Pouvoir et altérité dans une région ouest-africaine*. Paris: L'Harmattan, pp. 185–202.

Haji, A., 1997. 'Pouvoir de bénir et de maudire: cosmologie et organisation sociale des Oromo-Arsi.' *Cahiers d'Études Africaines*, 37(146), pp. 289–318.

Hamer, J., 2007. 'Dezentralization as a Solution to the Problem of Cultured Diversity: An Example from Ethiopia.' *Africa* 77(2), pp. 207–25.

Hardung, C., 1998. 'Exclusion sociale et distance voulue. Des rapports entre les Gannunkeebe et les Fulbe.' In E. Boesen, C. Hardung and R. Kuba, eds, *Regards sur le Borgou. Pouvoir et altérité dans une région ouest-africaine*. Paris: L'Harmattan, pp. 203–19.

Hardung, C., 2002. 'Everyday Life of Slaves in Northern Dahomey: Using Oral Testimony.' *Journal of African Cultural Studies* 15(1), pp. 35–44.

Hardung, C., 2003. 'Le Pilon et la voix – sur le travail des anciens esclaves dans un contexte rituel peul.' In H. d'Almeida-Topor, M. Lakroum, and G. Spittler, eds, *Le Travail en Afrique noire. Représentations et pratiques à l'époque contemporaine*. Paris: Karthala, pp. 93–106.

Hardung, C., 2006. *Arbeit, Sklaverei und Erinnerung. Gruppen unfreier Herkunft unter den Fulbe Nordbenins*. Cologne: Rüder Köppe Verlag.

Irvine, J. T., 1990. 'Registering Affect: Heteroglossia in the Linguistic Expression of Emotion.' In L. Abu-Lughod and C. Lutz, eds., *Language and the Politics of Emotion*. Cambridge: Cambridge University Press, pp. 126–161.

Klein, M., 2005. 'The Concept of Honour and the Persistence of Servility in the Western Sudan.' *Cahiers d'Études Africaines*, 45(179–180), pp. 831–51.

Kuba, R., 1996. *Wasangari und Wangara: Borgu und seine Nachbarn in historischer Perspektive.* Münster and Hamburg: LIT.

Kyburz, O., 1997. 'La Fabrication de la foulanité.' *Journal des Africanistes* 67/2, pp. 101–26.

Law, R. and Lovejoy, P., 1999. 'Borgu in the Atlantic Slave Trade.' *African Economic History*, 27, pp. 69–92.

Lombard, J., 1965. *Structures de type «féodal» en Afrique noire. Etudes des dynamismes internes et des relations sociales chez les Bariba du Dahomey.* Paris: Mouton.

Lovejoy, P. and Hogendorn, J., 1993. *Slow Death for Slavery. The Course of Abolition in Northern Nigeria, 1897–1936.* Cambridge: Cambridge University Press.

Meillassoux, C., 1973. 'Y a-t-il des castes en Inde?' *Cahiers Internationaux de Sociologie*, XIV, pp. 5–30.

Mines, M., 1988. 'Conceptualizing the Person: Hierarchical Society and Individual Autonomy in India.' *American Anthropologist*, 90, pp. 568–77.

Moraes Farias, P. F. de, 1998. 'For a Non-culturalist Historiography of Béninois Borgu.' In E. Boesen, C. Hardung and R. Kuba, eds, *Regards sur le Borgou. Pouvoir et altérité dans une région ouest-africaine.* Paris: L'Harmattan, pp. 39–69.

N'Gaïde, A., 2003. 'Stéréotypes et imaginaires sociaux en milieu haalpulaar. Classer, stigmatiser et toiser.' *Cahiers d'Études Africaines*, 172, pp. 707–38.

O'Hear, A., 1997. *Power Relations in Nigeria. Ilorin Slaves and Their Successors.* New York: University of Rochester Press.

Popitz, H., 1992. *Phänomene der Macht.* Tübingen: J.C.B. Mohr.

Rasmussen, S. J., 2004. 'Reflections on Witchcraft, Danger and Modernity among the Tuareg.' *Africa*, 74(3), pp. 315–40.

Riesman, P., 1974. *Société et liberté chez les Peuls Djelgôbé de Haute-Volta. Essai d'anthropologie introspective.* Paris and La Haye: Mouton.

Riesman, P., 1990. 'Living Poor while Being Rich. The Pastoral Folk Economy.' In A. Jacobson-Widding and W. Van Beek, eds, *The Creative Communion. African Folk Models of Fertility and the Regeneration of Life.* Uppsala: Almqvist and Wiksell, pp. 323–34.

Roumeguere-Eberhardt, J., 1987. 'Dialectiques des pouvoirs et des sanctions chez les Maasai.' *Droit et Cultures*, 13, pp. 69–79.

Schareika, N., 1994. *Die soziale Bedeutung der Rinder bei den Fulbe (Bénin).* Münster and Hamburg: LIT.

Searle-Chatterjee, M. and Sharma, U., 1994. 'Introduction.' In M. Searle-Chatterjee and U. Sharma, eds, *Contextualising Caste: Post-Dumontian Approaches.* Oxford: Blackwell, pp. 1–24.

Simmel, G., 1950 (1907). 'Superordination and Subordination and Degrees of Domination and Freedom.' In K. Wolff, ed., *The Sociology of Georg Simmel.* London: Collier-Macmillan, pp. 268–300.

Stilwell, S., 2000. 'Power, Honour and Shame: The Ideology of Royal Slavery in the Sokoto Caliphate.' *Africa*, 70(3), pp. 394–421.

Weber, M., 1988 (1920). *Gesammelte Aufsätze zur Religionssoziologie.* Tübingen: Mohr (Paul Siebeck).

Notes

1 This essay is based on parts of my doctoral dissertation, published in 2006: *Arbeit, Sklaverei und Erinnerung. Gruppen unfreier Herkunft unter den Fulbe Nordbenins,* Koeppe Publishers. Research between 1991 and 1998 among the GannunkeeBe of

Northern Benin was funded by the Deutsche Forschungsgemeinschaft. I thank Sruti Bala for the English translation.

2 For an analysis of the municipal elections in Parakou see Bierschenk, 2004.

3 Bariba is an etic appellation (see Law and Lovejoy, 1999; Lombard, 1965, 43, footnote 1). Today it is applied to the farming Baatombu, the Boko (also called Bo'o) and the *wasangari*, the immigrant mounted warriors of the Borgu who claim common descent, although their real origin is not yet clarified (see also Kuba, 1996, 99ff.; Moraes Farias, 1998, 45ff.).

4 I use the term GannunkeeBe, which is the Fulfulde emic expression, instead of the term Gando, which is generally used in francophone Benin and is also common in the scientific literature. I do so to suggest that this essay does not deal with the Gando living in the Baatombu-area, who speak Baatonum as their mother-tongue and are fully integrated in Baatombu-culture.

5 On the relationship to land of the FulBe of Benin, see Bierschenk, 1997, 33; Boesen, 1999, 156f.

6 In the Sokoto caliphate, for instance, the absence of independent rights to land was one of the primary reasons for slaves not to leave their former masters, even after the formal abolition of slavery. Regulating land rights in Northern Nigeria was an important element in British colonial policy, serving to prevent mass uprisings by slaves (Lovejoy and Hogendorn, 1993, 127ff.; O'Hear, 1997, 14).

7 The mass rallies and political and cultural events of the *Laawol Fulfulde* (*Séminaire national linguistique fulfulde*) did little to alter this situation. These were meant to advance the civil rights of the FulBe at a national level and strengthen the cohesion of FulBe herders in conflict with farming communities. However, the rallies were also about issues related to FulBe identity, which the leaders of the *sous-commission linguistique fulfulde* themselves sought to define, sometimes in rigid ways. See Bierschenk, 1989; Hahonou, in this volume.

8 Concerning the destructive force of the curse harming animals and humans alike as form of social control in free communities see Dumas-Champion, 1985; Haji, 1997; Roumeguere-Eberhardt, 1987. The common principle that the curse has to be directed by a chief or an elder against a younger person is maintained in the ideology of slavery, as a slave is always considered the junior party in relation to a free man. On the question of the curse as a 'final attempt to restore social harmony' see Hamer, 2007, 11.

9 'Counting' here implies estimating the size of someone else's herd; but in the Pullo's reaction it implies gauging one's property. While herd owners do not keep a count of their animals, they have an exact idea of the size of their herd, since they are familiar with each individual animal. Only veterinary doctors count animals.

10 During colonialism, most FulBe groups sent to school the children of their *maccuBe* instead of their own offspring. Instead, GannunkeeBe chiefs kept children of their own slaves as domestic labour and quickly realised the opportunities that schooling would offer their own children.

11 Max Weber refers to the 'belief in the charismatic qualification of the clan' in the context of the generalised legitimisation of authority (*Veralltäglichung von Herrschaft*). These beliefs may take the place of individual 'bearers of charisma', of warlords or prophets and their capacity to exhibit 'extraordinary powers' (1988, 270).

12 Sometimes reference is made to the notion of *baraka*, which is common among the Muslims of North and West Africa. *Al baraka*, among the Tuareg, is primarily a quality of Islamic scholars and prominent chiefs, as Rasmussen (2004, 316f.) describes, and exists in parallel with other supernatural beliefs and practices. It functions as a form of ritual power grounded in moral discourse in Niger's Tuareg society.

13 The question of what sense it makes for descendants of slaves to consider themselves

as *maccuBe* is central to identity issues. As de Bruijn and Pelckmans pointed out: 'In ritual and in politics, the very ambiguity of their [the Riimaybe] "new" and "free" status comes to the fore: they are no longer real slaves, but then what, or who, are they? Non-slaves? Former slaves? [...] they are no longer what they used to be, but who, then, are they, what is the alternative?' (2005, 83). To assume the role of *maccuBe*, thereby ensuring their belonging to the FulBe community (see Hardung, 1998), is also a way to secure a social space that fills the vacuum described by de Bruijn and Pelckmans.

14   *EnDam* is a complex key concept for the FulBe. Depending on the context, it could mean any of the following: 'mother's milk', 'empathy', 'familial relationship', or 'the bond between brothers who have drunk the milk of the same mother'.

15   In some regions of Atakora, the ritual performance of *untal*, the pounding of sorgho by former female slaves, accompanying FulBe marriage ceremonies, is inscribed in the collective memory and creates a permanent awareness of having been slaves (Hardung, 2003).

16   This is a typical case of constructed identity, because of course the FulBe do till land.

17   I do not, however, wish to equate this term with *non-libres*, euphemistically employed by colonialists in place of *esclave/captif*, to represent 'domestic slaves', a form of slavery that was widely represented as unalterable, for reasons that will be dwelt on later in the essay.

18   For a comparative reading of both societal forms see Meillassoux, 1973. Diop, who has worked on the caste system in Africa, explicitly excludes the concept of caste in his analysis of slave–master relationships among the Wolof (1981, 105). Studies on the FulBe, on the other hand, employ the concept of caste particularly with reference to the stratification of FulBe groups, where a series of different endogamous occupational categories are to be found, apart from the division between the free and the unfree. Kyburz (1997) uses the term caste for the *Halpulaar*, placing it in quotation marks. Notions of 'impurity', the practice of weaving as hereditary specialisation and the prevalence of endogamy allow the classification of the GannunkeeBe as a quasi-caste. Riesman (1990, 324) also speaks of the descendants of slaves, the RiimaayBe, and the FulBe as two castes.

19   The free individual and the sense of shame are concepts of personhood common to many Sahelian groups. Concerning the notions of shame, honour and dishonour and their meaning in the slave–master relation in West African societies see Klein's comparative study (2005).

20   See Stilwell, 2000, for a description of the royal slaves of the Sokoto Caliphate, who evaded the common discourse of shame and honour and established their own status system in which they could acquire honour in spite of their slave status.

21   When a society disposes only of weak forms of sanction, as is the case for the Benin FulBe (Boesen, 1996, 201; Schareika, 1994, 46), and when social distinctions are easily transformed, ideas of 'pollution' often become particularly pronounced (Douglas, 1988, 151). Rules of avoidance and activities from which even the *maccuBe*, who usually performed all manual labour in the time of slavery, were excluded due to their 'impurity' (*maccuBe laaBaa*) concerned cows and milk, the core-realm of FulBe identity. In this context, until today, the most explicit rules of distance between the free and the descendants of the unfree have been maintained.

22   N'Gaïde (2003), who belongs to the Haalpulaar of the Senegal River, offers an insider perspective on the relational categories between members of different status groups of a FulBe community and on the dynamics of their interaction.

7

Contemporary Trajectories of Slavery in Haalpulaar Society (Mauritania)

Olivier Leservoisier

This chapter focuses on the contemporary situation of slavery among the Haalpulaar *maccuBe*[1] of Mauritania. It looks at the main forms of discrimination the *maccuBe* are facing today and at their resistance to it. First, then, we should remember that slavery is still a very topical issue in Mauritania. The latest official abolition of slavery only dates back to 1981 and more recently the Mauritanian National Assembly adopted, on 8 August 2007, a law criminalising slavery (see Klein, in this volume). More and more movements of emancipation among the descendants of slaves, in Moorish (Brhane, 1997) as well as in Haalpulaaren societies, have arisen in recent years. Today the question of slavery cannot be approached in the same way as in the late nineteenth century, when masters could exercise property rights on their slaves. It is nonetheless the case that groups of servile origin continue to face various forms of discrimination that, in today's contexts, give rise to increasingly frequent social conflicts. These conflicts reveal the persistence of inequalities and the ongoing relevance of the traditional Haalpulaar hierarchy,[2] which still characterise all those contexts where persons must be classified socially and attributed a place in the social order. At the same time, conflicts also constitute evidence that change has indeed been happening. In fact, most conflict situations are less the result of the nobles' power to force slaves to perform tasks, as was the case in the past, than they are the consequence of the claims of slave descendants to gain rights and responsibilities that had, until now, been denied to them. Yet contemporary social conflicts are primarily about crossing social boundaries, and only secondarily, if at all, about challenging and transforming these boundaries. By discussing various forms of discrimination and resistance, this chapter enquires into the tension between the maintenance of a hierarchical social order, and the process of social change and emancipation that the *maccuBe* are undergoing. It sets out to show that, in spite of the ongoing debate and negotiation over social categories, formal hierarchies have been maintained. This apparent paradox results from the simultaneous occurrence of strategies of emancipation *and* ambivalence in the ex-slaves' political actions, which reproduce the hierarchical foundations of society as a precondition for their own social mobility.

The Persistence of Stigma

First, we must say a few words about the stigma suffered today by the descendants of slaves. In Haalpulaar society slaves are described as having no sense of virtue, no sense of shame. It is thought that they can be identified through their body language and physical appearance: for instance, the skin on their hands is rough, the nape of their neck is thick and they have a strong build. These stereotypes contrast with the values of the nobles, which are based on the sense of honour and the control of their emotions (the renown *pulaaku* of FulBe societies). These stereotypes present social and cultural differences as natural and, by rooting prejudice in biology, they constitute a major obstacle to the emancipation of people of slave descent.

It is also interesting to note that groups of servile origin appear to have a definition of their identity that is different from the one constructed by the nobles.[3] The ex-slaves' own portrayal of themselves emphasises values such as courage (*caasal*), hard work (*liggey*), honour (*teddungal*) and solidarity (*ballotiral*). Moreover, groups of servile origin turn these very stereotypes against the nobles. For instance the *maccuBe* make fun of the fishermen elite by claiming they are rude. They say that *Cuballo muta futta pali*, which literally translates as 'a fisherman that dives into the water makes bubbles'; this amounts to saying that the fisherman farts in the water. Similarly, the *seBBe* (warriors of noble origin) are sometimes called *seBBe laalo*, after the baobab tree leaf, which is used to prepare millet couscous. This implies that the *seBBe's* nobility is somehow diluted or corrupted, since they are a mixture just like mixed millet. The *tooroBe* (marabouts, sing. *tooroodo*) are usually laughed at for their avarice: *Taarode Buri tooroodo*, 'a shower is better than the *tooroodo*', which implies that the marabout is always careful with money and doesn't give anything to others.

If stereotypes are not publicly stated, as was the case until very recently, they are nonetheless on everyone's mind. This accounts for the fact that some former slaves tend not to mix with other social groups, and would rather live and associate with members of their own group. It also partly explains why younger people who belong to different social categories avoid mixing with one another, contrary to what happens with the older generations.

Marriage

Matrimonial discrimination is expressed by the fact that marriages between nobles and *maccuBe* are not reciprocal. Noble men marry *maccuBe* women, but the reverse is forbidden: noble women are not allowed to marry a man who has an inferior status.

As we know, when a marriage between a noble man and a woman of servile status occurs, the woman's status can change: by giving birth to children recognised by her husband she is automatically emancipated and becomes a free woman. In Islam this is called emancipation via the womb. However, these emancipated women remain the object of certain forms of discrimination. For example, they are seen as not worthy of praise as noble women. Moreover, children from these mixed marriages usually keep away from their maternal relatives.

These forms of discrimination lead *maccuBe* men increasingly to condemn the absence of reciprocity in marriage alliances in spite of the abolition of slavery. Alliance with someone of slave status is considered dangerous, and this in part accounts for non-reciprocity in marriage. Such a belief is widespread among FulBe societies in Guinea (Botte, 1993) and in Benin (Hardung, 1997) where former masters fear that a former slave may benefit from this alliance so as to take revenge over earlier domination.

There are many examples of failed projects of alliance between *maccuBe* men and noble women. These failures highlight the limits of the rhetoric of the noble class on the alleged family links with their former slaves. They also show that social elites feel the need to re-assert their status when the question of crossing social boundaries is raised. Therefore it is not surprising that the few marriages contracted between a noble woman and a *maccuBe* man, were contracted without the consent of the bride's family. Furthermore, these marriages concern mostly the new generations. In principle, when a noble woman marries a former slave, she becomes isolated from her own family, which maintains a distance from her. Amadou's experience is a good example of the problems caused by this type of union.

Amadou is a veterinary nurse at Kaedi. He met his wife, who belonged to a group of maraboutic status, on his work. As he failed to obtain permission to marry her from his (then potential) parents-in-law, he decided to force the wedding, after making sure that a *qadi* (official authority in religious and legal matters) would be willing to recognise the union. At the time of the wedding, the bride-to-be's mother refused to organise at her home the ceremony that is usually made to gather money for her daughter's departure. The day of the wedding at Amadou's home, his parents-in-law sent a few gifts, but nothing compared to what is commonly done for a union between elite families.

Years have passed, but relations between Amadou and his in-laws are still tense. Amadou complains particularly about the way his parents-in-law (*esiraaBe*) remind him of their family links only in particular circumstances: 'Some of them will only act as my parents-in-law when they need my help but, if they don't, they will just wave at me when they see me'.

He is also concerned for his daughter when she visits her maternal grand-parents in their village of Belinabe, as some people may make fun of her because of her father's social position: 'I don't want her to be laughed at when she can hear them'. He only authorises her to go there if he is sure of the presence of his mother-in-law, as she is known as a *tooroodo* (member of a respected maraboutic group) and respected for that.[4]

Religious Discrimination

Along with other reasons discussed above, religious discrimination also under-pins the nobles' refusal to give their daughters or sisters in marriage to a *maccuBe* man. The *maccuBe* are often perceived as having little religious education. This view partly goes back to their original status as slaves: in Islamic Mauritanian societies, only 'infidels' could be enslaved, at least in theory.[5] Today, in spite of their ancient religious knowledge, which often compares with that of religious elites among their masters, the *maccuBe* still find it difficult to be recognised as Muslim clerics and believers by the rest of society. Three main issues are at stake here. First, nobles do not generally allow the *maccuBe* to lead the prayer. In certain cases tension over the identity and function of the *imam* is so high that the *maccuBe* have to build their own separate mosque.

Secondly, the public recognition of religious status is usually recorded in local historical memory, but this still constitutes a major challenge for the *maccuBe*. The *maccuBe* who have become marabouts find it difficult to obtain the same official recognition as the noble marabouts. Harouna, aged 76, who lives in Gurel Sane, a neighbourhood in Kaedi, is a living example of these difficulties.

Harouna was born in Kaedi and, at an early age, wanted to read the Quran. His parents thus decided to help him 'buy his freedom from their master', who agreed to emancipate him. As there were many obstacles to his studies, this 'buying back' was the condition of obtaining the freedom to study: 'in Kaedi, there were not many learned men among the masters. They did not want the *maccuBe* to learn.' At the age of 17 he started to train to become an Islamic scholar (*Afiz el Coran*, lit. master in Quran). In the early 1970s he was given the title of guide (*muqqadam*) of a Tijaniyya brotherhood. Back from Kaedi, he taught the Quran and cultivated the land. He is now a muezzin in Gurel Sane and gives blessings (*dou'ât*) after prayers. He has, however, never been the head of the mosque, which is under the supervision of the nobles. Today, Harouna bitterly admits that his knowledge has not been approved by the nobles:

I still have problems: if you want to show how knowledgeable you are, they [the noble] remind you that you were a former slave... and in such a situation, I, who am able to pass on my knowledge to the others (since I have the title of *muqqadam*), whenever I want to do so, I have to play it down or else the nobles will make a fuss about it.[6]

Today, younger generations increasingly try to honour the memory of religious figures belonging to their group. They organise pilgrimages (*ziara*) in honour of these figures. This, to them, is a means of obtaining public recognition for their marabouts, who are not otherwise mentioned in official history. Such initiatives constitute attempts on the part of former slaves to fight against the idea that slaves are 'people without history' (see Rossi, Introduction).

Finally, many *maccuBe* question the masters' discourse that uses religion to maintain power inequalities. They question the masters' rhetoric, which claims that salvation depends upon submission to their authority. A counter-discourse is heard more and more often stating the equality of all Muslims before God. This counter-discourse also condemns views that justify the legitimacy of slavery and/or related forms of discrimination.[7]

The Role and Position of *maccuBe* at Rituals and Ceremonies

The *maccuBe* have begun to challenge the tasks they usually have to perform in ceremonies such as baptisms or marriages. Along with some other professional groups, the *maccuBe* are expected to perform heavy tasks that are associated with low status: for example, carrying wood, fetching water, pounding millet and serving the hosts. The obligation to carry out these tasks is increasingly being questioned by younger *maccuBe*, who are members of so-called 'youth associations'. These associations clearly exemplify the ways in which social relations are being renegotiated. As is also the case at political elections, subordinated groups adopt modes of action that are much more complex and ambiguous than simple direct opposition.

These associations were created by *maccuBe* in the early 1990s in the city of Kaedi (the capital of the Gorgol region) and are integral to the struggles for emancipation of the last few years. They are open to young people from any social group. Originally, their official aim was to stop 'wasting resources' and to limit the excessive expenses of life-cycle ceremonies. They question the established social order by ending practices that are starting to be considered outdated, and they aim to achieve reciprocity and a fair distribution of tasks. At weddings, for example, what the guests give to the bride's and groom's mothers is kept by a group of members of the association until the end of the ceremony. This is meant to avoid the distribution of excessive amounts of money to the 'professional groups' (griots, weavers, blacksmiths). Association members fix in advance the amount that shall be paid to the members of these 'professional groups'. Should the latter receive more than what had been agreed, the offenders are fined. For example, if a man is caught giving money to a griot, who is praising him, he will have to pay a fine of ten times the amount he gave.

This control of expenses attracted some nobles, essentially the younger generations, who joined these associations as a way to save money: owing to their social status, a wedding ceremony may cost them very large sums. That said, the nobles who join these associations do not do so only for economic reasons but also because they disagree with certain former traditions. Thus, noble members take part in different tasks that used to be reserved to servile groups, except for slitting the throat of cattle, which remains a task performed exclusively by the elder *maccuBe*.[8] They are, nonetheless, allowed to cut up a head of cattle, and this is something new. The distribution of animal parts – which, as is well known, reflects the social hierarchy – has also been modified. Now, at ceremonies supervised by these associations, the noble may receive parts that were traditionally given to the *maccuBe*. For instance, they can now receive the neck or the lower parts of the legs. Lastly, the *maccuBe* are now allowed to pay their contributions like the nobles, which traditionally they did not do.

However, this reversal of roles during the ceremonies remains limited. In neighbourhoods where tradition has not yet been challenged and where the nobles still exercise some control on the *maccuBe*, youth associations are headed by nobles. The latter may take part in the activities, but refuse to become members of an association directed by a *maccuDo*. Besides, these associations are known for being ridden with conflict. *MaccuBe* often complain against certain nobles who do not fully accept the reciprocity game: for example, some noble members 'forget' to take part in low-status tasks when *maccuBe* from the same association celebrate a ceremony.

Land Tenure Discrimination

Land tenure has been at the heart of social renegotiations, particularly since the tenure reform of 1983. As elsewhere in Africa, this reform states that 'land belongs to the tiller'. In fact this reform has not benefited the most destitute sections of the population, but rather it supports the interests of private entrepreneurs. Nevertheless, the new legal framework strengthened the determination of slave-descendants to fight for their rights. It also forced former masters to modify their claims to land ownership and control. Thus, today, the majority of masters are not claiming back lands that were cleared by their former slaves. Moreover, former masters now allow former slaves to transfer rights to land to their descendants through inheritance, providing the land remains within the sphere of political control of the noble lineage that controls the territory.

As Roger Botte (1993) observes among the FulBe of Fuuta Jalon in Guinea, there is a tacit agreement which combines the principle of 'land to the tiller' with the principle of the inalienability of communal patrimony.

This agreement accounts for the fact that in societies characterised by a traditional division of tasks between noble farmers and people of servile origin (such as the Moors or the FulBe in Massina in Mali and Fuuta Jalon), descendants of slaves (*hrâtin, rimaayBe*) de facto become the main developers of these lands, and this gives them a certain economic emancipation (Pouget, 2001; Ruf, 1999). Conversely, in those Haalpulaar societies where agricultural work is carried out by both servile and noble categories, former servile groups find it harder to acquire land as farming land tends to remain under the direct control and management of nobles.

Tensions occur especially around the issue of land appropriation outside the community. This is the case with irrigated parcels (which were attributed to particular individuals by the Administration) and plots of land sold without the preliminary consent of the lineage head. In both cases, conflicts can even lead to the eviction of farmers from the community and the alienation of their land rights. This is what happened in Kaedi on the PPG (*Périmètre Pilote du Gorgol*) irrigated zone in 1997. In a survey of the beneficiaries of this area, several noble families did not register their former slaves who cultivated the lands to prevent them from obtaining a plot. Today, descendants of slaves forcefully condemn this situation and do not hesitate to contact the authorities to obtain justice.

Political Discrimination

The process of democratisation that took place in the early 1990s in Mauritania set the question of the political participation of subordinated groups at the core of the national agenda. However, it yielded ambivalent results. On the one hand, democratisation increased the integration of former slaves as citizens on a national scale. On the other, their frequent exclusion from the lists of eligible candidates strengthened their perception of marginality. Inequality of access to the position of elected representative thus worked as a catalyst for various disagreements and disputes that triggered the formation of social movements.

The development of new movements demonstrated that, whatever the actual state and practice of democracy in a country, the principle of 'one man, one vote' plays a determinant role in the process of emancipation of subordinate groups. The latter were quick to realise the importance of their demographic weight, which they used to apply pressure during elections. In the event of a disagreement with nobles over the choice of names in electoral lists, they can choose to support lists that are opposed to those they have been excluded from. They can even sometimes decide to leave the traditional groups, or *leyyi* in Haalpulaar, to which they are attached, and to create their own group (sing. *leynol*).[9] This is a crucial decision because the *leyyi* are, in principle, directed by noble families.

The political action of subordinate groups reveals the influence of inter-national actors in local political arenas. Hence, international migrants not only support financially the political goals of social movements, but they also influence the political imagination by introducing new ideas and strategies that contribute to the development of new political practices that destabilise local hierarchies. Thus, an increasing number of subordinate groups began claiming an equal share of political power in the name of equality, dignity and individual skills. Their demands are not limited to participation in the new political structures of the municipality, but they also aim to be represented in the traditional governance of the village. In other words, subordinate groups are making 'claims of citizenship' in village-level traditional political institu-tions, which would have been unimaginable a few years ago. By claiming equal rights at the level of 'traditional' power structures, they question the legitimacy of traditional leaders directly. This may result in widespread conflict, as shown in the case of Djeol below.

In 2000 a number of *SaafaalBe HormankooBe*[10] families in the village of Djeol (considered a servile group by the nobles) decided to leave the five *leyyi* to which they were attached in order to create their own *leynol*, with the aim of asserting their rights. This was an unprecedented and substantial move, given that the life of the village is built around the organisation of the *leyyi*. For instance, when it comes to distributing food aid, each *leynol* has its share. When a list of village representatives is drawn during elections, each *leynol* delegates one of its members to be one of the five representatives in a list of candidates. The fact that subordinate *SaafaalBe HormankooBe* families wanted to establish a new *leynol* caused violent reactions on the part of chiefly lineages, which took action against the *SaafaalBe HormankooBe*. They were denied access to food aid and excluded from some associations. These repres-sive measures were even taken in Europe against those migrants who had supported the cause of these families.

These migrants played a determinant part in the rise of the movement, supporting the families who stayed in Djeol. In fact, Djeol residents were able to count on the support of migrants who had settled in France since 1967, and whose financial help proved decisive in the pursuit of the movement's objec-tives. Following the sanctions in 1999, the movement opened several shops in Djeol, as well as a commercial association, to fight against the embargo that had been placed upon them. In addition, in 2002 it arranged the return of an uncle who had migrated to the Gambia where he worked as prawn fisher for forty years, and who was asked to assist his elder brother to guard family property in this period of insecurity (Leservoisier, 2005).

The example of Djeol shows that power struggles between social groups occur not only at the village level but may well involve a broad network of agents (youths, migrants, administration employees), different transnational spaces (Europe, Africa), and forms of political imagery.[11] These converging factors contribute to the ambivalence of political practices. In the case of Djeol, this is evident in the fact that the rebellious families demanded a share of power in the name of democratic principles, but they did not aim so much at subverting the current establishment as they wanted to gain a stake in it and a share in the control of village resources. These families never stopped asserting that they did not wish to question the internal organisation of the *leyyi*. Nevertheless, the conflict has not ended yet, and attempts at mediation have so far failed.

The case of Djeol shows that social negotiations have become increasingly complex, because of different contexts overlapping and of the intervention of multiple actors. This situation makes the resolution of conflicts hard to attain. One of the challenges faced by Haalpulaar society today is to find new forms of mediation capable of resolving ongoing conflict across status groups and at the same time to answer to the subordinated groups' growing need for political participation.

Identity Politics

Lastly, I would like to consider the reconfigurations of servile identities and related identity politics, which have been at the centre of recent political debates and struggles. The claims advanced in the name of reshaped identities exemplify different modes of resistance and testify to the heterogeneity of the servile groups. To simplify the situation, it is possible to distinguish across three main positions with regards to identity.

First, there are individuals who entirely refuse all forms of traditional classification and want to be considered as simple, ordinary citizens. These people often develop a form of 'avoidance behaviour', rejecting political and social participation in order to avoid exposing themselves to situations where they would be obliged to acknowledge their original status.

Conversely, a second type of position is maintained by those people who state their *maccuBe* origin openly. These are mostly elderly people used to this name, but also young people who rebel against discriminations. The latter refuse to deny their origins. This defence of the social category they belong to is matched by political considerations because, at elections, identification as a separate group is a precondition for obtaining seats in the municipal assembly and therefore gaining political representation for the group. If these young people proudly claim their belonging to the *maccuBe* group, they, nonetheless, refuse the hierarchical ideology of the elites. Thus, social categories can survive while being attributed new meanings by different individuals and groups.

A third position consists in rejecting the denomination *maccuBe* in favour of *SaafaalBe HormankooBe*, who are, as we have seen, one particular component within the servile category, possibly the descendants of black populations that had been raided by Horman Moroccan warriors. But the term *SaafaalBe HormankooBe* is also used to designate the *hrâtîn* – liberated slaves in Moorish society – who became integrated in Fulbe society. Interestingly, in today's political context, certain *SaafaalBe HormankooBe* who have become fully assimilated to Fulbe chose to reverse this historical process of identity transformation and deliberately call themselves *hrâtîn*. This choice reflects their desire to break away from the Haalpulaar hierarchical order and can be seen to have both social roots (a need to manifest otherness and uniqueness with regard to the broader Fulbe category) and political roots (a desire to obtain political representation).

Conclusion

I would like to return to the original focus of this essay on crossing social boundaries. These identity positionings, and particularly that of the *HormankooBe hrâtîn*, show how people who cannot cross social boundaries are led to create new boundaries within their own category. In the case we studied, this generates struggles over the definition of identity and their relative classificatory position between the *SaafaalBe HormankooBe*, who call themselves Haalpulaar, the *hrâtîn* and the *maccuBe* (Kamara, 2001; Leservoisier, 2000). These situations are all the more remarkable as the genealogical study of these groups reveals numerous kinship ties and sometimes common origins. Thus it is not rare to find that, within one family, some members claim to be *maccuBe* while their brothers and sisters pretend they are *SaafaalBe HormankooBe* or *hrâtîn*. In addition, particularly when they organise themselves into separate traditional communities (*leyyi*), these groups reject the presence of members of other groups and maintain a distance from them. This is what happened in Djeol where the *SaafaalBe HormankooBe* families refused to open their *leynol* to the *maccuBe* who wanted to join them. The *maccuBe* in question are emancipated but they chose to maintain their *maccuBe* names. However, they could equally have been *maccuBe* who are still considered slaves, in spite of the abolition of slavery in 1981. Some of them sometimes claim to belong to the *SaafaalBe HormankooBe* because the latter have been emancipated for a long time. But the *SaafaalBe HormankooBe* consider them as socially inferior. Paradoxically, within the servile category, the closer the groups (socially and genealogically), the harder it is to cross the classificatory boundaries that separate them.

This politics of exclusion, which may seem surprising if you consider how genealogically close these groups actually are, shows that gaining admission into a group depends on external acceptance. In order to be accepted, one has to be chosen by the members of the group. The actual origin of one's ancestors does not really matter. However, although the distinction between these servile groups relies on minor differences (such as precedence of emancipation, the reputation of being 'free', the general opinion of the group), these differences are nonetheless of paramount importance for the individuals concerned since they are constitutive of their identity. Last but not least, this exclusivist attitude highlights the ambivalence of some of the tactics of former slaves who, while advocating social justice and equality *between* status groups, reproduce hierarchical principles *within* their constituency.

References

Banegas, R., 2003. *La Démocratie à pas de caméléon. Transition et imaginaires politiques au Bénin*. Paris, Karthala.

Bayart, J.-F., 1996. *L'Illusion identitaire*. Paris, Fayard.

Botte, R., 1993. 'Stigmates sociaux et discriminations religieuses: l'ancienne classe servile au Fuuta Jaloo.' *Cahiers d'Études Africaines*, 34(133–35), pp. 109–36.

Botte, R., 2000. 'De l'esclavage et du daltonisme dans les sciences sociales. Avant propos.' *Journal des Africanistes*, 70(1–2), pp. 7–42.

Brhane, M., 1997. 'Narratives of the Past, Politics of the Present: Identity, Subordination and the haratines of Mauritania.' Unpublished PhD thesis, University of Chicago.

Burnham, P. and Last, M., 1994. 'From Pastoralist to Politician: The Problem of a Fulbe Aristocracy.' *Cahiers d'Études Africaines*, 34(133–35), pp. 313–57.

Douglas, M., 1966. *Purity and Danger: An Analysis of Concepts of Pollution and Taboo*. London: Routledge and Kegan Paul.

Goffman, E., 1975. *Stigmate, les usages sociaux des handicaps*. Paris: Minuit.

Hardung, C., 1997. 'Ni vraiment Peul, ni vraiment Baatombu. Le conflit identitaire des Gando.' In T. Bierschenk and P.-Y. Le Meur, eds, *Trajectoires peules au Bénin*. Paris: Karthala, pp. 109–38.

Holder, G., 1998. 'Esclaves et captifs au pays dogon. La société esclavagiste sama.' *L'Homme*, 145, pp. 71–108.

Kamara, O., 2000. 'Les Divisions statutaires des descendants d'esclaves au Fuuta Tooro mauritanien.' *Journal des Africanistes*, 70(1–2), pp. 265–89.

Leservoisier, O., 2000. 'Les *hrâtîn* et le Fuuta Toro, XIXème-XXème siècle: entre émancipation et dépendance.' In M. Villasante-de Beauvais, ed., *Groupes serviles au Sahara. Approche comparative à partir du cas des arabophones de Mauritanie*. Paris: IREMAM - CNRS éditions, pp. 147–67.

Leservoisier, O., 2005. '"Nous voulons notre part!" Les ambivalences du mouvement d'émancipation des *Saafaalße Hormankooße* de Djéol (Mauritanie).' *Cahiers d'Études Africaines*, 45(179–80), pp. 987–1014.

Pouget, C., 2001. 'Evolution des populations serviles dans les sociétés peules d'Afrique de l'Ouest et du Centre.' Unpublished PhD thesis, Université Paris X Nanterre.

Ruf, U. P., 1999. *Ending Slavery. Hierarchy, Dependency and Gender in Central Mauritania*. Bielefeld: Transcript Verlag.

Notes

1 The term *maccuBe* refers to the servile category in Haalpulaar society. This paper is based on my most recent research (2004–2005) on the situation of the descendants of slaves in the Gorgol area, which is located in the middle valley of the Senegal river.

2 The formal traditional Haalpulaar hierarchy divides society into three different orders: nobles, (free) professional groups and slaves.

3 The use of the term 'noble' in this paper refers to a generic category, that of the historical chiefs of the region, whose status was higher than those of other groups. It does not imply an association with other historical examples of 'nobility' (for a critique of comparative uses of the notion of 'aristocracy', see Burnham and Last, 1994).

4 Interview with A. N., Nouakchott, 10/2/04.

5 This principle therefore gave the slaves the reputation of practising witchcraft. Among the slaves, this reputation was particularly strong for those of Bambara origin. According to the testimonies of older *maccuBe* in Kaedi, witchcraft was used as an opposition force against their masters.

6 Interview Harouna, Kaédi, 16/12/04.

7 To date, I have not yet recorded, in either Kaedi or Djeol, a particular religious commitment among *maccuBe*. I have not noted a rise in the number of Islamic preachers, unlike other places in Mauritania (notably in Nouakchott) or more broadly in Africa. For example, in the same society in Mali, Gilles Holder (1998) notes that some descendants of slaves convert to Arabic wahabism, which is a form of Islam that denies the authority of religious leaders and advocates equality between Muslims.

8 This specialisation, which nobles deem degrading, illustrates what Mary Douglas underlines in *Purity and Danger* (1966) when she notes that the taboo, which varies across cultures, is a powerful political tool in so far as it contributes to creating a symbolic order that operates through exclusion from, and inclusion in, particular behaviours, roles, possessions, etc.

9 The *leyyi* are political groups of varying size, each having a noble family at its head. In the longer history of settlement, chiefly noble families integrated in their *leyyi* other families and different social groups, including large servile constituencies.

10 The *SaafaalBe HormankooBe* – which literally means the Horman Moors – might be the descendants of black populations, which had been captured by Horman Moroccan warriors, who were present in the Senegal valley in the early seventeenth century. These captives found refuge in Haalpulaar villages in the valley, where they were given the name of *SafaalBe HormankooBe*.

11 On this point, see Banégas, 2003; Bayart, 1996.

8

Slavery and Politics: Stigma, Decentralisation and Political Representation in Niger and Benin

Eric Komlavi Hahonou

In pre-colonial African societies, access to village spaces and 'spaces of sovereignty' was determined by sex (men rather than women), age (older rather than younger) and social status (free men rather than slaves), and not by egalitarian principles (Olivier de Sardan, 1994). Colonialism profoundly altered pre-existing forms of governance. However, it did not call into question considerations relative to 'political adulthood' (Olivier de Sardan, 1994, 120), which continued to set the rules of competition in local political arenas even after independence and successive waves of democratisation. In spite of numerous regime changes, women, young men and descendants of slaves remained politically marginal.

From the beginning of the 1990s, donor-led decentralisation appeared to both scholars and activists as the best way to promote democratisation 'from the bottom' (Wunsch and Olowu, 1990). Democratisation was presented as a cure to all the ills suffered by centralised African states. It was supposed to increase respect for human rights, to promote 'good governance', transparency and accountability (and thus stimulate the efficient management of public resources), to stimulate popular participation in development and to empower the most destitute and marginalised groups. Decentralisation, initiated from the exterior and taken up by internal forces (e.g. the case of Tuareg revolts in Niger and Mali), was eventually implemented by African governments. In the case of Benin and Niger, the reforms announced at national conferences from the beginning of the 1990s were not implemented until 2002–2003 and 2004, respectively. In both countries, groups of former slaves, until then politically marginalised and stigmatised, took advantage of the opportunities created by decentralisation to access political power at the local level.

Based on fieldwork conducted in Benin and Niger between 2002 and 2007, this essay[1] compares the processes of political emancipation followed by different groups of slave descent. In all of the three groups discussed in this chapter, slave descendants outnumber the descendants of old elites. While in the Songhay context the aristocracy has maintained its privileges and political power locally, former Tuareg[2] and Peul slaves were able to take over municipal councils. However, this renewal of leadership did not lead to major trans-formations in the management of local affairs. Instead, the new leadership reproduced the political culture and practices of governance that prevailed before decentralisation.

The Fieldsites

Bankilaré and Gorouol are two adjoining municipalities situated in Western Niger between the river and the borders of Burkina Faso and Mali. The Songhay sedentary population practices rain-fed agriculture and flood-recession farming along the banks of the river Gorouol. In regions where rain-fed agriculture is vulnerable to recurrent rain shortage and environmental degradation, flood-recession farming increases the subsistence security of the Songhay. Songhay farmers live in proximity to Fulbé and Kel Tamasheq groups, which used to be nomadic herders but recently became sedentary and started farming marginal lands. Historically, the Kel Tamasheq of the Niger Belt installed themselves on the Gourma bank (right bank of the river Niger) and gradually built powerful confederations that subjugated the Songhay, exacting tribute from them until the colonial conquest. Slavery played a central role in Songhay and Kel Tamasheq systems of production. Colonial domination at the beginning of the twentieth century put an end to the warrior economy, to the Kel Tamasheq supremacy and to slavery (Bernus, 1981). The country was 'pacified', and the French administration used local chieftaincies to rule the region. Sedentary populations were ruled by canton chiefs (*chefs de canton*) and village chiefs, whereas nomadic 'group chieftaincies' (*chefferies de groupement*) were created to administer nomadic and semi-nomadic tribes (Kel Tamasheq and Fulbé).

The municipality of Kalalé is situated in the department of Borgou of Northern Benin, in the Sudano-Sahelian region that borders Nigeria. The population is composed essentially of Baatombu groups (often called Bariba), Boo and Fulbé (more commonly called 'Peuls', and incorporating the Gando). Other ethnic groups in this region play a marginal political role. Local producers clear this vast forested area to cultivate foodcrops and cash crops (cotton in particular) and to practise livestock husbandry (cattle, sheep and goats) which plays a central role in the Borgou economy and Northern Benin more generally. The Fulbé are traditionally identified with semi-nomadic herding, even though they also practise subsistence and commercial agricul-ture. In pre-colonial times, Borgou was dominated by the Baatombu. The Fulbé, scattered in small groups and often without herds, provided herding labour to the Baatonu and Boo. Gradually, by establishing patron–client relations with the warriors (*wasangari*) and peasants of the Baatonu and Boo, they gained access to land and formed their own herds of cattle. Both raided and protected by the *wasangari*, the Fulbé of Borgu remained dominated until the arrival of French colonialists. In the process of assigning each group a chief who would serve as intermediary between the administration and local populations, the French created an independent Fulbé chieftaincy ex nihilo[3] (Bierschenk, 1993; 1997). These three groups possessed slaves that are referred to, collectively, as 'Gando'.

The Fulbé, Kel Tamasheq and Songhay, as several other Sahelo-Sudanese societies (Meillassoux, 1986), shared political and economic systems based on slavery. Pre-colonial conflicts and wars provided occasions to take prisoners who, unless they were freed, would become 'slaves'. Their descendants became 'captives'.[4] According to Rouch, 'whatever their previous status, they became the property of whoever defeated them' (Rouch, 1954, 48). Slaves constituted an important economic asset and they could be bought as farming, herding and domestic labour. Gradations of status existed also within the group of captives,[5] further stratifying the social hierarchy. The colonial administration ended slavery well after the official abolition of 1905. In spite of its humanistic and civilising ideology, the colonial administration turned a blind eye to the persistence of various forms of slavery for a long time, intervening only super-ficially when required by circumstances and/or by colonial interests (Bernus, 1981, 108–12; Hardung, 2002, 37–38; Olivier de Sardan, 1976, 15–18). Slavery, therefore, remained generally tolerated, often under various attenuated forms, even though some effort was put into limiting the abuses of the chiefs and allowing slaves who moved away from their former masters to control their own labour and the profits derived from it. This situation allowed a number of slaves to emancipate themselves economically from their masters while, at times, maintaining relations of a patron–client kind, or continuing to accept various forms of subordination. Slavery thus went on beyond colonialism, and certain forms of master–slave relationships are still observable today.[6]

Here I shall not comment on the polemic[7] initiated by Debord's film (2002) and the report of Timidria and Anti-Slavery International (2003) on the endur-ance of slavery in Niger and the magnitude of this phenomenon. It seems to me that, given the moral overtones of this subject, the ideological stance of the author tends to take precedence over methodological considerations.[8] Suffice it to note that, in the majority of cases, the people that define themselves as 'slave' (*iklan, maccuBe, jiyaaBe, banniyey*) in the course of an interview with an anthropologist or even a banal conversation in Niger or Benin are evoking their categorical status rather than their actual condition (people belonging to a master, working for him, lacking freedom of movement, etc.). In their survey on the state of slavery in Niger, Dandah and Galy rightly point out that 'slavery in Niger is not completely abolished in practice, and even less in people's mentality' (2003, 106). Various recent reports indicate that this statement would be equally appropriate for Northern Benin. This essay does not attempt to demonstrate the contemporary existence of situations of enslavement. Rather, it uses three case studies to illustrate and analyse the endurance of 'slavery' in popular representations and the recent political mobilisation of groups of servile origin.

The Persistence of Stigma

The terms 'Gando' and 'Bella' designate respectively individuals and groups of servile origin among the 'red Peuls', Boo and Baatombu on the one hand, and the Kel Tamasheq societies of Western Niger on the other. These terms, borrowed from the Baatonu (language of the Baatombu) and from Songhay-Zarma, regroup under a single denomination distinct social groups with different statuses: some belong to servile categories, others have been collectively freed by their masters, others still are independent. In daily interactions with outsiders, the status nuances conveyed in Fulfulde and Tamasheq are commonly glossed over. Once these groups are collectively designated as 'slave' and their members are uniformly represented as stigmatised, mistreated and scorned, they acquire the misleading appearance of a homogeneous whole.

Among the Songhay-Zarma, the dichotomous reasoning applied to the ideological distinction between nobles and captives tends to erase internal nuances (Olivier de Sardan, 1984). The terms that designate individuals of servile status in Songhay or Zarma contexts are euphemised (*almayaali*[9]), codified (*yegga* or 'centre-forward'[10]), omitted (I noted that, in a large proportion of interviews, speakers avoided naming people of servile origin, replacing a precise terminology with a commonly understood silence), or veiled (the ubiquitous term 'thing' replaces words that are too sensitive to be used in conversation). The majority of names designating servile groups in Songhay-Zarma, Fulfulde and Tamasheq are currently taboo among intellectuals in urban contexts. This is notably the case with *tam*, *horso*, *kongo* and *banniya* in Songhay-Zarma.[11] As a result of the work of the anti-slavery oganisation Timidria among the Kel Tamasheq of Niger the use of the term Iklan (sing. *Akli*) in public is strictly forbidden, under penalty of being openly confronted. Today the neutral term *Kel Tamasheq*, which encompasses all speakers of the Tamasheq language, or 'black Tuareg' are preferred to Iklan.[12] Similarly, in Peul contexts (Boo or Baatonu of Northern Benin), some people prefer speaking of 'black Peul' rather than using the terms *gannunkeeBe*, *maccuBe*, *Fulbé*, *yobu*, *yonobu*, which describe with greater precision the particular status of these groups (cf. Hardung, 1997, 113–22). These names carry pejorative connotations that are often internalised by their carriers (Hardung, 1997, 117), and their overt use in public situations induces considerable discomfort.

'It is not appropriate to talk about this!' This type of remark is common in the three groups considered here. A collective taboo surrounds the subject of slavery. When everybody knows, nothing has to be said. A set of symbolic elements function as constant reminders of the social differentiations particular to these societies both at the level of spatial organisation and at that of social interaction and self-representation (hairstyle, garments, jewellery, public demeanour, etc.), or in the organisation of work.

In the village or camp, social status is inscribed in the organisation of space. In Songhay rural villages nobles and 'slaves' live in separate neighbourhoods. In Bankilaré domestic slaves are generally situated west of the nobles' camps. Instead, the Gando are usually settled at the periphery of the red Peul's camps and the Baatonu or Boo villages. They are placed at the outskirts, towards the bush: in sum, they are physically banned from these societies of which they nonetheless constituted, and continue to constitute, a component essential to their development. Here and there some Songhay villages or Tamasheq camps are locally known for being composed only of slave descendants. As Bierschenk notes with regards to the Peul of North Benin, spatial structures play a constitutive role in social processes, as they make readable, in space, the principles of social organisation, thereby 'making those who inhabit these spaces believe that social constructs are "natural" and therefore inevitable, whereas they are nothing but the product of history[13] and culture' (Bierschenk, 1999, 196–97). This analysis could be extended to the three cases studied here. An example illustrates this point. In the Borgou a number of Gando farms located between Boo and Baatonu villages and Peul camps result from the auto-marginalisation operated by the Gando themselves. It is a phenomenon that occurs particularly among the *Yonobu*, who are children of the Boo and Baatombu assigned to the Peul at an early age because they were suspected of being sorcerers. The young *Yonubu* understands subsequently that he is not a full member of his adoptive Peul family (he cannot for example hope to marry a Peul woman), he is the genetic offspring of his Boo or Baatonu parents, who had rejected him and later wished to reintegrate him (in exchange for an ox given to his adoptive family). But his reintegration into the village proves difficult because, there, he is considered a Gando, an object of daily ridicule and scorn. Therefore he chooses to settle on the outskirts of other villages, creating new camps and clearing farms on unoccupied lands. 'Neither Peul nor Baatombu' (Hardung, 1997), the Gando places himself somewhere in between these two identities. His position at the margins of dominant societies reflects an emotionally charged psychological process that, according to some interpretations, is reflected in the meaning of the name 'Gando', namely 'outside is best!'[14]

Moreover, in Songhay villages every marriage, baptism,[15] religious celebration and burial[16] reiterates a person's place and rank in society. In Fulbé and

Kel Tamasheq societies slave women do not wear the same clothes, jewellery and hairstyle as noble women. Strict marriage endogamy also works as an expression of distance between different social categories. While noble men can marry women of servile status[17] (ennobling them through marriage), marriage between a man of slave descent and a noble woman often remains unthinkable from the perspectives of both 'nobles' *and* 'slaves' who have internalised the dominant ideology.

The social stigma attached to slave descent is also manifested in the division of labour. In Kel Tamasheq societies a free man will resist doing any farming and other agricultural labour, as this work is traditionally considered debasing and reserved for slaves. In fact, this is one of the causes for the impoverishment of the Kel Tamasheq nobles in Bankilaré: having lost their animals after the droughts of the early 1970s and 1980s, the *Imajeghen* were unable to reconstitute their herds through revenues derived from farming, in contrast to their 'slaves' who found a source of prosperity in this work.[18] This situation is less marked among the Fulbé of Northern Benin (where environmental conditions are not as harsh), who took up agriculture when their slaves were freed by the colonial administration. The social division of labour between elites and slave descendants is less flagrant in Songhay contexts, because here agriculture is traditionally practised by both groups. In urban centres, however, cleaning jobs and other demeaning tasks are reserved to slaves and foreigners (Hahonou, 2003).

If these aspects remain hidden or unspoken, they constitute tacit rules in the social and political arena. The whole of these 'un-saids' contributes to the production and reproduction of 'ideological discrimination' (Olivier de Sardan, 1984, 201). If, historically speaking, what distinguishes the free man from the slave is nothing but misfortune (a kidnapped child, a man defeated in war, a person born to slave parents, a child 'sorcerer' born among the Baatombu, etc.), ideology associates pejorative physical, moral and behavioural attributes with servile status. The slave bears the heavy load of being at the same time 'defeated', without lineage, without history, obscene, honourless, shameless and a liar.[19] He cannot conduct himself as a free man. He is portrayed as the antithesis of the noble (see Riesman, 1974, on Fulbé slaves; Olivier de Sardan, 1976, on Songhay slaves). As the slave *is* owned, he or she is denied the capacity to own land, to lead prayer or command free individuals. The ideology of slavery characterises the slave as an eternal outsider (Kopytoff and Miers, 1977a). This set of representations fosters a 'social racism' (Botte and Schmitz, 1994, 118) that is often extended to representations of slave descendants, producing an inferiority complex (Hardung, 1997, 128) that counterbalances the feeling of superiority of those of noble descent.

The internalisation of rules by different members of a community is flexible and varies across generations and levels of education. Referring to Western

Niger, Rouch highlighted the resistance of slaves to emancipation by the French administration, as it was considered that true liberation could only come from the master (1954, 49). Olivier de Sardan emphasised the obstacles to the achievement of 'psychological independence' by the slaves (1969, 47–48). Today in the rural milieu of Western Niger, as well as in Northern Benin, older ex-slaves, often illiterate, tend to perpetuate attitudes of loyalty, deference and respect towards their masters. The inferiority of one and superiority of the other are fully endorsed and, to return to Bierschenk's notion, they appear as a 'natural' social fact. Thus, in such contexts, slave and master will spontaneously employ terms and attitudes (body language) denoting their respective status. At the harvest, a slave may choose to offer a gift of cereals to his master to foster good relations with him in the future. Today these attitudes are induced less by actual subordination than by spontaneous or interested dispositions.

> Now the masters are finished! They don't exist anymore, in this area you only find them in Bankilaré [...] This is something we don't like, because when you haven't got a big man, whoever comes can take advantage of you. We prefer that he [the group chief] remains here, among us. (*Akli*, chef de tribu *Doufarafarak*, 2003)

The colonial administration almost always appointed 'traditional chiefs' chosen from the ranks of the old masters. In contexts marked by the recurrent predations of state agents at the expense of rural populations, and more particularly of so-called 'nomadic' peoples, the 'traditional' chief is perceived as a protector, the sole recourse in the face of abuses of power, sometimes violent, enacted by the 'wearers of uniform' (police, soldiers, customs agents, environmental agents, etc.). His status, his knowledge of the administration (of which he is an essential cogwheel) and the privileged relationships that he maintains with his superiors (the *sous-préfets* in the first place) gives the chief an intermediary position.[20] The chief is the privileged link between the state and local communities. All information, service or good directed to the population has to meet his preliminary approval. The chief has the role of the gatekeeper[21] and can allow or deny the transmission of anything destined for his subjects at will. He articulates the relations between his subjects and state services and reduces (or extends) the distance that separates them, in exchange for a financial remuneration, the cost of access to citizenship (Hahonou, 2006a, 104–20).

In Northern Benin the derogatory connotations of the status of 'slave descendant' drove an entire generation of intellectuals who had achieved a successful political and bureaucratic career into hiding their origins (for example, by speaking Baatonu rather than Fulfulde, changing name, living in the city and severing links with their village of origin). This attitude, rooted in the Gando 'identity complex' (cf. Hardung, 1997) is not, however, the only possible option for intellectuals. A number of Gando and Bella intellectuals have, on the contrary, opted for various forms of resistance. In the name of the ideals of justice and egalitarianism transmitted through modern education, Bella and Gando intellectuals in Niger formed political associations or parties to denounce the ongoing domination of former slaves by former masters and to claim a more equitable access to power. In Niger this resistance[22] took the form of associational militancy in favour of the emancipation of people of servile origins and gave rise to political parties addressed specifically to the 'black Tuareg' electorate. In Benin Peuls and Gando formed a common front in a political movement that took the form of a Fulfulde linguistic and cultural seminar, until a large group of Gando distanced themselves from the red Peuls, and Gando leaders created their own movements.

The Difficult Task of the Political Representation of Slaves in the Songhay Milieu

In spite of the greater demographic weight of former slaves, since the establishment of party politics in Niger (1946) all the representatives of the National Assembly from Gorouol have been chosen from the ranks of the aristocracy. No slave descendant was able to emerge politically (Hahonou, 2004a and b). 'Permanent juniors'[23] in Songhay-Zarma societies, slaves are traditionally excluded from power. The slave cannot envisage his accession to elder status. He will always remain dependent upon the master or his descendants. Power can only belong to a noble. In this context it is not surprising that former colonial soldiers of slave descent, who had been appointed chiefs by colonial administrators, were targeted by acute local criticism in the 1950s and 1960s. From the point of view of the aristocratic ideology, there is a complete incompatibility between servile status and the exercise of political functions. Nowadays, in spite of change,[24] these considerations are still widespread and the descendants of Songhay or Zarma slaves remain the object of discrimination in local political institutions.

The un-saids that structure the representations of 'slaves' among noble Songhay of Gorouol result in the quiet removal of ex-slaves from positions of responsibility through various manipulations. This occurs both in the constitution of local associations and of political parties:

> It is true and always a delicate subject [the place of slaves]. When the management committee of the Boogu ONG was formed in 1992, a nobleman got the leadership through various manipulations. Yatakala being 90% composed of captives, it was logical that they got the management roles at the level of presidency, vice-presidency... but after a covert debate we conspired to place myself in the best position. They said: 'That's it, we want you there because Yatakala must be on the frontline for the whole district, and we can't put

a "captive"! We have to set criteria so that you are in front, and it's up to you to meet these criteria'. So, we argued for the necessity to have someone capable of discussing with the Whites, the ONG, and reading documents.[25] There it is: during that whole time it was them [slave descendants of the village] who pushed me forward. And it is in this manner that I came to office. (member of the Boogu ONG bureau, interview at Yatakala, district of Gorouol, Niger, 2003)

Olivier de Sardan's writings on the ideological and symbolic survival of slavery in Songhay-Zarma societies remained essentially accurate (1984, 201–05). However, the multipartitism of the 1990s reshuffled local political forces. Just as in the 1990s young men of free origin tried to seize new political opportunities, the descendants of captives (mostly also young men) struggled to achieve political representation.

In Gorouol, if there are two major parties today, the MNSD and the PNDS, it is above all because of the problem of 'castes', and us... we understood this, and it's one of the reasons why we approached the PNDS [...] In the MNSD, there are older people and those who don't want to confront them. Us rebels, we side with the PNDS to try to change things. (a young politician of noble origin from Gorouol, Niamey 2003)

In Niamey the aristocratic intelligentsia militant within the MNSD Nassara[26] spread the rumour that the majority of the Songhay-Zarma of the Tillabéri region affiliated with the PNDS is of servile origin. Thus, every member of this party is suspected to be 'casted' or to sympathise with the illegitimate cause of those servile groups that are trying to overcome their conditions of origin. Thus, in Gorouol, social schisms are partly reflected in partisan demarcations. In this socio-cultural context national politicians are careful in their campaigns to subtly take advantage of existing social and political divisions to create their political clientage.

When I visit villages to ask people to support me, it must be known that I am noble... otherwise, those who consider themselves noble will not follow me. It's not easy! In introducing myself along with someone 'casted', things reinforce each other, and both sides contribute to sustaining the party. (the same PNDS politician from Gorouol, Niamey, 2003).

Yet the PNDS party did not win in Gorouol at the municipal elections of 2004. The MNSD Nassara, locally controlled by the aristocracy, gained all of the eleven seats of the municipal council. Hence all Songhay municipal representatives[27] are aristocrats or free men. In spite of the opportunities for political representation that became available thanks to the recent municipal elections, the opposition between slave descendants (*bagney*) and nobles (*borciney*) failed to find expression in the Gouruol municipal council.

The Political Emancipation of Kel Tamasheq of Servile Origin in Bankilaré

Referring to political representation among the Kel Tamasheq, Bourgeot notes that 'slaves [...] are, by definition, deprived of both political and economic freedom' (1995, 28). The 'captive' is situated outside politics (Bourgeot, 1995, 39). The repeated crises that the Kel Tamasheq have endured since 1904, such as major droughts (1900–03, 1913–14, 1931–32, 1972–73, 1984–85) and hostile colonial policies,[28] obliged masters to free a large part of their slaves (*Iklan*). The latter cleared the bush and became farmers or maintained their lives as nomadic shepherds, sometimes continuing to pay regular tributes to their masters. Some masters retained power over their economically emancipated slaves. Often this takes the form of protracted patron–client relationships[29] reflected in matters of political representation. By virtue of these relationships, the *Iklan* lend electoral support to their former *Imajeghen* masters. In the case of the Kel Tamasheq of Bankilaré, at the time of the legislative elections of 1989–91, 1993–95, 1995–96 and 1996–99, all council seats had been monopolised by the customary and religious chieftaincies. The Kel Tamasheq customary chiefs were able to take advantage of the new political deal that followed from the process of democratisation. From 1989, the eldest member of the chiefly family of the *Kel Igirer*[30] became a member of the National Assembly as his name was included in the national list presented by the MNSD party. From 1992–93, the Kel Igirer chieftaincy (*chefferie de groupement*) also managed to profit from the status of special circumscription[31] to monopolise the political representation of the group at the parliamentary level, with the support of the religious chiefs and to the detriment of the *Iklan* majority.[32] The *Imajeghen* and their allies, the *Ineslimen* (religious specialists), had to rely on their tributary and patron–client relationships with dependent groups (mostly *Imghad* and *Iklan*) to win the elections. Moreover, the ambiguous notion of 'mixed' status was used instrumentally to oppose the increasing weight of the *Iklan* in local politics. Thus, the two representatives elected in 1993, 1995 and 1996 shared the characteristic of being of mixed ancestry, born from *taklit*[33] mothers who had been freed by their *aneslim* masters. This granted them a double claim to the support of free and *Iklan* people.

Nonetheless, in the space of a decade the local balance of forces between masters and slaves progressively changed to the advantage of the latter. In Bankilaré, at the end of 1999, the struggle for the emancipation of slave descendants led by the Timidria association[34] finally resulted in the first slave descendant winning a seat in the National Assembly (cf. Hahonou, 2004a, 41–43). Even if the elected member belonged to the 'old school', the challenge to the *Imajeghen*'s and *Ineslimen*'s political supremacy came primarily from younger generations. In addition to Timidria's action, the election of an *Akli* benefited from the support of certain politicians from Gorouol.[35] However, the *Iklan's* victory at the legislative elections of the end of 1999 should not suggest a lack of internal divisions. Even the *Iklan* are divided into opposing conservative and progressive groups. The militant action of Timidria is still scarcely understood by many of them. For others, arrangements with the masters present more advantages than an uncertain struggle for emancipation:

> The people of Tahoua [referring to the Timidria association, whose national president is from Tahoua] come to insult people, to divide them by supporting the struggle against the 'Reds'. The Timidria, after their missions in Bankilaré, they tell women to take off the anklets that they wear on their feet. They are in their vehicles and they stop to forcibly remove the anklets from the women. And then, they also tell the women to remove their traditional hairstyles[36] and their clothes typical of *tiklan* women. These are the 'worst slaves' of Tahoua, who come to distribute money. One day, an old woman, one of the wet-nurses[37] of a son of the old-man [the *Chef de groupement*], replied to them: 'If you want me to remove the anklets, then change the color of my skin first!' (Kel Tamasheq politician of servile status, closely related to the chiefs of the Bankilaré group, 2003).

Until 2004[38] Timidria's action in Bankilaré remained fairly discrete and localised (focused upon the camps where the association leaders have relatives), often misunderstood, and even opposed by the creation of a development association[39] led by an *Akli* loyal to the *chefferie* of the *Kel Igirer*. Often assimilated to a political party, the ideology of Timidria seems dissonant with popular representations of politics, development aid or Muslim morality.

> 1st person: 'Yes, it is slaves who joined forces [Timidria] to fight to end slavery.
> 2nd person: Really? You know, we hadn't even understood this. We thought it was a party. [...]
> 1st person: Hasn't slavery been over for a long time?
> 2nd person: Maybe it's just against saying that word.
> 1st person: It's in the Qu'ran. Unless they're going to make the Qu'ran disappear so that they don't encounter the word. Slavery disappear? That would mean that these people are against the Qu'ran, against God. (extract from a discussion between two Kel Tamasheq women, Balleyara, 2003).

The message of Timidria, which challenges the verbal discrimination against slave descendants (the pejorative character of the term *Bella* or *Iklan* used to discredit and demean a person morally), is misunderstood. Neither development broker nor political party, Timidria has long remained an atypical actor in local politics. In other regions of Niger, politically engaged development brokers were quicker to reposition themselves at the political level (Tidjani Alou, 2000b, 303).

The formation of a political party of slave descendants, the PRD Mahiba – *parti tan Iklan* or 'slave party' (as the *Imajeghen* call it) – seen as the political wing of Timidria, marked an important symbolic turn, even if they could not yet impose themselves on the local and national political chessboards. The PRD Mahiba was created in 1996 from a section of the PUND Salama, itself originating from a division within the UDPS Amana, a political wing of the Touareg rebellion.[40] The three parties have in common the fact of being supported primarily by a Kel Tamasheq electorate. Following the Zinder congress of the PUND Salama (1995), militants from the Tillabéri department detached themselves from the leader Akoli Dawal[41] and created the PRD Mahiba. For the militants of Tillabéri (at the time, the administrative capital of the department of Western Niger), joining the PUND Salama had initially been motivated by a concern with the political under-representation of the Kel Tamasheq and their under-development compared to the Songhay. Since its creation, the party has been presided over by a native of Tillabéri. For the Bankilaré area, two state officers from the 'black Tuareg community' were its representatives (one of them was the first general secretary of the party, and it is said that the other owes his promotion in the state apparatus to his membership in the PRD Mahiba). In Bankilaré the electorate of the PRD generally followed the successive political memberships of its leaders: MNSD and ANDP, then PRD, and more recently MNSD (1999). Although it did not win the elections,[42] the emergence of the PRD Mahiba marked an important step in people's mindsets as an attempt to break with the former order. In this power quest, which follows the logic of 'political nomadism' (or opportunism), the return to the MNSD has above all allowed access to the financial resources required by the expensive and uncertain adventure of electoral campaigns.[43]

On the death of the first *Akli* representative of Bankilaré in 2001, his substitute (*député suppléant*), an active member of Timidria and of the PRD Mahiba, replaced him in office. Following allegations of corruption, the latter was disqualified from participating in the legislative elections of 2004. His successor, supporting the MNSD Nassara, was another activist of Timidria, coming from Bankilaré and sympathising with the PRD Mahiba. This politician was a doctor in ethnology who taught at the University of Niamey and played a decisive role in the municipal election campaign of July 2004 and the formation of the municipal executive bureau of which he is said to pull the strings.

The municipal council of Bankilaré which was elected at the end of 2004, after the resumption of the July elections (due to frauds denounced by the parties in competition), is composed of eleven elected representatives and two members by right: the deputy of Bankilaré and the chief of the *Kel Igirer* group. It is heavily dominated by the MNSD (8 of 11 seats), who won the bulk of *Iklan* votes, whereas the traditional chiefs and their allies, affiliated with the CDS, had to settle for three seats only (of which one was *Akli*). The post of mayor of Bankilaré was accorded to a slave descendant from Bankilaré employed at the Prefecture of Téra. Beyond having the support of the local member of Parliament, the MNSD candidates in the municipal administration benefited from the financial support of a Pullo who was originally from Bankilaré and became influential at the national level, acting as advisor to the prime minister, Hama Amadou, for several years.

Timidria, which had been in favour of accelerating the process of decentralisation 'likely to offer marginalised groups such as former slaves the possibility of taking part in the local administration of public affairs and to progressively erase the stereotypes that oppress them' (Dandah and Galy, 2003, 72), clearly played a central role in the process of the emancipation of slave descendants in Tamasheq contexts.

The Historical Revenge of the Gando of Kalalé

The political marginalisation of the Fulbé of the Borgou dates from the pre-colonial era, from the time when they were clients of the Baatombu and the Boo. Colonialism had provisionally interrupted their dependence and exploitation. In creating Fulbé chieftaincies (which did not exist before), the colonial administration had allowed them to establish direct relations with the state apparatus. The suppression of the chieftaincy in 1972 under a Marxist-Leninist regime constituted a step backward for this politically under-represented group. Exploited by the post-colonial administration, victims of all sorts of extortions by the military, civil servants and a corrupt justice, discriminated against in disputes arising from the damage caused by their animals on the fields of the Baatombu and Boo,[44] regularly deceived by unavoidable local intermediaries (the 'district chiefs', 'delegates' and other 'village chiefs'), the Fulbé remained locked in a stoicism rooted in the fulbé notion of *senteene*.[45] For a long time, the Fulbé accepted the marginalisation and the injustices bestowed upon them. It has even been possible to talk of 'auto-marginalisation of the Peul' (Bierschenk, 1995, 462; cf. Hardung, in this volume), who until recently stayed away from politics, thus being unable to end the humiliations they suffered. They attribute their exploitation to the historical error they committed by fleeing the 'school of Whites' (*janirde batuure*). Like the Songhay or Kel Tamasheq chiefs, the 'red Peuls' preferred sending to school the children of their slaves rather than their own. Their children's lack of schooling deprived them of 'intellectuals'[46] capable of representing their interests *vis-à-vis* the State and other groups that exploit them (Bierschenk, 1999, 208–09).

The collective awakening of the Fulbé occurred in December 1987 with the birth of the Laawol Fulfulde movement (lit. 'the way of the Fulbé').

Considered incapable of collective action, the Fulbé generated considerable surprise when they organised a massive gathering in Kandi, district-capital of Northern Benin, and expressed their claims in the course of a linguistic seminar (Bierschenk, 1992; Guichard, 1990). This event was made possible by the post-1980s change in Benin state politics against the earlier centralising approach and towards the promotion of internal diversity of national ethnicities and cultures (Bierschenk, 1995, 462–67). This opportunity was initially seized by a small group of fulbé intellectuals who, since the early 1980s, had joined an evangelical priest's struggle to promote literacy among the rural Fulbé of Northern Benin. Thanks to the support of some politicians, and in particular of the person who would become the president of the Laawol Fulfulde and who, at the time, was national deputy, the provisional committee obtained the authorisations and material support necessary to organise the Kandi seminar. At the local level, the huge mobilisation of 'Peul' and Gando, manifested through the support of traditional chiefs, massive popular participation and important material contributions (supplies, livestock, cash), was determinant in making the event happen. During the seven days of the conference, various commissions elaborated different themes, such as 'the origin of the Peuls of Borgou', 'the life of the Peul herder', 'schooling', etc. Literacy and education were established as 'key to the emancipation of nationality' (i.e. of the Fulbé group[47]). Through literacy, education would contribute to the reduction of the marginalisation and exploitation suffered by Fulbé for decades: 'The uneducated man is a blind man!'

The great Fulbé movement of Northern Benin that initially reflected a reaction against exploitation by the *HaaBe*[48] (the 'others', the 'non-Peuls') finally highlighted a different form of exploitation: that of Fulbé by Fulbé. This consideration led rapidly to internal disagreements in the Laawol Fulfulde. Thus, the second conference held in Kalalé in 1990 was disrupted by the participants of the first. The same ills listed three years earlier were still going on. Literacy and education, always seen as avenues to progress, had hardly advanced as a result of bureaucratic inertia. On one side, young people expressed consternation *vis-à-vis* the elders' management style. The latter established the committee as a sort of traditional tribunal which 'settled family disputes over wife stealing and the like, rather than the problem of Peul access to education'. Moreover, the funds of the committee, derived from various contributions (gifts of livestock, membership fees and donations, state-funded grants, etc.), had been embezzled by various members of the bureau. The youths who had criticised the elders of the committee were ostracised from the organisation. Instead, the Gando, frustrated by their continuing marginalisation, reiterated their demands to the committee. Gando intellectuals realised that the 'Peul' did not consider them full members of their group[49] and that their integration in the Laawol Fulfulde was merely a façade of unity, behind which divisions remained profound. Thus, the bureau of the committee remained dominated by the 'red Peuls' to the detriment of the 'blacks'. In preparation for the Banikoara conference of 1997, Gando delegations were received by the bureau committee in an attempt to overcome disagreements: 'They evoke Peul origins[50] and they don't talk about the Gando. They call us to finance conferences, but that's all! They cheat us and still dominate us...' Few things changed after this conference, and the expression of Gando frustration grew more intense as time went on.

In 2000–01 (after the death of the Laawol Fulfulde president), a restricted meeting between Gando and 'Peul' leaders took place in Parakou (the administrative centre of the Borgou prefecture, where a number of intellectuals work and live) to ensure that Gando representation be guaranteed in the management committee of the Laawol Fulfulde. However, it was another 'red' who took the leadership of the organisation. In spite of an agreement in principle following the meeting, the Gando soon afterwards detached themselves from the joint movement and formed their own organisations following the model of the linguistic conferences. This is how in this period the Idi Waadi association ('what we want has taken place') was formed led by Gando leaders from Nikki. A number of twin organisations that opposed the old order also emerged at the local level: Djanati ('peace finally come') in Kandi, Semmee Allah ('the force of God') in Kalalé, etc. These organisations served as political platforms for Gando leaders running in the municipal elections of December 2002– January 2003.

Semmee Allah is a branch of the Laawol Fulfulde created by Orou Sé Guéné, a college professor from Kalalé. Although the name evokes the accomplishment of the will of God, the group identifies with physical strength (*semmee*) and work (*golle*), which are the positive values emphasised by the Gando to distinguish themselves from other groups, as noted by Hardung (1997, 129–35). These values constitute a key element in the contemporary construction of Gando identity. After the colonial abolition of slavery, former slaves used their physical labour to further emancipate themselves. The Gando of Borgou quickly became wealthier than their former Peul and Baatombu masters (Lombard, 1965). But it is above all education, intellectual work, that allowed the Gando to progressively achieve a reversal of power relations. Through education the Gando gradually achieved state functions (Hardung, 1997, 137). Through education and knowledge of the past they were able to accept a collective identity until then defined essentially by the discourses and practices of exclusion of other groups (Boo, Baatombu and 'Peuls'). Gando intellectuals used their individual experience and understanding of the situation to help the whole group to emancipate itself and reappropriate an ethnic identity. This process of 'ethnicisation', to borrow Bierschenk's expression (1993), is now advanced among the Gando. This group, of which Hardung said that internal status differences constituted 'factors hindering group cohesion and the emergence of a collective identity' (1997, 117), was able to seize the opportunities offered by the processes of democratisation and decentralisation.

Just like the Kel Tamasheq of Bankilaré of servile origin, it was through associationism that the Gando began their process of political emancipation. Initially integrated in the unitary Laawol Fulfulde movement, where they could not fully express themselves,[51] the Gando progressively and collectively developed an ethnic identity of their own: 'neither Baatombu, nor Peul', but Gando. They took control of an ideological difference that until then had placed them outside, or banned them from the Boo, Baatonu and Peul societies. Nowadays, they assert their distinctiveness, confirming the tendency noticed by Hardung (1997, 137–38). As their repeated negotiations with the bureau dominated by Laawol Fulfulde aristocrats failed, they created an alternative movement founded on their ethnic uniqueness, particularly *vis-à-vis* the Peuls. As had happened with the organisers of the first linguistic seminar, the intellectuals who initiated the Gando movements became its leaders.

The composition of the Kalale municipal council reflects the demographic preponderance of the Gando:[52] of 17 municipal seats, nine are occupied by Gando. Orou Sé Guéné[53] – head of the RUND party[54] – fought his electoral campaign, working closely with his Gando 'brothers', under the banner of Gando political emancipation, struggle against the mismanagement of the cotton business, protection against the iniquities of the *HaaBe*, etc. He won seven seats and made a coalition with the delegates of two minor parties which had four seats in all, becoming the first elected mayor in the Kalalé municipality at the beginning of 2003.[55] However, the election of Orou Sé Guéné did not depend merely on the electoral weight of the Gando, but also on his capacity to recruit voters from other ethnic groups (Boo, Baatombu and other minorities).

If, for the descendants of the local aristocracy, the victory of a Gando threw shame on Kalalé, a slave descendant at the head of a collectivity was not an entirely new occurrence in Borgou. In Nikki, a neighbouring locality that had belonged to the Baatombu kingdom, a man of slave descent had achieved the highest position in local authority a few years earlier (at the time[56] Nikki was a *sub-prefecture*). Yet this historical precedent was short-lived because the sub-prefect was quickly replaced by a Nikki 'prince', promoted by the Minister of Interior Affairs. The latter seized the occasion of the expulsion of the Gando sub-prefect to reiterate publicly the incompatibility of individuals of servile status with leadership functions. This case caused great controversy in the Gando community of the Borgou, which took its revenge a few years later by 'voting ethnically' on the occasion of the municipal elections. Hence, the rise to power of slave descendants belongs to a tendency older than the recent trend induced by decentralisation.

New Elites, Old Forms of Governance

The appearance of municipalities in the institutional and political landscape of Benin and Niger is a recent phenomenon. One might think that it has led to the renewal of the local ruling elite. But in fact municipalities constitute only partial innovations, as local political arenas were already governed by a decentralised administration (the *sub-prefectures*, the *postes administratifs*), by a group of associative-style organisations and by the so-called *chefferie traditionelle*. Therefore, municipalities did not fill a political, administrative, organisational and institutional vacuum. Rather, they added themselves to multiple existing organisations in which local elites had already carved their niches. These multiple actors of local governance managed economic enterprises (organisations of cotton producers and herders) and the transport system (syndicates of transporters), they participated in public investment, administrated communities, etc. They immediately tried to take over the municipal bodies to which all of these sectors were legally transferred. On the one hand, the officers of the under-financed local administration converged around municipalities (to which the bulk of the resources of previous decentralised institutions had been transferred). Thus, former sub-prefects, general secretaries and other administrative officers of the sub-prefectures, as well as agents of technical services of the state, threw themselves into the political struggle for the first communal elections. Some of them were able to assume the main executive positions of the new municipalities (mayors and adjunct mayors). The profiles of newly elected municipal staff suggest that the leaders of the main local organisations took advantage of the political influence they had acquired within their old institutions to access new influential roles in the municipal councils (Hahonou, 2006b). Hence there wasn't an entire renewal but rather a displacement of local elites to new institutional positions. The migration of political actors to municipalities is inscribed in the broader transfer of competences and resources occasioned by the decentralisation process in Benin and Niger.

As local elites conquered the municipalities, they transposed their conceptions and practices of administration of public and collective resources to them. Thus, the administration of decentralised collectivities follows the logics that prevailed before their establishment in the administration of the sub-prefectures as much as in the organisations of cotton growers, water management committees, etc. Municipal governance inherited the dynamics of the political culture and moral economy which was anchored in local institutions in charge of the allocation of common property resources. These local practices are characterised by the diversion of funds, the systematic recourse to 'over-billing', the non-reimbursement of credit, various forms of neo-patrimonialism and nepotism, forms of clientelism that determine the redistribution of resources... These strategies are generalised and observable in all activities and all sectors.

In Benin the cotton sector is fairly indicative of these dynamics, which are part of the 'corruption complex' (Olivier de Sardan, 1996, 99) and rooted in forms of representation of the management of common resources down to the village level. 'In the village, becoming secretary of the village collective has become the ultimate ambition of the young students' (the mayor of a Borgou municipality, June 2006). The secretary of the village cooperative (*Groupement Villageois* or GV) is responsible for the administration of all inputs related to cotton farming (seeds, fertilisers, pesticides, country credits) as well as the management of incomes. The concrete aspects of these tasks allow the secretary and the other members of the management committee to enrich themselves under everyone's eyes with impunity.[57] Since the 1990s the conspicuous consumption of resources misappropriated by the administrative staff of producers' associations (funerary ceremonies, purchase of vehicles and audio and video equipment, etc.) has provoked the young cotton farmers' condemnation of the practices of the elders. These young, educated groups dismissed the old administration or formed new associations, where they reproduced the same practices and perpetuated the same 'model' of rapid social achievement.

> In all the North, it's like that. And it's tied to corruption. In certain GV, the presidents have been in office since 1984, when the texts allow for three-year mandates. But they don't want to leave. As everybody wants to be the boss, new networks are created so that people can lead! (former director of the Municipal Union of Kalale Cotton Producers, current 1st adjunct to the mayor of Kalalé, June 2006)

In Kalalé Gando leaders also fit in this dynamic of management turnover of the producers' associations. Of 74 producers' associations, more than half are Gando. It was to some of these groups that the Gando leaders, such as Ourou Sé Guéné, turned to finance their campaigns and enrol voters for the municipal elections of 2002. These associative organisations are real political instruments that allow for rapid personal enrichment, but also, and most of all, constitute a platform for the establishment of patron–client networks. In fact, the leaders of these structures have the tacit mandate to redistribute the associations' resources to their supporters, who turn to them when they need protection and/or assistance. Redistribution occurs primarily among relatives, as well as friends and allies recruited from within one's social or ethnic group. Neither the management of associations of Gando producers nor that of Gando cultural and identity movements (Idi Waadi, Djanati, Semmee Allah) could avoid this dominant model. 'They [the Gando] created their own way but they made the same mistakes by copying the behaviours of their masters.

They did the same thing, if not worse!' ('red' Peul, dissident member of the Laawol Fulfulde, April 2007).

These associative logics and practices are reproduced in municipal institutions, which, because of the competences and resources transferred to them, are seen as new income opportunities by local actors. Whatever the rhetoric used to access municipal power, the administration practices of elected Gando leaders do not differ from those of other administrations. They had not yet reached the end of their first mandate when this was already clear for all to see: '80 per cent of the mayors came to enrich themselves!' (officer of the National Association of Benin Municipalities, June 2006).

Since 2005, and after having already evaded dismissal by buying off some of the municipal advisors,[58] the Gando mayor of Kalalé was deposed following a 'vote of defiance' by the municipal council (14 votes against 3). As with a number of other mayors of Borgou, the mayor of Kalalé was blamed for his 'individualistic management' (gestion solitaire), that is, his tendency to keep for himself the benefits of his dominant position, 'binging alone' and excluding other municipal councillors from opportunities to 'devour the till'(i.e. municipal budget). His dismissal, orchestrated by central state powers via the prefecture of Parakou, was part of a series of depositions that affected particularly, but not exclusively, the Northern municipalities and was a political move aimed at destabilising the opposition before the presidential elections of March 2006. However, the transactions generated by these dynamics suggest that the redistribution of resources to political supporters had not been satisfactory from the viewpoint of the municipal council. In effect, it is generally expected that a mayor, 'put in business' by his allies in the council, will ensure an equitable distribution. In the political culture of municipalities, the 'accountability' of mayors is defined in terms of their capability to redistribute goods and services to other elected officials, as well as to their electors.

In Bankilaré or in Gorouol municipal institutions had only just been set up before embezzlement was already a routine affair. As municipalities were perceived primarily as a way to 'stuff one's belly', the embryos of municipal institutions established in Gorouol and Bankilaré sufficed to satisfy the objectives envisioned by local elected officials: to share municipal resources among themselves. In the municipalities of Benin and Niger considered in this essay the practices and modalities of distribution are very similar. In Kalalé and in the majority of the Benin municipalities executive power is limited to the posts of mayor and his adjuncts. The executive committee had to find a way to involve the other members of the municipal council in the management of resources. Some of the councillors (generally those belonging to the local branch of the governing party) were named 'district chiefs' and made responsible for the collection of municipal taxes at village markets. This allows two-thirds of the council to participate directly in the collection of local funds and to 'dip' into the 'municipal pot'.[59] In Niger the councillors of Gorouol decided to assign their substitutes to the position of collectors of market taxes. This decision, formalised by an ordinance signed by the mayor, ensures the provision of 'political rewards' expected by the substitutes. The decision was positively welcomed by the national direction of the MNSD Nassara, Niger's governing party. It is common knowledge in Niger that the market tax collectors, whose official remuneration should be a percentage of the taxes collected, actually set their own 'salary'.[60] Of course these measures, taken by the municipal councils, are hardly compatible with the stated objective of increasing municipal income.

> Subsitutes: they are nothing in the municipality. But this, it's the spirit of sharing, it's to maintain their respect. It presupposes that the councilors fatten themselves, and give tickets to substitutes in compensation. It's a political recompense! (Chief of the Gorouol district, Kolmane, September 2006)
>
> This mess is not unique to these two communes [Gorouol and Bankilaré], you also find it in Méhana and Dargol, it happens a little bit everywhere! (General Secretary of the Téra prefecture, Niger, September 2006)

In the practice of municipal administration, being of slave descent or not is inconsequential. Municipalities are political arenas endowed with resources that ought to be seized. In Kalalé or Bankilaré, belonging to a servile category is no longer an obstacle for accessing these resources, and it might, in fact, be an asset (identity as a political resource and as a means to gain votes). Those who had to settle for the neck of the sheep can now obtain choice cuts.[61] It is in this sense that a historical revenge has taken place.

The relations established between governors and governed in the municipalities are in continuity with past habits. They are characterised by a 'feudal' political regime, that is, following Maquet (1961), they are relations organised 'between two parties with unequal power, relations of patronage on one side, and of loyalty and service on the other'. What counts most is the personal tie between patron and client. Yet in most cases today the patron is no longer the master and the client not necessarily the slave or vassal. The examples discussed above show that these patronage relations are highly variable (alliances between young nobles and slaves, struggles internal to chiefly groups, opportunism of migrants, factionalism) and unstable (contestations, counter-alliances, depositions). Access to local powers by people of servile origins obliged to protect their voters will probably have an impact on their social integration (intermarriages, political and religious functions and roles). It will initiate a centripetal movement of these groups from the margins to the centre of society, bearing witness to the progressive erasure of servile stigma and gradual access to citizenship on the part of servile groups, a process that political anthropology will have to investigate and document.

Conclusions

From the perspective of the aristocratic ideology, which is still widespread in local societies (including among individuals and groups belonging to less stratified societies), slave status is seen as incompatible with political leadership. Relegated to the lowest ranks and the least desirable jobs, slave descendants remained stigmatised and until recently marginalised in the political space. The recent municipal elections in Benin and Niger highlighted a number of meaningful social and political changes. The principle by which the status of a group may entail its marginalisation at the economic and political level seems not to apply any more. In various contexts, groups that appeared to be the least likely to exercise power have finally seized it. Today in Bankilaré the aristocratic elites are a small minority in the municipal council, which is largely dominated by people of iklan status, and in Kalalé there isn't a single Pullo nobleman on the council. On the contrary, noble Songhay still dominate the municipal political arena in Gorouol.

Differences across contexts (Songhay of Gorouol vs. Fulbé of Kalalé and Kel Tamasheq of Bankilaré) indicate that democratisation and decentralisation per se are not sufficient conditions for the emergence of marginal groups in local political arenas. They merely constitute favourable frameworks for the expression of dynamics already at work at the local and global levels, including long-term transformations of past hierarchies, political hegemonies and subordinate relations in stratified societies. The introduction of new rules of access to political power (equality of social actors as voters, electoral premium on demographic weight, role of education) is likely to bring about a profound transformation of the social order. New hierarchies and social inequalities are beginning to take shape: the political leaders of servile origin dominate local political arenas and have started to impose themselves at the national level, to the detriment of former masters progressively relegated to a political minority. A counter-ideology affirms itself and new legitimacies appear: 'Who is a slave today? If the noble is illiterate and poor, he will become the slave of a slave!' (Gando leader of Kalalé, May 2007).

In the contemporary discourses and representations of the majority of Gando or *Iklan*, slavery figures as bound to poverty. This association changes the original meaning of the institution. As relations of patronage are no longer based on traditional status hierarchies, the question of citizenship will undoubtedly pose itself as primary. However, in spite of the appearance of new actors in positions they did not occupy before and of the social 'reshuffling' this entails, uses of power and administrative practices tend to remain the same. The struggle for change is less about changing the modes of local governance than about gaining a share of political power by those who had been excluded from it.

The study of the political emancipation of slave descendants requires a long-term approach. Colonialism and the abolition of slavery incontestably set a break with the past, allowing the physical liberation and economic emancipation of slaves without truly disrupting social hierarchies. In Kel Tamasheq and Fulbé societies the political emancipation of (male) slaves occurred in the broader context of the impoverishment of the masters, who constitute a small minority of the population, and the relative economic ease of the ex-slaves; the dissolution of tributary and dependent relations; and most importantly the development of movements defending the interests of social groups that were long subjugated (the Tuareg rebellion; the creation of Timidria in Niger; the Fulbé cultural and linguistic movement; as well as the Gando associations of Northern Benin). These political arenas functioned as privileged spaces for the emergence of collective consciousness in the dominated class. Within it the psychological passage from the 'identity complex' to the affirmation of the self achieved at first by individual intellectuals transformed itself in a collective movement that undermined past ideological constructs. The intellectuals of servile origin who became leaders of these movements were able to develop or strengthen patron–client relations based on kinship, ethnicity and social proximity. They developed an emancipation rhetoric that reversed the previous discourse. The new 'enemy' is easily recognisable: in Bankilaré it is 'red', it collects taxes, extorts its subjects rather than protecting them, monopolises politics without redistribution; in Kalalé it is again the 'reds', who at an earlier stage had substituted themselves for the *HaaBe*, who despise the Gando, cheat them and exploit them. A wind of revolution and revenge has blown. Politically active former slaves seem anxious to restructure traditional hierarchies and erase progressively the social stigma cast upon them.

A new egalitarian ideology that values instruction, economic power and demographic (electoral) weight today dominates the aristocratic ideology. It is improbable that the Songhay of Gorouol will be able to resist the changes that have transformed neighbouring societies once a community of slave descendants is able to affirm itself there, too, by breaking silences and taboos. These societies are witnessing profound socio-political changes that increase the complexity of identities, progressively transforming local governance, access to citizenship and ways of practising politics locally, and in Africa as a whole.

References

Baldus, B., 1969. 'Soziale Struktur und Ideologie.' Unpublished PhD thesis, University of Kiel.

Baldus, B., 1977. 'Responses to Dependency in a Servile Group: the Machube of Northern Benin.' In Miers and Kopytoff, eds, pp. 435–58.

Bayart, J. F., 1989. *L'Etat en Afrique. La politique du ventre*. Paris: Fayard.

Bernus, E., 1963. 'Quelques aspects de l'évolution des touaregs de l'Ouest de la République du Niger. Evolution récente des relations entre éleveurs et agriculteurs en Afrique Tropicale: l'exemple du Sahel nigérien.' *Etudes Nigériennes*. Niamey: IRSH, pp. 91–152.

Bernus, E., 1981. *Touaregs nigériens, unité culturelle et diversité d'un peuple pasteur*. Paris: Orstom.

Bierschenk, T., 1992. 'The Ethnicisation of Fulani Society in the Borgou Province of Benin by the Ethnologist.' *Cahiers d'Études Africaines*, 32(127), pp. 509–20.

Bierschenk, T., 1993. 'The Creation of a Tradition: Fulani Chieftaincy in Northern Dahomey/ Bénin since Early Colonial Rule.' *Paideuma*, 9, pp. 177–244.

Bierschenk, T., 1995. 'Rituels politiques et construction de l'identité ethnique des Peuls du Bénin.' *Cahiers des sciences humaines*, 31(2), pp. 457–84.

Bierschenk, T., 1997. 'Introduction.' In T. Bierschenk and P. Y. de Meur, eds, *Trajectoires peules au Bénin. Six études anthropologiques*. Paris: Karthala, pp. 5–19.

Bierschenk, T., 1999. 'Structures spatiales et pratiques sociales chez les Peuls du nord du Bénin.' In R. Botte, J. Boutrais and J. Schmitz, eds, *Figures Peules*. Paris: Karthala, pp. 195–209.

Bierschenk, T. and Le Meur, P. Y., eds, 1997. *Trajectoires peules au Bénin. Six études anthropologiques*. Paris: Karthala.

Bierschenk, T., Chauveau, J. P. and Olivier de Sardan, J. P., 2000. ' Les Courtiers entre développement et Etat.' In T. Bierschenk, J. P. Chauveau and J. P. Olivier de Sardan, eds, *Courtiers en développement. Les villages africains en quête de projets*. Paris: Karthala et APAD. pp. 5–42.

Bosen, E., 1989. 'Der Weg der Fulbe.' *Ethnischer Konservatismus in einer pluralen Gesellschaft (VR Benin)*. Berlin: Das arabische Buch (Socialanthropologische Arbeitspapiere 19).

Boesen, E., 1997. 'Identité et démarcation: les pasteurs peuls et leurs voisins paysans.' In Bierschenk and Le Meur, eds, pp. 21–47.

Botte, R., 1994. 'Stigmates sociaux et discriminations religieuses: l'ancienne classe servile au Fuuta Ialoo.' *Cahiers d'Études Africaines*, 34(133–35), pp. 109–36.

Botte, R., 2003. 'Le Droit contre l'esclavage au Niger.' *Politique Africaine*, 90, pp. 127–43.

Botte, R. and Schmitz, J., 1994. 'Paradoxes identitaires.' *Cahiers d'Études Africaines*, 34(133–35), pp. 7–22.

Bourgeot, A., 1995. *Les sociétés touarègues. Nomadismes, identité et résistance*. Paris: Karthala.

Boyer, F., 2005. 'L'Esclavage chez les Touaregs de Bankilaré au miroir des migrations circulaires.' *Cahiers d'Études Africaines*, 45(3–4), pp. 771–803.

Brandt, H., 1956, *Nomades du Soleil*. Lausanne: Clairefontaine.

Dandah, M. L. and Galy, K. A., 2003. *L'Esclavage au Niger: aspects historiques, juridiques et statistiques*. Niamey: Anti-Slavery International and Association Timidria.

De Haan, L., van Driel, A. and Kruithof, A., 1990. 'From Symbiosis to Polarization? Peasants and Pastoralists in Northern Benin.' *The Indian Geographical Journal*, 65, pp. 51–65.

Gluckmann, M., Mitchell, J. C. and Barnes, J. A., 1949. 'The Village Headman in British Central Africa.' *Africa*, 19, pp. 89–106.

Guichard, M., 1990. '"L'Ethnicisation" de la société peule du Borgou (Bénin).' *Cahiers d'Études Africaines*, 30(117), pp. 17–44.

Hahonou, E. K., 2003. 'La Question des déchets et de l'assainissement à Tillabéri.' *Etudes et travaux du LASDEL*, 9, Niamey.

Hahonou, E. K., 2004a. 'Les Pouvoirs locaux dans le Gorouol.' *Etudes et travaux du LASDEL*, 20, Niamey.

Hahonou, E. K., 2004b. 'Les Dynamiques politiques locales dans les futures communes rurales de Bankilaré et du Gorouol.' *Etudes et travaux du LASDEL*, 28, Niamey.

Hahonou, E. K., 2005. 'Les Pouvoirs locaux dans la commune de Tillabéri.' *Etudes et Travaux du LASDEL*, 33, Niamey.

Hahonou, E. K., 2006a. 'En attendant la décentralisation au Niger… Dynamiques locales, clientélisme et culture politique.' Unpublished PhD thesis, EHESS, Marseille.

Hahonou, E. K., 2006b. 'La Décentralisation à la sauce béninoise. Point de vue socio-anthropologique sur les dynamiques sociopolitiques dans le Nord Bénin.' Paper presented at the conference *Les pouvoirs locaux et la décentralisation au Niger et en Afrique de l'Ouest*, October 2006, Niamey.

Hahonou, E. K., 2008. 'Les Premiers Pas de la commune de Gorouol.' *Rapport d'étude du LASDEL pour la DDC*, Niamey.

Hahonou, E. K. and Souley, A. 2003. 'Etude socio-anthropologique sur les associations cantonales dans le Tagazar et le Tondikandia.' *Etudes et travaux du LASDEL*, 24, Niamey.

Hardung, C., 1997. '"Ni vraiment Peul, ni vraiment Baatombu". Le conflit identitaire des Gando.' In Bierschenk and Le Meur, eds, pp. 109–38.

Hardung, C., 2002. 'Everyday Life of Slaves in Northern Dahomey: The Process of Remembering.' *Journal of African Cultural Studies*, 15(1), pp. 35–44.

Kopytoff, I. and Miers, S., 1977a. 'Introduction. African "Slavery" as an Institution of Marginality.' In Miers and Kopytoff, eds, pp??.

Kopytoff, I. and Miers, S., eds, 1977b. *Slavery in Africa. Historical and Anthropological Perspectives*. Madison, WI: University of Wisconsin Press.

Lombard, J., 1965. *Structures de type féodal en Afrique noire. Etude des dynamiques internes et des relations sociales chez les Bariba du Dahomey*. Paris-La Haye: Mouton.

Mair, L., 1968. *Primitive Government*. London: Penguin Books.

Maquet J., 1961. 'Une Hypothèse pour l'étude des féodalités africaines.' *Cahiers d'Études Africaines*, 2(6), pp. 292–314.

Meillassoux, C., 1986. *Anthropologie de l'esclavage. Le ventre de fer et d'argent*. Paris: PUF.

Mendras, H., 1976. *Sociétés paysannes. Eléments pour une théorie de la paysannerie*. Paris: Armand Colin.

Nicolaisen, J. 1962. 'Structures politiques et sociales des Touareg de l'Air et de l'Ahaggar.' *Etudes Nigériennes*, 7, Ifan: Niamey.

Olivier de Sardan, J. P., 1969. *Système des relations économiques et sociales chez les Wogo (Niger)*. Paris: Institut d'Ethnologie.

Olivier de Sardan, J. P., 1975. 'Captifs ruraux et esclaves impériaux du Songhay.' In C. Meillassoux, ed., *L'Esclavage en Afrique précoloniale*. Paris: Maspéro, pp. 99–134.

Olivier de Sardan, J. P., 1976. *Quand nos pères étaient captifs (récits paysans du Niger)*. Paris: Nubia.

Olivier de Sardan, J. P., 1982. *Concepts et conceptions songhay-zarma (histoire, culture, société)*. Paris: Nubia.

Olivier de Sardan, J. P., 1983. 'The Songhay-Zarma Female Slave: Relations of Production and Ideological Status.' In C. Robertson and M. A. Klein, eds, *Women and Slavery in Africa*. Madison, WI: University of Wisconsin Press, pp. 130–43.

Olivier de Sardan, J. P., 1984. *Les Sociétés songhay-zarma (Niger-Mali) Chefs, guerriers, esclaves, paysans...* Paris: Karthala.

Olivier de Sardan, J. P., 1994. 'Séniorité et citoyenneté en Afrique précoloniale.' *Communications*, 59, pp. 119–36.

Olivier de Sardan, J. P., 1996. 'L'Economie morale de la corruption en Afrique.' *Politique Africaine*, 63, pp. 97–116.

Riesman, P., 1974. *Société et liberté chez les Peuls Djelgôbé de Haute-Volta. Un essai d'anthropologie introspective*. Paris-La Haye: Mouton.

Robinson, P. T., 1975. 'African Traditional Rulers and the Modern State: The Linkage Role of Chiefs in the Republic of Niger.' Unpublished PhD dissertation, Columbia University.

Rouch, J., 1954. *Les Songhay*. Paris: PUF.

Tidjani Alou, M., 2000a. 'Démocratie, exclusion sociale et quête de la citoyenneté: cas de l'association Timidria au Niger.' *Journal des Africanistes*, 70(1–2), pp. 173–95.

Tidjani Alou, M., 2000b. 'Courtiers malgré eux. Trajectoires de reconversion dans l'association Timidria au Niger.' In T. Bierschenk, J. P. Chauveau and J. P. Olivier de Sardan, eds, *Courtiers en développement. Les villages africains en quête de projets.* Paris: Karthala, pp. 279–304.

Urvoy, Y., 1936. *Histoire des populations du Soudan central (Colonie du Niger).* Paris: Larose.

Van Rouveroy van Nieuwaal, E. A. B., 1999. 'Chieftaincy in Africa: The Three Facets of a Hybrid Role.' In R. Van Dijk and E. A. B. Van Rouveroy van Nieuwaal, eds, *African Chieftaincy in a New Socio-Political Landscape.* Hamburg: LIT, pp. 21–48.

VerEecke, C., 1994. 'The Slave Experience in Adamawa: Past and Present Perspectives from Yola (Nigeria).' *Cahiers d'Études Africaines,* 34(133–35), pp. 23–53.

Wunsch, J. S. and Olowu, D., 1990. *The Failure of the Centralized State. Institutions and Self-Governance in Africa.* San Francisco: Institute for Contemporary Studies Press.

Notes

1 Translated from French to English with the valuable and much-appreciated help of Benedetta Rossi.

2 Local actors often employ the contrast red/black (or its variant white/black) to characterise ethnic and moral distinctions. The ethnonyms 'Tuareg' or 'Peul' usually evoke 'reds'. From the point of view of intellectuals of servile origin, the politically correct term to designate all social categories of their society is Kel Tamasheq, that is, individuals who speak the Tamasheq language. Similarly, in Fulbé society (the term Peul, used in French, comes from 'Pullo', sing. of Fulbé), there is the same emphasis on colour distinctions (exaggerated and empirically unfounded). People talk of 'red Peuls' and 'black Peuls'. These categories have in common that they speak the same Fulfulde language. There is no such distinction in Zarma and Songhay societies where masters and slaves have the same complexion. Here I shall use the emic terms Fulbé and Kel Tamasheq to designate the whole population of native speakers of Fulfude or Tamasheq. I use the term 'Peul' to highlight the contrast with the Gando group.

3 Village and camp chiefs were designated locally, as well as a superior Peul regional chief (Bierschenk, 1993).

4 Meillassoux (1986, 325) uses the term 'captive' in the different sense of the person who has been captured but has not yet been acquired by a master. It is generally acknowledged that at the beginning of the 1900s the difference between 'slave' and 'captive' in official colonial discourse was broadly artificial and tied to the ideology prevalent at the time. In current Nigerien French usage, the terms 'slave' and 'captive' tend to be used interchangeably. In this essay, I use the term 'slave' to imply a particular social status: categorical slavery.

5 For an exhaustive description of different servile categories, see Rouch (1954) and Olivier de Sardan (1976; 1984) for the Songhay; Bernus (1969; 1981) for the Kel Tamasheq of the Niger belt; Baldus (1969; 1977) and Hardung (1997) for the Fulbé of North Benin.

6 I was able to observe cases of domestic servitude among Nigerien Kel Tamasheq, and particularly the *Ineslimen* (religious specialists) and certain *Imajeghen* (warrior aristocracy) at the outskirts of Bankilaré. Florence Boyer's writings (2005) also attest the occurrence of this phenomenon among the *Ineslimen* of Ingui— Ezak, near Bankilaré. Such situations are still widespread in various regions of the country and it is not uncommon to come across herders of servile status taking care of the herds of their 'master'. Today these dependent relations are marked by ambiguity (Hahonou, 2006a).

7   The documentary 'Masters and Slaves', directed by B. Debord in 2002, stages 'slave liberations' by the anti-slavery association Timidria. These freed 'slaves' are female 'domestics' who serve in the home of their masters where they carry out various kinds of household chores, and water and wood transport, without being paid. Both this film and the report by Timidria and the ONG Anti-Slavery International (2003) were contested by the Nigerien intelligentsia and several anthropologists.

8   This also applies to Botte's 2003 article on Nigerien slavery, based on highly controversial evidence that fuelled a heated debate. 'Negationists' deny the contemporary relevance of slavery, claiming that the 'proofs' supplied to document the phenomenon are inadequate. To be sure, it is misleading to say that in Bankilaré 'the *iklan* are forbidden to drill wells, reserved for "nobles"; they must settle for a contaminated lake...' (Botte, 2003, 129). On a short research tour accompanied by members of Timidria, Botte was probably unable to gather adequate information. In fact, some *tiklan* women from neighbouring camps do take water from the lake, but they do so primarily to avoid having to pay the fee collected at the well by an administrator, who happens to be of slave descent. Water here is provided in drums of 20 litres or barrels of 200 litres, whatever the social status of the clients. Yet the social division of tasks is so marked that it is only the *iklan* who go to fetch water at the well, just as only *tiklan* women grind millet.

9   The term *almayaali* refers to all dependent groups (cf. Olivier de Sardan, 1982).

10   The term *yegga* (which designates the number 'nine' in Zarma-Songhay language) is used to refer to people of servile status. Dominant ideologies portray slaves as incomplete beings. The number 'ten' (*iwey*) characterises completeness and is sometimes employed to qualify an accomplished man (*timme*). However, in Niamey young people use *yegga* to refer to the 'centre-forward' (the number nine corresponding to the position of centre-forward in football). Status ideologies are deeply rooted, and old expressions are adapted to changing times and made relevant to the culture of younger generations.

11   For more details on the distinctions between 'slave' and 'captive' in Songhay -Zarma, see Rouch, 1954, and Olivier de Sardan, 1975; 1976; 1984.

12   These expressions are factually inaccurate insofar as it is possible to find black 'masters' and red 'slaves'. Status is tied to a person's history, not to his/her skin colour. But the red/black opposition is used ideologically to simplify and naturalise differences.

13   The emancipation of slaves in Fulbé and Kel Tamasheq societies during the colonial period occurred through progressive departures of slaves from their masters' camps (Bernus, 1981, 111–12; Hardung, 1997). Today physical mobility remains a means for the *iklan* of Bankilaré to evade their masters' impositions (Boyer, 2005).

14   Other meanings associated with Gando are discussed in Hardung, 1997, 122.

15   At baptism or marriage ceremonies, *griots* reconstruct the genealogies of the families involved. As descendants of slaves are 'without ancestors', they cannot conduct ceremonies in the same manner as free people.

16   In a number of Gorouol villages nobles and captives are not buried in the same places. This is true also for the Kel Tamasheq, whereas among the Gando small burial details distinguish a noble's tomb from that of a commoner (Hardung, 1997, 115).

17   In each of the societies studied the offspring descending from the union of a noble man and a slave woman inherits the status of the father.

18   This is also true for the Gando of the Borgou who have become wealthier than their former masters (Hardung, 1997, 133–34; Lombard, 1965, 405).

19   In Peul, Kel Tamasheq and Zarma-Songhay societies the slave is supposed to lack shame and reserve (*haawi* in Zarma, *senteene* in Fulfulde).

20   See Gluckmann, Mitchell and Barnes, 1949, and Mair, 1968, for early studies of the chief's intermediary role in Africa. While Van Rouveroy van Niewaal (1999) applies

this analytical framework to contemporary African chiefs by highlighting the negative implications of this position, I am inclined to see it as advantageous and a source of power for the chief.

21   This notion is used by Bierschenk, Chauveau and Olivier de Sardan (2000, 18) who develop Mendras' (1976) idea that notables act as 'screens' in French rural societies. The image of the gatekeeper is also in Robinson (1975, 291–92), who qualified the intermediary position of the traditional administrative *chefferie* in Africa, and particularly in Niger, as a 'switch' joining electric circuits. For an application of the notion of gatekeeper to the religious *chefferies* of the Maraboutic groups of Bankilaré, see Hahonou, 2004a.

22   Not to be confused with the 'Touareg rebellion' of Niger (1991–95), during which status distinctions in Kel Tamasheq society were generally erased.

23   Expression of Olivier de Sardan (1975).

24   As a consequence of the schooling of slaves and their recruitment in the colonial administration, at Niger's independence Songhay and Zarma masters and slaves shared power at the top levels of the state apparatus. But slaves, with few exceptions (for example Boubou Hama, president of the National Assembly under the First Republic, who was, however, under constant attack for his servile origins), tended to occupy secondary roles (cf. Olivier de Sardan 1984, 205).

25   Contrary to the majority of noble Songhay Peul or Kel Tamasheq families, the Songhay of the Gorouol started sending their own children to 'the White's school' (the nearby French Catholic Mission) very early. In this case, the descendants of nobles were better prepared than other groups to assume positions of power at independence.

26   The MNSD Nassara is the former state-party (1989–91). Having lost influence after the 1993 presidential elections (won by Maman Ousmane of the Rahama CDS) and under the Baré régime (1996–99), since the 1990s the MNSD has become the dominant party in Gorouol and Bankilaré, and in Niger as a whole. The PNDS Tarraya is a party that claims to be of socialist inspiration. Led by a native of Tahoua, it gained considerable power at the national level with the exception of Western Niger.

27   Somewhat paradoxically, the communal council of Gorouol is headed by its only Bella member (i.e. a Kel Tamasheq of slave descent), who took advantage of the incessant struggles between the two rival wings of the Songhay *chefferie de canton* (cf. Hahonou, 2008).

28   Colonial policy was ambiguous and sometimes contradictory on this issue (cf. Bernus, 1969, 40–42). For example, after 1908–09, several *Bella* tribes were declared independent in the Gourma, whereas in the 1940s in the surroundings of Bankilaré the colonial administration decided to support Tuareg religious owners of *Bella*, in contradiction of France's egalitarian principles, to avoid setting in motion rapid social changes that would have been difficult to control.

29   Tentatively, I am inclined to interpret contemporary axes of electoral support and patron–client relations as originating from the ties of fictive kinship between former domestic slaves and their masters (Nicolaisen, 1962, 8; Olivier de Sardan, 1984, 12). Relations of fictive kinship obtain also between Peuls and Gando in North Benin (survey data).

30   In colonial and post-colonial administrative reports the *Kel Igirer* are collectively called *Tinguereguedesh* (sometimes *Tinguereguedesh-Logomaten* or *Loghmaten*). The ethnological literature generally followed this convention (cf. Bernus, 1963; Urvoy, 1936). However, this is a truncated expression provided by the local Kel Tamasheq, defeated and suspicious of colonialists. The term *Tinguereguedesh* (which signifies 'I am under the protection of') designates the 'tent slaves' who carry out domestic chores in the masters' camps, and who situate themselves generally in the immediate proximity of the camp. The same thing happened in the case of the *Doufarafarak* (literally 'behind the livestock enclosure'), who today prefer being called *Kel Ansongo* (Hahonou, 2004a,

15–16). To be cautious, masters gave colonialists the names of their slaves, which then remained. The same attitude is at the origin of slave children's attendance at school in the place of the sons of chiefs.

31 The status of special circumscription was accorded to the PA of Bankilaré in 1992 by the ordinances n. 92-058 and 92-059 of 9 December 1992, becoming an electoral district and obtaining seats at the National Assembly. These legal measures have allowed local minority groups to benefit from a special representation at the National Assembly since the 1993 legislature.

32 Due to the sensitivity of this subject, the proportions between 'nobles' and 'slaves' are highly controversial. Concerning Songhay societies, Olivier de Sardan argues that 'the captives formerly represented more than half the population' (1983, 132). Referring to the Kel Tamasheq, Bernus (1981, 388) notes that in the 1960s more than 80 per cent of the Kel Tamasheq of Western Niger were *Iklan*. Numerous originally servile groups of the left riverbank fled their masters and placed themselves under the protection of dominant groups of the right riverbank, acquiring liberated status (Bernus, 1981, 395), which distinguishes them from the *Iklan* acquired in wars and raids or inherited. Bernus (1981, 393) classifies the *Imallagazan* and *Ibahawan* as *Iklan*. In fact, the latter two groups were the slaves of the *Imghad Iloghmatten* at their arrival in the Gourma (cf. Hahonou, 2004a).

33 *Taklit*: feminine of *akli*, which signifies slave in the Tamasheq language. On the genetrix role of the captive, see Bernus, 1981, 92. *Aneslim*: Kel Tamasheq religious specialist (plur. *Ineslimen*).

34 The Timidria association (lit. 'fraternity' in Tamasheq) was created in 1991. It militates for the recognition of the rights of servile people as full citizens and members of Kel Tamasheq societies of Niger. For a general study of the discourse and strategies in favour of *iklan* citizenship, see Tidjani Alou, 2000a and b). For a more detailed analysis of Timidria's activity in Western Niger, see Hahonou, 2003; 2004a; 2005.

35 For strategic reasons the former MNSD deputy Wassalké Boukari, a Songhay from Gorouol and an ex-minister, allied himself with the local opposition to Bankilaré's chieftaincy led by Elhaji Ghoumar (who became national deputy in 1999). The alliance's objective was to win the support of the Kel Tamasheq electorate in the struggle for the 'municipalisation' of the administrative post of Bankilaré (cf. Hahonou, 2004a and b).

36 Individual status can be 'read' on the body from top to bottom. Particular hairstyles, clothes and jewels symbolise slavery and bondage, and are opposed to those of free and/or elite women. For example, ankle bracelets, often in plastic today, recall the irons formerly worn by the Kel Tamasheq slaves. While Timidria militants denounce this as an expression of hegemony, women and men of servile status may well interpret symbolism differently from masters and possibly valorise it as a source of distinctive identity.

37 Masters maintain privileged relationships with the wet-nurses of their children. This relationship (called *hasan-nda-hini* in Songhay, cf. Olivier de Sardan, 1983) is based on the notion that that milk forms a solid bond between children nursed by the same woman (the child of the noble and the child of the slave wet-nurse). The 'pact of milk' is at the basis of joking relationships and political alliances in Kel Tamasheq societies. The quote makes implicit reference to this loyalty. The oral history of Bankilaré reports that two twins, who were slave wet-nurses, were the founding ancestresses of the *Iklan* tribes closest to the *amenokal* (chief) of the *Kel Igirer*.

38 Whereas slavery has practically disappeared in the village of Bankilaré, it persists in neighbouring camps. Timidria's action (awareness-raising, surveys, creation of schools) is limited to the Kel Tamasheq camps from which the association's leaders come, and to the village of Bankilaré, which has greater media exposure. Thus, in Lemdou and Ingui-Ezak (cf. Boyer, 2005), vestiges of slavery are still observable. Slavery is particu-

larly resilient in camps led by the religious chieftaincies (*Ineslimen*) of the *Kel Igirer* group. This is a consequence of the fear of the religious leaders' intermediary position between God and the profane (cf. Hahonou, 2006). Boyer (2005) observes that in these camps, emancipation is often only temporarily achieved in the course of seasonal migration to Côte d'Ivoire.

39   This is the Tartit association, whose president is also the president of the Bankilaré section of the CDS (party represented by candidates of the chefferie *amajigh* (aristocrats) and the chefferie *anelism* (religious chiefs from Ingui-Ezak) at the municipal elections of 2004). As Timidria in the past, this association functions as a 'development broker', acting as contact point for some aid projects in Bankilaré,

40   Identity claims 'transcend the internal hierarchies of Touareg societies, cristallising the social convergence generated by state politics. [...] The new ties and networks of solidarity engendered the feeling of belonging to the same group, forming a community of blood and destiny' (1995, 436-440) wrote Bourgeot in 1990, in the wave of enthusiasm of the nascent Tuareg rebellion. However, identity discourses, trying to create cohesion and unify a divided people against an oppressive state, gave way to less idealistic realities in which social hierarchies are reaffirmed daily. It is in this context that another identity was reinforced, that of the Kel Tamasheq of servile origin, in pursuit of political emancipation from their masters.

41   'White Tuareg', aristocrat, former minister, founder of the PUND Salama, native of In Gall (Department of Agadez).

42   When the first municipal elections were held in February 1999, the PRD Mahiba did not gain any of the 11 seats in the municipal council (Sahel Dimanche 19/02/1999). The RDP Jama'a party of President Baré gained power after the 1996 coup and gained nine seats, whereas the MNSD and the PNDS won one seat each. These results were nullified in March and President Baré was deposed by a military coup in April 1999.

43   The first deputy of Bella origin in the Tillabéri department, which includes Gorouol and Bankilaré, was elected in 1995. He was elected as representative of the PUND Salama, known locally as 'Ce gaa party', literally the 'party of those who go by foot', with reference to the scarce financial resources of the party (Hahonou, 2005, 40–47).

44   The Baatombu and Boo were able to manipulate the structures of the modern state, revolutionary and post-revolutionary, better than other groups (cf. De Haan et al., 1990).

45   The notion of *senteene* or *semteende* (Fulfulde of Northern Nigeria) refers to the typical Peul restraint and reserve in manifesting one's needs, emotions and various physical requirements (eating, urinating, etc.); cf. Boesen, 1989; Brandt, 1956, 35; VerEecke, 1994, 30.

46   The term 'intellectual' is used in Benin and Niger with reference to literate and school-educated people.

47   Extract from the report of the Conference of the National Sub-Committee of Linguistics (Fulfulde)- Laawol Fulfulde, non-paginated. In these 'revolutionary' times, the term 'nationality' was used to designate the ethnic group. Thus, the People's Republic of Benin was conceived as a multi-national state.

48   In other contexts the term *HaaBe* or *BaleeBe*, translated as 'blacks', includes slaves (cf. Botte, 1994, 116; VerEecke, 1994, 30). Here, due to the inclusive categories adopted by Benin's administration, and to the emphasis on group unity that prevailed at the Fulfuldé conference, the term *HaaBe* does not encompass the Gando.

49   'How can they want to be Peuls? These are *je'aaBe* (slaves) and that's evident' (cited in Boesen, 1997, 42). 'A Gando is a Gando' (cited in Hardung, 1997, 112).

50   Bierschenk mentions that the presentation of 'Peul history and culture' was an important part of the programme, which celebrated Peul values, the idealisation of 'fulanity' and the construction of ethnic identity (1993, 15, 26).

51   The report of the Conference of the Laawol Fulfulde linguistic national sub-committee

(December 1987) states clearly that the history of the Gando remains to be written. Bierschenk notes that the shape given by Peul intellectuals to the Kandi conference hardly left any space for possible disagreements and criticisms (1995, 479–81).

52 The colonial and post-colonial adminstrations classified the Gando among the 'Peul'. Today the proportions of slave descendants and nobles are still unknown. However, in Kalalé, where the 'Peul' officially represent 68 per cent of the population (census of 1992), the red Peul represent a small minority and the Gando are by far the most numerous.

53 Orou Sé Guéné presided over the Association for the Economic and Social Development of the District of Kalalé (ADESKA) for many years. He was a member of the national bureau of the Laawol Fulfulde (responsible for propaganda and information), of the Idi Waadi association, and possibly other associations. He was always close to organisations of cotton producers, supporting the electoral campaigns of some of their leaders.

54 The national president of the RUND party, who is not from Northern Benin, contributed financially to the creation of the Idi Waadi association.

55 After the legislative elections of March 2007, Orou Sé Guéné and his colleague, mayor of the neighbouring municipality of Nikki, became the first Gando representatives for their regions.

56 Another Gando had been sub-prefect at an earlier time, towards the end of President Kérékou's revolutionary regime. Coming from another stigmatised ethnic group (Somba), Kerekou had intentionally placed a Gando to administer the historic centre of the Baatombu kingdom.

57 It is not uncommon for the members of village organisations to mobilise themselves for the liberation of their leaders when these are detained by the police.

58 'Mr. Mayor, we are hungry! If you don't give each of us 300.000 F CFA as FARD Alafia did, we shall be against you in the vote for your impeachment' declared a dozen municipal councillors. The mayor had to give account for the misappropriation of 53 million F CFA that represented a subvention to the municipal budget by the Communal Union of Cotton Producers.

59 I recorded this expression at an interview with an officer of the Decentralisation Mission (Cotonou, June 2006). This metaphor, which refers to the communal budget, fits clearly within the framework of the 'politics of the belly' (Bayart, 1989).

60 The most common procedure for pocketing money illegally consists in charging traders and other market visitors more than the value printed on their receipts (inactive values). When tax collectors have to pay the money they have collected into the municipal accounts, they only turn in the equivalent of the inactive values that were officially sold.

61 In Kel Tamasheq and Songhay ceremonies, the neck of the sheep is traditionally reserved for slaves, whereas the best pieces (fillet, leg) are for the masters.

9

Slavery and Migration: Social and Physical Mobility in Ader (Niger)[1]

Benedetta Rossi

> *Tafiya ta fi zama*
> Travelling is better than staying still
> (Hausa proverb of Ader)

One of the ways in which hierarchy was, and still is, expressed in the Ader region of the Republic of Niger is in terms of relative control over one's own and other people's mobility. In contexts where movement, rather than a settled lifestyle, is a habitual state, 'how one moves' constitutes a critical dimension of 'who one is'. An emphasis on mobility in the constitution of identity means that power manifests itself as relative control over one's own and other people's movements. The restructuring of relations of governance and production induced by colonialism did not, in spite of colonial efforts in this sense, lead to population settlement, but it redirected the axes of control over people's mobility. The elites, who practised transhumance and asserted their freedom to move through war, saw their mobility curtailed and controlled by colonial administrators. People of slave status, whose movements had been tied to the will of their masters, followed different patterns. Until the 1940s some ex-slaves were employed in compulsory labour. Others, having gained independence from their former masters, started migrating to northern Nigeria, seasonally or permanently.

Throughout the nineteenth century slave labour was embedded in transhumance and long-distance trade. In northern Ader, in areas bordering the desert, hamlets of semi-sedentary servile groups farmed lands and tended livestock that belonged to their masters, functioning as a reservoir of labour, cereals and animals for Tuareg masters leading nomadic lifestyles. The mobility of various subordinate groups was a dependent mobility, constrained by the mobility of elites and freemen. The masters' yearly trajectories gave rise to patterns of crossed mobilities, the elite's movements generating a set of subordinate movements. Dependent persons were not free to choose when and how to move. While the latter's movements were not physically restrained, the semi-desert habitat that surrounded them, the military superiority of the masters and the regional legitimacy of the *imajeghen*'s rule made escape difficult and rare in the nineteenth century.

In the early 1900s Tuareg elites were defeated by the French and progressively lost control over people and camels, their main forms of wealth. The promulgation of emancipation decrees had consequences for the status of slaves primarily in and around urban centres, where such decrees could be enforced. These centres became poles of attraction for ex-slaves now able to move independently and seeking avenues of social mobility where their status was unknown. Many slaves whose masters had been defeated by the French did not leave Ader permanently but started engaging in seasonal migration. The imposition of taxation in French currency created an unprecedented need for cash. High rates of population growth led to the occupation of progressively less productive lands and the diversification of sources of subsistence. These changes supported the adoption of seasonal labour migration to areas of greater economic development.

While the hierarchy that governed Ader political and economic systems was substantially restructured throughout the 1900s, the capacity to move independently and to control the movements of others has remained a fundamental mark of power. What has changed is who moves and how. Poorer groups in rural Tahoua face yearly production deficits. In the absence of formal employment opportunities and planned aid programmes, subsistence deficit is met through two main forms of seasonal labour migration, *cin rani* and *bida*. *Cin rani* encompasses short distances and usually involves the entire family. It has low-status connotations and is aimed primarily at ensuring that food needs are met during the dry season. For people of slave descent it involves a temporary family resettlement to places where wealthier patrons, sometimes ex-masters, provide employment and/or support. *Bida*[2] is practised by young men travelling without their families to other African countries, where they work for wages, sometimes for several years. These two types of seasonal labour migration differ in how they relate to the historical experience of servile groups. In Ader *cin rani* is sometimes explicitly likened to the pre-colonial movements of slaves. When it involves moving to work seasonally for ex-masters, this association is not merely metaphorical. Instead, *bida* started acquiring its present magnitude in the second and third decades of the twentieth century, when independent mobility became an option for slaves. Youths of slave descent who practise *bida* experience a break from the stigma of slave status. Yet, at destination, many of them are confronted with xenophobia and exploitation. Physical mobility grants access to social mobility, but projects of mobility – at once physical and social – are not always successful. Subjectless structures, such as national borders, corruption and the initial investment required for long-distance migration, limit poor people's mobility. The most vulnerable actors face the highest constraints on movement, and remain locked in the orbit of old and new patrons. On the other hand, successful migrants control their own movements and, eventually, those of cohorts of clients. They gradually erase the memory of their slave status, which remains a 'public secret' in their village of origin.

The remaining part of this essay is divided in three sections. The first section explores the patterns of mobility characteristic of Ader's pre-colonial hierarchy. The second section looks at the consequences of colonial conquest for the intertwined mobilities of elites and slaves, and discusses the case of the Izanazzafan to exemplify the articulations of status and mobility for dependent groups. The third section sets contemporary patterns of mobility in historical perspective.

Hierarchy and Mobility in Pre-colonial Ader

Ader coincides roughly with the southern part of the administrative Region of Tahoua falling between the fifteenth parallel to the north and the national border with Nigeria to the south. The main languages are Hausa, which is a lingua franca, and Tamasheq. Fulfulde-speaking Fulani are a minority. Despite colonial attempts to normalise a settled lifestyle, mobility in Ader was, and has remained, much more than a coping strategy. In its multiple forms, mobility is a state of being, and settlement is temporary and restricted to few social categories. These include women more than men, the elderly more than youths, the sick more than the healthy, and people in particular professions, such as officers working in the public administration. Studying Ader society also means observing how people move. The Aderawa[3] are known across Niger for their propensity to move, and are often qualified as prototyp- ical migrants or *grands exodants*. This section examines the patterns of mobility that preceded French conquest.[4] It focuses on the dependent mobility of slaves and its integration in pre-colonial systems of governance and production. Some contemporary forms of mobility are in continuity with this pre-colonial past. Others, particularly international seasonal labour migration, result from changes introduced under French colonialism, considered in the subsequent section.

In the second half of the nineteenth century Ader social structure consisted of an inter-ethnic hierarchy, at the top of which were the Tuareg warrior elites (*imajeghen*) of the Kel Gress (southeastern Ader) and of the Iullemmeden Kel Dinnik (northern Ader). Hausa chieftaincies and villages owed tributes to ruling *imajeghen*, who controlled the greatest part of valuable resources. Dependent Tuareg groups of slave- or liberated-slave status were organised according to gradations of servility (cf. Baier and Lovejoy, 1977; Bernus, 1981, 92). Some slave groups (Tamasheq pl. *iklan*, also known as Bella in Songhay and Buzu or Buzaye in Hausa)[5] lived attached to their master's family, while others lived in semi-nomadic hamlets scattered between the edge of the Sahel and the Sudanic savannah. These, unlike the *iklan* living with their masters, were responsible for their own subsistence. When needed, they provided farming and/or herding labour for their masters.

Iullemmeden and Kel Gress organisation was founded on the hierarchical relation between small groups of *imajeghen* and variously classified dependent villages with usufruct rights over lands that fell in the area of influence of their respective *imajeghen*. Among these, three principal categories could be distinguished (cf. Bonte, 1976): (a) semi-permanent camps of slaves working for their patrons (farming and herding); (b) villages of liberated slaves owing their former patrons a part (usually one tenth) of the agrarian produce and various kinds of extraordinary contributions on special occasions in the *imajeghen*'s life-cycle (marriage, birth of a child, war, etc.); and (c) villages of Hausa or Hausa-phone peasants conquered and obliged to give a tenth of the produce and pay different kinds of tributes to the *imajeghen*.[6] The Kel Gress livelihood system was more diversified than that of the Iullemmeden and included livestock husbandry, agriculture and caravan trade. Their closeness to Nigeria promoted the trade of cattle with northern Nigerian cities and the development of important markets where the Kel Gress sold animals, salt and crafts, and bought cereals and cloth. Their herds followed a double migratory pattern, moving southwards in the winter and northwards in the summer, for the salt cure. The Iullemmeden derived their livelihood from dairy husbandry, which they integrated with the consumption of wild seeds and cereals obtained from dependent farming villages. Warfare and raids against free groups granted them access to additional resources. While they did not practise caravan trade (Nicolas, 1950, 197), they participated in the summer salt cure, which before the 1970s represented a collective movement of all Tamasheq speakers.[7]

Masters disposed of the productive and reproductive capabilities of their slaves, the most marginal of which could be sold. Up to a certain number of slaves were controlled by masters individually. Some *tawsiten* (Tuareg lineage units) controlled entire hamlets of slaves, which functioned as reservoirs of labour and resources. This system was common in Northern Ader under Iullemmeden Kel Dinnik control. Here, closeness to the Sahara desert meant that lands were scarcely productive and the system of production was highly specialised. Iullemmeden *imajeghen* were not caravan traders and relied on herding and the exaction of resources from groups settled in their area of control. They had precedence over dependants in the consumption of scarce provisions during famines (cf. Baier and Lovejoy, 1975; 1977). Ecological constraints limited the potential of sharecropping as an economic strategy.[8] This system was maintained through the threat of violence, accounting for brutal conditions of enslavement and the quasi-absence of the category of liberated slaves (*ighawelen, iderfan*). This contrasts with Southern Ader, dominated by the Kel Gress, where land productivity and closeness to Nigeria favoured economic diversification and the conversion of slaves into tributary farmers.

Kel Gress society included large contingents of manumitted slaves, who had been turned into tributary dependants. While these did not have to be fed and supported, the elites could still appropriate farming surplus by setting the terms of the hierarchical relation. As exploitative as this relation may have been, freed slaves controlled their own bodies, progeny and, in some cases, productive resources. Sharecropping increased farming productivity and therefore benefited Kel Gress masters. Conversely, in the arid regions controlled by the Kel Dinnik, a free farmer was less valuable than a slave whose property and person could be disposed of by the masters. At the southern edge of Iullemmeden control, some Hausa farming villages provided varying amounts of cereals to the *imajeghen* after the harvest. When the masters' demands were not met promptly, villages were raided.[9]

Neighbouring Iullemmeden Kel Dinnik and Kel Gress political systems were confronted with different environmental conditions, resulting in distinct politics of slavery. The system of production had consequences not just for how sovereignty was exercised, but also for kinship and marriage. In Kel Gress society, with its large cohort of free and freed tributaries, elite endogamy was necessary for the maintenance of political and economic privilege in the hands of a small minority. From the masters' perspective, marriage with slaves reinforced the endogamic principle, keeping privileges in the patrilineal line. The freed tributary or sharecropper may have owed a large share of the harvest to the master but, at least *de iure*, was economically independent. Marriage with this group would have diluted elite supremacy through redistribution. These concerns were less prevalent among the Iullemmeden, not just because freed slaves were a smaller constituency, but also because elite supremacy was maintained through the monopoly of violence and related ethos of masters' invincibility. Kel Gress and Kel Dinnik strategies to enforce sovereignty differed: the former acted slightly more as patrons than as warlords, as they benefited from their dependants' willingness to collaborate in their diversified economy. This balance was reversed for the Kel Dinnik, who had fewer incentives to maintain 'willing dependants' in the arid areas they controlled. Here, resources were scarce and slaves were primarily (though not only) valued as an additional resource.

Oral testimonies in Ader convey a vivid sense of fear and powerlessness amidst constant threats of violence in the form of unexpected exactions, raiding, kidnapping and warfare between opposed *imajeghen* groups and involving certain groups of dependants as military support. The type of migration known today as *bida* could not be practised. As summed up by an elder of slave descent, 'in the times of fear, people wouldn't go anywhere' (*lokacin da anka tsoro-tsoro, ba a tafi ko'ina*).[10] A slave needed his/her master's permission to leave his/her usual residence. Intercepted fugitives, if found out by representatives of their masters, would be obliged to return to their homes and possibly punished. Even crossing areas outside their master's sphere of influence was risky, as they could be caught by the elites of other Tuareg groups and re-enslaved, returned to their masters or sold (cf. Adamu, 1979, 174). Some informants stated that *bida* would have been meaningless as money was not needed in the past.[11] This confirms the association of this type of movement with 'searching for money', or *'neman kudi'*, which is the common definition of *bida*.[12]

The potential mobility of servile groups varied according to the status, identity and mobility patterns of their masters; the original mode of enslavement of the slaves; and the positioning of a particular category of slaves in their masters' life and economic organisation. Every hierarchical relation established a specific pattern of crossed mobilities. A first distinction is between slaves who lived in separate settlements and slaves who lived attached to their masters' families, following them in their displacements, carrying out domestic tasks for them and taking care of their animals. The latter lived in symbiosis with their masters and had very little autonomy, but they were safer in times of hardship, as masters had to provide food, clothing and protection. Conversely, communities of slaves leading semi-nomadic lifestyles at the desert's edge enjoyed greater independence but were more vulnerable to recurrent shocks. The frequency of contact with the masters varied, but my research suggests that it could have been as low as two or three times per year, depending on the slave settlement's position within the *imajeghen*'s area of nomadisation. These slaves had to provide for their own subsistence through herding and/or farming. They hosted their masters when the latter chose to camp in their settlement and made available to them any resource (including people) the masters wished to consume or take with them.

Another important distinction is between the slaves of *imajeghen* and *ineslemen* (religious groups). Kel Dinnik *imajeghen* led a nomadic existence, moving their camps to fit their yearly activities. The *ineslemen*, or religious specialists, received the majority of their slaves from the *imajeghen* in compensation for religious work and protection.[13] Some *ineslemen* were closely associated to particular elite groups and sometimes followed them throughout their movements. Other groups of *ineslemen* lived in settled hamlets near those of their slaves, who did all the work for them. *Ineslemen* sometimes toured within areas of religious influence of particular individuals and/or groups, collecting alms and various goods in compensation for religious services and teaching. In these movements they were followed by some of their slaves. Sometimes informants referred to this 'dependent movement' as *cin rani*.

In one village elderly men discussed how, before emancipation, it was almost impossible to practise *bida*, but they did go on *cin rani* following their master. The anachronistic use of the terms *bida* and *cin rani* to designate, respectively, independent and dependent movements sheds light on the associations evoked by these two types of migration in contemporary Ader. Masters, *ineslemen* of the Kel Eghlal Enniger group, would spend weeks or even months in villages to the south of their usual residence, around Gadamata and Ibohamane, never further south than Madaoua.[14] The master lived in a village, staying at the place of a host with whom he had long-term visiting ties, while slaves camped on the village's outskirts. The master visited the camp of his slaves only for specific needs. Meanwhile, the slaves could work for local village families, as herders or carrying out manual labour, and were remunerated in cereals. When the master decided to go back, slaves who disposed of donkeys carried the cereals back home as grain reserves. Whatever they could not carry they sold for money. However, upon return, the masters took from them a varying amount of what they had earned, in money or kind.[15]

Until the end of the 1800s power was manifested through control over movement. The role and identity of the *imajeghen* in the past is often represented today by the use of expressions indicating freedom to move and make others move. Informants characterise *imajeghen*, in contrast to other groups, consistently as those who 'wouldn't stay put in a single place' (Hausa, *'ba su zamna wuri guda'*). Kel Dinnik warrior elites are represented as capable of crossing the desert freely on their camels, their wills and bodies equally unrestrainable, moving to unfold independent designs. Kel Gress economy, geared to the control of caravan trade, thrived by shifting people and resources across space. The mobility of subordinate components within these two confederations was auxiliary to that of the elites. Among subjected groups the freest to move were Hausa tributary chiefs and traders. Yet even free tributaries and allies avoided moving against the interest of Tuareg warlords for fear of retaliation or of losing the protection of powerful local leaders and becoming exposed to external attacks. The lifestyle of powerless free dependants was integrated in the economic system of the elites through the obligation to pay tributes and provide services. At the bottom of this hierarchy slaves moved for their masters. Independent movement would have been so dangerous that it left no trace in people's memory and folktales.[16] Comparing the physical movements of slaves and masters at a smaller scale than that of spatial mobility, people of slave descent portray their bodies at work in opposition to the stillness of masters (Hausa, *munka aiki, sunka zamna*: 'we worked, they sat still'). Accounts of the past evoke masters free to roam the land, unhindered by the obligation to carry out productive labour, and slaves busy working (*aiki*), farming (*noma*) and herding (*kiwo*), themselves owned and controlled like cattle. Depending on the circumstances, status and mood of the speaker, these representations are invoked to exalt or denigrate either masters or slaves. A single interpretation of the past and of the ranked identities that inhabited it has yet to settle. Moreover, the consequences of colonial intervention introduced new standards of power against which status was recalibrated.

Colonial Impacts on Mobility

At the beginning of the twentieth century the French administrative structure was super-imposed on pre-existing political formations. In 1919 the Military Territory of Niger[17] was divided into nine administrative units called *cercles* (Agadez, Dosso, Gouré, Maradi, N'Guirmi, Niamey, Tahoua, Tillabéry and Zinder), subdivided into a varying number of *secteurs*, later renamed *subdivisions*, administered by officers of lieutenant rank (Fluchard, 1995, 18; Fuglestad, 1983, 80). A *secteur* comprised 'indigenous' political entities, named provinces, tribes, cantons or groups (*groupements*), under the authority of so-called 'traditional chiefs' (*chefferie traditionelle*). The *cercle* of Tahoua was divided into two subdivisions: the southern section, where settled farming prevailed, was classified as *subdivision sédentaire*. The northern zone, which included a vast desert area inhabited primarily by pastoral nomads, was a *subdivision nomade*. To account for pockets of population whose lifestyle did not match the broader categorisation of their subdivision, groups perceived as settled or nomadic were classified, respectively, as *cantons* or *groupements*. Colonial intervention did not simply encapsulate local hierarchies in new administrative structures, but it also provoked a substantial reshuffling of power, rewarding groups that submitted and crushing those who resisted colonial rule. In Ader 'winners' comprised the Lissawan, some Hausa chieftaincies and some Tuareg *ineslemen* groups; the main 'losers' were the Kel Dinnik *imajeghen* (cf. Bernus, 1990, 160; Urvoy, 1936, 305).

The imposition of this new administrative grid did not suffice to achieve de facto governance over Ader society. In order to exercise command the French were forced to move continuously. In spite of their military supremacy they had to comply with the logic of mobility that prevailed in the regions they had conquered. In turn, governance primarily involved attempts on the part of French administrators to alter and control the movements of various groups.

'Il faudrait pouvoir se mettre dans la peau du nomade'[18]

Having conquered Ader, the French had to move to maintain order in this region. In the years before 1918 French administrators and their indigenous allies were constantly on the move to track and crush the resistance organised by the chiefly groups of the Iullemmeden. The Kel Gress submitted early, thereby protecting their commercial interests and diversified economy. But Iullemmeden elites derived their wealth from the extraction of resources from slave constituencies and dependent populations. Their economic and political systems were incompatible with French occupation, military sovereignty and administrative structures. Allied to the Western Iullemmeden (Kel Attaram of Mali), the Kel Dinnik resisted. Initially, they retreated into the desert, dismissing French attempts to negotiate. The French had enormous diffi-culty tracking individual resistance leaders in the Sahara. Here, the *imajeghen* maintained some freedom of movement and action. Conversely, in southern sedentary regions the population had submitted to French control and newly created chieftaincies collaborated with the French against the Iullemmeden.

The difficulty of controlling the North resulted in a dual line of action. On the one hand, French administrative reports reveal a relentless intelligence aimed at tracking the movements and activities of individual dissident chiefs. This intelligence work relied both on the surveillance of French administra-tors and their camel corps (*pelotons méharistes*) and on information provided by collaborating Hausa and Tuareg population. On the other hand, offensive actions of Tuareg 'rebels' were followed by brutal retaliations, justified as acts of deterrence. Reports of 'counter-raids', or *contre-rezzous*, organised to pursue and punish Tuareg raids (*rezzous*) are frequent in pre-1917 administrative correspondence. However, the fact that these raids occurred, and sometimes remained unpunished, exemplified the limits of French command and the ongoing capacity of Tuareg chiefs to move freely and continue extracting resources from the population. This intermittent insurrection of the Kel Dinnik elites, followed by some loyal dependants, reached a climax in the events of 1916–17. Two events are particularly meaningful.

In January 1917 Alfourane, Amenokal of the Kel Dinnik, and his travel companions met Amajalla, a Tuareg of slave status serving as a guide in the French military, carrying a message from the Commandant de Cercle de Tahoua. Amajalla was decapitated and the Amenokal continued his journey.[19] Only two weeks later, under full French military mobilisation (a state of siege had been declared in the entire *Territoire du Niger* on 25 December 1916), a series of attacks hit the *cantons* of Keita and Tamaske. These two cantons, which fell into the sedentary subdivision, had been under direct control of the Kel Dinnik *imajeghen*. Following the French invasion and the *imajeghen*'s retreat northwards, local chiefly groups received chieftaincy titles and prerogatives from the French. In particular, the Lissawan of Keita collaborated with the French, assisting them to track the Iullemmeden and pacify the region. On 1 February 1917 Keita was pillaged and burned down. On 14 February a second Iullemmeden raid reached Keita in the morning. Afadandan, the Lissawan canton chief, was killed.[20] These events made a huge impression on locals.

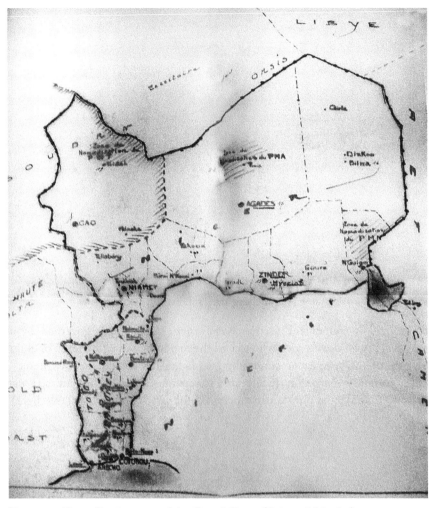

Figure 9.1 Nomadisation area of the Camel Corps (*Peloton Méhariste*)

In spite of their superior military technology the French had been unable to restrain the *imajeghen*, who seemed capable of crossing the country, raiding and pillaging at will. French command resolved that the only way to stop the revolt would be to crush the *imajeghen*. On 12 April a French brigade led by Capitaine Sadoux surprised the Kel Dinnik *imajeghen* and their families and followers next to Tanout. In a telegram describing this operation Sadoux reported that 'Forty-six (46) *imajeghen* – or the quasi-totality of the Eastern *imajeghen*[21] – have been killed, as well as fifty-six (56) of their *imghads* and other dependants'.[22] Following the Tanout massacre, Tahoua was permanently 'pacified'.

If 1917 marked a threshold in French rule, administrators had to continue moving to govern. And a large part of their government still consisted in

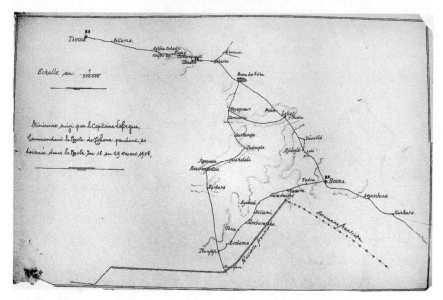

Figure 9.2 *Tournée de service* in the sedentary subdivision (1906)

controlling movement. Thus, the *Subdivision Nomade* was governed by a *Commandant de Subdivision* who toured the region by camel for seven or eight months of the year, accompanied by guards and, if needed, an interpreter.[23] Three *pelotons méharistes* were allocated to separate 'nomadisation areas' (*zones de nomadisation*) and constantly supervised the *subdivision nomade* (see fig. 1).

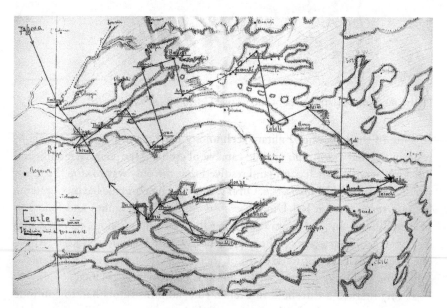

Figure 9.3 *Tournée de service* in the sedentary subdivision (1937)

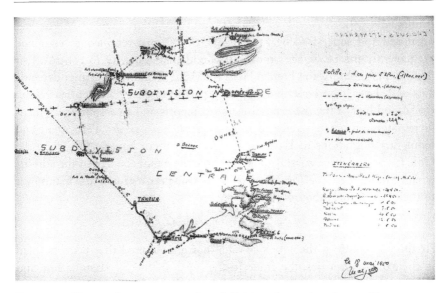

Figure 9.4 *Tournée de service* across the subdivisions (*nomade* and *centrale*)

The *commandant* of the *subdivision sédentaire* underwent periodic (usually, monthly) *tournées de service* through which he followed the state of the region and dealt with any matters arising (see figs 2, 3, 4), travelling by horse and relying on the hospitality of indigenous chiefs throughout his tours.

While constantly on the move themselves, French administrators never perceived population mobility as a 'normal' state, and struggled in various ways to limit and control it. In 1903 the French still hoped that locals would soon realise the benefits of a sedentary lifestyle:

> The best option will be to encourage the nomads to adopt a settled lifestyle, with the aim of controlling these 'desert ghosts'.[…] The contrast between a well-established and well-practised tranquillity and a straying and unstable life, wandering from one lake to another, always on the run, always worried and on guard against the imminent raids of neighbouring tribes, will push them in a relatively short time to modify their wandering habits and turn to a less agitated lifestyle. (Noel, *Rapport sur la situation politique du Troisième Territoire Militaire*, 1902, my translation)

Yet, contrary to their expectations, most aspects of life in the *cercle*, its sedentary subdivision as much as the nomadic one, continued to occur in motion. Unable to stop movement, the administration strove to regulate it. In 1916 all merchants had to dispose of circulation permits (*cartes de circulation*) in order to exercise their trade (*Journal de Cercle de Madaoua*, 10 August 1916). The yearly transhumance to the In Gall region for the salt cure, in which all Tuareg herders participated, was officially started and accompanied by the officer commanding the *Subdivision Nomade*,[24] and the pilgrimage to Mecca was organised and supervised by French officials.[25] Moreover, having restrained permanently the *imajeghen*'s movements and their capacity to control their dependants' mobility, the French faced the rising mobility of former dependants and slaves, who benefited from the 'pacification' of the country.[26] From the second half of the 1920s administrative reports and correspondence focus increasingly on what is referred to as *la question des exodes*. Permanent and temporary migrations to English territory (Northern Nigeria first, then the Gold Coast and other coastal zones) became the major concern of the administrators of the *Cercle de Tahoua*, who feared losing tax revenues and manpower to their British neighbours.

'La question des exodes'

At the beginning of the 1900s colonial powers required that taxes be paid in their own currencies, the franc to the north of the Say-Baroua line and the pound sterling to the south. The introduction of head taxes and forced military conscription and compulsory labour had a mixed impact on mobility. People migrated both in order to pay taxes for themselves and their family, and to avoid paying taxes or to escape military recruitment and forced labour (Skinner, 1960, 377; Wallerstein, 1965, 151). Regions at the border between French and British territories witnessed substantial displacements of French subjects moving to the other side of the border and settling permanently in neighbouring British territory, where the fiscal pressure was less harsh and army enrolment was voluntary (Prothero, 1957, 253; Skinner, 1960, 379). This exodus alarmed French administrators.

Former slaves whose mobility had been constrained by their masters started migrating as soon as they felt secure enough to unfold independent entrepreneurial strategies. In the mid-1920s the first seasonal migrants began travelling on foot to Northern Nigeria, for periods of about two months. Many people of slave descent were still attached to their masters' families. For this group, migration was a way to cut resilient ties of bondage. Yet a large proportion, possibly the majority, of ex-dependants of the Kel Dinnik stayed. After the 1917 defeat of former masters in Tanout some servile fractions that had a collective tribal name and lived in independent hamlets appear to have been granted free status by the French (see the case of the Izanazzafan discussed below).[27] The masters' dispersal meant that no one would claim ownership of the lands where these *imajeghen*'s slaves had been settled.[28] The situation differed for domestic slaves or slaves of local maraboutic groups, whose power had increased as a consequence of French conquest and *imajeghen* defeat. Many of these slaves did not hesitate to complain about their masters' abuses directly to the French administrators. Their claims figure prominently in the daily entries of the *Journal de Cercle de Tahoua*, particularly in the first two decades of the 1900s. Resettling was hardest for families of domestic slaves as all or some family members might still be working for their traditional masters. Most of the complaints recorded in Tahoua refer to the forced separation of the families of domestic slaves. Slave families freed from the masters' control and resettled in a separate household were likely to settle in Ader. But when masters refused to renegotiate relations with their slaves, the latter often moved away. Administrators were concerned with the mainten-ance of the unity of slave families primarily as a means to reduce permanent migration:

> The families of domestic slaves are currently almost always divided: the woman rarely joins her husband if the couple belong to two different masters. Children are too often separated from their mothers following circumstantial events in the masters' family life (e.g. marriage, inheritance). [...] In fact, we shall only be able to consider this situation redressed when the *iklan* of today have become tributaries, living with their families and their herds in the orbit of their old masters, whom they will continue to assist through compensated domestic and herding work. Even then, their situation will perhaps not have fully evolved, but the *iklan* will be sufficiently attached by their family ties and other interests for us to be able to stop fearing their mass departure to the South. (Capt. Delon, *Rapport de tournée, 11 Février 1948*, my translation)

Former slaves did not migrate simply to abandon their masters but also to avoid forced enrolment and taxation. Buzu villages and individuals ranked low in local hierarchies and were the easiest targets of recruitment operations carried out by indigenous chiefs. In the Tahoua region forced recruitment and military conscription were immensely resented. Many villages organ-ised armed resistance and attacked recruiting agents, including canton and village chiefs. The situation remained the same throughout the whole colonial period, and in the early 1940s villagers were frequently sanctioned for refusing to provide information on reserves hiding to avoid (re-)integration in the military.[29] According to one administrator who served in Tahoua in the 1930s, when the migration question was at the top of the agenda, forced labour and military recruitment were, together with a strict fiscal policy, the main causes of migration.[30] Entire families and single individuals who resented French exactions voted with their feet and moved to the 'sunnier skies' (*cieux plus cléments*) of British Nigeria:

> We have achieved a result that we probably did not seek, but which was foreseen, foretold, and fatal, namely, the flight of our administered subjects [*administrés*], first, by imposing a military conscription that they did not want, and, second, by extracting from them taxes that one part of the popula-tion cannot afford. [...] We committed the inexcusable mistake, in 1931, of

requesting the same amounts of taxes after a year of famine as we did after prosperous years. We have partly ruined the country. All these mistakes are paid for, either through insurrection, when this is the taxpayers' last resort, or through flight to sunnier skies [*cieux plus cléments*]. (De Loppinot, *Rapport de Tournée, 23 Novembre 1933*, my translation)

The numbers migrating to Nigeria received increasing attention in the first half of the 1930s. In a letter to the Governor General of AOF dated 21 October 1933 de Loppinot provides evidence that, since 1916, 25,000 people had left the *cercle*, that is, more than 20 per cent of the *cercle*'s population in 1933.[31] Most migrants had moved to Nigeria, 10,000 of them to escape the military recruitments of 1916–17. Eventually, the administration implemented policies aimed at encouraging the return of emigrants and fugitives, with some degree of success. In a letter dated 16 April 1936 the Governor General of AOF wrote to de Loppinot:

You inform me that, following the publicity you have given to my instructions concerning migrants willing to return, you have noticed, in the last census, the return of several families of the *Canton de Laba* and of numerous bellah [*sic*] tents. It is with satisfaction that I take note of these first results concerning a movement that will continue to increase, and about which I wish to be kept updated by every means in considerable detail, through your three-monthly reports and tour reports, as well as by ad hoc letters. You will ensure that you provide the exact numbers [of migrants], indicating the date when the runners [*transfuges*] left; the regions where they seek refuge; the reasons for their departure. If the latter was occasioned by the sanctions of the chiefs; and finally, what has pushed them to return to their country. I attach great importance to this question of exodus [*question des exodes*], and it is necessary that you provide all useful details to allow me to report to the Chief of the Federation. (*Gouv. Gen. Court à De Loppinot, 16 Avril 1936*, my translation)

It is noteworthy that the first reference to seasonal labour migration as an important phenomenon is found in a British annual report from Sokoto province also dated 1936. According to Prothero,

it may be inferred that the general lack of reference is indicative of the fact that seasonal migration, though not unknown, was at least on an incomparably smaller scale in the early decades of the century than at the present day. *If the same numbers were involved then as now, they would certainly have commanded more attention. However, it was not until 1936 that this was forthcoming*. (Prothero, 1958, 18–19, my emphasis)

Swindell, studying the same region, also notes that the early 1930s must have marked 'a clear watershed' in the history of West African migrations (Swindell, 1984, 17). It may appear puzzling that 1936 appears in independent French and

English administrative correspondence as a threshold in the movements across the French–British frontier in the Sokoto area. It is possible that this acknowledged growth in Niger–Nigeria migrations be related to the promulgation of ordinance No. 19, to which the literature has so far paid scarce attention.[32] The news of conditions favourable to slaves may have spread relatively quickly to French areas close to the border, like Ader, which had been 'sending areas' of temporary migrants and traders since earlier times. The heightened movements recorded in 1936 may reflect a rise in permanent migrants, attracted by the prospect of abandoning slave status. But 'permanent' and 'temporary' migrants are not independent categories. Permanent migrants serve as a support base to networks of seasonal migrants; and some migrants who originally intended to leave permanently may have returned in response to colonial measures implemented to attract migrants back to French territory.

Colonial correspondence and oral testimonies show that one of the first steps of ex-slaves beginning to take control of their lives consisted in taking control of their movements. Many slaves whose masters refused to renegotiate the terms of the servile relationship after the formal abolition of slavery in 1905 and the enforcement of French governance simply left. Most of them appear to have moved primarily to Northern Nigeria but more research is needed to reconstruct their trajectories and experiences. Slaves who did not want to exchange the impositions of old masters for the demands of French rulers, also moved to *cieux plus clements*. Finally, slaves who remained in Ader after ties to former masters had been severed (following the masters' dispersal or the slaves' initiative) started taking up seasonal labour migration.

During the 1930s the French strove to contain migration, partly because it was seen as detrimental to French economic interests, but also because settlement was considered the norm and movement an exceptional state. By the end of the 1930s colonial reports started treating seasonal labour migration as physiological more than pathological. In 1938 Thiellement, *Comm. de Cercle de Tahoua*, defines young seasonal migrants to Nigeria as *navetanes* trying to escape the control of family elders and gain access to Nigerian currency. Unlike his predecessor, de Loppinot, Thiellement sees seasonal migration as integral to local social organisation, even if he invariably discusses possible incentives that would encourage these *navetanes* of Ader to stay.[33] In the 1940s administrative reports signal with satisfaction returns of migrants 'to their native land after having tried their luck abroad, apparently without success!' alongside ongoing seasonal migration to the Sokoto area.[34] In this period the theme develops of seasonal migration as an expression of juvenile thirst for adventure that needs to be patiently tolerated by benevolent administrators.[35]

In the mid-1940s reports start distinguishing between two forms of migration: short-period or short-distance seasonal movements (within the *cercle*) and migration to Nigeria and other countries, notably Dahomey and the Gold

Coast, of longer duration.[36] Yet these reports do not ask which categories of actors opt for one or the other migration strategy and why. As mentioned in the previous section, for people of servile origins these patterns of physical mobility corresponded to distinct strategies of social mobility. *Cin rani* signals the resilience of local forms of patronage often evolved from former dependent relationships. *Bida* promises autonomy and greater profits to migrants whose economic, social and physical conditions make long-distance travel possible.

Dependence and Mobility: The Case of the Izanazzafan

The case of the village of Wassoumamane sheds light on the historical origins of the distinction between *bida* and *cin rani*, and of the different ideological connotations of these two types of seasonal labour migration.[37] Today Wassoumamane hosts some people of the Izanazzafan group, who used to be slaves of the Tillimidis (or Tellemidez) *imajeghen* section of the Iullemmeden. The Izanazzafan of Wassoumamane have long-established ties to the old village of Agouloum. Before French conquest at least four different groups resided in Agouloum, two of which spoke Tamasheq while the other two spoke Hausa. The indigenous inhabitants of Agouloum appear to have been Hausa Bageyawa and Djibalawa groups, who had Buzu slaves at their service. Some Lissawan chiefly families also resided in Agouloum with their slaves. The fourth group settled in the area were the Izanazzafan Buzaye.

In the late nineteenth century the Iullemmeden *imajeghen* collected cereal tributes from all Agouloum groups of free status at least once a year. When they visited Agouloum they were hosted by the Hausa chief. While it was generally recognised that the Izanazzafan were attached to the Tillimidis, they also did remunerated work for the free Hausa. After the dispersal of the Iullemmeden, some Izanazzafan families settled in the village of Wassoumamane, not far from Agouloum. In March 1901 the French attributed to the Lissawan chiefly family exclusive political authority and land ownership over today's cantons of Keita, Laba and Tamaske.[38] In the following years the people of Wassoumamane and most of the villages falling into Keita's canton stopped giving an indeterminate amount of the harvest to their former masters and began paying the Lissawan chief a yearly tribute corresponding to 10 per cent of the harvest. According to some Izanazzafan elders this was generally more than what they owed to the Tillimidis, and was exacted with greater rigour.

Even after they settled in Wassoumamane some Izanazzafan families continued to return to Agouloum on *cin rani* during the dry season. The parents of today's elders followed three types of movements. From Wassoumamane, some of them left at the beginning of the rains and led their own and their relatives' cattle to pastures in the northern region of In Gall (transhumance). Others left after the harvest and went to Agouloum on *cin rani*, where they continued carrying out remunerated work for Hausa people in kind and, later, in cash. To the Hausa of Agouloum these migrants are known as descendants of the slaves of the Tillimidis. This status is undeniably stigmatising but it also signals a long relation of trust and reciprocal obligation, in some cases of friendship and respect. Finally, some started going on *bida* to Nigeria. Some of today's elders, and the deceased parents of people in their forties and fifties, were the first generation to go on *bida* to Kaduna, Jos, Maradi and Agadez. They went on foot and usually did not stay away for longer than three months, and brought back cash earned through manual labour. The case of Wassoumamane is not unique and explains why *cin rani* has low-status connotations. It is a type of mobility associated with slavery and/or poverty. Free Tamasheq- (including liberated slaves and groups of *imghad* status) and Hausa-speaking groups also practised *cin rani*, but only in case of subsistence failure and necessity.

In Ader *cin rani* seems to involve the reactivation of long-term regional servile and/or clientelistic relations. *Cin rani* is not the only institution that increases food security. In a dry region like Ader droughts and harvest failures constitute recurrent shocks, and, even in years characterised by higher-than-average rainfall, rains are sporadic across villages. This accounts for a variety of endogenous coping strategies in pastoralist and farming contexts. Another example is the institution of *kone*, which consists of a millet gift made by people living in areas where the harvest was abundant to relatives or close friends who faced a scarce harvest. But *kone* implies a symmetric relation between giver and receiver and the expectation of reciprocation should future harvests reverse the fortunes of the exchange parties. Most Buzu youths today prefer *bida* to *cin rani* because, as long-distance migrants, they become part of a mass movement of seasonal labourers in which servile origins are temporarily concealed. Potential earnings from *bida* are substantially higher, although the risk of returning empty-handed is also greater. Importantly, from the perspective of most of my informants, it does not expose their wives to the humiliation of working as domestic servants at destination, which is usually the case for *cin rani*.

In Conclusion: Status and Mobility in Historical Perspective

In Ader today pure nomadic pastoralism has become rare, but is still practised by a minority of Fulani and Tuareg herders. Long-distance trade has remained labour intensive, even though motor vehicles, national borders, monetisation, taxes, customs and 'corruption fees' changed business conditions. Seasonal labour migration is the largest form of collective movement in the region of Tahoua, and possibly Niger as a whole. Harvest failures, economic retrenchment and reduced employment opportunities following from the implementation of privatisation and liberalisation programmes inflated the phenomenon of migrant labour and extended the duration of the migrants' stay abroad. At destination migrants from the same region may coalesce. When this happens, shared cultural characteristics partly override traditional status boundaries. However, upon return, migrants are re-integrated in their village of origin, usually without a substantial renegotiation of the low status of ex-slaves (Boyer, 2005).

In many cases, ties with former masters have not been entirely severed, and old relations continue to exist in muted forms. New forces and actors emerged and old social and political structures have been transformed. People of free and slave descent have entered the 'informal sector' as paper-less seasonal migrants and unskilled labourers in West Africa's cities. In Ader, relative wealth and status are still manifested by the ability to choose if and when to move, and poor people's movements are conditional on material necessity and/or the decisions of others. Some contemporary types of mobility exhibit consider-able historical continuity with their pre-colonial forms. Other trajectories are the outcome of the reorganisation of labour relations over the last century. If transhumant pastoralism and trade are in continuity with their pre-colonial antecedents, labour migrations result from the restructuring of older forms of governance and production. One axis of discontinuity is marked by the transition from slave to free labour.

In the case of *cin rani* I recorded examples of circuits that reproduce the trajectories of slave groups following their masters, or of dependent labour relations between slaves and free seasonal employers. While in the majority of cases, today, such movements reflect the autonomous choice of contemporary migrants (*masu cin rani*), their inferior status is implicit in the type of relation established. The economic and social subordination of men and women practising *cin rani* is often explicitly acknowledged, even by people of free descent forced to join this movement by circumstantial necessity. Ideologically, the obligation to employ, or at least feed, *masu cin rani* is sometimes likened to the moral and religious obligation that characterised past forms of slavery known as *bayun yunwa*, namely, people offering themselves as slaves to powerful individuals in exchange for protection and food during famines.[39] The asymmetry of each particular relation established through *cin rani* varies on an ad hoc basis. Yet *cin rani* is a shorter-distance movement that requires smaller initial investments and can be afforded by poorer people.[40] Even linguistically, *cin rani* implies a strategy to ensure consumption throughout the year, particularly relevant to groups recurrently or exceptionally exposed to subsistence failure.

Bida has high barriers to entry due to the greater investments required to finance travel and subsistence at destination and is generally characterised as an independent entrepreneurial activity. *Bida* is practised equally by people of free and slave origins. To men of slave descent it offers a temporary break from a context where, in some cases, their identity still carries the stigma of slavery. Some older generation migrants used their migration earnings to ransom themselves and members of their family and sever ties with their former masters. However, younger migrants emphasise the hardship and humiliation suffered abroad, where many of them become victims of xenophobia, corruption and insecurity. At destination their status as unskilled manual labour sometimes obliges them to accept exploitative employment conditions. Perhaps paradoxically, long-distance migration reinforces their idealisation of life in the village and appreciation for the familiarity and (skewed) reciprocity that distinguish hierarchical relations at home.

Specific patterns of physical mobility are indicative of people's status and identity. At the same time, they serve as strategies of social mobility. Status manifests itself also in terms of relative capacity to choose how and when to move. Contemporary trade- and production- related mobility (farming and, primarily, herding) have evolved from pre-colonial institutions. Some old circuits and markets have remained central to transhumance and exchange. But the conditions and actors populating the dry and dusty roads of Ader have changed. Its society is no longer 'dominated by the few [Tuareg] aristocratic leaders who in effect acted as managers of large firms' (Baier and Lovejoy, 1975, 554). Nor does it contain the new firms and managers characteristic of today's industrialised contexts. Seasonal migration is the result of economic transformations and the restructuring of labour relations that, I have argued, started taking their current shape in the 1920–1930s. Migration flows have absorbed ex-slaves and freemen coping with production deficit and structural unemployment. Ex-slave migrants choose between re-inhabiting old forms of dependent relations through *cin rani* and joining the mass of manual labourers seeking their fortune in today's West African cities (*bida*). Yet, conditions of choice are not of their own making. Ader society partakes of past and contemporary hierarchies, with their respective ideologies and institutions. These are constantly crossed, physically and symbolically, by seasonal migrants and other people on the move.

References

Abraham, R., 1949. *Dictionary of the Hausa Language.* London: University of London Press.

Adamu, M., 1979. 'The Delivery of Slaves from the Central Sudan to the Bight of Benin in the Eighteenth and Nineteenth Centuries.' In H. Gemery and J. Hogendorn, eds, *The Uncommon Market: Essays in the Economic History of the Atlantic Slave Trade.* New York: Academic Press.

Baier, S. and Lovejoy, P., 1975. 'The Desert Side Economy of the Central Sudan.' *The International Journal of African Historical Studies,* VIII(4), pp. 551–81.

Baier, S. and Lovejoy, P., 1977. 'The Tuareg of the Central Sudan: Gradations in Servility at the Desert's Edge (Niger and Nigeria).' In I. Kopytoff and S. Miers, eds, *Slavery in*

Africa: Historical and Anthropological Perspectives. Madison, WI: University of Wisconsin Press.

Bernus, E., 1970. 'Recits historiques de l'Azawagh.' *Bulletin de l'IFAN serie B,* 32(2), pp. 434–85.

Bernus, E., 1981. *Touaregs nigériens: unité culturelle et diversité régionale d'un peuple pasteur.* Paris: ORSTOM.

Bernus, E., 1990. 'Dates, Dromedaries, and Drought: Diversification in Tuareg Pastoral Systems.' In J. Galaty and D. Johnson, eds, *The World of Pastoralism: Herding Systems in Comparative Perspective.* New York: Guilford Press.

Bernus, E., 1996. 'La Zone pastorale touaregue: évolution ou mutation?' In C. Arditi et al., eds, *Les Dynamiques du changement en Afrique sub-saharienne.* Paris: L'Harmattan.

Bonte, P., 1976. 'Structure de classe et structures sociales chez les Kel Gress.' *Revue de l'Occident Musulman et de la Méditerranée,* 21, pp. 141–62.

Boyer, F., 2005. 'L'Esclavage chez les Touaregs de Bankilaré au miroir des migrations circulaires.' *Cahiers d'Études Africaines,* 45 (179–80), pp. 771–803.

Chailley, M., 1968. *Histoire de l'Afrique occidentale française 1638–1959.* Paris: Editions Berger-Levrault.

Decalo, S., 1979. *Historical Dictionary of Niger.* African Historical Dictionaries No. 20. London: The Scarecrow Press.

Fluchard, C., 1995. *Le PPN/RDA et la décolonisation du Niger 1946–1960.* Paris: l'Harmattan.

Fuglestad, F., 1983. *A History of Niger 1850–1960.* Cambridge: Cambridge University Press.

Gregoire, E., 1992. *The Ahalzai of Maradi. Traditional Hausa Merchants in a Changing Sahelian City.* London: Lynne Rienner.

Lorimer, F. and Karp, M., eds, 1960. *Population in Africa.* Boston: Boston University Press.

Lovejoy, P. and Hogendorn, J., 1993. *Slow Death for Slavery: The Course of Abolition in Northern Nigeria, 1897–1936.* Cambridge: Cambridge University Press.

Manvell, A., 2005. 'Action Spaces, Differentiation, and the Dryland Farm: A Case Study From the Dakoro Region of Niger.' Unpublished PhD thesis, University of East Anglia.

Nicolaisen, J., 1963. *Ecology and Culture of the Pastoral Tuareg.* Copenhagen: Nationalmuseets Skrifter.

Nicolas, F., 1950. *Tamesna: les Ioullemeden de l'Est ou Tuareg Kel Dinnik.* Paris: Imprimerie Nationale.

Olofson, H., 1985. 'The Hausa Wanderer and Structural Outsiderhood: An Emic and Etic Analysis.' In M. Chapman and M. Prothero, eds, *Circulation in Third World Countries.* London: Routledge and Kegan Paul.

Prothero, M., 1957. 'Migratory Labour from North Western Nigeria.' *Africa* 27(253), pp. 251–61.

Prothero, M., 1958. *Migrant Labour from Sokoto Province, Northern Nigeria.* Northern Region of Nigeria: The Government Printer.

Rain, D., 1999. *Eaters of the Dry Season: Circular Labour Migration in the West African Sahel.* Boulder, CO: Westview.

Roberts, R. and Klein, M., 1980. 'The Banamba Slave Exodus of 1905 and the Decline of Slavery in the Western Sudan.' *The Journal of African History,* 21(3), pp. 375–94.

Rossi, B., forthcoming. 'Tuareg Trajectories of Slavery: Preliminary Reflections on a Changing Field.' In I. Kohl and A. Fisher, eds, *Tuareg Moving Global.* New York: I.B. Tauris.

Séré de Rivières, E., 1965. *Histoire du Niger.* Paris: Berger-Levrault.

Skinner, E., 1960. 'Labour Migration and its Relationship to Socio-cultural Change in Mossi Society.' *Africa,* 30, 388(3), pp. 375–401.

Souchet, R., 1948. 'Les Lissaouanes et le Canton de Keita. Esquisse d'une histoire de l'Ader.' Unpublished mimeograph.

Swindell, K., 1984. 'Farmers, Traders, and Labourers: Dry Season Migration from North-West Nigeria 1900–33.' *Africa*, 54(1), pp. 3–19.

Urvoy, Y., 1936. *Histoire des populations du Soudan central (Colonie du Niger).* Paris: Larose.

Wallerstein, I., 1965. 'Migration in West Africa: The Political Perspective.' In H. Kuper, ed., *Urbanization and Migration in West Africa.* Berkeley: University of California Press.

Archival sources

ANN: Archives Nationales de Niamey

Brouin, Comm. *Cercle Tahoua, Rapport de tournée, Mai 1943,* ANN 1E28.54.

Court (Gouv. Gen. AOF) à de Loppinot, 16 April 1936.

Delon, *Rapport de Tournée, 11 Février 1948,* ANN 1E37.22.

Escher, Admin. Adj., *Rapport de tournée, Oct. 1938,* ANN 1E22.101

Gagneux, M. Le, *Rapport sur le pélérinage à la Mecque en 1948, incl. télégrammes et circulaires sur l'organisation du pélérinage,* ANN 4E13.3

Journal de Cercle de Madaoua, Secteur de Tahoua, 10 August 1916.

Journal de Cercle de Madaoua, Secteur de Tahoua, Année 1917, 17 January 1917.

Journal de Cercle de Madaoua, Secteur de Tahoua, 14 February 1917.

Loppinot, A. de, *Rapport de Tournée, Février 1933,* ANN 1E15.65.

Loppinot, A. de, *Rapport de Tournée, Mars 1933,* ANN 1E15.92.

Loppinot, A. de, *Rapport de Tournée, 23 Novembre 1933,* ANN 1E13.75.

Loppinot, A. De (Comm. Cercle de Tahoua), à Gouv. Gen. Court, 21 October 1933, ANN 1E1.

Noel, Lieut. Col., *Rapport sur la Situation Politique du Troisième Territoire Militaire, 4ᵉ Trimestre 1902,* 19 February 1903.

Rapport d'Ensemble du 1e Semestre 1946, ANN 1E32.21.

Rapport Semestriel d'Ensemble, Cercle de Tahoua, 1e Semestre 1940, ANN 1E24.29.

Regnault, Commis de Services Civils, *Rapport de tournée de recensement dans le canton de Laba, septembre 1945,* ANN1E31.54.

Rollet, Elève Adm., *Rapport de tournée, Mai 1941,* ANN1E25.52.

Thiellement, Comm., *Rapport de tournée, Août 1938,* ANN 1E22.97.

Thoine, Capt. Comm. de Cercle d'Agadez à M. le Gouv. du Niger, 20 February 1930, ANN 2E3.4.

Notes

1   Research for this article was conducted in repeated periods of fieldwork and archival research since 1995, and primarily during my most recent visit (Jan. 2005–Dec. 2005), funded by an ESRC Research Fellowship (grant number: RES-000-27-0147-A). I would like to thank Paul Lovejoy and Andrew Irving for commenting on earlier drafts of this chapter.

2   David Rain's distinction between *cin rani* and *digga* or *bida* differs from the one outlined here. He attributes to *cin rani* many of the characteristics described here for longer-distance seasonal movements (*bida*, or *digga*) and characterises *digga* as 'distress moves, driven by household food shortages' (Rain, 1999, 134). This is in contrast with my findings and those of other researchers, which suggest that *digga* and *cin rani* constitute respectively, longer- and shorter-distance circuits, with *cin rani* emphasising food security and *bida* focusing on profit: see, for example, Lorimer and Karp, 1960, 73; Manvell, 2005, 237; Prothero, 1957, 251–61; 1958, 17. Olofson's distinction between *cin rani* and *yawon neman kudi/abinci* is also relevant (Olofson, 1985, 56). Ader migrants use the term *digga* rarely, as a synonym of *bida*. They use *bida* to refer to long-distance,

almost exclusively male, seasonal labour migration aimed at accumulating wealth. It is possible that in the more productive and developed Maradi region studied by Rain the contexts at destination of *digga* and *cin rani* appear similar to migrants. In Ader these two movements are seen as polarised and aimed, alternatively, at money-making in economically developed areas (*bida*), or at ensuring subsistence by keeping one's reserves intact in the dry season while working regionally (*cin rani*). Cf. for example fieldnotes 16/4/2005.

3 The ethnonym 'Aderawa', 'people of Ader', is ambiguous. Within Ader the term 'Aderawa' is only applied to specific sub-sections of the population. However, outside Ader, the term 'Aderawa' tends to be used indiscriminately to refer to people coming from this region (with the exception of lighter-skinned Tuareg). Seasonal migrants from Ader are usually called 'Aderawa' at destinations, and the Ba-Adere (Hausa, male sing. for Aderawa) has come to be seen, and to see himself, as the prototypical seasonal migrant. This is not a recent situation. In the *Dictionary of the Hausa Language* published in 1949, Abraham provides the following definitions for the two forms of mobility discussed here: '*Ya tafi cin rani*' is translated as 'in order to eke his corn out, he has gone to spend the hot season elsewhere in exercise of his trade' (Abraham, 1949, 722). On the other hand, for '*tuma da gora*', he translates freely 'fast travelling Adrar people' (Abraham, 1949, 849). Prothero argues, I believe correctly, that there must have been an error in Abraham's text, 'for the people in the North of Sokoto Province and extending northward into the *Colonie du Niger* are Adarawa' (Prothero, 1957, 254, footnote). Hence, Abraham referred to the people of the Adar region (not to be confused with the Adrar) as prototypical migrants, or *exodants*. More recently, Manvell suggests that in Dakoro Ader is seen as exemplary for the practice of *digga* (another term for *bida*), see Manvell, 2005, 245.

4 Most of the data for this section consists of testimonies, interviews and informal discussions collected since 1995 in the course of fieldwork carried out in various villages of Ader. This data can usefully be contrasted with the work of other historians and anthropologists of southern Niger. Due to the contemporary sensitivity of the topic of slavery in Niger, I do not disclose the identity and location of my informants in order to protect their privacy. When necessary, I refer to the date when information was recorded in fieldnotes.

5 The terms Bella and Buzu refer, *strictu sensu*, to 'the slaves of the Tuareg' (cf. Bernus, 1981, 62). Sometimes Hausa speakers qualify the Tuareg generally as 'Buzu' in a derogatory sense (Bernus, 1981, 63). Both terms should not be seen as a direct translation of either the Tamasheq term *iklan*, slave, nor of the terms used to refer to liberated slaves (*ighawelen, iderfan*). The terms Buzu (Hausa) and Bella (Songhay) fail to convey an exact translation of the subtle gradations of servility of Tuareg society. Hence, they tend to conflate slave and ex-slave groups under the same label. Cf. Rossi, forthcoming.

6 Iullemmeden and Kel Gress Tuareg differed in their internal structure, in the numeric consistency of different sub-sections and in their political and economic organisation. See Bernus, 1981, 72–81; Nicolaisen, 1963, 393–442.

7 The salt cure is the summer migration of herds to areas with a high concentration of sodium chloride and sodium sulphate present in the surface layers of the soil and in wells and springs. These mineral salts have a laxative effect and stimulate the elimination of intestinal parasites, cf. Bernus, 1990, 163.

8 I use the term 'sharecropping' loosely, to suggest that dependent farmers were obliged to share a varying proportion of their harvest with the ruling *imajeghen*. Unlike the slaves, freed slaves owned their part of the crop, and this was an incentive to maximise production. However, in the context of this chapter, 'sharecropping' does not imply a particular land tenure regime.

9 My research suggests that the quantities of cereals, primarily millet, or other resources

(e.g. butter) demanded varied from year to year. In most cases, representatives of *Kel Dinnik* chiefs, usually of *enadan* (Tamasheq, artisan) status, would bring a certain number of leather bags (Hausa sing. *taiki*, plur. *tayukka*) to village headmen, responsible for filling them with cereal grains and keeping them until collection. I tried to find out if the amount requested was fixed. Apparently it wasn't. Once an elder commented that at the mere sight of the *imajeghen*'s men, villagers rushed to collect the best of their possessions for fear of the consequences of disappointing Tuareg chiefs, cf. fieldnotes 4/10/2005.

10   Fieldnotes 27/10/2005; cf. 10/6/2005.

11   28/10/2005.

12   The Hausa term *bida* itself is a synonym of *nema*, meaning to look for or search for.

13   For example, fieldnotes 11/4/2005 and 19/5/2005.

14   Madaoua is usually referred to as *bakin Hausa*, or the southern border with the Hausa area.

15   Fieldnotes 27/10/2005.

16   The story of a legendary Tuareg warrior, Fellan, tells of how this *amajer* (sing. of *imajeghen*) had been captured in war and enslaved as a child by the Kel Attaram, where his real status was ignored. One day Fellan's master asked him to prepare his horse for battle against the Kel Air, who were on their way to raid the Kel Attaram's camp. But while the master was in the tent, Fellan jumped on the horse and, alone, defeated the aggressors. This is only a detail of Fellan's long and well-known story (cf. Bernus, 1970, 467ff.). Suffice it to note here that Fellan's bravery and 'instinct' to move independently is seen as a proof of his 'real' nobility.

17   Niger first appeared as a separate geopolitical entity in 1900 when, on 20 December, a decree created the *Territoire Militaire Autonome du Niger* within the *Colonie du Haut-Sénégal et Niger*. It was transformed into *Territoire Militaire du Niger* in 1911, and then into *Territoire du Niger* in 1920. In 1922 it became *Colonie du Niger* (Colony of Niger), with administrative and financial autonomy, under the direction of a *lieutenant-gouverneur* and under the higher authority of the general governor of the *Afrique Occidentale Française*, or AOF (French West Africa), resident in Dakar. See Chailley, 1968, 413; Decalo, 1979, 14; Séré de Rivières, 1965, 244.

18   Capt. Delon, 1948.

19   *Journal de Cercle de Madaoua, 17 Janvier 1917;* cf. fieldnotes 30/9/2005 and 10/10/2005.

20   *Journal de Cercle de Madaoua, 14 Février 1917;* cf. Urvoy, 1936, 214.

21   Here 'Eastern *imajeghen*' is a reference to the imajeghen, or warrior elites, of the Eastern Iullemmeden (Kel Dinnik), as opposed to the Western Iullemmeden of Mali (Kel Ataram).

22   Télégramme du Capt. Sadoux Concernant les Operations dans la Region Est du Secteur, 13 Avril 1917.

23   Cf. de Loppinot, *Rapport de Tournée, Février 1933.*

24   The *Chef de la Subdivision Nomade de Tahoua* wrote periodic reports to the *Commandant de Cercle de Tahoua*, and every year provided a detailed account of the unfolding of the salt cure. This information was summarised in the six-monthly *Rapport d'Ensemble* written by the *Commandant de Cercle*.

25   See, for example, *Rapport de Mr. Le Gagneux sur le pélérinage à la Mecque, 1948.*

26   'Avant notre arrivée, par suite de l'insécurité du pays, les tribus restaient relativement groupées. Actuellement, autant par esprit d'indépendance que pour éviter ou retarder le payement de l'impôt, fournir aux prestations, réquisitions, etc… le nomade s'écarte et quitte facilement sa tribu ou le Cercle. Les règlements actuels lui en donnant le droit. Il n'a qu'une déclaration à faire. C'est à mon avis une erreur […]'. Thoine à Gouv. du Niger, 20 February 1930.

27   A number of colonial communications and reports note that particular slave groups

tied to Iullemmeden *imajeghen* sections had been liberated in 1918. I have not yet identified how these 1918 'liberations' occurred, if they were supported by formal legal acts or were simply a consequence of the 1917 repression of the Kel Dinnik.

28 Several specific aspects of slave mobility in Ader can be interestingly compared with equally specific aspects discussed in Roberts and Klein's study of the Banamba slave exodus. This would require a detailed comparison of the factors involved in the inter-action between patterns of slave mobility and particular forms of enslavement (the particular organisation of slave–master relations). This detailed comparison is beyond the scope of this essay. However, it is possible that the exodus from northern Ader would have been larger and more often definitive (as was the case in Banamba) had the French not permanently crushed the masters, thereby indirectly making it easier for the (ex-) slaves to access productive resources. See Roberts and Klein, 1980, 375–94.

29 See, for example, the section on '*Recrutement et Questions Militaires*' in the *Rapport Semestriel d'Ensemble, Cercle de Tahoua, 1e Semestre 1940*.

30 De Loppinot, *Rapport de Tournée, Mars 1933*.

31 De Loppinot à Gouv. Gen. Court, 21 October 1933.

32 'With Ordinance No. 19, "all persons born in *or brought into* Northern Nigeria" were free. It was no longer necessary for individuals to pay their ransoms or acquire certificates of freedom in the Islamic courts. Ordinance No. 19 was the last piece of legislation in the long history of legal-status abolition in Northern Nigeria' (Lovejoy and Hogendorn, 1993, 261, and note 113). The north–south movement of 1936 could not, instead, be related to harvest failures in northern areas, as 1936 was characterised by exceptionally abundant rains, reaching 231mm in Agadez and 611mm in Tahoua (see Bernus, 1996, 48).

33 Comm. Thiellement, *Rapport de tournée, Août* 1938; cf. Admin.-adj. Escher, *Rapport de tournée, Oct. 1938*: Escher notes that all youths migrated temporarily to Nigeria following a bad harvest to earn money to pay taxes that would otherwise been paid through the sale of cereals. While de Loppinot blamed taxation for inducing migration, here migra-tion is seen as a 'healthy' measure that ensures taxes are paid also after poor harvests.

34 Rollet, *Rapport de tournée, Mai 1941*.

35 'C'est un vieux courant solidement ancré dans les habitudes, c'est un peu d'aventures en des terres lointaines, et la jeunesse aime à vagabonder.' Brouin, *Rapport de tournée, Mai 1943*.

36 See, for example, Regnault *1945, rapport de tournée de recensement dans le canton de Laba*. The *Rapport d'Ensemble du 1e Semestre 1946* observes that the continuation of seasonal migration in spite of forced labour's abolition suggests that it should be seen as 'a real tradition, rather than a pressing necessity'.

37 Based on research conducted in Wassoumamane and Agouloum primarily in September and October 2005. Some information on the Izanazzafan is available in colonial censuses and other archival documents.

38 In 1913 the cantons of Laba and Tamaske were rendered independent from the Lissawan and appointed their own canton chiefs; cf. Souchet, 1948, 18–20.

39 For example, see fieldnotes 8/9/2005. During the 2005 crisis a number of better-off families in Keita agreed to feed, and sometimes host, in exchange for domestic help, poor women with young children who had come from marginal villages whose husbands were away as migrants (*bida*) and unable to send remittances. These agree-ments were ambiguously characterised as forms of *cin rani*, or as examples of mutual support explicitly assimilated to the practices of *bayun yunwa*. This example reveals the gendered implications of migration: some women were forced to rely on *cin rani* while their husbands were away on *bida*.

40 Most labour relations in Ader are of a patron–client kind, as exemplified by the *mai gida* (or *uban gida*, or head of household) – *bara* (servant) relationship, which character-ises asymmetric business relations between parties that are assumed free (cf. Gregoire, 1992, 54). However, *cin rani* has clearer connotations of need and dependence.

10

Discourses on Slavery:
Reflections on Forty Years of Research

Philip Burnham

Many of the publications on the topic of slavery in African Studies during the 1970s were primarily concerned to analyse the socio-legal and political-economic positioning of slaves in various pre-colonial or proto-colonial settings (e.g. Meillassoux, 1975; Miers and Kopytoff, 1977a). They were therefore written either from an historical perspective or by using a rather vaguely defined notion of the ethnographic present. In this literature particular emphasis was placed on exploring the question of whether pre-colonial African systems of slavery were comparable, in terms of social status and degree of exploitation, to the systems of plantation slavery in the New World or in antiquity (e.g. Finley, 1968). On the other hand, what one was encountering in relation to slavery as a fieldworker in Africa during the 1960s and 70s was, for the most part, more related to discourses on slavery than to its continued practice. Nonetheless, it remained the case that the concept of 'slave' was still quite prominent in daily usage in many of the African social contexts where I was working. And in the late 1980s, during two periods of field research in the Caribbean, I found this also to be the case. This experience in a social setting which otherwise stood in marked contrast to my work in Africa further piqued my interest in 'slavery' as a keyword.[1] In this essay I draw on my experiences of field research in Africa and the Caribbean over forty years to reflect on the social significance of contemporary usages of notions of 'slavery' that I have encountered in diverse social contexts.

My essay considers a series of cases or instances drawn from my field-notes where I have encountered a prominent reference to 'slave/slavery'. These range from a case of contested succession to a village chieftaincy, through mobilisation of the word in situations of inter-ethnic conflict or extortion, through cases of contestation over natural resources, through focus on the topic by campaigning non-governmental organisations, and on to competing interpretations of the term within the context of a public festival in Trinidad celebrating the 150th anniversary of the abolition of slavery. In line with the general theme of this book, this material raises points for reflection on some recent African trajectories of slavery, with particular emphasis on how the concept has become variably embodied in institutions and discourses in diverse social settings.

From the outset of my first fieldwork in 1968 in the Meiganga (now Mbere) District of Cameroon I encountered the term 'slave/slavery' on a regular basis.[2] In this multi-ethnic setting which had been much affected by slave raiding and trading up into the first few decades of the twentieth century, there were still a significant number of persons living during the 1960s who had had firsthand experience of slavery. This situation offered numerous opportunities for oral historical research, and the local and national archives contained rich veins of documentary resources to be mined. Much of this historical material has been published in earlier articles and books (e.g. Burnham, 1995 and 1996), but the aim of my present chapter is to consider changing implications of persistent discourses of slavery up into the twenty-first century. Virtually all my old informants with firsthand experience of slavery are now dead, although a few who were taken as slaves as small children around 1930 were still living when I was last in the field in 2004. However, socially significant discourses about slavery continue up to the present day in Cameroon, and a primary aim of this essay is to consider and analyse the trajectories and changing ideological loadings of this term.

As the generations that had had direct experience of slavery died out, more space appears to have opened for evolution of meanings. With a strong word like slavery we perhaps shouldn't expect radical shifts, but certain semantic dimensions have gained greater weight than others. Lovejoy (1981, 11–15; cf. Miers and Kopytoff, 1977a;, Smith, 1965) discusses three key dimensions of slavery: the property dimension, the power dimension (degrees of freedom and nature of domination) and coercion (manipulation of violence). While the property and the coercion dimensions have totally disappeared in the contexts I am familiar with, nuances of the power/domination aspect of slavery continue to be expressed up to the present day. The implications of past slave status for contemporary social identities have evolved differently in different contexts. In some places discourses on slavery are not salient, and the slave origins of certain individuals and groups have been blurred or forgotten. Elsewhere the notion of 'slavery' has become part of racialised discourses of status and identity or has otherwise acquired new semantic connotations.

Gbaya Slavery: The Case of DK

One of the early experiences during my first period of field research (Burnham, 1980a) among the Gbaya people of Cameroon in 1968–70 that still sticks in my mind was my encounter with DK. My wife Jennifer and I were living in a small Gbaya village of some 150 inhabitants and, as we began to make the acquaintance of the villagers, we soon met this very old man. DK was senile and had lost the use of his legs, but he still managed to move about in a crab-like manner, dragging himself around his compound where he spent his days. Gbaya tend to view the senile elderly as objects of mirth, and DK used to attract the mocking attentions of some children in the village, who would comment on his spindly legs, his toothless gums and his often incomprehensible utterances. Passing adults might half-heartedly seek to disperse such pesky children, but they themselves were not averse to making joking remarks at DK's expense. And in early chats with various villagers, we soon learned that it was not only DK's senility that was a subject of wry remarks; it was also the fact that DK was a Laka captive.

The term 'Laka' as used by the Gbaya people of Meiganga refers to a diverse collection of ethnic groups which inhabit the plains region northeast of the Mbere River valley, on either side of the Chad–Cameroon frontier. Throughout much of the nineteenth century and continuing up to the First World War this densely populated plains region was a preferred location for large-scale slave raiding, primarily by the Fulbe of the Ngaoundere and Rei Bouba chiefdoms (Burnham, 1995; Burnham, 1996, 19, 26; Froelich, 1954, 15; Lenfant, 1909; Serre, 1997, 146). Gbaya clans living to the south of the Laka, in a region that today comprises east-central Cameroon and north-west Central African Republic, often participated in these raids as tributaries and allies of the Fulbe chiefdom of Ngaoundere. The bulk of the slaves taken in these raids passed into circuits of political tribute within the Sokoto Caliphate or were sold to Muslim slave traders for export and sale to private slave owners throughout the West African savanna zone and beyond. Other captives became the property of Ngaoundere's Gbaya allies, who might sell them to Hausa traders (primarily for payments of cloth) or who might incorporate them into their own clans. DK had been captured as a child in one of these large raids in the early twentieth century and had lived as a member of his captor's clan ever since.

When we knew DK in 1968 he still had two Gbaya wives, one who was only slightly younger than himself, and one (a crippled woman) who was still of child-bearing age, as witnessed by a malnourished infant who struggled for sustenance from her mother's flaccid breasts. As I gradually began to record the genealogies of the village inhabitants, I soon found to my surprise that DK, a Laka slave, was the father of the village's well-respected headman, who lived in a large compound adjoining DK's.

The social organisation of the Gbaya at the time of DK's capture was a politically uncentralised descent-based system in which slavery was mitigated by progressive incorporation into the captor's clan via a fictive kinship relationship (cf. Burnham, 1980a; Miers and Kopytoff, 1977b, 22–25). As DK's case shows, however, this mode of incorporation did not serve to efface the memory of a captive's origins. Moreover, as I delved further into the dynamics of Gbaya settlement patterns and local politics (Burnham, 1980a, chapter 4), I came to learn that, over the previous decade, DK's slave status had been the cause of a series of struggles over succession to the village headmanship and subsequent village fissions on the part of clan segments that had been unsuccessful in these struggles. Two other villages located (in 1968) several kilometres from the village where we were residing were comprised of those disgruntled clan segments, whose members, when asked, proclaimed that they would never live under the leadership of a son of a slave. Indeed, one of the elders living in these neighbouring villages took considerable pleasure in recounting his involvement in the slave-raiding expedition in which DK and other Laka slaves had been captured.

DK died within the year and his death was celebrated some months later by the memorial ritual reserved for senior Gbaya men who have left many descendants. The ceremonial unfolded without reference to DK's slave origin. In 1974, on a return trip to the field, I found that a major village reorganisation had taken place in conjunction with the paving of the motor road that passed through the village. The road project was used as a pretext by the Cameroon administration to insist on the coalescence of a series of small neighbouring villages into one nucleated settlement, and the disgruntled clan segments had been forced to rejoin their clansmen who had continued to live under the headmanship of DK's son. The dissident clansmen had symbolised their rejection of this enforced situation by choosing to live on the opposite side of the road from the headman's compound but, in the ensuing decades, the knowledge and social relevance of DK's slave status for younger generations appears to have faded. This is not to say that the knowledge of DK's slave origin may not still remain available to be mobilised by those who remember it should a situation arise where such information could prove advantageous.

I have witnessed several occasions in various parts of Cameroon where similar oral histories, although normally considered of little relevance on a day-to-day basis, have indeed been used to strategic effect in disputes over land rights, marriage relations, sharing of 'common' property or access to political office (e.g. Burnham and Graziani, 2004). However, in the DK case and in most other Gbaya social contexts, there is no public, institutionalised commemoration of the historical legacy of slavery that can serve as a memory vehicle, and it seems likely that, within a few more decades, DK's social status along with those of the other slave ancestors in Gbaya genealogies will be forgotten.

In the preceding sentence I wrote 'most Gbaya social contexts' but, while doing research in the Eastern Province of Cameroon around Bertoua, the provincial capital, in the 1980s, I encountered a different situation where a history of domination has been inscribed in a more enduring way on the social landscape. A key concept in this context is the Gbaya term *ndem nam*, which refers to a settlement composed of conquered or subordinated people of diverse origins (Burnham et al., 1986, 100; Burnham, 1996, 186; Copet-Rougier, 1987). Although separate slave villages were not an institution characteristic of most of pre-colonial Gbaya society, the Gbaya chiefdom of Bertoua, which stood in a tributary relationship with the Fulbe state of Ngaoundere in the late nineteenth century, settled its own conquered tributaries and slaves in a ring of *ndem nam* villages around Bertoua – much as the Fulbe did with their *rumnde* slave settlements around Ngaoundere. This pattern emerges clearly when one consults both early colonial and more recent maps (Moisel, 1910–13; National Geographical Centre of Cameroon, 1977) but, in the present day, the implications of servitude associated with the term *ndem nam* are not very widely remembered in Gbaya society.

Certainly, the social cleavage implied by the *ndem nam* term is not nearly as accentuated today as what one encounters in the case of former slave villages in the Southwest Province of Cameroon. There one finds a pattern of paired neighbouring villages carrying names such as 'Big X' versus 'Little X', where Big refers to free autochthonous status and Little refers to former slave and/ or stranger status. The remaining social disabilities of formerly servile populations in Southwest Province are more marked, with controls being exercised on who may be admitted as a resident of an autochthonous village accompanied by associated disadvantages in relation to land tenure and other rights affecting stranger populations. Interestingly, large commercial plantations are the dominant feature of the socio-economic landscape in Southwest Province, and numerous labour migrants have long been recruited particularly from the Northwest Province to work on these plantations. This is the same source from which had originated, in pre- and early colonial times, many of the slaves and forced labourers who were transported to the Atlantic coast of the Southwest Province by slave traders and German colonial labour recruiters (Rowlands, 1979, 14–17; Warnier, 1975). Persons of Northwestern ancestry living in the Southwest Province, even if born in the Southwest Province, may still suffer stigma up to the present day, although the contrast between 'natives' (*autochtones*) versus 'strangers' (*allogènes*) now tends to be the preferred terminological gloss (Geschiere and Nyamnjoh, 2000) rather than the concept of slavery.

Although I have not personally carried out research on this issue, anthropologists working in the Southwest Province of Cameroon have reported an interesting transformation of local discourses on slavery which associates slavery with current conceptualisations of witchcraft. Thus, for example, as summarised by Geschiere (1995, 196–202; see also Balz, 1984; de Rosny, 1981; Warnier, 1989), victims of *nyongo* and *ekong* witchcraft among the Duala,

Bakweri, Bakossi and other ethnic groups of southern Cameroon are believed to be exported by the witches, with their hands tied, to work as slaves on invisible plantations across the ocean or on Mount Kupe in Cameroon. Geschiere emphasises that this version of witchcraft is intimately associated with what are viewed locally as processes of immoral personal enrichment as a result of involvement with the modern economy.

Considering these cases in somewhat more general terms, I believe it is possible to dissect out two separate, albeit related, processes which give different inflections to modern trajectories of slavery discourses in these politically uncentralised, descent-based Cameroonian societies. On the one hand, we have seen how the mobilisation of popular memories and/or of genealogical knowledge can provide an ideological basis for the pursuit of concrete political disputes, competitions over resources or even witchcraft accusations. On the other hand, in a more diffuse manner, local concepts of slavery, having been shorn of legal/institutional support following the formal abolition of slavery during the colonial period (however belated and often half-hearted in application – see e.g. Eckert, 1999), have merged into concepts of ethnic identity and difference and remain available for mobilisation in ethnic political discourses today. Judging from my observations in Cameroon and elsewhere, this second process appears to be quite a general, although not inevitable, tendency in post-emancipation settings, and I will return to this issue in more detail once we have reviewed other ethnographic cases.

Modern Transformations of Slavery among Fulfulde-Speaking Peoples in North-Central Cameroon

While the case of DK permitted me to review some of the modern changes in discourses about slavery that I have encountered over the years among the Gbaya in the Adamaoua and Eastern Provinces of Cameroon, it is also of relevance to consider the somewhat different trajectories of the slavery concept that have unfolded in the same region among the various Fulfulde-speaking groups in this area. The two principal Fulfulde-speaking groups that I will consider here are the Mbororo pastoralists, many of whom still practise a seasonally mobile lifestyle, and the Fulbe, a heterogeneous population of settled agro-pastoralists and traders that continues to recognise the traditional legitimacy of the various Fulbe states (lamidates) that dominated this region in the pre-colonial period. Fuller details on these peoples are presented in my monograph *The Politics of Cultural Difference in Northern Cameroon* (Burnham, 1996).

The Mbororo Case

During my first period of fieldwork in Cameroon during the late 1960s my wife and I lived for several months in an ethnically mixed village which owed its origin to the institution of slavery. In pre-colonial and early colonial times it was a common practice among the pastoral Mbororo to purchase slaves, particularly children, who served their masters as herdboys, domestic servants and/or concubines and who might eventually be settled in fixed agrarian settlements (known as *labbaare* in Fulfulde) around which their Mbororo masters would continue their seasonally transhumant lifestyle. Indeed, in the late 1960s I was able to make the acquaintance of an old Kanuri man resident in the Meiganga region who had been a slave trader in this zone up into the 1930s. He reported that he had been involved in the kidnapping of numerous, mainly Gbaya, children, usually with the collusion of avaricious headmen or senior kinsmen of the child, and he then traded these children primarily to the Mbororo.

In any case, the multi-ethnic village where we were residing had originally been a settlement inhabited principally by a few pastoral Mbororo families, some of whose members were too infirm to participate in mobile pastoralism, and their slaves. In 1969 this village still had a small core group of seden-tarised Mbororo residents from which the village headman was recruited. Several elderly residents of the village were publicly identified as former slaves of the Mbororo and, although now free of any legal disabilities that could hinder their relocation, they had voluntarily chosen to remain in the village, maintaining what might best be described as a relationship of clientage (but not fictive kinship) with their former masters. While researching in neighbouring encampments of still-mobile Mbororo pastoralists, I also encountered several individuals who were the now-adult offspring of former slave concubines of the Mbororo and whose way of life and economic status were now indis-tinguishable from those of Mbororo of non-servile ancestry. Such persons were viewed as kin by their fellow Mbororo clansmen of non-slave ancestry, and it is only in relation to the choice of first marriage partners among the Mbororo that these persons of slave ancestry experience discrimination in the present day. Mbororo parents of free ancestry would not normally accept a first marriage for their daughters with a man of slave ancestry (see Burnham, 1996, 109–10).

As in the case of DK presented above, by the 1960s the trajectory of this former system of slavery among the Mbororo seemed to be headed in much the same direction as that among the Gbaya. Apart from some remaining discrimination in marriage choice as just mentioned, slave status lacked a firm structural grounding in the politically uncentralised and relatively non-hierar-chical setting of Mbororo society and, as more time passes, successive genera-tions of descendants of slave concubines are likely to move towards full assimilation. On the other hand, as I have described in my 1996 monograph, Mbororo continue to exhibit a marked degree of racialised ethnic discourse linked with their concept of cultural and racial distinctiveness (*pulaaku*). In numerous day-to-day contexts such as the telling of folktales or ethnic jokes as well as in judgements of an individual's character, the black slave remains an archetypal figure (for example, see Bocquené, 2002, 178–79, 225–26). Whereas according to *pulaaku* the Mbororo place a high value on the qualities of intelligence, self-control, finesse and moral conduct, the black slave is viewed in Mbororo discourse as embodying the very negation of these positive values. This ideology is at the root of an exclusivist ethnic discourse, which continues to demarcate a sharp boundary between the Mbororo and their non-Fulbe neighbours (Burnham, 1996, 106–10 *et passim*).

Centralised Fulbe State Systems

Apart from the politically uncentralised pastoral Mbororo just discussed, a large majority of the Fulfulde-speaking population in northern Cameroon is comprised of sedentary agro-pastoralists and merchants of the Fulbe category, whose historical origins derive from the various states of the Sokoto Caliphate. As I have described elsewhere (Burnham, 1995), slavery played a central role in these states prior to their conquest by the Germans at the turn of the last century. Slave raiding and trading were at the heart of their economies, with slaves being used both as a major source of agricultural and domestic labour within their captors' farms and households as well as for tribute payments from the various Cameroonian lamidates to their political overlords, the Emir of Adamawa at Yola and the Sultan of Sokoto.

Following the ousting of the Germans during the First World War, the French colonial administration soon moved to formally abolish slavery in Cameroon. Over the next few decades in certain parts of northern Cameroon this resulted in an increased rate of population mobility as freed slaves moved away from the sites of their domination and sought to establish new lives elsewhere (see Podlewski, 1966 and 1971, who discusses the continuing demographic consequences of this situation). On the other hand, as a result of the very limited numbers of colonial officers present in northern Cameroon until after the Second World War, the French utilised a *de facto* system of indirect rule to administer the region, a practice that ensured the persistence of many of the traditional structures of the Fulbe lamidates. Among these traditional administrative structures was an extensive set of titled slave offices whose incumbents owed allegiance directly to the ruler (*laamiiDo*). Such slave officials could act as something of a counterbalance to the power of the titled free officials in the royal court whose interests, in some contexts, might be opposed to those of the *laamiiDo* (Burnham, 1972, 310). Of particular relevance for this essay is the title *dogari laamiiDo*, which can be translated as a traditional policeman of a Fulbe ruler. These officials were normally persons who had been born in captivity, i.e. second-generation slaves (*rimaayBe*), or who were the offspring of slave concubines who had been manumitted by their masters. In any case, lacking a supporting network of kin, the primary loyalties of such *dogari'en* (plural of *dogari*) were to their royal masters.

To a significant degree this system of indirect rule relying on traditional Fulbe state structures has been perpetuated even into the post-independence period, as the Cameroon government has found it useful in certain areas of northern Cameroon. Nowhere is this more true than in the vast territory of the Fulbe lamidate of Rei Bouba where, in return for his close collaboration with the para-statal cotton company SODECOTON (Koulandi, 2006; Seignobos, 2006) and his assurance of favourable results at election times (Amnesty International, 1997; Article XIX, 1995), the *laamiiDo* of Rei Bouba continues to be given great latitude in controlling affairs in his domain even by the present southern, Christian-dominated regime of President Paul Biya.

Central to the day-to-day administration of the Rei Bouba lamidate today are the *dogari'en* police force/royal emissaries, who are charged with the exaction from the local population of the (now illegal) *zakkat* tax, road tolls, market taxes, as well as labour levies to work the fields or perform other services for the *laamiiDo*. *Dogari'en* also assert their right to allocate farmland and house plots in the name of the *laamiiDo* in villages in his territory, in contravention of Cameroonian national law. Persons who attempt to resist such exactions risk a beating, imprisonment in the traditional prisons of the *laamiiDo*, or even death, since the *dogari'en* have repeatedly shown themselves to be extremely diligent and severe in enforcing what they claim to be the traditional prerogatives of the *laamiiDo*. It is also the case that, at election times, *dogari'en* are very active and brutal in suppressing the campaigning activities of all candidates standing in the Mayo Rey District except those from the ruling party. The special relationship that the *dogari'en* (also termed *nelaaBe*) in Rei Bouba enjoy with the *laamiiDo* is said to rest on an oral tradition (Abdoullaye and Mohammadou, 1972, 16–17, 254–56) according to which, during a pre-colonial war between Rei Bouba and Yola, it was the slaves of the *laamiiDo* rather than the free Fulbe dignitaries of his court who supported him in his greatest time of need (see also Shimada, 1993).

As I observed this system in operation in 1998–2002 (see also Seignobos, 2006), it becomes quite difficult to distinguish the prerogatives of the *laamiiDo* from those of the *dogari'en*, since these police normally operate in rural settings where their actions are not monitored by any superior official and where they are largely free to commit abuses in furtherance of their personal interests. In other words, up to the present, *dogari'en* in Rei Bouba have a strong vested interest in continuing to identify themselves as *maccuBe laamiiDo* (slaves of the ruler), a status that authorises what today must frankly be termed a system of gangsterism.

The two cases just presented drawn from Fulfulde-speaking societies in northern Cameroon highlight some notable contrasts in the recent trajectories of slavery discourses in these two situations. They also offer interesting parallels with the analysis presented in M. G. Smith's well-known article 'Slavery and Emancipation in Two Societies', originally published in 1954 (Smith, 1965). Smith compared the social positioning of slaves in Jamaica and Hausaland with a view to understanding the substantially different modes and degrees of integration of ex-slaves in these two societies after emancipation. Working within the framework of his plural society model, Smith (1965, 159) emphasised that 'Despite formal similarities in their legal definition, the institutions of slavery in Mohammedan Zaria and Jamaica . . . (bore) markedly different functional relations with other institutions in the two societies'.

In particular, Smith (1965, 136–37, 147–48) emphasised the significance of the universalist and assimilationist values of Islam in promoting a relatively smooth transition towards social integration of ex-slaves in post-emancipation Hausaland.

> The Hausa slave by virtue of his assimilation to Islam found his relation to his master humanized and transmuted in the direction of guardian–ward relations, and was thereby further induced to assimilate Hausa culture voluntarily, to such an extent that he could be and, in fact, was entrusted with military command and territorial administration. In contrast, the exclusion of the Caribbean slaves from the Christian community to which their masters belonged involved and created differences of humanity and kind between the two groups which were expressed in the systematic exploitation of slaves as real property from which the maximum social and economic satisfactions were to be extracted. For Hausa, Islam prescribed an eclectic attitude toward race, and ordained cultural and social homogeneity. For the Caribbean, Christian ideology was only one of several competing systems of value and belief, and often enough it lent support to the ideologies of race or laissez-faire which sought to sanction and rationalize the plurality of Caribbean social and cultural systems.

In contrast to the Hausa case as described by Smith, which is characterised by what I have termed an 'inclusivist' orientation (Burnham, 1996, 6 *et passim*) towards the assimilation of its servile population in both the pre- and post-emancipation periods, the Fulfulde-speaking peoples of northern Cameroon can display markedly exclusivist attitudes to their former slave populations, which tend to be closely linked with their attitudes towards racial difference. Unlike the Hausa with their 'eclectic' attitude towards race, as Smith puts it, we find especially among the Mbororo a well-developed racialist ideology that continues to inform their interpretation of slavery despite the weakening structural/institutional supports for such an attitude. In the present day I would argue that the hierarchical implications inherent in the concept of slavery have largely come to be grafted onto Mbororo concepts of ethnicity, with the concept of slavery serving to symbolise radical difference in this context.

The situation is more complex among the Fulbe. To begin with, in a context such as that of Rei Bouba where the Fulbe rulers in particular have for many generations taken wives and concubines from their conquered non-Fulbe subjects, phenotypic differences between Fulbe freemen and non-Fulbe ex-slaves have markedly diminished. Then too, in a manner similar to that described by Smith for the Hausa, the universalist doctrines of Islam among the more religious Fulbe have encouraged the development of more inclusivist attitudes towards the formerly servile populations now incorporated within Fulbe society. This is not to say that one cannot still encounter racialist discourses today in Fulbe society that are quite similar to those in Mbororo society (see, for examples, Eguchi, 1974; Lacroix, 1965, 21, 153, 426). However, these are often balanced or even subordinated to the universalist, inclusivist discourse of Islam. In the quite extreme case we have considered of the *dogariʹen* in Rei Bouba, the persistence and, indeed, active defence of their self-identification as slaves is clearly linked to a situation of marked economic and political advantage.

Impacts of Globalised Discourses on Slavery in Cameroon

The references to international non-governmental organisations (NGOs) such as Amnesty International and Article XIX in my discussion of the Rei Bouba case above bring to the fore another, increasingly prominent aspect of discourses on slavery operative in present-day Cameroon. Particularly over the last several decades, it has been noteworthy that, primarily through the intervention of external NGOs working in the human rights or environmentalist fields, a diverse array of social practices in different parts of the country are being held up for scrutiny.

At about the same time that certain academic authors writing about African slavery (e.g. Miers and Kopytoff, 1977b) were arguing for the need for more careful definitions and precise distinctions in this field (in order to emphasise, for example, that most forms of African slavery were more benign than the plantation slavery of the New World), certain campaigning NGOs were seeking to expand the category, often by metaphorical extension, to assist their efforts to combat an increasingly varied array of forms of exploitation. The NGO Anti-Slavery International (ASI), the modern name for the Anti-Slavery Society founded in 1823, has been quite explicit about its tactics in this regard (Anti-Slavery International, n.d.: 14):

> The Working Group on Slavery has met regularly in Geneva since 1975 and the Anti-Slavery Society played a large part in establishing this group. It was the first international body since 1939 dedicated to the elimination of slavery and, as it heard evidence from many NGOs, enabled the definition of slavery to become ever wider. Its meetings are public and can attract press

coverage, and so appeal to NGOs in their search for support and awareness of their work. As a consequence the word 'slavery' now covers many
practices which would not immediately be associated with it . . .

In this way, campaigning NGOs such as ASI have been able to bring into
their ambit of concern quite a range of forms of labour exploitation and abuse
– for example, child labour and fosterage, dependent labour, or exploitative
wage levels – in addition to slavery itself.

I well recall a telephone conversation in London in the early 1980s with
an employee of ASI, which was considering launching a campaign under the
anti-slavery banner against the exploitation of the Baka Pygmies of southeastern Cameroon by neighbouring sedentary agriculturalist villagers. This
was part of a more general initiative of ASI at this time to extend its work to
cover indigenous peoples. In the course of this conversation I was seeking to
learn what were the criteria being used by ASI to extend the concept of slavery
so as to include the Baka case. However, I soon discovered, as the above quotation suggests, that definitional explicitness was not a key concern of ASI in
this context. Indeed, quite the opposite was the case and, as I have observed in
several instances over the years, flexible usage and/or metaphorical extension
of categorical terms such as 'slavery' or 'indigenous peoples' (Burnham, 2000;
Kendrick and Lewis, 2004; Lewis, 2005) can be very useful for campaigning
NGOs both for the purpose of raising funds and for supporting claims
regarding the legitimacy of their involvement in particular issues. As far as
the Baka are concerned, as far as I know, ASI has never yet mounted such
a campaign, so perhaps my urging to them on the telephone that to apply
the term 'slavery' to the experience of the Baka would be quite inappropriate
and possibly counter-productive did have some effect. Nonetheless, for the
purposes of our present discussion of keywords, this NGO example does serve
to highlight the ways in which globalised discourses in fields such as human
rights can potentially come to impact on local usages of key terms, recasting
understandings and opening up new lines of transformation.

Celebrating Emancipation in Trinidad

While the preceding case has raised the issue of the potential impacts of
globalised discourses concerning slavery on local concepts, this process
is obviously not solely related to the actions of NGOs. For my last case, I
venture outside the African continent to raise issues concerning competing
globalised discourses on slavery. While most of the field research I have
conducted during my career has been located in Africa, in 1988–89 I carried
out a year's fieldwork in the Caribbean, on the islands of Trinidad and Tobago.
By chance, my stay in Trinidad happened to coincide with a national celebration of the 150th anniversary of the end of the apprenticeship system, the point

at which African slaves on the island received full emancipation. The festivities consisted of a diverse set of events stretching over several days, with much of the emphasis of the celebrations being placed on Trinidad's African heritage. In this connection several honoured guests from Nigeria had been invited by the festival organisers, including Yusufu Bala Usman, Reader in History at Ahmadu Bello University, Omotoso Eluyemi, Professor of Archaeology at Ife (now Obafemi Awolowo) University, and Okunade Sijuwade Olubuse, the Oni (traditional ruler) of Ife. The culmination of the three-day festivities, presided over by Prime Minister A. N. R. Robinson and televised on Trinidad national TV, provoked acrimonious debate in the media due to the inclusion of elements of Afro-Trinidadian Orisha ritual, a religious denomination which in other circumstances was distinctly marginal or even discriminated against in mainstream Trinidadian society (see, for example, Thomas, 1987).

Of particular interest for our present concerns, however, was the major public seminar organised at the University of the West Indies on the theme of 'The African Past and the African Diaspora', which attracted active participation not only from the local academic community but also from a wide array of politico-cultural organisations espousing diverse ideologies – Garveyism, Black Power, Pan-Africanism, Marxism and various versions of neo-traditional African religion. As soon became apparent in the seminar presentations and subsequent discussion, the concept of slavery was of quite varied and often opposed significance for the diverse attendance, and Dr Yusufu Usman soon provoked an uproar by stating that the Emancipation Day celebration organisers had made a grave mistake in inviting the Oni of Ife as an honoured guest. Usman argued that no doubt the festival organisers had invited the Oni on the mistaken presumption that he was a modern analogue of a traditional African ruler whereas, in reality, Usman considered him to be a modern example of the African commission agents and middlemen who had collaborated with European slave traders to sell Afro-Trinidadians' ancestors into slavery. Usman went on to attack racialised versions of African history, stating that Africa is a multi-racial continent and that pan-Africanism must be based on the recognition of the common historical experience of slavery and colonial oppression of African peoples and not on the mistaken notion of a single black race. Usman's presentation provoked an outpouring of the diverse views represented in the auditorium, but prominent among them were discourses arguing for the persistence among Afro-Trinidadians of 'racial memories' of slavery. As the noted Trinidadian economist Dr Ralph Henry stated, 'I won't defer to anyone's opinion as to how I should behave unless they too have had the experience of being a slave in the last 200 to 300 years.'

Conclusion

Such heated debates are nothing new for researchers working in Afro-Caribbean or Afro-American contexts, or indeed for researchers working in certain African countries. However, placed in juxtaposition with the case material drawn from Cameroon, I think they highlight some interesting points. Whereas for many Afro-American and Afro-Caribbean commentators there has been a prominent concern for many decades to promote a positive social valence for histories of slavery and trans-Atlantic historical connections, such historicising reflexes are notably absent in the Cameroon contexts we have considered. Histories of the masters (e.g. Abdoullaye and Mohammadou, 1979; Bassoro and Mohammadou, 1980) still tend to be emphasised rather than histories of slaves, and claims to empowerment based on slave ancestry and race such as those that featured so prominently in the Trinidadian Emancipation Day seminar seldom find expression in Cameroon. The political power of the Rei Bouba *dogari'en*, self-identified as slaves (*maccuBe laamiiDo*), rests not on a concept of Black empowerment but on their clientelistic relations with an autocratic Fulbe ruler who has successfully maintained an independent niche of power within the Cameroon state despite damning campaigns by various international NGOs. Conversely, as Yusufu Usman argued so controversially, there was a notable irony in the fact that the Afro-Trinidadian organisers of the Emancipation Day celebrations had sought to embellish their event by inviting the Oni of Ife, whose qualifications for office were based on dubious practices in Usman's view. Given Usman's own Marxist and pan-African political leanings and his reputation as a critic of bad governments and corruption in the Nigerian context (*Nigeria Daily News*, 2005), it is apparent that we are here dealing with a notable case of clashing globalised discourses on the interpretation of slavery – discourses that, for the most part today, are being formulated both with reference to conflicting understandings of the past as well as differing socio-political agendas in the present.

As Smith cogently argued in his comparison of slavery and emancipation in Hausaland and Jamaica, the racial factor in slavery tends to receive variable weighting depending on the ideological context in which it is set. Among the Gbaya, Islam has not played a prominent role as in the Fulbe or Hausa examples mentioned above. Yet inclusivist logics characteristic of Gbaya kinship and political organisation account for the progressive incorporation of people of slave origins into the society of the free, without major stigmatising consequences for their everyday life. And in the examples from the Fulfulde-speaking peoples of Cameroon we have considered, we found the racialist elements of the ideology of *pulaaku* to stand in contradiction to the inclusivist doctrines of Islam, with this uneasy mix playing itself out rather differently among the Mbororo than among the Fulbe. Although, as

I have argued, concepts of ethnic identity and race can come to be principal carriers of meaning with respect to modern discourses on slavery, we have also noted the development and increasing prominence of other semantic reflexes of slavery as a keyword. The international human rights movement, as we have seen, can be a productive source of meaning as can international development discourses linked to the campaign for financial reparations to African countries for the effects of the slave trade (*African Studies Quarterly*, 1999).

Slavery clearly remains a powerfully evocative term. But what it evokes varies widely with social context. In Cameroon, for example, despite a desultory and now largely moribund effort to gain UNESCO World Heritage Site status for the slaving port of Bimbia in the Southwest Province, there is virtually no involvement in the slavery heritage tourism industry (Forss et al., 2005) that has become so prominent in other West African countries such as Ghana and Senegal. Nor have Cameroonians played much of a role in the international slavery reparations campaign. Given the present calculus of ideological interests and discourses relating to slavery in Cameroon, such a situation is not surprising, and one might hazard a prediction that the particular ways in which 'socially and historically constituted knowledge about "slavery" is embodied in institutions and everyday practices' in present-day Cameroon (to quote from the initial statement of our seminar's theme) are likely to encourage the persistence of such attitudes for the foreseeable future.

References

Abdoullaye, H. and Mohammadou, E., 1972. *Les Yillaga de la Bénoué: Ray ou Rey-Bouba*. Yaounde: Ministère de l'Information et de la Culture.

African Studies Quarterly, 1999. 'A Roundtable on Reparations'. *African Studies Quarterly*, 2(4).

Amnesty International, 1997. *Cameroon: Blatant Disregard for Human Rights*, http://web.amnesty.org/library/index/engAFR170161997?openandof=eng-2af

Anti-Slavery International, n.d. *The History of Anti-Slavery International*, http://www.antislavery.org/homepage/antislavery/history.pdf

Article XIX, 1995. *Northern Cameroon: Attacks on Freedom of Expression by Governmental and Traditional Authorities*, http://www.article19.org/pdfs/publications/cameroon-attacks-on-foe.pdf

Balz, H., 1984. *Where the Faith Has to Live*. Basel: Basel Mission.

Bassoro, M. A. and Mohammadou, E., 1980 *Garoua: tradition historique d'une cité peule du Nord-Cameroun*. Bordeaux: Centre National de la Recherche Scientifique.

Bocquené, H., 2002. *Memoirs of a Mbororo: the Life of Ndudi Umaru: Fulani Nomad of Cameroon* (English translation of *Moi un Mbororo* by Philip Burnham and Gordeen Gorder). New York and Oxford: Berghahn Books.

Burnham, P., 1972. 'Racial Classification and Ideology in the Meiganga Region, North Cameroon'. In P. Baxter and B. Sansom, eds, *Race and Social Difference*. London: Penguin Books.

Burnham, P., 1980a. *Opportunity and Constraint in a Savanna Society: The Gbaya of Meiganga, Cameroon*. London: Academic Press.

Burnham, P., 1980b. 'Raiders and Traders in Adamawa: Slavery as a Regional System'. In J. Watson, ed., *Asian and African Systems of Slavery.* Oxford: Basil Blackwell and Mott.

Burnham, P., 1991. 'L'Ethnie, la religion et l'état: le rôle des Peuls dans la vie politique et sociale du Nord-Cameroun.' *Journal des Africanistes,* 61(1), pp. 73–102.

Burnham, P., 1995. 'Raiders and Traders in Adamawa: Slavery as a Regional System.' *Paideuma,* 41, pp. 153–76 (revised and updated version of Burnham, 1980b).

Burnham, P., 1996. *The Politics of Cultural Difference in Northern Cameroon.* Edinburgh: Edinburgh University Press for the International African Institute.

Burnham, P., 2000. 'Whose Forest? Whose Myth? Conceptualisations of Community Forests in Cameroon.' In A. Abramson and D. Theodossopoulos, eds, *Land, Law and Environment: Mythical Land, Legal Boundaries.* London: Pluto Press.

Burnham, P., Copet-Rougier, E. and Noss, P., 1986. 'Gbaya et Mkako: contribution ethno-linguistique à l'histoire de l'Est Cameroun.' *Paideuma,* 32, pp. 87–128.

Burnham, P. and Graziani, M., 2004. 'Legal Pluralism in the Rain Forests of Southeastern Cameroon.' In K. Homewood, ed., *Rural Resources and Local Livelihoods in Africa.* Oxford: James Currey.

Copet-Rougier, E., 1987. 'Du clan à la chefferie dans l'est du Cameroun.' *Africa,* 57(3), pp. 345–63.

de Rosny, E., 1981 *Les Yeux de ma chevre.* Paris: Plon.

Eckert, A., 1999. 'Slavery in Colonial Cameroon, 1880s to 1930s'. In S. Miers and M. Klein, eds, *Slavery and Colonial Rule in Africa.* London: Frank Cass.

Eguchi, P., 1974. *Miscellany of Maroua Fulfulde (Northern Cameroon).* Tokyo: Institute for the Study of Languages and Cultures of Asia and Africa.

Finley, M., 1968 'Slavery.' *International Encyclopedia of the Social Sciences,* 14, pp. 307–13. New York: Macmillan.

Forss, K. et al., 2005. *Evaluation of the Slave Route Project: 1994–2004.* Paris: UNESCO.

Froelich, J. C., 1954. 'Le Commandement et l'organisation sociale chez les Foulbé de l'Ada-maoua.' *Etudes Camerounaises,* 45–46.

Geschiere, P., 1995. *Sorcellerie et politique en Afrique.* Paris: Karthala.

Geschiere, P. and Nyamnjoh, F., 2000. 'Capitalism and Autochthony: The Seesaw of Mobility and Belonging.' *Public Culture,* 12(2), pp. 423–52.

Kendrick, J. and Lewis, J., 2004. 'Indigenous Peoples' Rights and the Politics of the Term "Indigenous".' *Anthropology Today,* 20(2), pp. 4–9.

Koulandi, J., 2006. 'Coping with Social Complexity and Ethnic Diversity: Rural Resettlement, Cotton Cultivation and Coping Strategies in the Village of Tongo-Kaiwan and the Benue River Basin, Northern Cameroon.' Unpublished doctoral dissertation, University of Tromsø, Norway.

Lacroix, P. F., 1965. *Poésie peul de l'Adamawa.* 2 vols. Paris: Juillard.

Lenfant, Comm., 1909. *La Découverte des grandes sources du centre de l'Afrique.* Paris: Hachette.

Lewis, J., 2005. 'Whose Forest is it Anyway? Mbendjele Yaka Pygmies, the Ndoki Forest and the Wider World.' In T. Widlok and W. Tadesse, eds, *Property and Equality, Vol. 2 Encapsulation, Commercialisation, Discrimination.* Oxford: Berghahn Books.

Lovejoy, P., ed., 1981. *The Ideology of Slavery.* Beverly Hills: Sage.

Meillassoux, C., ed., 1975. *L'Esclavage en Afrique précoloniale.* Paris: Maspero.

Miers, S. and Klein, M., eds, 1999. *Slavery and Colonial Rule in Africa.* London: Frank Cass.

Miers, S. and Kopytoff, I., eds, 1977a. *Slavery in Africa: Historical and Anthropological Perspectives.* Madison, WI: University of Wisconsin Press.

Miers, S. and Kopytoff, I., 1977b. 'Introduction' to Miers and Kopytoff, eds.

Moisel, M. 1910–13. *Karte von Kamerun 1:300,000.* Berlin: Dietrich Reimer.

National Geographical Centre of Cameroon, 1977. *Map of Cameroon, 1/500,000 series, Bertoua sheet*. Yaounde: National Geographical Centre.

Nigeria Daily News, 2005. 'Obituary: Yusufu Bala Usman (1945–2005): Human Rights Activist.' http://www.nigeriadailynews.com/leaders/ad.asp?blurb=96.

Podlewski, A. M., 1966. *La Dynamique des principales populations du Nord-Cameroun (entre Bénoué et Lac Tchad)*. *Cahiers ORSTOM* (Sciences Humaines Series), II (4).

Podlewski, A. M., 1971. *La Dynamique des principales populations du Nord-Cameroun (Piémont et Plateau de l'Adamaoua)*. *Cahiers ORSTOM* (Sciences Humaines Series), VIII, numéro spécial.

Rowlands, M., 1979. 'Local and Long Distance Trade and Incipient State Formation on the Bamenda Plateau in the Late 19th Century.' *Paideuma*, 25, pp. 1–19.

Seignobos, C., 2006. 'Une négociation introuvable: l'exemple du Mayo-Rey dans le nord du Cameroun'. Paper presented at the international conference, *Le Frontières de la Question Foncière*, Montpellier http://www.mpl.ird.fr/colloque_foncier/Communications/PDF/Seignobos.pdf

Serre, J., 1997 *Explorations au coeur de l'Afrique: le commandant Lenfant*. Paris: Harmattan.

Shimada, Y., 1993. 'Jihad as Dialectical Movement and Formation of Ethnic Identity among the Fulbe.' In P. Eguchi and V. Azarya, eds, *Unity and Diversity of a People: The Search for Fulbe Identity*. Senri Ethnological Studies No. 35. Osaka: National Museum of Ethnology.

Smith, M. G., 1965 (1954). 'Slavery and Emancipation in Two Societies'. In M. G. Smith, ed., *The Plural Society in the British West Indies*. Berkeley: University of California Press.

Thomas, E., 1987. *A History of the Shouter Baptists in Trinidad and Tobago*. Tacarigua: Calaloux Publications.

Warnier, J. P., 1975. 'Precolonial Mankon: The Development of a Cameroon Chiefdom in its Regional Setting.' Doctoral dissertation. University of Pennsylvania.

Warnier, J. P., 1989 'Traite sans raids au Cameroun.' *Cahiers d'Études Africaines*, 113, pp. 5–32.

Williams, R., 1976. *Keywords: A Vocabulary of Culture and Society*. London: Fontana.

Notes

1 My approach in this paper has been inspired in part by Raymond Williams' book *Keywords: a Vocabulary of Culture and Society* (1976), a work that was a reaction to Williams' experience of returning to Britain after overseas service during the Second World War and being struck by the marked changes in meaning that had taken place in a range of socially significant English words during his four-and-a-half years of absence. In fact, these shifts in the meaning of keywords were a function of more general patterns of social change that had been unfolding during the first half of the twentieth century or longer. But the counter-intuitive impact on Williams of these changes in meaning was heightened by the sharp psychological disjuncture of his war experience, and it was this that led him to explore the social correlates of semantic change illustrated by a list of some 132 common words. While the word 'slavery' was not one of Williams' keywords and, happily, I have not undergone a traumatic period of war service, I nonetheless feel that there is something to be gained in considering the significance of this word's general and variable usage as reflected in my forty years' span of fieldnotes, an exercise that may allow us to highlight tendencies towards rapid change or relative conservatism in different social contexts.

2 The archives of the (then) Sub-Prefecture of Meiganga, the Cameroon National Archives in Yaounde, as well as the (then) IRCAM Archives in Yaounde contained numerous reports on the attempts of the French colonial administration to suppress

slave raiding, kidnapping and the slave trade in northern Cameroon. A particularly noteworthy case was that of the Gbaya chief Bangozou (*Gbaŋgozu*), the prominent leader of the Lobo clan around the present-day village of Djohong along the Mbere River valley. Bangozou was implicated in numerous cases of trading kidnapped children and was eventually killed by native police in 1930. See, for example, Dossier APA 11781/H, 'L'Affaire Bangozou', Cameroon National Archives and Dossier VT/19/49, 'Tournée Geli, Octobre 1932', Meiganga Sub-Prefecture Archives.

Glossary of Foreign Words

This glossary is provided to facilitate reading. Definitions are not exhaustive and may fail to convey semantic nuances. As mentioned in the Note on Language, the meanings of some of the entries below are currently disputed. At different times these terms may have had different meanings (e.g. words used today to designate 'slave descendants' may have meant 'slave'), and this is reflected in their current polysemy. Entries are listed under the singular or plural form, depending on the frequency with which they appear in the text.

Arabic

'abd: slave
baraka (or *al baraka*): blessing
'itq: emancipation
jihad: war or action for the Faith
kufr: unbelief, idolatry
nasab: genealogical link
qabila: tribal group
qadi: Muslim judge ruling in Islamic legal and religious matters
sayyid: master
tarikh: written history
ulama: Muslim scholars
dar-al-Islam: lands ruled by Islam

Akan (Twi)

abosom: divinities or lesser gods
asamanfo: ghosts, ancestors
hyire: white clay

kente: Ghanaian cloth
Mmoatia: 'little folk' in the Asante forest
mogya: blood
nifa: right side (associated with superiority)
benkum: left side (associated with inferiority)

Ewe

trokosi: ritual servitude associated with Ewe shrines

Fulfulde

almaami: imam, title of FulBe Islamic ruling elite.
annasaraaBe: the White, by extension, Europeans and Americans
arani: stranger
asakal: dime
ballotiral: solidarity
bardeeji: griot, jester
batu: council of dignitaries
caasal: courage
ceerno: title of the Islamic TooroBBe aristocracy of nineteenth-century Fuuta Tooro; today designates village chiefs
cehilagal: friendship
cootigu: ransom
dawol: wage labour paid on a daily basis
demal gerte: seasonal migrations to the Wolof peanut basin, lit. 'cultivating peanuts'
dewol: matrilineage
dimo (plur: *rimBe*): free human
dokkal: gift
du'aare: blessing
dou'ât: blessings
enndam: milk kinship
esiraaBe: parents-in-law
fasiraaBBe: informal training of youths paired by age
feDDe: age groups
galle: compound or guest-house
gallunkooBe: slave descendants
gannunkeeBe: (former) slaves, slave descendants
golle: work
gorol: paternal lineage
Haalpulaar'en: see Note on Language

harâtîn or *hrâtîn* (sing. *hartani*): slave descendants and descendants of freed slaves

jaggorde: electoral councils

jatigi: landlord-patron

jawdi: wealth, comfort

jeeri: rainy season

jiyaaBe or *jeyaaBe* (sing. *jiyaaDo*): slaves and descendants of slaves, owned persons

JiDi WaDi: association of Gando farmers of Northern Benin

jom leydi: landowners

jom wuro: village chief, citizen

joomiraaBe (sing. *joomiraawo*): (former) masters

juuwde: shallows

kilifa: master

kosam: cow's milk

kulol: fear.

kuttol: ritual slaughter of animals at ceremonies

HaaBe: the others, the non-Peul

horBe (sing. *korDo*): female slave

laamiido: ruler

Laawol Fulfulde: cultural and political movement of the FulBe of Northern Benin, lit. 'the way of the FulBe'

lamaare FulBe: supremacy of the FulBe

leydi: territory

leynol (plur. *leyyi*): lineage, group with common ancestry, political unit following the same ruling family

liggey: work

lubal: loan

maabuBe: caste of weavers and pottery makers

maccuBe: slaves and slave descendants

noraan: dry season

passijo: companion

pulaaku: 'FulBe-ness', FulBe code of behaviour, quality of FulBe identity

rempeccen: sharecropping

sanyooBe: weavers

seBBe (sing. *ceddo*): former warrior groups

semmee: physical strength

senteene: shame

subalBe (sing. *cuballo*): fishermen groups

suudu: 'chambres', room or guest-houses of Senegalese migrants

taalibe: disciple

teddungal: honour

tooroBBe (sing. *tooroodo*): high-ranking religious (maraboutic) groups

untal: pounding of cereals done by (former) slaves at the (former) masters' ceremonies

waalo: Senegal River floodplains

wasangari: (former) mounted warriors

yaa'oore: curse

yobu: domestic slaves, usually slaves of Baatombu farmers

yonobu: slave

yoosiyooBe: 'slaves of the slaves', slaves of the GannunkeeBe

ziara : pilgrimages

Hausa

aiki: work

bara: servant

bayun yunwa (dial. Ader): lit. 'slaves of hunger'; acceptance of dependency (servitude, slavery) by people faced with extreme poverty and hunger

bida: form of seasonal migration

Buzu, Buzaye, or Bugaje: (former) slaves of the Tuareg, often ethnicised

bawan sarki: slave of the sarki

cin rani: lit. 'eating the dry season', form of seasonal migration

digga: see *bida*

kiwo: herding

mai gida: household head

noma: farming

sarki: Hausa chiefly title, sometimes translated as 'emir' in Islamic political bodies. In the twentieth century *sarki* is translated as *chef de canton*, a title attributed to so-called 'customary chiefs' (*chefferie traditionelle*) in the administration of colonial and post-colonial Niger.

taiki (plur. *tayukka*): large leather bags used to contain grains in the past

Songhay-Zarma

Bella: (former) slaves of the Tuareg, often ethnicised

borciney: elites, (descendants of) nobles

haawi: shame, honour

horso: (former) slave

banniya (plur. *bagney* or *bannyey*): (former) slave

Tamasheq

enadan (or *inadan*, sing. *enad*): artisans

iderfan: liberated slaves

ighawelen: liberated slaves

iklan (sing m. *akli*; sing f. *taklit*): slaves

imajeghen (sing. *amajer*, *imuhag*): elite, nobles (this is the meaning prevalent in the regions discussed in the volume. In other areas, the term *Imajeghen* is also used as ethnonym for the Tuareg in a more encompassing sense.)

imghad (sing. *amghid*): tributaries

ineslemen (or *ineslimen*, sing. *aneslim*): Islamic class of religious specialist, maraboutic groups

Kel Tamasheq: those who speak Tamasheq language; see Note on Language

tawsit (plur. *tawsiten, tiwsatin*): Tuareg lineage unit; usually translated as 'tribe'

temushaga: Tuareg code of honour

Wolof

jaam: slave

Index

Printed and bound by CPI Group (UK) Ltd, Croydon, CR0 4YY

09/06/2025

14685812-0003